FUNCTIONAL PROGRAMMING
Application and Implementation

Prentice-Hall International
Series in Computer Science

C. A. R. Hoare, Series Editor

Published

BACKHOUSE, R. C., *Syntax of Programming Languages: Theory and Practice*
DUNCAN, F., *Microprocessor Programming and Software Development*
HENDERSON, P., *Functional Programming: Application and Implementation*
JONES, C. B., *Software Development: A Rigorous Approach*
WELSH, J. and ELDER, J., *Introduction to PASCAL*
WELSH, J. and McKEAG, M., *Structured System Programming*

Future Titles

de BAKKER, J. W., *Mathematical Theory of Program Correctness*
JACKSON, M. A., *System Design*
NAUR, P., *Studies in Program Analysis and Construction*
TENNENT, R., *Principles of Programming Languages*

FUNCTIONAL PROGRAMMING
Application and Implementation

PETER HENDERSON
University of Newcastle upon Tyne

Prentice/Hall International

ENGLEWOOD CLIFFS, NEW JERSEY   LONDON   NEW DELHI
SINGAPORE   SYDNEY   TOKYO   TORONTO   WELLINGTON

Library of Congress Cataloging in Publication Data

HENDERSON, PETER   1944–
   Functional programming

   Bibliography: p.
   Includes index
   1. Electronic digital computers—Programming
   I. Title
   QA76.6.H46   001.6'42   79-16840
ISBN 0-13-331579-7

British Library Cataloguing in Publication Data

HENDERSON, PETER
   Functional programming

   1. Electronic digital computers—Programming
   I. Title
   001.6'42   QA76.6
ISBN 0-13-331579-7

ISBN 0-13-331579-7

PRENTICE-HALL INTERNATIONAL, INC., *London*
PRENTICE-HALL OF AUSTRALIA PTY., LTD., *Sydney*
PRENTICE-HALL OF CANADA, LTD., *Toronto*
PRENTICE-HALL OF INDIA PRIVATE LIMITED, *New Delhi*
PRENTICE-HALL OF JAPAN, INC., *Tokyo*
PRENTICE-HALL OF SOUTHEAST ASIA PTE., LTD., *Singapore*
PRENTICE-HALL, INC., *Englewood Cliffs, New Jersey*
WHITEHALL BOOKS LIMITED, *Wellington, New Zealand*

Typeset by HBM Typesetting Ltd.,
Chorley, Lancashire
Printed and bound in Great Britain
by A. Wheaton and Co. Ltd., Exeter

80 81 82 83 84 5 4 3 2 1

CONTENTS

PREFACE   ix

1 FUNCTIONS AND PROGRAMS   1

1.1   Programming with Functions   2
1.2   Programming with Procedures   8

2 A PURELY FUNCTIONAL LANGUAGE   13

2.1   Symbolic Data   13
2.2   Elementary Selectors and Constructors   18
2.3   Elementary Predicates and Arithmetic   21
2.4   Recursive Functions   23
2.5   More Recursive Functions   26
2.6   Accumulating Parameters   33
2.7   Local Definitions   37
2.8   Higher-Order Functions and Lambda Expressions   40
2.9   Dot Notation   48
       Exercises   54

3 SIMPLE FUNCTIONAL PROGRAMS   59

3.1   Dimensional Analysis—an Example of Structured Programming and
       Structured Program Testing   60
3.2   Tree Searches—a Comparison of Programs for Breadth-first and
       Depth-first Searches   71
3.3   The Singletons Program   84
       Exercises   90

4 THE REPRESENTATION AND INTERPRETATION OF PROGRAMS   93

4.1   Abstract and Concrete Forms of Programs   95
4.2   Binding   103
4.3   An Interpreter for the Lisp Variant   110
      Exercises   122

5 CORRESPONDENCE BETWEEN FUNCTIONAL PROGRAMS AND IMPERATIVE PROGRAMS   126

5.1   An Interpreter for an Imperative Language   127
5.2   Functional Equivalents of Imperative Programs   133
5.3   Transforming Imperative Programs into Functional Programs   136
5.4   Supporting Functional Programs on Conventional Machines   149
      Exercises   157

6 A MACHINE ARCHITECTURE FOR FUNCTIONAL PROGRAMS   163

6.1   Overview of the Machine   163
6.2   The SECD Machine   167
6.3   A Compiler for the Lisp Variant   176
6.4   Programming the Compiler   187
6.5   Completing the Semantic Description   190
      Exercises   196

7 NON-DETERMINISTIC PRIMITIVES AND BACKTRACK PROGRAMS   198

7.1   Non-deterministic Primitives   198
7.2   Interpretation of Non-deterministic Primitives   203
7.3   Backtrack Programs   206
      Exercises   212

8 DELAYED EVALUATION—A FUNCTIONAL APPROACH TO PARALLELISM   214

8.1   Delayed Evaluation   215
8.2   Interpretation of Delay and Force   218
8.3   Lazy Evaluation   223
8.4   Networks of Communicating Processes   231
      Exercises   239

9 HIGHER-ORDER FUNCTIONS   242

9.1   On Types of Functions   243
9.2   Describing the Syntax of a Language   251
9.3   Describing the Structure of a Picture   255
      Exercises   265

10 PROGRAMMING LANGUAGES AND PROGRAMMING METHODS   268

10.1 On Clarity of Expression   269
10.2 On Data Domains   272
10.3 The Dominant Assignment   277
      Exercises   280

11 A FUNCTIONAL PROGRAMMING KIT   281

11.1 The List Space   282
11.2 The Principal Control Operation   288
11.3 The Input of S-expressions   289
11.4 The Input of Tokens   295
11.5 The Output of S-expressions   298
11.6 The Output of Tokens   300
11.7 The Conversion Routines   301
11.8 The Execution Cycle   303

12 BASIC MACHINE SUPPORT FOR THE FUNCTIONAL PROGRAMMING KIT 313

12.1 Storage for Lists 313
12.2 The Garbage Collector 319
12.3 The String Store 321
12.4 Building and Testing a Lispkit System 323
12.5 Bootstrapping and Optimization 331

APPENDICES 334

1 Answers to Selected Exercises 334
2 The Lispkit Compiler 339
3 Bibliography 342

INDEX 347

PREFACE

My principal motivation in writing this book has been to collect together many of the important ideas which have been devised for writing programs in a purely functional, or applicative, style. These ideas have arisen from two largely separate areas of our discipline, the study of programming language semantics and the programming of artificial intelligence applications. The book includes a complete coverage of the functional style of programming, the structure of functional languages, their application and implementation, and such advanced concepts as delayed evaluation, non-deterministic programs and higher-order functions.

My approach is a pragmatic one, being more concerned with the application and implementation of functional programming than its theoretical foundation. Thus the book describes the fundamental techniques used in building functional programs, then goes on to describe how functional languages can be implemented on conventional computers and finally describes more advanced features of such languages by defining their meaning in terms of their implementation.

Functional languages are used in the study of programming language semantics in two distinct ways. One way is to define an interpreter for the language being studied, a role for which functional languages are ideally suited. An alternative is to define, for each program in the language being studied, an equivalent function or functional program. In either case, it is the extreme simplicity and power of a functional language which makes it suitable for such semantic specification.

In artificial intelligence applications there is a need to manipulate complex, usually symbolic, data structures with equally complex algorithms. McCarthy's development of the programming language Lisp, whose basic structure is that of a functional language, overcame much of the complexity inherent in these applications. The use of a purely functional style of programming is natural for applications largely characterized by a process of repeatedly deriving complex data structures from other complex data structures. Today, the techniques of functional programming have a wider relevance and will become increasingly important as technology allows us to move towards very much higher level programming languages.

My belief is that a fuller understanding of the semantics of functional languages, and by extension all programming languages, is developed if one studies the connections between the languages and their implementations. To ensure that all the connections are established, the book includes a complete description of an implementation of a purely functional language called Lispkit Lisp. This implementation (of a significant variant of the programming language Lisp) is presented in the form of a kit which the diligent reader, with access to a computer, can easily assemble for himself. Two essential components of the kit, the compiler in source and object form, are reproduced in an appendix. All that is necessary to build the kit is to write a simple simulator for an abstract machine and then load the compiler into it. The compiler will then compile itself and any other Lispkit Lisp program, thus enabling the reader to experiment with the programs and languages described in the book. Construction details are contained in Chapters 11 and 12. The reader may find it valuable to refer to these chapters from time to time in order to supplement his understanding of the precise meaning of some of the concepts of functional programming.

While Lispkit Lisp is used as a concrete example of a functional language to be implemented, the language used throughout the book for writing functional programs has a somewhat more readable syntax. There are simple rules of transliteration between this notation and Lispkit Lisp, so that any programs written in the book, or required by the exercises, can be run on a Lispkit Lisp system.

I have used the material in this book over a number of years, in a course on the semantics of programming languages, taught to undergraduate computer scientists. The practical basis of the course means that the new concepts can easily be related to those which are familiar from a study of more conventional programming. In addition, the ability to experiment with the interpreters and compilers described here, and to alter the semantics of the language being studied, means that a very positive appreciation of the delicate nature of the semantics of a programming language is gained. For undergraduates in general the book will help to relate their otherwise separate studies of the theory of programming, compilers, programming languages, data structures and machine architecture. For postgraduates, whose area of specialization is programming, programming languages, artificial intelligence or machine architecture, the book will form an introduction to many essential topics in the use of functional languages both as a programming and as a specification tool. The home computer enthusiast looking for a practical introduction to computer science theory or for a very high level language for experimentation should also find building the kit a useful and rewarding exercise.

It probably requires a two semester course to cover all the topics included in the book. However, as the diagram of strong dependencies between chapters shows, it is possible to omit various sections depending upon where the emphasis is to be placed. In my own course, which runs for approximately one semester, I try to teach the use of functional programming as a practical and useful skill and thus put a lot of emphasis on doing examples and exercises and on experimenting with interpreters and compilers. For this, Chapters 2,4,5 and 6 are used, with selected material from Chapters 8 and 9. The students are of course given access to a Lispkit Lisp implementation for experimentation both by using it and by making modifications to it. It should be feasible, in a longer course, to ask the students to assemble the Lispkit Lisp system for themselves. This task should be ancillary to the study of the functional programming style and to the understanding of the semantics of programming languages.

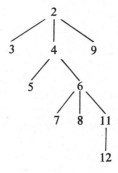

strong dependencies between chapters

Many people have helped me in the production of this book by reading various drafts and giving me their valuable advice. In particular Tony Hoare and Simon Jones have made significant contributions. Fred King's efficient implementation of Lispkit Lisp has been invaluable. I am grateful to Julie Lennox who typed and corrected many drafts and to all my colleagues in the University of Newcastle upon Tyne who have provided a stimulating environment in which to work.

PETER HENDERSON

1   FUNCTIONS AND PROGRAMS

Early computers were very small and very slow in comparison with modern machines. The most important concern of the programmer was therefore to make the running program as efficient as possible. As computers became faster and bigger, it became possible to forsake a little efficiency in return for a more clearly expressed program. The program, being thus easier to understand, was more economical to build and to maintain. High-level languages such as Fortran, Algol, Cobol, PL/1 and Pascal were developed. Because high-level language programs translate to machine-language programs, their users accept a loss in execution speed of some two to ten times. This willingness to accept less efficient but more easily understandable programs is a trend which will accelerate in the near future as we reap the benefits of technological improvements in the design of electronic components.

Current trends in technology are such that the cost of hardware is diminishing dramatically. In addition, computers are continually becoming faster and bigger, so much so that we can anticipate whole orders of magnitude improvements in their performance in the early 1980s. Thus, as the underlying hardware becomes more efficient, for many applications the trend towards clearer, easier to understand programs which make much less than optimal use of the hardware will continue. We can anticipate therefore, that the trend in high-level languages will be to provide features that are progressively more user-oriented and at higher levels. In particular, one may hope that these languages will become simpler and more uniform. It is characteristic of conventional programming languages, such as those already mentioned, that they effect a compromise between user orientation and machine orientation, leading to a great variety of inter-related features in each language. Languages which do not effect such a compromise with

1

the capabilities of the machine have the property that, in general, their programs run more slowly than those which do.

The kind of programming language with which we shall be concerned in this book is one which makes less of a compromise with the conventional machine and thus provides a higher-level interface with the user. The language is referred to as a purely functional language because the notion of a function is the primary building block for programs in that kind of language. Functional languages are the most widely studied class of very high-level languages. Programs that would be long and difficult to write in a conventional high-level language can often be much shorter and clearer when written in a functional form. Thus a functional language can truly be said to be at a higher level than those conventional languages we have mentioned. The price which we pay of course is that their implementation leads to programs which are correspondingly less efficient in their use of hardware. The technology trends which we have described are making this efficiency loss less important than it has been and, for many applications in the future, will make it of no great importance at all.

We begin in this chapter to review the mathematical notion of a function and to show how programs can be built as compositions of functions. We shall define what a functional programming language is in Section 1.1. In Section 1.2 we shall discuss what a functional programming language is not, by comparing it with conventional high-level languages. In particular, we shall be concerned with those features of high-level languages which are more machine oriented. The remainder of the book is devoted to a study of how a purely functional language can be used for a wide class of practical applications and how it can be supported with acceptable efficiency on conventional machines. The thesis which we shall maintain is that such programs are clearer expressions of their purpose than conventional programs and as such are easier to understand, easier to maintain and easier to build correctly in the first place.

1.1 PROGRAMMING WITH FUNCTIONS

The concept of a function is one of the fundamental notions of mathematics. Intuitively, a *function* is a rule of correspondence whereby to each member of a certain class there corresponds a unique member of another class. That is to say, given two classes of individuals, respectively called the *domain* of the function and the *range* of the function, each member of the domain is made to correspond by the function to exactly one member of the range. The correspondence shown in Fig. 1.1 defines a function, call it f, whose domain is the class of individuals $\{a,b,c,d\}$ and whose range is the class $\{p,q,r\}$. The important property of a correspondence which characterizes it as a function is that the individual in the range of the function is uniquely determined by the individual in the domain. This fact allows us to denote by $f(x)$ the

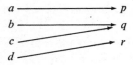

Fig. 1.1

individual in the range of f which corresponds to the individual x in the domain of f. We say that f maps x to $f(x)$ or that $f(x)$ is the image of x under f. More common usage in computing is to say that $f(x)$ is the result of applying f to the argument x.

There are many ways in which a trivial function such as that above can be displayed. For example we can list the correspondences as a sequence of pairs

$$(a,p) , (b,q) , (c,q) , (d,r) ,$$

or we can tabulate the function as in Table 1.1, which amounts to the same thing.

Table 1.1

x	a	b	c	d
$f(x)$	p	q	q	r

An alternative is to write the correspondence as a set of equations:

$$f(a)=p, \quad f(b)=q, \quad f(c)=q, \quad f(d)=r.$$

Each of these displays suffers from the weakness that the constraint on the correspondence, that $f(x)$ is uniquely determined by x, is not clearly expressed and thus not easily checked. When the domain is large it is not obvious, at a glance, that any particular display properly denotes a function. When the domain is infinite, of course, we cannot use such a display at all. For such functions we can therefore use such displays to enumerate only a sample of the correspondences established by the function.

Let us consider a more realistic example. The function *square* has as domain the class of all integers (positive, zero and negative) and as range the class of all non-negative integers. The individual in the range of *square* which corresponds to x in the domain of *square*, is just $x \times x$. Thus, for example we have:

$$square(3) = 9, \; square(6) = 36, \; square(-2) = 4.$$

We cannot of course display the whole correspondence of *square*, because the domain is infinite. However, we can define all the correspondences by writing a rule (or definition) such as

$$square(x) \equiv x \times x$$

Here we have defined precisely how to compute the image of x for any x in the domain of *square*. The image of x is obtained simply by squaring x, that is, multiplying it by itself. In writing this definition we have made use of a variable x, to stand for any individual in the domain, and have written the rule for computing the corresponding individual in the range as an expression using this variable. Such a variable is usually called a parameter of the definition.

A defining rule, or definition, such as the one we have given for *square*, is the standard way in which we shall present functions. With such a presentation, the domain and range are implicit and not always obvious. The fact that we intend square to have the integers as domain is expressed only in the supporting narrative, and the fact that the range is thereby the non-negative integers, although derivable from the form of the rule, is certainly not explicit in it. We should have used the same defining rule if we were defining square over the real numbers. In general, with the functions we shall define, it will be sufficient if we characterize their domain and range informally in the supporting narrative. Indeed, we shall often nominate as domain and range classes which are larger than they need be in that some individuals in the nominated domain of the function have no corresponding individual in the range or some individual in the range is the image of no individual in the domain. For example, we might say that *square* maps the integers (as domain) to the integers (as range). Here the range unnecessarily includes the negative integers. Similarly the function

$$reciprocal\,(x) \equiv \frac{1}{x}$$

may be said to map the real numbers to the real numbers. Yet, the real number 0 is not in the domain of *reciprocal*, because *reciprocal*(0) is not defined by the above rule. We say that a function for which we have nominated as domain the class A is *partial* over A, if there is some individual in A for which the image under the function is not defined. A function which is not partial over A is said to be *total* over A. We shall not make much use of these terms, but it is important to note that in general the functions which we shall define in this book will be partial over the classes which we nominate as their domains.

Consider another example. The function *max*, if applied to a pair of real numbers, will return the larger of the two. Thus, for example,

$$max\ (1,3) = 3, \quad max\ (1.7,-2.0) = 1.7.$$

The rule for this can be most conveniently expressed using two parameters.

$$max(x,y) \equiv \begin{cases} x, \text{ if } x \geqslant y \\ y, \text{ otherwise.} \end{cases}$$

This is a cumbersome way to write the definition which can be avoided if we allow ourselves the use of a conditional form such as **if** . . . **then** . . . **else**, with which we are familiar from conventional programming languages.

$$max(x,y) \equiv \textbf{if } x \geqslant y \textbf{ then } x \textbf{ else } y.$$

As in the definition of square, the right-hand side of this rule is an algebraic expression involving parameters, x and y. On this occasion the **if** . . . **then** . . . **else** form requires that we evaluate $x \geqslant y$, obtaining true or false, and accordingly select between the subexpressions x and y to compute the result of any particular function application.

For example, the application $max(1,3)$ is evaluated as follows, using the above rule. The form of the application (also called a *function call* in programming-language parlance) tells us that x and y are to be associated with the values 1 and 3 respectively. Thus the evaluation of $x \geqslant y$ requires us to evaluate $1 \geqslant 3$ which is of course false. Consequently we select the value of y, that is 3, as the result of the application. We have determined that $max(1,3) = 3$.

We are beginning to see how we can program with functions. We define a basic repertoire of useful functions, such as *square* and *max*, and by presenting them with suitable arguments, compute their results in the manner outlined above. A function is a kind of program which accepts input (its arguments) and produces output (its result). To be able to construct more powerful programs, then, it is necessary to be able to define new functions using old ones. Ultimately of course the new functions must rely for their evaluation on only the basic functions, but it is obvious that this can be achieved by building a hierarchy of definitions. Consider, for example. the following definition

$$largest(x,y,z) \equiv max(max(x,y),z)$$

As its name implies, *largest* determines which of its three arguments (which must be real numbers) is largest. It does this by using the function *max*, first to determine the larger of the first two arguments, then to determine the larger of this intermediate result and the third argument.

The definition of *largest* illustrates one of the fundamental methods of building new functions from old ones. It is the method of *function composition*. By nesting one application of *max* within another we have made a composition of *max* with itself. In general, functions may be composed to any depth with each other. For example, the largest of six real numbers a,b,c,d,e and f may be determined using any of the compositions which follow:

$$max(largest(a,b,c), \; largest(d,e,f))$$
$$largest(max(a,b), \; max(c,d), \; max(e,f))$$
$$max(max(max(a,b), \; max(c,d)), \; max(e,f)).$$

To be able to program with functions we need to be able to define a suitably rich set of basic functions and then to use function composition to define new functions in terms of these. Thus we may build ourselves a whole library of useful functions, some of which, probably built upon layers of others, are considered to be sufficiently powerful to be called programs—purely functional programs. The question arises, do we need more than just a repertoire of basic functions and the ability to compose them in order to define a library of functional programs? The answer is that we do not and it is the purpose of the remainder of this book to illustrate just that point.

The chosen repertoire of basic functions is of course very important. For practical purposes, both to make implementation on conventional computers reasonably efficient and to ease the problems of program design, the basic repertoire must be quite powerful. In Chapter 2 we shall introduce a set of basic functions, often taken as standard in functional programming, which are adequate to define functional programs for many important applications. Other choices of basic repertoire are possible, and this matter is discussed further in Chapter 10.

Among the basic functions, we must include those of arithmetic. We are accustomed in mathematics, and in programming, to writing algebraic expressions involving the arithmetic operators, such as:

$$a+b\times c$$
$$(2\times x+3\times y)/(x-y).$$

Of course, the operators $+$, $-$, $\times$ and $/$ are functions, each having as domain the ordered pairs of real numbers and as range the real numbers. We can make this observation explicit by defining them as functions:

$$add(x,y)\equiv x+y, \quad mul(x,y)\equiv x\times y,$$
$$sub(x,y)\equiv x-y, \quad div(x,y)=x/y.$$

Using these function names instead of the operators, the above algebraic expressions become

$$add(a,mul(b,c))$$
$$div(add(mul(2,x),mul(3,y)),sub(x,y)).$$

Rewriting the expressions in this way clearly shows what Landin has called the applicative structure of expressions in mathematical (and programming) languages. Every expression in such a language can be broken up into constituents which are either operators or operands. The operands denote values while the operators denote functions. The structure of an expression is simple: it is composed from operators applied to operands.

An important notion associated with applicative structure is that the value of an expression (its meaning) is determined solely by the values of its constituent parts. Thus, should the same expression occur twice in the same context, it denotes the same value at both occurrences. A language which has this property for all its expressions is usually referred to as an *applicative language*. Here, we shall refer to it as a *purely functional language*. Both names are useful, emphasizing the dominant role played by functions and by applications of functions. In the next section, before beginning our study of functional programming in a purely functional language, we shall briefly review the structure of conventional programming languages and discuss the extent to which they are not purely functional.

1.2 PROGRAMMING WITH PROCEDURES

Conventional high-level programming languages all provide a construct
called procedure or subroutine, a notion which is based largely on the idea
of a function. Indeed, it is often the case that these procedures are used to
implement new functions in the sense in which we have defined functions in
the previous section. In (1.1)–(1.3) the function *max* is programmed respectively in Fortran, PL/1 and Pascal. These definitions are such that they

---

$$
\begin{aligned}
&REAL\ FUNCTION\ MAX\,(X,Y) \\
&REAL\ X,Y \\
&IF\,(X.GE.Y)\ GO\ TO\ 10 \\
&\quad MAX = Y \\
&\quad RETURN \\
&10\quad MAX = X \\
&\quad RETURN \\
&\quad END
\end{aligned}
\tag{1.1}
$$

$$
\begin{aligned}
&MAX:\ PROCEDURE\,(X,Y)\ RETURNS\,(REAL); \\
&\qquad DECLARE\ X,\ Y\ REAL; \\
&\qquad DECLARE\ Z\ REAL; \\
&\qquad\quad IF\ X \geqslant Y\ THEN\ Z = X;\ ELSE\ Z = Y; \\
&\qquad\quad RETURN(Z); \\
&\qquad END;
\end{aligned}
\tag{1.2}
$$

function *max(x,y:real)*: *real*;
begin
    if $x \geqslant y$ **then** *max*:$=x$ **else** *max*:$=y$ (1.3)
end

---

implement pure functions. For example, the Fortran function can be called
by some such assignment as

$$
M = MAX\,(MAX\,(A,B),C)
$$

to determine the largest of three values. However, only a very limited class
of functions can be defined in these languages, and for practical programs
we have to resort to a more general use of procedures.

We begin to depart from the notion of a pure function when we define procedures which, rather than returning a result, instead assign a value to one of their parameters. For example, we might define MAX so that the call $MAX(A,B,M)$ computes the larger of A and B and assigns it to M, as shown in (1.4)–(1.6) respectively in Fortran, PL/1 and Pascal. Computing

---

```
      SUBROUTINE MAX(X,Y,Z)
      REAL X,Y,Z
      IF (X.GE.Y) GO TO 10
      Z=Y                                    (1.4)
      RETURN
   10 Z=X
      RETURN
      END
```

```
      MAX: PROCEDURE (X,Y,Z);
             DECLARE X,Y,Z REAL;            (1.5)
                 IF X ⩾ Y THEN Z=X; ELSE Z=Y;
      END;
```

```
      procedure max(x,y:real; var z:real);
      begin                                  (1.6)
          if x⩾y then z:=x else z:=y
      end
```

---

the largest of three values is then programmed as the call $MAX(A,B,M)$ followed by the call $MAX(M,C,M)$. We could argue that this is just a syntactic variation on the way of writing function applications and that the true notion of function has not been lost. All we have lost is a certain convenience in writing that composition of applications which computes the largest of three values.

We depart a little further from the notion of pure function when we define MAX to be a procedure such that the call $MAX(A,B)$ computes the larger of A and B and assigns that value to A as we have done in (1.7)–(1.9).

Thus the calls $MAX(A,B)$ and $MAX(A,C)$ in sequence determine the largest of three values (leaving the result in A) but may have consequently over-written the original value of A. Again we could maintain that the notion of

---

```
      SUBROUTINE MAX(X,Y)
      REAL X, Y
      IF (X.GE.Y) GO TO 10
      X=Y                                              (1.7)
  10  RETURN
      END
```

```
      MAX: PROCEDURE (X,Y);
          DECLARE X,Y REAL;                            (1.8)
              IF X< Y THEN X=Y;
          END;
```

```
procedure max(var x:real; y:real);
begin                                                  (1.9)
    if x<y then x:=y
end
```

---

pure function has not been lost but only hidden, since the result of the call $MAX(A,B)$ is still determined uniquely by the initial values of the arguments. Programs composed from pure functions simply define how new values are to be computed from old values. The procedures (1.4) – (1.9) however, do not simply compute values, but also have a side effect of assigning to one of their parameters. When composing programs from such procedures we must think in terms of the incremental changes made to variables by successive assignments. That is to say, we are *computing by effect* rather than just *computing values*. Despite their use of local assignments the procedures (1.1)–(1.3) have no side effect and hence are implementations of pure functions.

A more striking example of the phenomenon of computing by effect is given by a procedure which alters the value of a variable which is not one of its parameters. In (1.10)–(1.12) we have defined the procedure MAX so that the call $MAX(A,B)$ assigns the larger of the values in A and B to the variable

```
        SUBROUTINE MAX(X, Y)
        REAL X, Y
        COMMON M
        REAL M                                          (1.10)
        IF (X.GE. Y) GO TO 10
        M = Y
        RETURN
   10   M = X
        RETURN
        END
```

```
        MAX: PROCEDURE (X, Y);
                DECLARE X, Y REAL;                      (1.11)
                        IF X > Y THEN M = X; ELSE M = Y;
        END;
```

```
        procedure max(x,y:real);
        begin                                           (1.12)
            if x ⩾ y then m: = x else m: = y
        end
```

M. The variable M is not a parameter. Thus, the largest of three values is now computed by the call $MAX(A,B)$ followed by the call $MAX(M,C)$ leaving the result in M. A procedure with a definition such as this leads to programs which are very difficult to understand. But the features which allow us to define such obscure procedures in conventional programming languages have usually been added to those languages for the very good reason that without them certain programs could not make adequately efficient use of the machine.

The purely functional language which we shall define in the next chapter does not compute by effect. The programmer may only define functions which compute values uniquely determined by the values of their arguments. Consequently, many of the familiar concepts of conventional programming languages are missing from our purely functional language. Most important, assignment is missing. So is the familiar programming notion of a variable as something which holds a value which is changed from time to time by assignment. Rather, the variables in our purely functional language are like the mathematical variables we used in the previous section as parameters in function definitions. They are used only to name the argument values of functions and are associated with these constant values for the duration of the evaluation of the algebraic expression which defines the result of the function.

To compensate for these omissions, our purely functional language has two features of significant power. The first is its data structuring capability. The second is an ability to define what are called higher-order functions. The power of the data-structuring capability lies in the fact that entire data structures are treated as single values. They may be passed to functions as arguments and returned from functions as results. More significantly, once a data structure has been built it cannot be altered, its value will remain inviolate. It will of course be incorporated in other structures, but as long as the program requires its value, its value will be available. This particular device is of fundamental importance to the usability of the purely functional language and requires a great deal of care in implementation if adequate efficiency is to be gained. Much the same can be said of higher-order functions. A higher-order function is one which either takes a function as argument or produces a function as its result. The use of such functions can lead to programs that are remarkably short and succinct for the computation which they perform. Their correct implementation will be a matter which concerns us greatly in the ensuing chapters.

Future programming languages will, of necessity, present a compromise between a language in which programs can be most clearly expressed and one which can be efficiently implemented. However, the hardware costs in this equation are changing radically and can be expected to continue to change, in that basic hardware will become cheaper, faster and bigger by whole orders of magnitude in the near future. It is time therefore to look again at our programming languages and ask what higher-level features we can now afford to incorporate in order to ease the task of building certain kinds of program. The class of languages referred to as applicative or purely functional have been extensively studied. Programs in these languages can be an order of magnitude shorter than programs to perform the same task written in conventional languages. They are correspondingly simpler to write correctly, to understand and hence to maintain. The purpose of this book is to demonstrate this power, to describe the techniques needed to program in such a language, to relate those techniques to some theoretical studies of programming and to fully describe a way in which such languages can be implemented on conventional machines.

2 A PURELY FUNCTIONAL LANGUAGE

This chapter is devoted to the introduction of an abstract notation which will be used throughout the book for the expression of functional programs. In the previous chapter we used an informal notation and defined functions which mapped numeric values to numeric values. We shall require a richer domain than the usual machine representation of numbers in order to be able to write interesting programs and so, for the sake of definiteness, we use a particular form of symbolic data which was invented by McCarthy for the programming language Lisp. This form of data, which is usually called "S-expressions"(S for "symbolic"), has the advantage of being very simple but very general. We begin by describing how to write symbolic expressions and then introduce the basic functions used to manipulate them. Again we have chosen exactly the basic functions provided by Lisp, thus ensuring that they are familiar when, in a later chapter, we introduce our own variant of the Lisp language as an example for semantic specification. The remainder of this chapter is devoted to methods of constructing ever more powerful functions. We therefore discuss a variety of topics including recursion, higher-order functions and how to choose parameters, all of which are intended to make the reader completely familiar with the methods and notation of functional programming. The notation introduced in this chapter is used throughout the remaining chapters of the book.

2.1 SYMBOLIC DATA

We shall define a class of symbolic expressions which are called *S-expressions* and which form the data domain for the functional programs which we shall later construct. Each of the following three lines contains an S-expression:

> (*JOHN SMITH IS* 33)
> ((*DAVE* 17) (*MARY* 24) (*ELIZABETH* 6))
> ((*MY HOUSE*) *HAS* (*BIG* (*BROWN DOORS*)))

The most obvious common property which one notices in these examples is the use of parentheses. Indeed, the use of parentheses in S-expressions is absolutely fundamental. If the position of, or the number of, parentheses is altered in any way, then the structure of and consequently the meaning of the S-expression will be changed. This section is devoted to describing the rules for constructing S-expressions in the form in which they are predominantly used throughout the book. A small extension which proves very useful in later chapters is postponed until Section 2.9.

Apart from parentheses in the above examples, each S-expression is constructed from elementary items called *atoms*. The following are examples of atoms.

JOHN	-127
SMITH	*MYCATALOG*
33	*APPLE*13
MY	

Atoms are of two types, either *symbolic* or *numeric*. A symbolic atom is usually a sequence of letters, although it may contain other characters, including digits, just as long as it includes at least one character which distinguishes it from a number. A symbolic atom is considered to be indivisible. We shall never decompose it into its constituent characters. Rather, the only operation we shall perform on symbolic atoms is to compare two to see whether they are the same or different. A numeric atom is a sequence of digits, possibly preceded by a sign, and is taken to denote the corresponding decimal integer, as we would expect. In general, S-expressions contain a mixture of symbolic and numeric atoms, although we shall have occasion to use S-expressions in which all the atoms are of one kind.

The very simplest form of S-expression is just a lone atom. A more elaborate form of S-expression is a simple list of atoms. This is formed by writing the atoms in a sequence and enclosing the sequence in one set of parentheses. Hence

(JOHN SMITH IS 33)

is a sequence of four atoms. The layout of the S-expression on the page, in particular the spacing, is not significant, except that it is necessary to have at least one space between adjacent atoms, in order to distinguish them. Further examples of simple lists are as in (2.1). The first is a list of eight atoms, all symbolic. The second is a list of five atoms and the third a list of just one atom, *BANANA*. The fourth example is different from the third, being a list of six symbolic atoms, each being just one character long.

(*JOHN SMITH EATS*
    BREAD AND BUTTER
    QUITE OFTEN)   (2.1)
(14 *DEGREES AND* 50 *MINUTES*)
(*BANANA*)
(*B A N A N A*)

S-expressions of a significantly more elaborate variety can be constructed when we allow the items of a list to be not just simple atoms, but S-expressions themselves. Thus

((*DAVE* 17) (*MARY* 24) (*ELIZABETH* 6))

is an S-expression because it is a list of three items, each cf which is itself an S-expression. Again, the layout of this S-expression on the page is not important. However, the parentheses are vitally important. As written, it is a 3-list of items each of which is a 2-list, whereas

(*DAVE* 17 *MARY* 24 *ELIZABETH* 6)

is a 6-list of atoms, which we shall see is a fundamentally different structure. Consider now the construction of a more elaborate example. Since *BIG* and (*BROWN DOORS*) are both S-expressions, it follows that (*BIG* (*BROWN DOORS*)) is an S-expression. Now since (*MY HOUSE*) and *HAS* are S-expressions,

((*MY HOUSE*) *HAS* (*BIG* (*BROWN DOORS*)))

is an S-expression. Lists may become nested in each other to great depths in practice with a consequent multiplicity of parentheses. The difficulty in reading very long S-expressions we shall see is far outweighed by the ease we have in processing them.

The general rules for constructing S-expressions can be summarized in the following recursive definition:

1. an atom is an S-expression;
2. a sequence of S-expressions enclosed in parentheses is an S-expression (a list).

In Section 2.9 we shall extend this definition slightly but, for the vast majority of examples in this book, the S-expressions we shall use will be those defined by this rule.

When writing a program probably the first consideration we will make is how our data are going to fit into the format of S-expressions. Consider for example if we were to write a program to sum a sequence of integers. In what form would we present these data to the program? Probably as a list of integers. For example

$$(127\ 462\ 45\ 781\ -18\ 842\ 96)$$

or

$$(18\ 17\ 16\ -16\ -17\ -18)$$

for this structure will be the simplest one to process.

Suppose we wish to choose an S-expression representation for simple algebraic formulas. Here we have to recognize that formulas are made up of constants, variables and binary operators. Let us represent constants and variables by atoms and place a binary operator in the first position in a list followed by its operands. Further, let us choose particular symbolic names for the operators. We can summarize one way in which formulas can be represented by S-expressions by giving for each possible formula its corresponding S-expression, as shown in Table 2.1.

Table 2.1

Formula	S-expression
Constant	Number
Variable	Symbol
$p+q$	(ADD p q)
$p-q$	(SUB p q)
$p \times q$	(MUL p q)
p/q	(DIV p q)
p^q	(EXP p q)

Here, in the formula column, p and q stand for parts of the formula and in the S-expression column for the corresponding S-expression form of that part. Thus, the fact that

$$2 \times x + 1$$

has the form $p_1 + q_1$ where $p_1 = 2 \times x$ and $q_1 = 1$, and that p_1 has the form $p_2 \times q_2$ where $p_2 = 2$ and $q_2 = x$ means that we represent this formula by

$$(ADD\ (MUL\ 2\ X)\ 1)$$

By a similar argument we see that

$$x^2+2x-31$$

can be represented by

$$(ADD\ (EXP\ X\ 2)\ (SUB\ (MUL\ 2\ X)\ 31))$$

It can also be represented by

$$(SUB\ (ADD\ (EXP\ X\ 2)\ (MUL\ 2\ X))\ 31)$$

and many other possible forms. Any program which we write to manipulate this formula should be able to handle all these different forms.

As a third, quite different, example, consider a program written to deal with data concerning a chess game. First, we need to be able to denote each piece by symbols for its value and colour, for example $(KING\ WHITE)$ and $(PAWN\ BLACK)$. Next, we need to be able to denote the position of each piece. We could choose to represent the coordinates by pairs of integers (assuming rows and columns of the board numbered 1 to 8 in some fashion). Thus, various squares may be represented by (4 7), (2 1) etc. Now the entire board can be represented by making up a list of pairs, pairing each piece with its position. Thus the configuration shown in Fig. 2.1. might be represented as in (2.2).

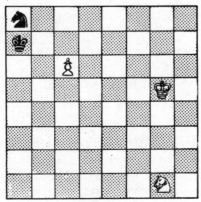

Fig. 2.1

$$
\begin{aligned}
(\ \ &((KING\ WHITE)\ (4\ 7)) \\
&((KING\ BLACK)\ (2\ 1)) \\
&((PAWN\ WHITE)\ (3\ 3)) \qquad\qquad (2.2)\\
&((KNIGHT\ WHITE)\ (8\ 7)) \\
&((KNIGHT\ BLACK)\ (1\ 1))\ \ )
\end{aligned}
$$

Of course, there are many different ways we can choose to represent the same data, and which choice we actually make is almost entirely determined by the processing we are to do. This particular choice of chess data might be suitable for certain kinds of processing and unsuitable for other kinds.

2.2 ELEMENTARY SELECTORS AND CONSTRUCTORS

In order to manipulate S-expressions we will introduce some primitive functions for dismantling and reassembling them. Then we will show how it is possible to define new functions in terms of these primitive functions. For example it will be possible to define the function

$$length(x)$$

which, when applied to a list x will return an integer value equal to the number of items in the list. That is, for example, the following S-expressions have the *lengths* shown in Table 2.2.

Table 2.2

x	$length\ (x)$
$(A\ B)$	2
$(A\ B\ C\ D)$	4
$((A\ B)(C\ D))$	2
(A)	1

When giving examples of the results of functions, we shall make use of this tabular form. Here, listed under x, are some sample S-expressions and corresponding to them under $length(x)$ is the result of calling the length function with that value for x. We see that only the top level items in the list are counted, and not the elements of sublists.

The function $length(x)$ is not primitive. Before we can define it, we need to introduce some primitive functions on S-expressions. These functions are given their traditional Lisp names, even though these are, at first, a little unusual. You will grow used to them, even grow to like them. The first function we need allows us to select the first member of a list. It is the *car* function (Table 2.3).

Table 2.3

x	$car\ (x)$
$(A\ B)$	A
$(A\ B\ C)$	A
$((A\ B)(C\ D))$	$(A\ B)$
(A)	A

Thus, *car* may be applied to a list and its result is the first (or leftmost) item in the list. We see that the selected item may be an atom or a list. The *car* of an atom is not defined. Corresponding to the *car* function, we have the *cdr* function. The *cdr* of a list is the list that one gets by omitting the first member of its argument list. The *cdr* of an atom is not defined. The name of this function is usually pronounced "cudder". Thus *car* and *cdr* are com-

Table 2.4

x	$cdr(x)$
$(A\ B)$	(B)
$(A\ B\ C)$	$(B\ C)$
$((A\ B)(C\ D))$	$((C\ D))$
(A)	NIL

plementary. If we have a list with a single item in it, then the *cdr* of the list is the (special) atom *NIL*. With just these two primitive functions, we can select any item in a list, provided we know it is there. For example, the third item in a list x is

$$car(cdr(cdr(x)))$$

For, suppose x is $(A\ B\ C\ D)$; then $cdr(x)$ is $(B\ C\ D)$ and $cdr(cdr(x))$ is $(C\ D)$. Therefore $car(cdr(cdr(x)))$ is C, which is the third item of the original list.

We shall allow ourselves to introduce new, non-primitive functions by writing function definitions. For example

$$third(x) \equiv car(cdr(cdr(x)))$$

defines the function $third(x)$ explained above. The function being defined appears to the left of $\equiv$ and the definition to the right. The definition is made in terms of primitive functions, other defined functions and the parameters of the function being defined. Consider, for example, the following definitions, intended for manipulating S-expressions which are lists with just two members each of which in turn is a list with just two members. An example is

$$((A \ B)$$
$$(C \ D))$$

whose shape suggests the names we have chosen for our functions, as listed in (2.3). Of course, such functions may be undefined if they are applied to S-expressions of the wrong shape.

$$first(x) \equiv car(x)$$
$$second(x) \equiv car(cdr(x))$$
$$topleft(s) \equiv first(\ first(s))$$
$$topright(s) \equiv second(first(s)) \tag{2.3}$$
$$bottomleft(s) \equiv first(second(s))$$
$$bottomright(s) \equiv second(second(s))$$

Now we come to the primitive constructor function *cons*. This function takes two S-expressions as arguments and combines them to form a single S-expression in such a way that the original components can be regained using *car* and *cdr* (Table 2.5).

Table 2.5

x	y	$cons \ (x,y)$
A	$(B \ C)$	$(A \ B \ C)$
$(A \ B)$	$((C \ D))$	$((A \ B)(C \ D))$
$(A \ B)$	$(C \ D)$	$((A \ B) \ C \ D)$
A	NIL	(A)

In general, the second argument of *cons* will be a list or the special atom *NIL*. The result of *cons* is then the list one obtains by including its first argument as a new first member in this list. Hence if y is a list of length n, then $cons(x, y)$ is a list of length $n+1$, regardless of the value of x. Because of this it is convenient and conventional to think of *NIL* as the list of length zero, or the empty list. It *is* a symbolic atom but it also fills this special role of denoting the empty list.

As an example of the use of *cons*, consider the definitions

$$twolist(x,y) \equiv cons(x,cons(y,NIL))$$
$$square(a,b,c,d) \equiv twolist(twolist(a,b),twolist(c,d))$$

The function *square* builds structures which can be decomposed using *topleft*, *topright, bottomleft* and *bottomright*. These functions have been given simply as examples of the use of *car*, *cdr* and *cons*: they will not be used later in the book. It is important however to have a thorough understanding of the primitive functions *car*, *cdr* and *cons* before reading further.

2.3 ELEMENTARY PREDICATES AND ARITHMETIC

In order to be able to process lists of varying structure, it is necessary to be able to test S-expression values to determine (a) whether they are atoms or lists, and (b) whether they are equal. The function *atom(x)* is called a predicate because it returns the value true or false. We shall denote true by the atom *T* and false by the atom *F*. The function *atom(x)* is true only if *x* is a symbolic or numeric atom. Some examples are given in Table 2.6.

Table 2.6

x	$atom(x)$
A	T
(A)	F
(A B C)	F
DICTIONARY	T
NIL	T
127	T
(127)	F

We use such a predicate to test the symbolic value before we apply a function to it which would otherwise be undefined. Consider, for example the function

$$f(x) \equiv \textbf{if } atom(x) \textbf{ then } NIL \textbf{ else } car(x)$$

which returns the first member of a list if applied to a list, but returns *NIL* if applied to an atom. Whereas *car(x)* is undefined for some S-expressions (a partial function), *f(x)* is defined for all S-expressions (a total function). Note that *atom(x)* does not distinguish between numeric and symbolic atoms.

Table 2.7

x	y	$eq(x,y)$
A	A	T
A	B	F
127	127	T
127	128	F
127	A	F
(A B)	A	F
(A)	A	F
A	(A B)	F

We can also compare two atoms to see if they are equal or not. We shall write this in the form

$$eq(x,y)$$

and must be particularly careful about its definition. One or other of the values compared by eq must be an atom. If both values are lists the result is undefined. Otherwise, the result of $eq(x,y)$ is true only if x and y are both the same atom, and false if either they are different atoms, or one of them is not an atom (see Table 2.7). The usual way in which this predicate is used is illustrated by the next definition.

$$size(x) \equiv \textbf{if } eq(x,NIL) \textbf{ then } 0 \textbf{ else}$$
$$\textbf{if } eq(cdr(x),NIL) \textbf{ then } 1 \textbf{ else } 2$$

This function returns the value 0, 1 or 2 according to whether its argument is a list of 0, 1 or more items. Now, we are getting reasonably close to being able to define the function *length*, with which we began the section. First however, let us enumerate the arithmetic functions which we shall allow.

The arithmetic operators $+$, $-$, $\times$, $\div$ (or **div**) and **rem** will be used. These compute respectively the sum, difference, product, quotient and remainder of their integer operands. The operator **rem** is defined by

$$x \textbf{ rem } y = x - (x \div y) \times y,$$

that is, it is the remainder on division of x by y.

If we wish to define a function which returns a twolist of the quotient and remainder of x divided by y, we write

$$quotrem(x,y) \equiv twolist(x \div y, x \textbf{ rem } y)$$

Examples of this function are as shown in Table 2.8.

Table 2.8

x	y	$quotrem(x,y)$
17	3	(5 2)
17	-3	$(-5$ 2)
-17	3	$(-5$ $-2)$
-17	-3	(5 $-2)$

We see that the quotient q and remainder r satisfy the relationship $x = q \times y + r$.

We shall also use the predicate $x < y$ to determine if x is less than or equal to y, for numeric atoms only. It is undefined for operands which are either symbolic atoms or lists. As an example of its use consider the function

$$distance\ (x,y) \equiv \textbf{if}\ x < y\ \textbf{then}\ y - x\ \textbf{else}\ x - y$$

whose value is the magnitude of the difference between x and y. Similarly, predicates can be built using the other usual relational operators for numerical values $<$, $>$ and $\geq$. However, in later chapters (4 and 6) when we introduce our variant of Lisp and an interpreter and compiler for it, we restrict that language to $<$ in order to reduce the size of these implementations. In consideration of this, the examples in the book are also written using only $<$ and $=$.

2.4 RECURSIVE FUNCTIONS

Let us consider now how we shall define the function $length(x)$, applicable to a list, and returning as its result the number of items in that list. We require a function which, in particular, yields the values given in Table 2.9.

Table 2.9

x	$length(x)$
$(A\ B\ C\ D)$	4
$(B\ C\ D)$	3
$(C\ D)$	2
(D)	1
NIL	0

This sequence of values suggests the following algorithm: successively take the *cdr* of x and count how many times this must be done before *NIL* is reached. It does not, however, immediately suggest a way of programming this algorithm as a recursive function. In general, when dealing with a list x, we consider the two cases $x = NIL$ and $x \neq NIL$ separately. In the second case, since we can take the *cdr* of x and this will be a list, we can apply the function being defined recursively. This recursion will terminate because, with each recursive call, the list will become one item shorter.

We can apply this design technique to $length(x)$ as in (2.4). The case

---

$$
\begin{aligned}
&\text{case(i)} \quad x = NIL \qquad length(x) = 0 \\
&\text{case(ii)} \quad x \neq NIL \\
&\qquad\qquad\qquad\quad \text{suppose } length(cdr(x)) = n \\
&\qquad\qquad\qquad\quad \text{then } length(x) = n + 1
\end{aligned}
\qquad (2.4)
$$

$x = NIL$ is trivial here. The case $x \neq NIL$ allows us to assume the result of a recursive call applied to $cdr(x)$. Here we assume that $length(cdr(x))$ is n, in which case the length of x must be just one more. Now, this leads us to write the definition of $length(x)$ as follows.

$$length(x) \equiv \textbf{if } eq(x,NIL) \textbf{ then } 0 \textbf{ else } length(cdr(x)) + 1$$

We can apply this design technique to another similar function, $sum(x)$, which takes as argument a list of integers and returns as result their sum (Table 2.10). Since NIL represents the empty list, in this case the list with

Table 2.10

x	$sum(x)$
(1 2 3)	6
(2 −2)	0
NIL	0

zero numbers in it, its sum is zero. Considering the cases leads to the analysis given in (2.5).

case(i)	$x = NIL$	$sum(x) = 0$
case(ii)	$x \neq NIL$	
		suppose $sum(cdr(x)) = n$
		then $sum(x) = car(x) + n$

(2.5)

This is very similar to $length$. The case $x = NIL$ is trivial. The case $x \neq NIL$ leads us to determine that the sum of a list x is just its car added to the sum of its cdr. We write this as a function definition as follows:

$$sum(x) \equiv \textbf{if } eq(x,NIL) \textbf{ then } 0 \textbf{ else}$$
$$car(x) + sum(cdr(x))$$

As a third example, consider the function $append(x,y)$ which takes two arguments, x and y (both lists), and produces as result the single list which

Table 2.11

x	y	append (x,y)
$(A\ B\ C)$	$(D\ E)$	$(A\ B\ C\ D\ E)$
$(A\ B)$	$(C\ D\ E)$	$(A\ B\ C\ D\ E)$
NIL	$(\ A\ B\ C)$	$(A\ B\ C)$
$(A\ B\ C)$	NIL	$(A\ B\ C)$
NIL	NIL	NIL

has all the items of x followed by all the items of y (Table 2.11). Since append has two arguments, both lists, we have to do a case analysis (2.6) on each.

$$
\begin{aligned}
&\text{case (i)} \quad x = NIL \\
&\quad \text{subcase (i.i)} \quad y = NIL \quad\quad append(x,y) = NIL \\
&\quad \text{subcase (i.ii)} \quad y \neq NIL \quad\quad append(x,y) = y \\
&\text{case (ii)} \quad x \neq NIL \quad\quad\quad\quad\quad\quad\quad\quad\quad\quad (2.6) \\
&\quad \text{subcase (ii.i)} \quad y = NIL \quad\quad append(x,y) = x \\
&\quad \text{subcase (ii.ii)} \quad y \neq NIL \\
&\quad\quad \text{suppose } append(cdr(x),y) = z \\
&\quad\quad \text{then} \quad append(x,y) = cons(car(x),z)
\end{aligned}
$$

Here, we can write down the result for each subcase directly except the last (ii.ii), where we made use of recursion. Although it was possible to take the *cdr* of both x and y, it was only necessary to actually take the *cdr* of x. Here the recursion is guaranteed to terminate by the finiteness of x. In carrying out this design, at each stage we consider what we know and whether we can write down the answer directly. If we know that some list is not *NIL*, then we consider whether we can write down the answer indirectly in terms of the *cdr* of that list. In case (ii.ii) then, there are three candidates whose values we might assume we can compute by recursive call:

$$append(cdr(x),y)$$
$$append(x,cdr(y))$$
$$append(cdr(x),cdr(y))$$

Fortunately, we found a way of expressing the result we require in terms of one of these (the first). The second and third are no use to us.

Here we have designed the function which would be written as

$$
\begin{aligned}
append(x,y) \equiv \ &\textbf{if } eq(x,NIL) \textbf{ then} \\
&\quad \textbf{if } eq(y,NIL) \textbf{ then } NIL \textbf{ else } y \textbf{ else} \\
&\textbf{if } eq(y,NIL) \textbf{ then } x \textbf{ else} \\
&\quad cons(car(x),append(cdr(x),y))
\end{aligned}
$$

Now, this is not the usual way in which append is written because most designers notice that when $x = NIL$, $append(x,y) = y$ whether y is NIL or not. That is, the subexpression

if $eq(y,NIL)$ **then** NIL **else** y

can be replaced by y giving

$append(x,y) \equiv$ **if** $eq(x,NIL)$ **then** y **else**
if $eq(y,NIL)$ **then** x **else**
$cons(car(x),\ append(cdr(x),y))$

Furthermore, some designers prefer to use the fact that when $x \neq NIL$

$append(x,y) = cons(car(x),append(cdr(x),y))$

whether y is NIL or not. This means the test on y can be omitted and the definition rewritten.

$append(x,y) \equiv$ **if** $eq(x,NIL)$ **then** y **else**
$cons(car(x),append(cdr(x),y))$

All three versions define equivalent functions. That is they all give the same result. One may be considered more easily understood than another. The first may be preferred because it is explicit about cases, the third because it is shortest. The second and third however have a fundamentally different efficiency. The second version avoids computation in the case $y = NIL$ at the expense of extra computation, for redundant tests, when $y \neq NIL$. The third formulation avoids redundant (repeated) tests on y but will nevertheless recursively rebuild x even when y is NIL.

2.5 MORE RECURSIVE FUNCTIONS

It is often convenient when defining a function to introduce extra function definitions just to ease our task. For example, when defining $append(x,y)$ we might utilize an extra function $appendnonnull(x,y)$ which appends x and y assuming y is not NIL. Thus we would have the definitions

$append(x,y) \equiv$ **if** $eq(y,NIL)$ **then** x **else**
$appendnonnull(x,y)$
$appendnonnull(x,y) \equiv$ **if** $eq(x,NIL)$ **then** y **else**
$cons(car(x),appendnonnull(cdr(x),y))$

Note that this combines the efficiencies of the second and third versions of *append* given in the previous section. It is usual, in functional programming, to define new functions in terms of old and thus to establish a set of functions defined in terms of each other, on the way to defining a principal function. Thus a functional program consists of a set of functions, one of which is considered to be the raison d'être of the others. This is the function which the programmer expects to be evaluated, as it were, as the main program, where all the remaining functions act as subroutines for it.

The problem of choosing the subfunctions when designing a main function is the eternal problem of how to structure programs well. Sometimes, standard subfunctions suggest themselves, but more often it is the case that a wisely chosen, special-purpose subfunction can considerably simplify the structure of the set of functions as a whole. If the functions chosen in this book seem to have this property then it is usually because many previous choices have been rejected. Indeed, this is the only advice the author can offer with respect to producing well-structured functional programs: try to continuously improve what you have. In this section we shall consider the design of some more elaborate functions.

An interesting function to consider, because we shall meet it again, is *reverse(x)*, which produces as a result the list *x* in reverse order (Table 2.12).

Table 2.12

x	$reverse\ (x)$
$(A\ B\ C)$	$(C\ B\ A)$
$((A\ B)(C\ D))$	$((C\ D)(A\ B))$
NIL	NIL

Note that, if the list has elements that are lists, the elements of these lists are *not* reversed. Since *x* is a list we must do a case analysis. If *x* is *NIL*, then reverse(*x*) is *NIL*, trivially. If *x* is not *NIL*, then we can make use of *reverse(cdr(x))*. Well, reverse(*cdr(x)*) is the beginning of reverse(*x*) and we would have completed our task if only we had a function with which we could put *car(x)* at the end of *reverse(cdr(x))*. At this point in the design we have recognized the need for a function

$$putatendof\ (x,y)$$

which takes a list *x* and an item *y* and makes *y* a new last member of *x*. Some examples of the action of this are given in Table 2.13. If we assume we can

Table 2.13

x	y	putatendof (x,y)
(A B C)	D	(A B C D)
((A B)(C D))	(E F)	((A B)(C D)(E F))
NIL	A	(A)

design such a function, but postpone its design a while, we can write out our completed design (2.7) of reverse(x).

---

case (i) $x = NIL$ reverse(x) = NIL
case (ii) $x \neq NIL$ (2.7)
   suppose reverse(cdr(x)) = z
   then reverse(x) = putatendof (z,car(x))

This would be written as the function definition

reverse(x) $\equiv$ **if** eq(x,NIL) **then** NIL **else**
                 putatendof (reverse(cdr(x)),car(x))

Now we can design putatendof.

This function has two arguments, the first of which is a list and the second of which is any S-expression. Therefore our case analysis will be on its first argument. In fact, it is so similar to our previous designs that we can write its design (2.8) immediately.

---

case (i) $x = NIL$ putatendof (x,y) = cons(y,NIL)
case (ii) $x \neq NIL$ (2.8)
   suppose putatendof (cdr(x),y) = z
   then putatendof (x,y) = cons(car(x),z)

This design gives us the function definition.

putatendof (x,y) $\equiv$ **if** eq(x,NIL) **then** cons(y,NIL) **else**
                      cons(car(x),putatendof (cdr(x),y))

Now the definition of reverse uses putatendof as a subfunction, and therefore it is the two functions together that constitute a program to reverse a list.

Incidentally, we could have defined *putatendof* in terms of *append*, as follows:

$$putatendof\,(x,y) \equiv append(x,cons(y,NIL))$$

in which case the program for *reverse* would have consisted of three function definitions. It is, however, more conventional to put the call of *append* directly into the *reverse* function and dispose of the *putatendof* function, giving the program (2.9).

$$reverse(x) \equiv \textbf{if } eq(x,NIL) \textbf{ then } NIL \textbf{ else}$$
$$append(reverse(cdr(x)),cons(car(x),NIL)) \qquad (2.9)$$
$$append(x,y) \equiv \textbf{if } eq(x,NIL) \textbf{ then } y \textbf{ else}$$
$$cons(car(x),append(cdr(x),y))$$

With this last program we can do an interesting calculation. The function $append(x,y)$ calls itself recursively n times if n is the length of the list x. Hence, we discover that whenever we use $append(x,y)$ it will call *cons* n times. Now consider $reverse(x)$. By a similar argument, $reverse(x)$ calls itself recursively n times where n is the length of the list x. Hence *reverse* does n calls of *cons* too, but it also does n calls of *append*. For each of these n calls of *append* the length this of first argument is respectively $0,1,2,\ldots,n-1$. Thus the number of times *cons* is called by *append* on behalf of *reverse* is

$$0+1+2+\cdots+(n-1) = \frac{n(n-1)}{2}.$$

The total number of calls of *cons* made by *reverse* is therefore

$$n + \frac{n(n-1)}{2} = \frac{n(n+1)}{2},$$

which is a very big number (Table 2.14).

Table 2.14

length(x)	Number of calls of cons by reverse(x)
10	55
100	5050
1000	500500

To reverse a list of length n we would expect to make n calls of *cons*. The number of extra calls made by *reverse* thus seems extravagant. We shall see in Chapter 12 that calls of *cons* can be expensive, but before then, in Section 2.6, in fact, we shall see how to reprogram *reverse* to avoid calling *cons* in a program which would be obviously faster even if calling *cons* were not known to be expensive.

Let us turn now to a more typical application for S-expressions. We will design a function *atomsin(t)* which takes as argument a list of atoms t and returns as result a list which contains one occurrence of each of the atoms occurring in t (Table 2.15).

Table 2.15

t	*atomsin*(t)
(A B A B A C A)	*(A B C)*
(THE CAT AND THE FIDDLE AND ALL)	*(THE CAT AND FIDDLE ALL)*

The way in which we use the list which this function constructs is quite a common use of S-expressions. The result of *atomsin(t)* is a set, represented as a list with no repetitions. Recognizing this guides us in our choice of sub-functions. Now let us design *atomsin(t)* by a case analysis on t, as in (2.10).

$$
\begin{aligned}
&\text{case (i)} \quad t = NIL \quad\quad atomsin(t) = NIL\\
&\text{case (ii)} \quad t \neq NIL\\
&\quad \text{suppose} \quad atomsin(cdr(t)) = s\\
&\quad\quad \text{then} \quad atomsin(t) = addtoset(s, car(t))
\end{aligned}
\quad\quad (2.10)
$$

Here, the case $t = NIL$ is trivial as usual. In the case $t \neq NIL$ where we have supposed that the list of atoms used in $cdr(t)$ is s, to compute the list of atoms used in t we must add $car(t)$ to s if it does not already occur. We have assumed we can define an appropriate function *addtoset(s,x)* to do this for us. So far, we have designed

$$atomsin(t) \equiv \textbf{if } eq(t,NIL) \textbf{ then } NIL \textbf{ else}$$
$$addtoset(atomsin(cdr(t)),car(t))$$

Now the function *addtoset(s,x)* is trivial if we assume we have a function with which we can test whether x is a member of the set s.

We have

$$addtoset(s,x) \equiv \textbf{if } member(x,s) \textbf{ then } s \textbf{ else } cons(x,s)$$

It remains to design *member(x,s)*. Remember that while *s* is being used logically as a set, it is still a list and so the usual case analysis (2.11) can apply.

---

case (i)   *s* = *NIL*   *member(x,s)* = *F*
case (ii)   *s* ≠ *NIL*
    suppose   *member(x,cdr(s))* = *b*
        then   *member(x,s)* =   (2.11)
            if *b* **then** *T* **else**
            if *x* = *car(s)* **then** *T* **else** *F*

This is correct as we have written it, but it leads to a somewhat inefficient function if we simply write it as it appears.

member(x,s) ≡ **if** *eq(s,NIL)* **then** *F* **else**
          if *member(x,cdr(s))* **then** *T* **else**
          if *eq(x,car(s))* **then** *T* **else** *F*

By simply reordering the tests we can avoid the need to search the whole of *s* when *x* is a member of *s*. We write

member(x,s) ≡ **if** *eq(s,NIL)* **then** *F* **else**
          if *eq(x,car(s))* **then** *T* **else**
          if *member(x,cdr(s))* **then** *T* **else** *F*

Indeed, the function can be tidied up a little more, into the form in which it usually appears, by recognizing that

   if *b* **then** *T* **else** *F*

always has the same value as *b*, when *b* is a logical-valued expression.

member(x,s) ≡ **if** *eq(s,NIL)* **then** *F* **else**
          if *eq(x,car(s))* **then** *T* **else** *member(x,cdr(s))*

We have completed the program for *atomsin(t)*, which consists of the three functions *atomsin*, *addtoset* and *member*. Let us consider briefly a generalization. Let us extend *atomsin(t)* so that it will work also for lists whose members are lists, indeed will work to any depth of nesting of lists. That is to say, *t* is a general list structure and *atomsin(t)* is a list of those atoms which occur at least once in *t*. Hence the result is again a set represented as a list of atoms (Table 2.16).

Table 2.16

t	$atomsin(t)$
$(ADD\ (MUL\ X\ 2)$ $(MUL\ X\ X))$	$(ADD\ MUL\ X\ 2)$
$(((A\ B)\ A)(A\ (B\ A)))$	$(\ A\ B)$

Let us redesign $atomsin(t)$, as in (2.12). Now, we have had to deal with

case (i) $t = NIL$ $atomsin(t) = NIL$
case (ii) $t \neq NIL$
    suppose $atomsin(cdr(t)) = s$
        then   subcase (i.i) $car(t)$ is an atom   (2.12)
                    $atomsin(t) = addtoset(s,\ car(t))$
                subcase (i.ii) $car(t)$ is a list
                    suppose $atomsin(car(t)) = s'$
                        then $atomsin(t) = union(s',s)$

the case when $t \neq NIL$ in two subcases. When $car(t)$ is an atom we have the same result as before. When $car(t)$ is a list, however, we must call $atomsin(car(t))$ to determine the set of atoms used in the car of t. Now, we have two sets s and s' and we must compute the result by forming the set union of them, that is the set which contains all the elements of both s and s'. Hence we have designed the function

$atomsin(t) \equiv$ **if** $eq(t,NIL)$ **then** NIL **else**
      if $atom(car(t))$ **then** $addtoset(atomsin(cdr(t)),car(t))$ **else**
      $union(atomsin(car(t)),atomsin(cdr(t)))$

To complete this extension we must design $union(u,v)$, where u and v are sets. This is straightforward since it is so similar to many of the functions we have designed so far. We have the case analysis (2.13).

case (i) $u = NIL$ $union(u,v) = v$
case (ii) $u \neq NIL$ (2.13)
    suppose $union(cdr(u),v) = w$
        then $union(u,v) = addtoset(w,car(u))$

Thus, if $u \neq NIL$ we compute the union of $cdr(u)$ and v and then add $car(u)$ to this set. This gives us the function

$$union(u,v) \equiv \textbf{if } eq(u,NIL) \textbf{ then } v \textbf{ else}$$
$$addtoset(union(cdr(u),v),car(u))$$

This extended program for $atomsin(t)$ uses four functions whose definitions are repeated in (2.14)–(2.17).

$atomsin(t) \equiv \textbf{if } eq(t,NIL) \textbf{ then } NIL \textbf{ else}$ (2.14)
  $\textbf{if } atom(car(t)) \textbf{ then } addtoset(atomsin(cdr(t)),car(t)) \textbf{ else}$
  $union(atomsin(car(t)),atomsin(cdr(t)))$

$union(u,v) \equiv \textbf{if } eq(u,NIL) \textbf{ then } v \textbf{ else}$ (2.15)
  $addtoset(union(cdr(u),v),car(u))$

$addtoset(s,x) \equiv \textbf{if } member(x,s) \textbf{ then } s \textbf{ else } cons(x,s)$ (2.16)

$member(x,s) \equiv \textbf{if } eq(s,NIL) \textbf{ then } F \textbf{ else}$
  $\textbf{if } eq(x,car(s)) \textbf{ then } T \textbf{ else}$ (2.17)
  $member(x,cdr(s))$

2.6 ACCUMULATING PARAMETERS

In this section we introduce an interesting programming technique often used in functional programming. We begin to illustrate the technique by reprogramming $reverse(x)$. The basic idea is to define a subsidiary function with an extra parameter which is used to accumulate the required result. In the case of reverse we define a function $rev(x,y)$ with the property that x is the list being reversed and y is the parameter accumulating the reversed list. We have the function definition

$$rev(x,y) \equiv \textbf{if } eq(x,NIL) \textbf{ then } y \textbf{ else}$$
$$rev(cdr(x),cons(car(x),y))$$

in terms of which we can define $reverse(x)$:

$$reverse(x) \equiv rev(x,NIL)$$

It is rather easier to see how this function operates than to design it. When $rev(x,y)$ is called, y has accumulated in reverse order all the elements so far seen of the list being reversed. Hence if x is NIL then y has accumulated the result as a whole, whereas if x is not *NIL* we can accumulate the *car* of x into y and call *rev* recursively to deal with the *cdr*. We see that successive calls of *rev* have the values given in Table 2.17 for x and y if *reverse* is called originally with $(A\ B\ C\ D)$.

Table 2.17

x	y
$(A\ B\ C\ D)$	*NIL*
$(B\ C\ D)$	(A)
$(C\ D)$	$(B\ A)$
(D)	$(C\ B\ A)$
NIL	$(D\ C\ B\ A)$

In the case of $rev(x,y)$, the second parameter y is the accumulating parameter. The problem in designing such functions lies in recognizing what the subfunction with accumulating parameters computes as its result. Here we have not applied our usual methodical design by analysis of cases but rather plucked $rev(x,y)$ out of the air, then described how it works.

To apply our analysis by cases we must decide what the general result of $rev(x,y)$ is when given an arbitrary value for y. The result of $rev(x,y)$ when x and y are both lists (possibly empty) is a list with all the elements of x appearing in reverse order followed by all the elements of y (in their original order). Formally we can write

$$rev(x,y) = append(reverse(x),y)$$

although this is not a suitable definition of $rev(x,y)$ since we need it to define *reverse*. Now we can carry out our design (2.18) of $rev(x,y)$ by a case analysis on x. This requires some explanation. It is more a proof of the validity of

---

case (i) $x = NIL$ $rev(x,y) = y$
case (ii) $x \neq NIL$
  suppose $rev(cdr(x),z) = append(reverse(cdr(x)),z)$ (2.18)
    then $rev(x,y) = append(reverse(x),y)$
                      $= append(reverse(cdr(x)),cons(car(x),y))$
                      $= rev(cdr(x),cons(car(x),y))$

---

the function given at the beginning of this section than a design of it, because the transformations made in case(ii) are fairly sophisticated. Let us take the cases in order.

When $x = NIL$, since we require that

$$rev(x,y) = append(reverse(x),y),$$

then we conclude simply that $rev(x,y) = y$. However, when $x \neq NIL$, since we still require the above equality we must assume that

$$rev(cdr(x),z) = append(reverse(cdr(x)),z)$$

for any z. This is the kind of assumption one makes in a mathematical proof by induction, and it is valid for such a proof. What we are doing is assuming we can define rev for any first argument shorter than x and then showing that we can define it for x. Now, by recognizing that

$$append(reverse(x),y) = append(reverse(cdr(x)),cons(car(x),y))$$

we conclude that the choice

$$z = cons(car(x),y)$$

is suitable to define $rev(x,y)$ in terms of $rev(cdr(x),z)$.

To conclude this definition of *reverse* using accumulating parameters, let us calculate the number of times it calls *cons*. Clearly *reverse*(x) does all its calls of *cons* in $rev(x,NIL)$. However, $rev(x,y)$ calls itself recursively n times, where n is the length of x. Thus $rev(x,y)$ calls *cons* exactly n times and hence so does *reverse*(x). This compares with $\frac{1}{2}n(n+1)$ calls by our earlier definition of *reverse* (2.9). It is an enormous saving.

Now let us apply the technique of accumulating parameters in a case where it is typically most useful. This is the case when we want to define a function which accumulates more than one result. In a previous section we defined *sum*(x), which calculated the sum of a list of integers. A similar function can be defined for computing the product (see Exercise 2.1). Let us consider the definition of a function *sumprod*(x) which returns as its result a two-list whose first member is the sum of x and whose second member is the product of x. That is we want to define *sumprod*(x) so that

$$sumprod(x) = twolist(sum(x),product(x))$$

To do this using accumulating parameters we introduce a subsidiary function $sp(x,s,p)$ with two additional parameters which will accumulate the sum and the product respectively. That is, we shall try to define sp so that

$$sp(x,s,p) = twolist(s + sum(x), p \times product(x))$$

and then we shall be able to make the definition

$$sumprod(x) \equiv sp(x,0,1)$$

We design sp by a case analysis (2.19) on x.

---

case (i) $x = NIL$ $sp(x,s,p) = twolist(s,p)$

case (ii) $x \neq NIL$ (2.19)

   suppose $sp(cdr(x),s',p') = twolist(s' + sum(cdr(x)), p' \times product(cdr(x)))$

   then $sp(x,s,p) = twolist(s + sum(x), p \times product(x))$

                 $= twolist(s + car(x) + sum(cdr(x)), p \times car(x) \times product(cdr(x)))$

                 $= sp(cdr(x), s + car(x), p \times car(x))$

As before, we have made a fairly lengthy derivation which, as well as requiring insight as to which subfunction to define, requires that we recognize and use simple identities, when $x \neq NIL$

$$sum(x) = car(x) + sum(cdr(x))$$
$$product(x) = car(x) \times product(cdr(x))$$

This has led us to design

$$sp(x,s,p) \equiv \textbf{if } eq(x,NIL) \textbf{ then } twolist(s,p) \textbf{ else}$$
$$sp(cdr(x), s + car(x), p \times car(x))$$

Again, a remarkably simple and interesting function. Here, as well as avoiding two searches of the list x, implied by computing

$$twolist(sum(x), product(x))$$

we have avoided a lot of unnecessary assembling and dissassembling of 2-lists that would be necessary if we were to try to program them without accumulating parameters. That is, without accumulating parameters we would have produced some such definition as

$$sumprod(x) \equiv \textbf{if } eq(x,NIL) \textbf{ then } twolist(0,1) \textbf{ else}$$
$$accumulate(car(x), sumprod(cdr(x)))$$
$$accumulate(n,z) \equiv twolist(n + car(z), n \times car(cdr(z)))$$

The version with accumulating parameters builds only one 2-list, the final result, whereas the later version builds $n+1$ 2-lists where there are n elements in the original list x.

2.7 LOCAL DEFINITIONS

Often it is useful to be able to compute the value of an expression and give it a name so that its value can be used repeatedly. We had an example of this at the end of the previous section. When we programmed $sumprod(x)$ without accumulating parameters we found it necessary to define the subsidiary function $accumulate(n,z)$ to avoid the inefficiency in the following definition:

$$sumprod(x) \equiv \textbf{if } eq(x,NIL) \textbf{ then } twolist(0,1) \textbf{ else}$$
$$twolist(car(sumprod(cdr(x)))+car(x),$$
$$car(cdr(sumprod(cdr(x)))) \times car(x))$$

With this definition the expression $sumprod(cdr(x))$ is computed twice. It would take a very sophisticated compiler to avoid this by recognizing the common subexpression. This doubling up of the recursive call to $sumprod$ ultimately has an exponential effect, increasing the number of recursive calls from n, for a list x of length n, to 2^n for the same list. To provide a more convenient device for avoiding such efficiency problems than the introduction of subsidiary functions, we allow local definitions to be made using **let** or **where** clauses. We rewrite the above definition in either of the forms (2.20), (2.21).

$$sumprod(x) \equiv \textbf{if } eq(x,NIL) \textbf{ then } twolist(0,1) \textbf{ else}$$
$$\{\textbf{let } z = sumprod(cdr(x)) \qquad\qquad (2.20)$$
$$twolist(car(z)+car(x),car(cdr(z)) \times car(x))\}$$

$$sumprod(x) \equiv \textbf{if } eq(x,NIL) \textbf{ then } twolist(0,1) \textbf{ else}$$
$$\{twolist(car(z)+car(x),car(cdr(z)) \times car(x))$$
$$\textbf{where } z = sumprod(cdr(x))\} \qquad\qquad (2.21)$$

The choice between these is a matter of taste: they both have the same meaning. A local definition, using the variable z, is introduced. The scope of this definition is just the expression enclosed in the braces. The **let** form allows us to write the definition before using it, the **where** form after using it. Whatever we say concerning the one syntax will apply equally to the other. Here z is defined to be the value of $sumprod(cdr(x))$, implying that this is evaluated only once and then the two parts of this result, the partial sum *car(z)* and partial product *car(cdr(z))* are used within the scope of *z*. The use of **let** or **where** clauses provides a facility similar to the block structure of Algol. We shall have to give a more careful definition of the scope rules but this we delay until we have looked at other examples.

We can make this single function definition of *sumprod(x)* even more reminiscent of the two-function version given in the last section, by introducing a local definition for the number *n* selected from the list *x*, as in (2.22).

$$sumprod(x) = \textbf{if } eq(x,NIL) \textbf{ then } twolist(0,1) \textbf{ else}$$
$$\{\textbf{let } n = car(x) \qquad\qquad (2.22)$$
$$\textbf{and } z = sumprod(cdr(x))$$
$$twolist(n + car(z), n \times car(cdr(z)))\}$$

The definitions within a block are separated by **and**. Sometimes we use local definitions simply to make a function more readable. We can do this with *sumprod* by introducing new local variables *s* and *p* to hold the partial sum and partial product contained in *z*, as in (2.23).

$$sumprod(x) \equiv \textbf{if } eq(x,NIL) \textbf{ then } twolist(0,1) \textbf{ else}$$
$$\{\textbf{let } n = car(x)$$
$$\textbf{and } z = sumprod(cdr(x)) \qquad\qquad (2.23)$$
$$\{\textbf{let } s = car(z)$$
$$\textbf{and } p = car(cdr(z))$$
$$twolist(n + s, n \times p)\}\}$$

Here it is necessary to nest the definitions of *s* and *p* so that they can refer to the value of *z*. The explanation for this is that, in a **let** block, when we have a set of definitions, the variables defined are only accessible within the expression qualified by the definitions and not within the definitions themselves.

$$\{\textbf{let } x_1 = e_1$$
$$\textbf{and } x_2 = e_2$$
$$\vdots \qquad\qquad\qquad (2.24)$$
$$\textbf{and } x_k = e_k$$
$$e\}$$

In (2.24) we have written $x_1, \ldots, x_k$ for locally defined variables,

$e_1,\ldots,e_k$ for the expressions which define them and e for the qualified expression. The variables $x_1,\ldots,x_k$ can only be used in e, where they are taken to have the value of $e_1,\ldots,e_k$ respectively.

With these features we are able to construct a very simple function for symbolic differentiation. We shall only deal with formulas which have variables, constants and the operations $+$ and $\times$. Thus we must implement the differentiation rules (where Dx means the derivative with respect to x):

$$Dx(x)=1$$
$$Dx(y)=0 \qquad\qquad y\neq x \; (y \text{ a constant or variable})$$
$$Dx(e_1+e_2)=Dx(e_1)+Dx(e_2)$$
$$Dx(e_1\times e_2)=e_1\times Dx(e_2)+Dx(e_1)\times e_2$$

and we can construct our program in such a way that these rules appear fairly directly. First we must decide upon the representation of data but this is straightforward after our discussion of the first section. Thus we shall use the representations:

$$\text{constant}\rightarrow\text{number}$$
$$\text{variable}\rightarrow\text{symbol}$$
$$e_1+e_2\rightarrow(ADD\; e_1\; e_2)$$
$$e_1\times e_2\rightarrow(MUL\; e_1\; e_2)$$

First we write two useful subsidiary functions which we use to form sums and products respectively.

$$sum(u,v) \equiv cons(ADD,\; cons(u,cons(v,NIL)))$$
$$prod(u,v) \equiv cons(MUL,\; cons(u,cons(v,NIL)))$$

Now we can write the function $diff(e)$, which computes the derivative of e with respect to X as in (2.25).

$diff(e) \equiv$ **if** $atom(e)$ **then**
      if $e=X$ **then** 1 **else** 0
  else if $eq(car(e), ADD)$ **then**
    $\{sum(diff(e1),\; diff(e2))$
      where $e1=car(cdr(e))$ (2.25)
      and $e2=car(cdr(cdr(e)))\}$
  else if $eq(car(e), MUL)$ **then**
    $\{sum(prod(e1,diff(e2)),prod(diff(e1),e2))$
      where $e1=car(cdr(e))$
      and $e2=car(cdr(cdr(e)))\}$
  else $ERROR$

We have avoided a detailed and obvious case analysis in the design of this function. Some observations are, however, in order. The function *diff* (*e*) has been organized to return the atom *ERROR* if presented with invalid arguments. In fact, this atom may appear embedded in the result if the malformed argument was malformed only in a nested subcomponent. The function has also been organized so that, using local definitions, the rules of differentiation are represented reasonably succinctly in the form of the function.

2.8 HIGHER-ORDER FUNCTIONS AND LAMBDA EXPRESSIONS

Consider the function

$$inclist(x) \equiv \textbf{if } eq(x, NIL) \textbf{ then } NIL \textbf{ else}$$
$$cons(car(x)+1, \; inclist(cdr(x)))$$

When applied to a list of integers, it produces a list of the same length and with corresponding entries exactly one higher than the list it was given. The effect is illustrated in Table 2.18.

Table 2.18

x	$inclist(x)$
(1 2 3)	(2 3 4)
(0 −1 −2)	(1 0 −1)
(127)	(128)

Similarly

$$remlist(x) \equiv \textbf{if } eq(x, NIL) \textbf{ then } NIL \textbf{ else}$$
$$cons(car(x) \textbf{ rem } 2, \; remlist(cdr(x)))$$

produces from x a list of the remainders when each entry in x is divided by 2 (see Table 2.19).

Table 2.19

x	$remlist(x)$
(1 2 3)	(1 0 1)
(0 −1 −2)	(0 −1 0)
(127)	(1)

The similarity of these two functions and our ability to imagine many more similar functions leads us to consider a general-purpose function where the actual operation carried out on each element of the list is made a parameter of the general-purpose function. Here, this general purpose function is called *map* and is defined by

$$map(x,f) \equiv \textbf{if } x = NIL \textbf{ then } NIL \textbf{ else}$$
$$cons(f(car(x)),map(cdr(x),f))$$

This has exactly the same form as the definitions of *inclist* and *remlist*, but the function applied to each element of the list x is undecided, it is the parameter f. We can therefore redefine *inclist* and *remlist* in terms of *map* as follows:

$$inc1(z) \equiv z+1$$
$$inclist(x) \equiv map(x,inc1)$$
$$rem2(z) \equiv z \textbf{ rem } 2$$
$$remlist(x) \equiv map(x,rem2)$$

Functions which take other functions as arguments are examples of what we shall call higher-order functions. In functional programming the judicious use of higher-order functions can lead to programs which are both extremely simple and powerful.

As another example of a higher-order function consider the following operation of reduction (the idea and the name are in fact taken from the programming language APL). We define $reduce(x,g,a)$ where x is a list, g is a binary function, and a is a constant, so that the list $x = (x_1 \ldots x_k)$ is reduced to the value

$$g(x_1, g(x_2, \ldots g(x_k,a) \ldots))$$

Thus, in particular if we define

$$add(y,z) \equiv y+z$$

then we would have

$$reduce(x,add,0) = sum(x)$$

The design of *reduce* is straightforward:

$$
\begin{aligned}
&\text{case (i)} \quad x = NIL \qquad reduce(x,g,a) = a \\
&\text{case (ii)} \cdot \; x \neq NIL \\
&\qquad \text{suppose} \quad reduce(cdr(x),g,a) = z \\
&\qquad\qquad \text{then} \quad reduce(x,g,a) = g(car(x),z)
\end{aligned}
$$

This gives us the definition

$$reduce(x,g,a) \equiv \textbf{if } x = NIL \textbf{ then } a \textbf{ else}$$
$$g(car(x),reduce(cdr(x),g,a))$$

Having this higher-order function makes the definition of *sum* and *product* trivial.

$$add(y,z) \equiv y+z$$
$$sum(x) \equiv reduce(x,add,0)$$
$$mul(y,z) \equiv y \times z$$
$$product(x) \equiv reduce(x,mul,1)$$

Interestingly enough, it also handles *sumprod(x)*. We have to recognize that, in this case, the result of *reduce* is a *twolist* and that therefore the arguments of the function *g* will be an integer and a 2-list, but we already have the appropriate function at the end of Section 2.6.

$$accumulate(n,z) \equiv twolist(n+car(z),n \times car(cdr(2)))$$
$$sumprod(x) \equiv reduce(x,accumulate,twolist(0,1))$$

One small disadvantage of using higher-order functions—the need to define and give names to the function supplied as an actual parameter to the higher-order function—can be overcome with the use of lambda expressions, which we shall now describe. So far, we have always introduced functions with the device of definition, such as

$$f(x_1, \ldots, x_n) \equiv e,$$

where f is the function being defined, $x_1, \ldots, x_k$ its parameters and e the expression defining it. The name f is then considered to be global (it can be used anywhere), whereas the names $x_1, \ldots, x_n$ are local (they can be used only in e). If we want to define a function which is not available globally, as yet we have no way of doing it.

A lambda expression is an expression whose value is a function. To understand this notion we have to understand that a definition, such as that given above, of a function f assigns to f (later we shall say binds to f) a value which is a function. The value assigned to f by the above definition is the value represented by the lambda expression

$$\lambda(x_1, \ldots, x_k)e$$

A function is a rule for computing a value for some arguments. The lambda expression encapsulates this rule by displaying the parameter names (here $x_1, ..., x_k$) and the expression, given in terms of these parameters, which computes the value. The lambda expression

$$\lambda(z)z+1$$

evaluates to the function which, if called with a particular value as argument, returns that value increased by one. That is, it is the function assigned to *inc*1 in the definition given at the beginning of this section. Hence we have found an immediate use for a lambda expression—as an actual parameter to a higher-order function. We can redefine *inclist*(x) by

$$inclist(x) \equiv map(x, \lambda(z)z+1)$$

Similarly, we can write

$$remlist(x) \equiv map(x, \lambda(z)z \text{ rem } 2)$$
$$sum(x) \equiv reduce(x, \lambda(y,z)y+z, 0)$$

A lambda expression denotes the same function value regardless of the names chosen for its parameters, just as long as they are distinct. Thus

$$\lambda(x)x+1$$

and

$$\lambda(z)z+1$$

denote the same function and can be interchanged, whenever they occur. In particular we can use $\lambda(x)x+1$ as the actual parameter of *map* in the definition of *inclist*, but with a little more confusion than necessary because of the two x's:

$$inclist(x) \equiv map(x, \lambda(x)x+1)$$

We will allow ourselves to use lambda expressions anywhere that a function value is needed. In particular we can use them in combination with **let** or **where** blocks to make local definitions of functions. Consider rewriting *inclist* above as

$$inclist(x) \equiv \{map(x, inc1)$$
$$\textbf{where } inc1 = \lambda (z)z+1\}$$

which, whilst it does not avoid the introduction of the name $inc1$ for the function argument to *map*, does make the scope of that name less than global. Indeed, the name $inc1$ is available only in the expression $map(x,inc1)$ itself.

When a local function definition introduces a recursive function we must use a modified form of **let** or **where** block. We indicate this modified form of block by using the keywords **letrec** and **whererec**. We can rewrite the definition of $sumprod(x)$ given at the end of Section 2.6 to make the function $sp(x,s,p)$, which is of no general usefulness, local to the definition of *sumprod*:

$$sumprod(x) \equiv$$
$$\{sp(x,0,1)$$
$$\textbf{whererec } sp = \lambda(x,s,p) \textbf{ if } eq(x,NIL) \textbf{ then } twolist(s,p) \textbf{ else}$$
$$sp(cdr(x),s+car(x),p \times car(x))\}$$

The difference between **where** and **whererec** (and **let** and **letrec**) is simply one of the scope of names. If we use **where** and **let** as in (2.26), the names

$$
\begin{array}{lll}
\{e & \{\textbf{let} \quad x_1 = e_1 & \\
\textbf{where } x_1 = e_1 & \textbf{and } x_2 = e_2 & \\
\textbf{and } x_2 = e_2 \quad \text{or} & \vdots & \quad (2.26) \\
\vdots & \textbf{and } x_k = e_k & \\
\textbf{and } x_k = e_k\} & e\} &
\end{array}
$$

$x_1,\ldots,x_k$ are available for use with the values $e_1,\ldots,e_k$ only in the qualified expression e. In the case of **whererec** and **letrec** (2.27), however, the names

$$
\begin{array}{lll}
\{e & \{\textbf{letrec } x_1 = e_1 & \\
\textbf{whererec } x_1 = e_1 & \textbf{and } x_2 = e_2 & \\
\textbf{and } x_2 = e_2 \quad \text{or} & \vdots & \quad (2.27) \\
\vdots & \textbf{and } x_k = e_k & \\
\textbf{and } x_k = e_k\} & e\} &
\end{array}
$$

$x_1,\ldots,x_k$ are used for the values $e_1,\ldots,e_k$ throughout e and $e_1,\ldots,e_k$. If each of $e_1,\ldots,e_k$ is a lambda expression and thus each $x_1,\ldots,x_k$ is a function, then any of the expressions $e_1, \ldots, e_k$ can call any of the functions $x_1, \ldots, x_k$. This is invariably the way we shall use **letrec** and **whererec**.

The **rec** postfix stands for recursive and is intended to indicate that the local definitions are mutually recursive. We shall see that this leads to some complication in the interpretation of functional programs. It can also lead to some confusion on the part of the user. When should one use **rec** and when not? It is a good rule to use **rec** only when necessary, that is when defining local recursive functions, and then to make sure that all parallel definitions are also function definitions. That is, to be safe, all the local definitions in a **letrec** or **whererec** should be functions. Consider for a moment the strange definition

$$\{\{x \text{ whererec } x = x + 1\} \text{ where } x = 0\}$$

Since **whererec** has been used both the x's in $x = x + 1$ are the same one. This is clearly a meaningless expression. On the other hand

$$\{\{x \text{ where } x = x + 1\} \text{ where } x = 0\}$$

is perfectly all right having the value 1. The x's in $x = x + 1$ are not the same one, that on the right being the one defined in the outer block.

Usually, as we have discovered, a functional program consists of a set of mutually recursive functions with one of those functions having been designated as the principal one being defined. We can use **whererec** or **letrec** to form an expression whose value is the principal function being defined and where the subsidiary functions are hidden within the expression. If the set of functions which are being defined is $f_1, \ldots, f_k$ and f_1 is the principal function in this set, we write the definition as in (2.28).

$$\{f_1$$
$$\textbf{whererec } f_1 = \ldots \qquad \qquad (2.28)$$
$$\textbf{and } f_2 = \ldots$$
$$\vdots$$
$$\textbf{and } f_k = \ldots \}$$

The final version of *atomsin(x)*, collected at the end of Section 2.5, can be rendered in this form as in (2.29).

{*atomsin* **whererec**
         atomsin = λ(*t*) **if** *eq*(*t*,*NIL*) **then** *NIL* **else**
                   if *atom*(*car*(*t*)) **then** *addtoset*(*atomsin*(*cdr*(*t*)),*car*(*t*)) **else**
                   union(*atomsin*(*car*(*t*)),*atomsin*(*cdr*(*t*)))
         and *union* = λ(*u*,*v*) **if** *eq*(*u*,*NIL*) **then** *v* **else**   (2.29)
                   addtoset(*union*(*cdr*(*u*),*v*),*car*(*u*))
     and *addtoset* = λ(*s*,*x*) **if** *member*(*x*,*s*) **then** *s* **else** *cons*(*x*,*s*)
     and *member* = λ(*x*,*s*) **if** *eq*(*s*,*NIL*) **then** *F* **else**
                   if *eq*(*x*,*car*(*s*)) **then** *T* **else**
                   member(*x*,*cdr*(*s*))}

Finally, in this section we wish to introduce another kind of higher-order function, a function-producing function. That is, a function whose result is a function. Consider the definition

$$inc(n) \equiv \lambda(z)z + n$$

Here *inc* is certainly a function, it expects an integer argument, *n*. However, its result is a function. For example *inc*(3) is a function which, when called returns *its* argument plus 3. That is, the value of

$$\{f(2) \textbf{ where } f = inc(3)\}$$

is 5. Similarly, we can redefine *inclist* by writing

$$inclist(x) \equiv map(x, inc(1))$$

Note that, if we were to write *inc* as a local definition to *inclist* (not very likely, but here it illustrates a point) we would write

$$inclist(x) \equiv \{map(x, inc(1))$$
$$\textbf{where } inc = \lambda(n)\{\lambda(z)z + n\}\}$$

This clearly shows that the body of the function assigned to *inc* is itself a lambda expression. Here we have enclosed it in an extra set of braces just to make it easier to determine where each lambda expression begins and ends.

An interesting issue has crept into our notation without our really being aware of it. We have used the lambda expression

$$\lambda(z)z + n$$

above without remarking on the fact that here we have a function defined in terms of a variable which is not one of its parameters, in this case n. Such a variable is called a global (or free) variable of the function. Here it is not very global when we consider the context in which $\lambda(z)z+n$ is used, but nevertheless it can present a problem. The problem is clearly exemplified by the expression

$$\{\textbf{let } n=1$$
$$\{\textbf{let } f=\lambda(z)z+n$$
$$\{\textbf{let } n=2$$
$$f(3)\}\}\}$$

The value of $f(3)$, and hence the value of the whole expression, is either 4 or 5, depending upon which n is chosen as the one to be added to 3 when f is called. We think of a lambda expression as being an expression which evaluates to a function value and here we think of that value being assigned to f. We shall assume that the function value so computed has all global variables resolved. That is the function is that which one obtains by replacing all global variables by their values when evaluation of the lambda expression takes place. Hence, in evaluating the above expression we first make the local definition of $n=1$, then we evaluate the lambda expression, assigning to f the function value denoted by

$$\lambda(z)z+1$$

Next, n is redefined to be 2 and then f is called with actual parameter 3. Because of the assignment of $\lambda(z)z+1$ to f this call returns the value 4. This form of evaluation of lambda expressions in which global variable values are determined at the place of definition, rather than the place of call, is called *proper* or *static* binding. This is a semantic feature of functional programming which greatly affects the overall design of its implementation and hence one we shall return to repeatedly in the remainder of the book.

Let us conclude this section with the definition of a higher-order function which has functions as both arguments and results. We define

$$dot(f,g) \equiv \lambda(x)f(g(x))$$

This is the so-called function dot product (or composition of functions). It takes as arguments two functions and produces as result the function which applies both of these functions in succession. That is, it applies f to the result of g. For example

$$increv \equiv dot(inclist,reverse)$$

is a function which first reverses a list and then increments each of its elements by one.

Table 2.20

x	$increv(x)$
(1 2 3)	(4 3 2)
(127 −127)	(−126 128)

Similarly, if we define, like $inc(n)$

$$rem(n) \equiv \lambda(z)z \text{ rem } n$$

then

$$dot(inc(1),rem(2))$$

is a function which has the same effect as

$$\lambda(z) \ (z \text{ rem } 2)+1$$

so that

$$map(x,dot(inc(1),rem(2)))$$

will take each element of a list and increment by 1 its remainder on division by 2 (Table 2.21).

Table 2.21

x	$map(x,dot(inc(1), rem(2)))$
(1 2 3)	(2 1 2)
(127 128 129 130)	(2 1 2 1)

Higher-order functions are a very important topic which bear heavily upon the considerations we must make when implementing a purely functional language on a computer. This is why we have discussed them here. We shall return to their use repeatedly throughout the book. In particular, Chapter 9 is devoted to applications of higher-order functions.

2.9 DOT NOTATION

We come now to a useful extension to the notation for S-expressions. In Chapter 4 we shall make a good deal of use of this extension when writing

S-expressions. This section is included here for completeness. A full study of it can be delayed until dot notation is encountered in later sections. The need for the extension arises out of the fact that we have no way of representing the value of *cons(x,y)* when *y* is an atom, except when *y* is *NIL*. We shall represent the value of

$$cons(A,B)$$

by the S-expression

$$(A.B)$$

with a dot between the atoms. Note that this is distinct from the value

$$(A\ B)$$

which is the result of the expression

$$cons(A,cons(B,NIL))$$

Now, we have a phenomenon which we have not had until now — two different ways of representing the same data value. The value of

$$cons(A,NIL)$$

can be represented by either

$$(A)\quad\text{or}\quad(A.NIL)$$

That is to say, these are different ways of writing the *same* value. A similar phenomenon occurs in the decimal representation of integer numbers where we consider

$$127\quad\text{and}\quad0127$$

as representing the same value, leading zeros being ignored.

The extension to the notation which we will make is in fact more general than this. For example, we shall represent the value of

$$cons(A,cons(B,cons(C,D)))$$

by

$$(A\ B\ C.D)$$

That is, the end of the list, not being *NIL*, is written following a dot. Again we have that

$$(A \ B \ C.NIL) \quad \text{and} \quad (A \ B \ C)$$

are different representations of the same value. In general the value of the expression

$$cons(e_1,e_2)$$

is represented by the dotted pair

$$(v_1.v_2)$$

where v_1 and v_2 are the S-expression values of e_1 and e_2, regardless of what kind of values these are.

Table 2.22

x	y	$cons(x,y)$
A	B	$(A.B)$
A	NIL	$(A.NIL)$
A	$(B.NIL)$	$(A.(B.NIL))$
A	$(B.C)$	$(A.(B.C))$
$(A.B)$	C	$((A.B).C)$

However, we apply the following abbreviations. The S-expression

$$(v_1.(v_2.(v_3. \ \ldots \ (v_k.v_{k+1}) \ \ldots \ )))$$

is written as

$$(v_1 \quad v_2 \quad v_3 \quad \ldots \quad v_k.v_{k+1})$$

Note the solitary dot. Also, the S-expression

$$(v_1 \quad v_2 \quad v_3 \quad \ldots \quad v_k.NIL)$$

is written as

$$(v_1 \quad v_2 \quad v_3 \quad \ldots \quad v_k)$$

as it has been all along. These rules can be summarized as follows. A dot, followed immediately by an opening parenthesis, can be omitted as long as the opening parenthesis and its corresponding closing parenthesis are also omitted. A dot followed immediately by the atom *NIL* can be omitted as long as the *NIL* is also omitted. Hence we see that the value of

$$cons(A,cons(B,cons(C,NIL)))$$

is represented by

$$(A.(B.(C.NIL)))$$

which abbreviates successively to

$$(A\ B.(C.NIL))$$
$$(A\ B\ C.NIL)$$
$$(A\ B\ C)$$

Indeed all of the S-expressions shown in Fig 2.2 represent the same value. that is the value of the above expression. Each arrow shows which form is

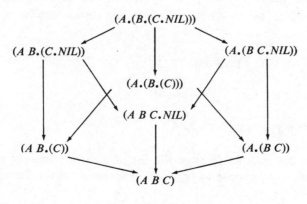

Fig. 2.2

obtained from which by application of one of the rules. In general, we shall always use the shortest form, that is the one with as many dots eliminated as possible.

The way in which we shall make most use of dot notation is when we wish for example to refer to the first two elements of a list of arbitrary length. We shall write

$$(x_1 \ x_2.y)$$

rather than

$$(x_1 \ x_2 \ x_3 \ \ldots \ x_k)$$

so that x_1 denotes the first list element, x_2 the second and y the rest of the list (here $(x_3 \ \ldots \ x_k)$). It is sometimes convenient to build pairs using *cons* rather than *twolist*. To a large extent it depends upon whether or not such pairs are to be printed. For example, if we wanted to make a list of pairs of symbolic atoms with integer values, we could choose to use a list of 2-lists

$$((X \ 1) \ (Y \ 17) \ (Z \ -127))$$

or a list of dotted pairs

$$((X.1) \ (Y.17) \ (Z.-127))$$

The choice is a matter of taste. The dotted pairs may require less storage space in most implementations, but if symbols are paired with general S-expressions rather than with atoms, the *twolist* version can be more legible. Compare

$$((X \ A) \ (Y \ (B \ C)) \ (Z \ NIL))$$

with

$$((X.A) \ (Y \ B \ C) \ (Z))$$

which is the abbreviated form of the list of dotted points. In general, an implementation will choose to print an S-expression as the shortest possible form.

Since now we can represent the result of any *cons* operation, we can write functions of general S-expressions. An S-expression is either

1. an atom, or
2. a dotted pair of two S-expressions (the result of a *cons*).

Hence, when designing functions of S-expressions (as opposed to just lists).

we have a different case analysis to consider. Let us design a function (see (2.30)) which counts the number of atoms in an S-expression—call it *atomsize(s)*.

---

case (i)   *s* is an atom $atomsize(s) = 1$

case (ii)   *s* is not an atom   (2.30)

   suppose $atomsize(car(s)) = m$

   and $atomsize(cdr(s)) = n$

   then $atomsize(s) = m + n$

So the cases to consider are just atom and non-atom. In the non-atom case we call the function being defined recursively for both the *car* and the *cdr* of the argument. We have designed the following function:

$$atomsize(s) \equiv \textbf{if } atom(s) \textbf{ then } 1 \textbf{ else}$$
$$atomsize(car(s)) + atomsize(cdr(s))$$

Note that, if we apply this to a list or list of lists, etc., then the *NIL*s which terminate each list also get counted.

We have observed earlier that $eq(x,y)$ is a predicate which can be applied only if at least one of its arguments is an atom. That is to say it is undefined if both its arguments are S-expressions in the sense that whether it returns *T* or *F* is not defined. However, we can design a function *equal(x,y)* which returns *T* if both *x* and *y* are identical S-expressions in the sense that if we compare each of them we find exactly the same atoms in exactly the same positions. We apply our case analysis as in (2.31).

---

case (i)   *atom(x)* $equal(x,y) = eq(x,y)$

case (ii) $\neg atom(x)$

   subcase (ii.i)   *atom(y)* $equal(x,y) = eq(x,y)$ (2.31)

   subcase (ii.ii) $\neg atom(y)$

      suppose $equal(car(x),car(y)) = t_1$

      and $equal(cdr(x),cdr(y)) = t_2$

      then $equal(x,y) = \textbf{if } t_1 \textbf{ then } t_2 \textbf{ else } F$

In case (i) and (ii.i) we know that one of *x* or *y* is an atom and therefore we can simply use *eq*. In case (ii.ii), since neither *x* nor *y* is an atom, we use *equal* recursively to compare the *car*s and the *cdr*s. Now *x* and *y* are equal if both their *car*s are equal and their *cdr*s are equal. That is, we want to write

$$equal(x,y) = t_1 \text{ and } t_2$$

Instead, we have written

$$equal(x,y) = \textbf{if } t_1 \textbf{ then } t_2 \textbf{ else } F$$

which is easily seen to have the same value. This is more consistent with the design of the rest of the function (but reflects the fact that we anticipate some problems with **and**—see Chapter 5). The function we have designed is shown in (2.32).

$$
\begin{aligned}
equal(x,y) \equiv\ &\textbf{if } atom(x) \textbf{ then } eq(x,y) \textbf{ else} \\
&\textbf{if } atom(y) \textbf{ then } eq(x,y) \textbf{ else} \\
&\textbf{if } equal\ (car(x),car(y)) \textbf{ then} \\
&\quad equal(cdr(x),cdr(y)) \textbf{ else } F
\end{aligned}
\qquad (2.32)
$$

While we could have written this using local definitions for t_1 and t_2, as in (2.33), we should *not* do so. This form of definition implies that both the *car*s

---

$$
\begin{aligned}
equal(x,y) \equiv\ &\textbf{if } atom(x) \textbf{ then } eq(x,y) \textbf{ else} \\
&\textbf{if } atom(y) \textbf{ then } eq(x,y) \textbf{ else} \\
&\{\textbf{let } t1 = equal(car(x),car(y)) \\
&\quad \textbf{and } t2 = equal(cdr(x),cdr(y)) \\
&\quad \textbf{if } t1 \textbf{ then } t2 \textbf{ else } F\ \}
\end{aligned}
\qquad (2.33)
$$

---

and the *cdr*s are compared, whereas the earlier form implies that if the *car*s are found not to be equal, then the *cdr*s are not even compared.

Note that, in either function definition, the second comparison $eq(x,y)$ is always false, and should thus be replaced by F.

EXERCISES

2.1 Design a recursive function *product*(x) which will form the product of a list of integers.

2.2 Design a function *declist(x)* which takes a list of integers *x* as argument and produces as result a list each of whose members is one less than the corresponding element in *x* (see Table 2.23).

Table 2.23

x	*declist(x)*
NIL	*NIL*
(1 2)	(0 1)
(4 5 6)	(3 4 5)

Generalize this so that the amount by which each element is decreased can be given as an extra parameter to declist.

2.3 Design a function *position(x,y)* which takes as arguments an atom *x* and a list of atoms *y*. Its result is the position of the atom *x* in the list *y*, counting the first position as number 1. Assume that *x* does occur in *y* (see Table 2.24).

Table 2.24

x	*y*	*position(x,y)*
A	(A B C)	1
B	(A B C)	2
F	(A B C D E F)	6

2.4 Modify the above function so that it returns the value 0 if *x* does not occur in *y*.

2.5 Design a function *index(i,y)* which takes as arguments an integer *i* and a list *y*. It returns the *i*th member of the list *y*, assuming *y* is at least of length *i*.

2.6 Write a function *flatten(x)*, where the argument *x* is a list with sublists nested to any depth, such that the result of *flatten(x)* is just a list of atoms with the property that all the atoms appearing in *x* also appear in *flatten(x)* and in the same order.

Table 22.5

x	*flatten(x)*
(A(B C)D)	(A B C D)
(((A B)C)(D E))	(A B C D E)
((((((A))))))	(A)

2.7   Design a function *frequencies*(*t*) which takes as argument a list of atoms *t* and produces a list of all the atoms occurring in *t* each paired with the frequency of its occurrence (see Table 2.26). Since the result is a set of pairs it is not important in what order these pairs appear.

Table 2.26

t	*frequencies*(*t*)
(*A B A B A C A*)	((*A* 4) (*B* 2) (*C* 1))
(*THE CAT AND THE*	((*THE* 2) (*CAT* 1) (*AND* 2)
FIDDLE AND ALL)	(*FIDDLE* 1) (*ALL* 1))

2.8   Design functions to perform the usual set operations on lists of atoms used to represent sets in the way they have been used in Section 2.5, that is without repetition. Set *union* has been done. Set *intersection* produces from sets *u* and *v* the set which contains all those atoms which are in both *u* and *v*. Set *difference* produces from *u* and *v* the set which contains all those atoms in *u* which are not in *v*. The function *exclusiveunion* produces from *u* and *v* the set which contains all the atoms in either *u* or *v* but not in both. That is

$$exclusiveunion(u,v) = difference(union(u,v), intersection(u,v))$$

2.9   Design a function *singletons*(*t*) which takes as argument a list *t* and produces as a result a list of all the atoms which occur exactly once in *t*. Note that, while it is possible to use *frequencies*(*t*) and then select only those atoms with unit frequency, a better program can be obtained by tackling this one more directly.

2.10   Reprogram *singletons*(*x*) defined in Exercise 2.9 so that it uses accumulating parameters. This time two such parameters are needed, one to accumulate those atoms seen exactly once and those seen more than once. Compare the number of calls of *cons* used by your solutions with and without accumulating parameters.

2.11   Define a function *mapset*(*x*,*f*) which takes as argument a list *x*, considered to be a set, and produces as result the set, again represented as a list, obtained by applying *f* to each member of *x* (see Table 2.27). Note that the order of elements in a list representing a set is immaterial.

Table 2.27

x	*mapset*(*x*,λ(*z*)*z* **div** 10)
(1 57 84 61 53 6)	(0 5 8 6)
(101 102 103 104 105)	(10)
(78 87 79 −97)	(7 8 −9)

2.12 Design a function *reduce2(x,g,a)* which when applied to the list

$$x = (x_1 \quad \ldots \quad x_k) \text{ produces the value } g(\ldots g(g(a,x_1),x_2)\ldots, x_k)$$

Consider $reduce2(x,\lambda(y,z)10 \times y + z,0)$ when x is a list of single-digit positive integers. What value is computed? What if we use *reduce* instead of *reduce2*?

2.13 Abbreviate the following S-expressions:

$$((A.(B.NIL)).((C.(D.NIL)).NIL))$$
$$(((A.NIL).NIL).B)$$
$$(A \ B \ C.(D \ E \ F.NIL))$$
$$((A.B).(C.D))$$

2.14 Redesign the *flatten(x)* function of Exercise 2.6, so that it will flatten a general S-expression (see Table 2.28). Note that, if a list is flattened its *NIL*s appear.

Table 2.28

x	$flatten(x)$
$(A.(B.C))$	$(A \ B \ C)$
$(A \ B)$	$(A \ B \ NIL)$
$((A.B)(C.D))$	$(A \ B \ C \ D \ NIL)$

If x is a general S-expression, *flatten(x)* is a list of all the atoms which occur in x, in the order in which they occur.

2.15 Design a function *samefringe(x,y)* which returns T if the same atoms occur in both x and y in the same order, regardless of the internal structure of x and y, and returns F otherwise, where x and y are arbitrary S-expressions. A correct but unsatisfactory definition is

$$samefringe(x,y) \equiv equal(flatten(x), flatten(y))$$

where flatten is as designed for the previous exercise. A general S-expression can be depicted by a binary tree. The binary tree equivalent to $(a.b)$ is

where if a and b are atoms they appear as leaves, whereas if they are dotted pairs they appear as subtrees. Thus the binary trees in Fig. 2.3, are given as titles the,

S-expressions to which they correspond. These trees all have the same fringe. If we
either relabel the leaves or reorder the labels they become fringe unequal. This is a

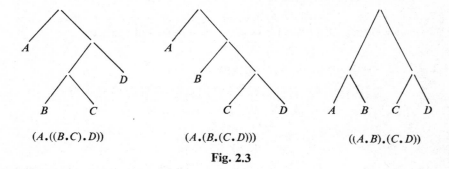

$$(A.((B.C).D)) \qquad (A.(B.(C.D))) \qquad ((A.B).(C.D))$$

Fig. 2.3

very difficult exercise, the problem being to avoid *flatten*ing a huge tree when it is
fringe unequal to the one with which it is being compared.

3 SIMPLE FUNCTIONAL PROGRAMS

In this chapter we will go through, in detail, three complete functional programs. Each program has been chosen to illustrate some particular programming techniques but should, nevertheless, be interesting in itself. The first program is to carry out a particular symbolic computation called *dimensional analysis*. This is the process of checking a formula or equation to see that all the quantities mentioned are combined in such a way that the fundamental units of mass, length and time are consistently used. For example, it is not allowed to add together a unit of mass and a unit of time. The programming techniques illustrated by this example are the basic principles of structured programming, the judicious separation of subproblems into easily specifiable subfunctions. This presents an opportunity to give some advice on testing well-structured programs and also introduces the notion of an association list, common to many applications.

The second example is of searching a tree, or graph, looking for a node with a particular property. Many problems can be cast in this form, and we mention just a few, using as our example the problem of determining which movements are required to rotate a tetrahedron into a prespecified orientation. This example gives us the opportunity to discuss in general the programming of searches in functional form and also the organization of a program which makes use of global variables.

The third example is a little more abstract. It is an example which has in fact appeared repeatedly in the exercises in Chapter 2 and hence one with which I hope the reader is familiar. It is the example of determining, for an arbitrary symbolic structure, the set of atoms which occur exactly once in that structure (the *singletons* function). This example affords us the opportunity to introduce the notion of using a function, where normally a data structure is used, to represent a set, and allows us to discuss that interesting programming technique.

3.1 DIMENSIONAL ANALYSIS—AN EXAMPLE OF STRUCTURED PROGRAMMING AND STRUCTURED PROGRAM TESTING

In engineering and applied mathematics, formulas describing real world phenomena are expressed in terms of quantities which have associated *dimensions*. These dimensions are expressed in terms of the fundamental units mass (M), length (L) and time (T). Thus area has dimension L^2 since it is the product of two lengths and velocity has dimension LT^{-1} since it is the ratio of length to time (e.g. feet per second). Note however, that these fundamental units take no account of whether the lengths are feet or metres or miles and so on. We could easily adopt a system which did take account of such things but we will not concern ourselves with that until later. Now an equation such as

$$v = u + ft$$

can be analyzed as follows.

This equation concerns motion in a straight line and tells us that if a body traveling with velocity u is accelerated with acceleration f for a length of time t, at the end of that time its velocity will be v. Hence we have the following dimensions for the quantities appearing in the formulas:

$$v = LT^{-1} \qquad\qquad u = LT^{-1}$$
$$f = LT^{-2} \qquad\qquad t = T$$

we see therefore that the dimension of the quantity ft is LT^{-1} and that the dimensions on each side of the equation balance. We conclude that the equation is dimensionally valid.

Another equation of motion in a straight line relates initial and final velocity to distance traveled rather than time taken. Its form is

$$v^2 = u^2 + 2fs.$$

Suppose, however, that we had incorrectly remembered this as

$$v^2 = u^2 + 2ft$$

we could determine the invalidity of this equation by dimensionsal analysis as follows. The dimension of u^2 is L^2T^{-2} and the dimension of $2ft$ is LT^{-1}. Therefore it is not permissible to add these quantities. The formula is dimensionally invalid.

We want to write a functional program which will do dimensional analysis. It is sufficient in fact to write a function which accepts an arithmetic expression and returns its dimension, for the two formulas given as examples here could be presented to such a function in the inverted form

$$0 = u + ft - v$$
$$0 = u^2 + 2ft - v^2$$

That is to say, only the right-hand side of the equation is analyzed. We must choose a representation for the arithmetic expressions to be analyzed and we must choose a representation for the dimensions of quantities. We will restrict ourselves to arithmetic expressions constructed from variables, constants and the operators $+$, $-$, $\times$, $\div$. In fact, we shall not distinguish between variables and constants, requiring both to be given dimensions and representing both by atoms. Hence, we will have the class of well-formed arithmetic expressions shown in Table 3.1, and the usual choice of representation for such expressions as explained in Section 2.1.

Table 3.1

well-formed expression	representation
variable and constant	atom
$e_1 + e_2$	$(ADD\ e_1\ e_2)$
$e_1 - e_2$	$(SUB\ e_1\ e_2)$
$e_1 \times e_2$	$(MUL\ e_1\ e_2)$
$e_1 \div e_2$	$(DIV\ e_1\ e_2)$

Hence the expressions $u+ft-v$ and $u^2+2ft-v^2$ will be represented by

$$(ADD\ U\ (SUB\ (MUL\ F\ T)\ V))$$
$$(ADD\ (MUL\ U\ U)\ (SUB\ (MUL\ 2\ (MUL\ F\ T))\ (MUL\ V\ V)))$$

Now, let us consider a data structure for representing dimensions. In general a dimension has the form $M^{n_1}\ L^{n_2}\ T^{n_3}$, where the integers n_1, n_2 and n_3 may be positive, zero or negative. Hence we could represent the dimension by a

3-list of integers. Thus, for example, velocity LT^{-1} would be represented by (0 1 -1) and force MLT^{-2} by (1 1 -2). Bearing this apparently trivial representation in mind, we proceed with the design of the analysis function which will turn out to be independent of the choice we make for this representation, a fact which we shall demonstrate by changing the representation later to a more powerful one.

An important design decision remains. How are we to determine the dimension of a variable appearing in a formula? Of course these dimensions must be given as an argument to the analysis function, so we must design a structure for this argument. Since each variable is associated with a unique dimension, this fact can be recorded in a list of pairs, each pair giving a variable and its associated dimension. Such a list is usually called an *association list*. In general we have the structure

$$((v_1\ d_1) \ldots (v_k\ d_k))$$

for an association list with k members, the variables (atoms) $v_1, \ldots, v_k$ and their dimensions $d_1, \ldots, d_k$. The principal function with which we manipulate such an association list is $assoc(v,a)$, where v is a variable whose associated value (dimension in this case) is required and a is the association list. If we assume that v is in the list a we have

$$assoc(v,a) \equiv \textbf{if } eq(v,car(car(a))) \textbf{ then } car(cdr(car(a))) \textbf{ else}$$
$$assoc(v,cdr(a))$$

If, however, we do not assume that v is in the list we can return some standard value to represent the fact that no association has been found. Here we choose to use the atom *UNDEFINED* for this purpose.

$$assoc(v,a) \equiv \textbf{if } eq(a,NIL) \textbf{ then } UNDEFINED \textbf{ else}$$
$$\textbf{if } eq(v,car(car(a))) \textbf{ then } car(cdr(car(a))) \textbf{ else}$$
$$assoc(v,cdr(a))$$

Now, we can postpone the design of any further subfunctions until we have dealt with the design of the main analysis function. Let us call the function to be defined $dim(e,a)$, where e is the expression to be analyzed and a is the association list. It must deal with five cases corresponding to the five forms of well-formed arithmetic expression, as shown in (3.1).

case (i)	e is a variable	$dim(e,a) = assoc(e,a)$
case (ii)	e is of the form $(ADD\ e_1\ e_2)$	suppose $dim(e_1,a) = d_1$ and $dim(e_2,a) = d_2$ then (1) d_1 and d_2 must be equal (2) $dim(e,a) = d_1$
case (iii)	e is of the form $(SUB\ e_1\ e_2)$	same as case (ii)
case (iv)	e is of the form $(MUL\ e_1\ e_2)$	suppose $dim\ (e_1,a) = d_1$ $dim(e_2,a) = d_2$ then $dim(e,a) = product(d_1,d_2)$
case (v)	e is of the form $(DIV\ e_1\ e_2)$	suppose $dim(e_1,a) = d_1$ $dim(e_2,a) = d_2$ then $dim(e,\ a) = ratio(d_1,\ d_2)$

$$(3.1)$$

Here we have determined that each of the four cases (ii)–(v) are similar in the respect that the dimension of a composite expression is a function of the dimensions of its components. In the case of MUL and DIV the appropriate functions $product(d1,d2)$ and $ratio(d1,d2)$ have yet to be designed. Similarly the function which is used in the case of ADD and SUB to determine if two dimensions are equal has not been defined. Let us call it $same(d1,d2)$, so that we can write the definition of $dim(e,a)$ as in (3.2). Note that here we have used, for example, the form $car(e) = ADD$ when strictly we should have written $eq(car(e),\ ADD)$. From now on, we shall use the two forms interchangeably in such tests.

$$
\begin{aligned}
&dim(e,a) \equiv \\
&\quad \textbf{if } atom(e) \textbf{ then } assoc(e,a) \textbf{ else} \\
&\quad \{\textbf{let } d1 = dim(car(cdr(e)),a) \\
&\quad\quad \textbf{and } d2 = dim(car(cdr(cdr(e))),a) \\
&\quad\quad \textbf{if } car(e) = ADD \textbf{ then} \\
&\quad\quad\quad \textbf{if } same(d1,d2) \textbf{ then } d1 \textbf{ else } UNDEFINED \\
&\quad\quad \textbf{else if } car(e) = SUB \textbf{ then} \\
&\quad\quad\quad \textbf{if } same(d1,d2) \textbf{ then } d1 \textbf{ else } UNDEFINED \\
&\quad\quad \textbf{else if } car(e) = MUL \textbf{ then} \\
&\quad\quad\quad product(d1,d2) \\
&\quad\quad \textbf{else if } car(e) = DIV \textbf{ then} \\
&\quad\quad\quad ratio(d1,d2) \textbf{ else } UNDEFINED\}
\end{aligned}
$$

$$(3.2)$$

The way in which this function works is fairly straightforward. In fact, it assigns dimensions to the innermost subexpressions first and then works its way progressively outward, determining the dimension of larger sub expressions until finally the dimension of the entire expression can be determined. We have treated constants as if they were variables and so an entry for each constant must appear in the association list.

Now we must design the remaining subfunctions *same*, *product* and *ratio*. If we assume the representation suggested earlier for dimensions, a 3-list of integers, then we arrive at the definitions in (3.3)–(3.7).

$same(d1,d2) \equiv$
   if $d1 = UNDEFINED$ **then** F **else**
   if $d2 = UNDEFINED$ **then** F **else**
   if $mass(d1) = mass(d2)$ **then**   (3.3)
      if $length(d1) = length(d2)$ **then** $time(d1) = time(d2)$
                          else F
      else F

$mass(d) \equiv car(d)$
$length(d) \equiv car(cdr(d))$ (3.4)
$time(d) \equiv car(cdr(cdr(d)))$

$product(d1,d2) \equiv$
    if $d1 = UNDEFINED$ **then** $UNDEFINED$ **else**
    if $d2 = UNDEFINED$ **then** $UNDEFINED$ **else**
    $threelist(mass(d1) + mass(d2),$ (3.5)
         $length(d1) + length(d2),$
           $time\ (d1) + time(d2))$

$ratio(d1,d2) \equiv$
    if $d1 = UNDEFINED$ **then** $UNDEFINED$ **else**
    if $d2 = UNDEFINED$ **then** $UNDEFINED$ **else**
    $threelist(mass(d1) - mass(d2),$ (3.6)
         $length(d1) - length(d2),$
          $time(d1) - time(d2))$

$threelist(x,y,z) \equiv cons(x,cons(y,cons(z,NIL)))$ (3.7)

These definitions are self-explanatory. Let us see how together they cope with the analysis of the expression

$$(ADD\ U\ (SUB\ (MUL\ F\ T)\ V))$$

with respect to the list of associations

$$((U\,(0\ 1\ -1))\,(V\,(0\ 1\ -1))\,(F\,(0\ 1\ -2))\,(T\,(0\ 0\ 1)))$$

The function $dim(e,a)$ constructs the dimensions given in Table 3.2.

Table 3.2

e	$dim(e,a)$
U	(0 1 −1)
F	(0 1 −2)
T	(0 0 1)
$(MUL\ F\ T)$	(0 1 −1)
V	(0 1 −1)
$(SUB\,(MUL\ F\ T)\ V)$	(0 1 −1)
$(ADD\ U(SUB\,(MUL\ F\ T)\ V))$	(0 1 −1)

When testing this program it is as well to test each of the subfunctions independently. Here the functions *mass, length, time* and *threelist* are sufficiently trivial that we might well avoid th'.s. However, since *same, product* and *ratio* are somewhat less trivial, testing them independently has the advantage that when we come to test *dim* we can rely upon their correct working. The function *assoc* should of course be tested independently and then the main function dim can be tested progressively, by first exercising it with simple data and then with each form of expression in turn. We shall return to a discussion of testing after we have elaborated this program some more.

Suppose, instead of just using the fundamental units M, L and T, we wish to use the usual absolute units and to analyze our formula to determine that all absolute units are consistent. Thus, for example, if lengths are measured in feet and time in seconds, then velocity is in feet per second and acceleration in feet per second per second. The formula

$$u+ft-v$$

is consistent if u and v are velocities in feet per second, f an acceleration in feet per second per second and t a time in seconds. If t' is a time in minutes we can use the conversion

$$t=ct'$$

where t is a time in seconds and c is a conversion constant ($=60$) which has dimension seconds per minute. Note that if we were using fundamental units such a constant would be dimensionless. Thus we see that we can do some useful additional analysis of our formula if we can cope with this extension. In the context of this book it is interesting because of the problem of data representation which it poses.

The data representation which we have is of course no use because we expect more than one kind of unit of, for example, length and hence we need to deal with more than just three units. Nor could we very satisfactorily extend this data representation to an n-list of integers, where each position is reserved for some predetermined unit, for this supposes both that we can enumerate all the units ever to be used by our program, and that this enumeration is reasonably short. Rather than try to do this here we shall instead try to deal with the units more explicitly. Note that a dimension can be written as a ratio of products of units. Thus

feet per second $\dfrac{\text{feet}}{\text{sec}}$

feet per second per second $\dfrac{\text{feet}}{\text{sec}^2}$

pounds per square foot $\dfrac{\text{lb}}{\text{feet}^2}$

Hence we could represent a dimension as a pair (i.e. 2-list) of lists, respectively the numerator and denominator of this ratio. The above dimensions become

$$((FEET)\,(SEC))$$
$$((FEET)\,(SEC\ SEC))$$
$$((LB)\,(FEET\ FEET))$$

respectively. This representation has the property that it can represent all the extreme cases which we require. For example,

$((FEET)\,NIL)$	is the basic unit, feet
$(NIL\,(SEC))$	is the unit, per second
$(NIL\ NIL)$	is the unit of a dimensionless constant.

On the other hand, it has some small difficulties, associated with the fact that it can be internally redundant; for example

$$((FEET)\,(FEET\ SEC))$$

is better written as

$$(NIL \ (SEC))$$

with the *FEET* "canceled". We will say that a representation in which no cancellations are possible is reduced and write a function *reduce(d)* which, given a dimension *d* will return a reduced representation of it.

In order to design *reduce(d)* we will assume that *d* is either the atom *UNDEFINED* or has the form *(t b)* where the numerator *t* and the denominator *b* are lists of atoms. The function *reduce* will simply take each of the atoms in the numerator in turn and see if it can be canceled from the denominator. Note that it is only necessary to consider the numerator in this way because if an atom can be canceled it must be present in the numerator before cancellation begins. By symmetry, it would have been equally satisfactory to consider the denominator in this way, but the point is that we need only consider one or other of them. First, we decide to deal with the case when *d* is *UNDEFINED* and then delegate the rest of the computation to a subfunction:

$$reduce(d) \equiv \text{ if } d = UNDEFINED \text{ then } UNDEFINED$$
$$\text{else } red(d)$$

Now consider the cases (3.8) which the function *red(d)* must deal with.

---

case (i)   *d* has form *(NIL b)*   it is already reduced

case (ii)   *d* has form *((u.t) b)*   suppose $d'' = red(d')$
                                                   where $d' = (t \ b)$

subcase (ii.i)
   u appears in denominator of *d''*; result is *d''* with *u*
   removed from denominator.   (3.8)

subcase (ii.ii)
   u does not appear in denominator of *d''*; result is *d''*
   with *u* added to the numerator.

We have considered two principal cases, that when the numerator is empty and that when it is not. When the numerator is *NIL*, the dimension is in reduced form, clearly. When the numerator is not empty we can call *red* recursively to reduce the dimension which excludes the first item of the numerator. Thus, in the above, d'' is in reduced form, and is the reduced form of d except for the incorporation of u, withheld when the recursive call was made. Now we have two possibilities: either u is or is not included in the denominator of d''. If it is, then we remove it to obtain the result. If it is not, then we must incorporate u in the numerator of d'' to obtain the result. Hence we have designed the function shown in (3.9).

$$red(d) \equiv \textbf{if } car(d) = NIL \textbf{ then } d \textbf{ else}$$
$$\{\textbf{let } d'' = red(twolist(cdr(num(d)),den(d)))$$
$$\textbf{if } member(car(num(d)),den(d'')) \textbf{ then} \qquad (3.9)$$
$$twolist(num(d''),remove(car(num(d)),den(d'')))$$
$$\textbf{else } twolist(cons(car(num(d)),num(d'')),den(d''))\}$$
$$num(d) \equiv car(d)$$
$$den(d) \equiv car(cdr(d))$$
$$twolist(t,b) \equiv cons(t,cons(b,NIL))$$

Thus we are in a position to reduce any dimension not considered to be reduced. There is no harm in applying *reduce* to a reduced dimension, but it is wasteful and we shall try to avoid it. We will so organize our program that, as soon as any new dimension is computed it will be reduced. Recall that $dim(e,a)$ calls the subfunctions $same(d1,d2)$, $product(d1,d2)$ and $ratio$ $(d1,d2)$ to manipulate dimensions. In fact, knowledge of the representation of dimensions is embedded entirely in these functions. In order to modify the program to work with our new representation, it is only necessary to reprogram these three functions.

The product of two dimensions is the most trivial: we simply append the numerator lists to obtain a new numerator and the denominator lists to obtain a new denominator. This new dimension may not be in reduced form and so we must reduce it. Finally, it is necessary to pay special attention to the case in which either of the arguments of $product(d1,d2)$ is *UNDEFINED*: the result is given in (3.10).

$$product(d1,d2) \equiv$$
$$\textbf{if } d1 = UNDEFINED \textbf{ then } UNDEFINED \textbf{ else}$$
$$\textbf{if } d2 = UNDEFINED \textbf{ then } UNDEFINED \textbf{ else} \qquad (3.10)$$
$$reduce(twolist(append(num(d1),num(d2)),$$
$$append(den(d1),den(d2))))$$

The ratio of two dimensions is computed similarly, except that we "cross-multiply", that is we form the numerator of the result from the numerator of $d1$ and the denominator of $d2$ and we form the denominator of the result from the denominator of $d1$ and the numerator of $d2$, as in (3.11).

$ratio(d1,d2) \equiv$
    if $d1 = UNDEFINED$ **then** $UNDEFINED$ **else**
    if $d2 = UNDEFINED$ **then** $UNDEFINED$ **else**   (3.11)
    $reduce\ (twolist(append(num(d1),den(d2)),$
        $append(den(d1),num(d2))))$

The design of $same(d1,d2)$, however, leads to some interesting programming. Because we have placed no significance on the order of units in the lists forming numerator and denominator of a dimension, we cannot simply compare numerator and denominator for equality. For example, the following dimensions are all equal:

$((LB)\ (FT\ FT\ SEC))$
$((LB)\ (FT\ SEC\ FT))$
$((LB)\ (SEC\ FT\ FT))$

What we must do then is to compare lists of atoms to see if they are the same except for order. One way to do this is to take the elements of the first list in turn, remove them from the second list and see if both lists become empty at the same time. This is reminiscent of "cancellation" and suggests that we consider if we can use *reduce* to do the work. We can, if we notice that two dimensions are equal if their ratio is dimensionless. That is, if we form $ratio(d1,d2)$ and obtain $(NIL\ NIL)$, then $d1$ and $d2$ must be the same dimension, for everything in the one has canceled everything in the other. Whether such an observation is "easy" to discover is difficult to say. However, the fact that it is easy to see once explained should make us not ashamed to use it here. As usual, we must take care of the special case $UNDEFINED$, as in (3.12).

$same(d1,d2) \equiv$
        if $d1 = UNDEFINED$ **then** F **else**
        if $d2 = UNDEFINED$ **then** F **else**   (3.12)
        $\{$**let** $d = ratio(d1,d2)$
        if $num(d) = NIL$ **then** $den(d) = NIL$ **else** $F\}$

In order to discuss the testing of this program it is useful to construct the function-call diagram for it (Fig 3.1). In this diagram, which is a graph with function names at its nodes, an arc from one node to another denotes the fact that the function at the tail of the arrow calls the function at its head. The trivial functions *num, den* and *twolist* are not shown.

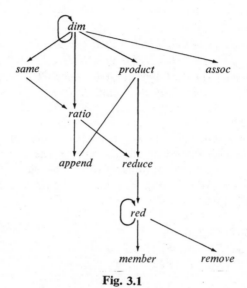

Fig. 3.1

In fact we have two alternative implementations of *same, ratio* and *product* using the two alternative representations. Assuming that we desire only to implement the second version of *dim*, which uses the more elaborate representation, then we have two distinct ways of proceeding with the testing. We can test entirely bottom-up or we can add an element of top-down testing. Here we will give a scenario for each approach, in order to indicate how such testing can take advantage of the structure of the program.

To test bottom-up we exercise first functions which call no others, and then functions which call only previously tested functions, and so on. Test data are chosen in such a way that, when a test fails (to produce the expected results) we are justified in suspecting the higher-level function which is new to this test. For example, with the above call structure, suppose we test *assoc* independently before we test *dim* which calls it. If we test *assoc* with the arguments

$$X \text{ and } ((X ((FT) NIL)) (Y ((SEC) NIL)))$$

and later test *dim* with the same data, the success by *assoc* and failure by *dim* justifies our suspicion of *dim*. Hence we have localized the likely cause of the fault. The sequence in which functions should be tested is easily determined from the above call structure. A function should be tested only when all the functions which it calls have been tested and, where possible, these subfunctions should have been made to handle the arguments which the calling function will give them. Recursion muddies this nice situation a little but, with a little thought, data can be chosen to progressively exercise the parts of a recursive function, causing it to recur $0, 1, \ldots$ more times. Similarly a set of mutually recursive functions can be progressively tested by judiciously chosen data. For example, if f calls g and g calls f as follows:

$$f(\ldots) \equiv \textbf{if} \ldots \textbf{then} \ldots g(\ldots) \ldots \textbf{else} \ldots$$
$$g(\ldots) \equiv \textbf{if} \ldots \textbf{then} \ldots f(\ldots) \ldots \textbf{else} \ldots$$

we must test f and g together, but can probably choose data so that testing f initially causes zero calls of g, then a single call of g, and this in turn makes zero calls of f and so on.

In the case of the particular example given in this section, we might sensibly suppose that *append*, *member*, *assoc* and *remove* have been tested previously or, if we do not make this assumption, we might test them independently. Next we should test *reduce* and *red*, probably together, since *reduce* is comparatively trivial. Once *reduce* is known to work we can, if we wish to continue bottom-up, test *product*, *ratio* and then *same*. Finally *dim* can be tested, exercising each of its arms progressively. The element of top-down testing suggested earlier arises if we choose to implement the simpler *product*, *ratio* and *same* functions just to test *dim*. Then, having tested *dim* and *reduce*, we can integrate them and, by supplying *dim* with suitable data, test the more elaborate *product*, *ratio* and *same* in this integrated set up rather than independently.

In this section we have been concerned with many things, the structuring of programs and the appropriate choice of subfunctions, the choice of data representations and the organization of program testing. In the remaining sections, while these techniques will be repeatedly deployed we will not explicitly discuss them. As a consequence, we will be able to go more quickly through the programs presented there and concentrate on the particular features they are designed to demonstrate.

3.2 TREE SEARCHES—A COMPARISON OF PROGRAMS FOR BREADTH-FIRST AND DEPTH-FIRST SEARCHES

First let us discuss what this section is not about: it is not about the programming of efficient searches. Although we shall be concerned with the searching of a tree in order to find a node which satisfies a certain property we shall not concern ourselves with the very important concept of organizing the search in order to encounter the most likely nodes first. Rather we shall simply be concerned with the way in which the two basic kinds of search, depth-first and breadth-first, can be programmed functionally, and with the structure of these functional programs. First we must set the scene and show how such searches arise. For this purpose we will use some elementary examples concerning the orientation of a tetrahedron. The development presented here is based on some ideas presented in Nilsson's book (1971), where many more very interesting applications are discussed.

Consider the regular tetrahedron shown in Fig 3.2. This is a triangular pyramid each of whose four faces is an equilateral triangle. We shall be concerned with rotations of the tetrahedron which are such that the positions of these four faces in space are interchanged. We may consider such a

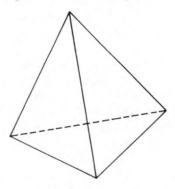

Fig. 3.2

tetrahedron to have a standard position with its faces pointing south, north-west, north-east, and downward. If we letter the faces a, b, c and d and place the tetrahedron on a plan such as that shown in Fig. 3.3, we can represent its standard position by the state $abcd$, that is, listing the face names in the order given above.

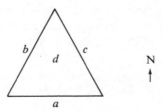

Fig. 3.3

Considering the operations we can perform on a tetrahedron, an obvious choice is to rotate 120° clockwise leaving the base in the down position. Calling this operation R we have the subgraph of state changes shown in Fig. 3.4, where each state change is obtained by rotating the first three face names.

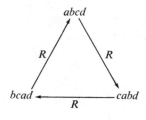

Fig. 3.4

Another operation, chosen because it will simplify the graph we must draw, which we will call F (flip), is to exchange the positions of the base and south facing slope. This operation maps *abcd* to *dcba* and in general, for any state, reverses the order of face names in that state. This flip operation however only makes accessible 12 states and 12 are still inaccessible (there are 24 permutations of the 4 face names). If we consider the tetrahedron drawn above (Fig. 3.2) we see why this is. As soon as any two face positions are fixed the other two are determined. But this is because we consider the tetrahedron to be solid. If it were thin rubber and had a hole in it, we could turn it inside out and transform the state *abcd* to the state *acbd*. Call this transformation C. It exchanges the north-west and north-east facing slopes without moving the base or south facing slope. Now it is simple, but tedious, to verify that the graph of the tetrahedron states is as shown in Fig. 3.5, where only 12 states have been drawn but the remaining 12 states can be considered to be in a parallel plane. The graphs in the two planes have identical shape, except that the direction of the R edges is reversed. Corresponding states in each plane are connected by a C transformation. The F transformations are shown as undirected, implying that they go both ways.

With this graph it is interesting to note that there is no shorter path from *abcd* to *cadb* (in the other plane, not shown, above *cdab*) than 5 transformations, for example *RRFRC* or *RFCRF*.

Although our main point here is to demonstrate the kind of graph which can be constructed to represent a problem from the real world in a symbolic form, the reader who has not been entirely convinced about the claims made for the states of the tetrahedron might find it useful to construct one. Rather than construct a single tetrahedron which can be turned inside out it is easier

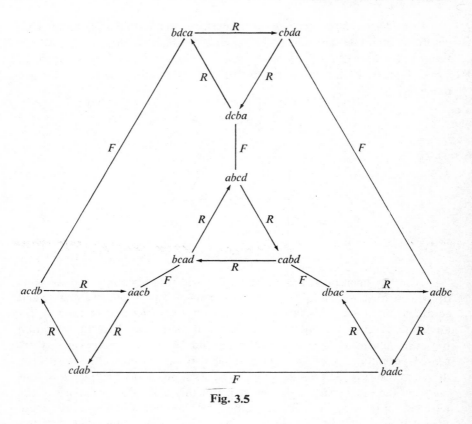

Fig. 3.5

to construct two (call them positive and negative) using the templates
shown in Fig 3.6. When folded into tetrahedra with the lettering outward

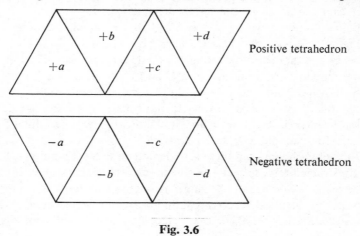

Fig. 3.6

(and held together by tape) these models can be manipulated on the plan shown on p. 72. The operations then have the following meaning:

R   rotate tetrahedron 120° clockwise on its base;
F   exchange positions of base and south facing slope;
C   change tetrahedra, in such a way that base and south facing slopes' names are not changed.

We shall return to the problem of the tetrahedron shortly. First we will generalize the problem in order that we can discuss searching in isolation from the particular details of this problem.

The particular generalization we wish to discuss is based on the recognition that many problems can be characterized by a graph of states similar to those we have drawn for the reorientation of the tetrahedron. This observation is developed in great detail in Nilsson's book (1971). Here we concentrate only on the more elementary forms of state graph discussed by Nilsson. We assume that we can characterize a problem by constructing a representation of a state (of the real world object) and that the result of applying an admissible operation to a state can be computed and the new state determined. In the example we have given, a state might be represented by a list of atoms, giving the orientation of the sides of the figure. It is easy to see how other problems could be modeled with an appropriately chosen state. In order to generalize the notion of applying an operation, we assume that a function $suc(s)$ is available which, if applied to a state s, returns the list of successor states of s. For example, in our tetrahedron graph, we would have the successor function

s	$suc(s)$
$(A\ B\ C\ D)$	$((C\ A\ B\ D)(D\ C\ B\ A)(A\ C\ B\ D))$

In general, for a given start state s, the function suc, applied successively, generates a tree. A branch of the tree terminates in state s only if $suc(s) = NIL$.

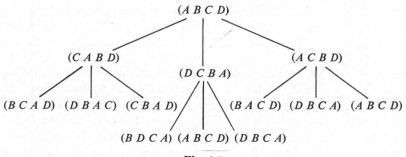

Fig. 3.7

The tree generated by *suc* for the tetrahedron is infinite and begins as shown in Fig. 3.7. Of course, it is only infinite because each state eventually gets repeated. For the moment we will assume that the *suc(s)* function is such that if applied successively it will eventually produce *NIL*, that is, that the tree is finite. When the *suc* function for a particular problem does not have this property, we will artificially modify it so that it does.

The kind of problem we wish to tackle is, given a start state, find a state reachable from the start state, which satisfies a certain property. Suppose the property to be satisfied is implemented as a predicate (logical function) *p(s)*. For example, if looking for a specific orientation of the tetrahedron, we might have

$$p(s) \equiv equal\ (s,(C\ A\ D\ B)).$$

There are two essentially different strategies we can adopt in searching for the state satisfying *p(s)*. The depth-first strategy investigates states in such an order that, when a list of successors is generated, the complete tree emanating from each is searched before the next is considered. The breadth-first strategy, on the other hand, investigates all the nodes at a certain distance (in terms of the number of applications of *suc*) from the start node, before investigating any nodes further removed.

It is generally considered that programming depth-first searches is more natural when using recursive functions, so let us tackle that first. We will define a function *find(s)* which, starting from state *s*, searches for the state satisfying *p(s)*. We use a subsidiary function *findlist(S)* which expects as argument a list of states *S* and applies *find(s)* to each state in the list until a state satisfying *p* is found, as in (3.13).

$$find(s) \equiv \textbf{if}\ p(s)\ \textbf{then}\ s\ \textbf{else}\ findlist(suc(s))$$
$$findlist(S) \equiv \textbf{if}\ S = NIL\ \textbf{then}\ NONE\ \textbf{else}$$
$$\{\textbf{let}\ s = find(car(S)) \tag{3.13}$$
$$\textbf{if}\ s = NONE\ \textbf{then}\ findlist(cdr(S))$$
$$\textbf{else}\ s\}$$

Here we see that *find(s)* first investigates *s* and only if that does not satisfy *p(s)* does it consider the states *suc(s)* using *findlist*. If *findlist(S)* finds that the set of states *S* is empty, then it returns the special value *NONE* to indicate no result is possible. If S is not empty, then *find* is applied to the first element of *S*. If *find* does not return *NONE*, then the result which it does return is the required state, otherwise we investigate the remaining members of *S*—altogether a very natural use of recursion. It is simple to determine that a depth-first search is indeed carried out, for the *find* function is applied successively to the first member of each successor set, before the remaining members are considered. Of course, the order of elements in the list returned by *suc* is irrelevant (although it will be crucial to the efficiency of the search) and we only concentrate on the *car*, as opposed to any other member, for convenience. In the (arbitrary) tree shown in Fig 3.8, the nodes are numbered in the order that they would be investigated by the above search.

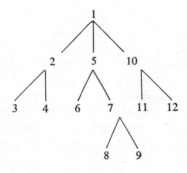

Fig. 3.8

Despite the naturalness of this function it is useful to reprogram it in a different form in order that we can discuss its relationship to the programming of a breadth-first search. This time we make use of the fact that *findlist*(*S*) deals with the elements of *S* in a particular order. We contrive to replace an item in *S* by its successors in such a way that *findlist* investigates the states in the correct order for the depth-first strategy. We have

$$find(s) \equiv findlist(cons(s, NIL))$$
$$findlist(S) \equiv \textbf{if } S = NIL \textbf{ then } NONE \textbf{ else}$$
$$\textbf{if } p(car(S)) \textbf{ then } car(S) \textbf{ else}$$
$$findlist(append(suc(car(S)), cdr(S)))$$

Here, all the work is done by *findlist*. The argument of *findlist* is a list of states which have still to be investigated. If this list is empty then there is no solution. If the first element of the list satisfies *p*, then this is the required result, otherwise all its successors are determined and placed at the front of the list being processed by *findlist*. Hence we have been more explicit about the order in which states are investigated and it is easily seen to be depth-first. This reprogramming has some demerits. The use of *append* can cause considerable overhead, as discussed in Section 2.5, and the nesting of recursive calls is no longer proportional to the depth of the sought node but to the number of nodes rejected before it is found. It does, however, make the description of a breadth-first search trivial. The program can be modified to do a breadth-first search simply by exchanging the arguments of the call of the append function. The call thus becomes

$$append(cdr(S), suc(car(S)))$$

and we see that for any particular call of *findlist*(S) each of the elements of S is taken in order by successive recursive calls and, after the last element of S, all the successors of elements of S have been built up into the argument for findlist. That is, all the next level states are available in order.

Now, for the kind of search for which these last two programs are comparable, that is an unsuccessful one, returning *NONE*, the program for the breadth-first search will be much slower than the depth-first program. This is because, on average, $cdr(S)$ is much longer than $suc(car(S))$ and hence *append* is required to do much more work. It would seem much more important therefore to remove the *append* from the breadth-first search than from the depth-first. This is not trivial, but is left nevertheless as an exercise for the reader, while we pursue the use of these programs on our specific application to tetrahedra.

The specific problem we wish to solve is, given two states of the tetrahedron, find the sequence of operations required to transform the first state to the second. At first sight, our programming of *find* does not seem to be useful in solving this problem. For suppose the start state is x and the state we are searching for is y; then setting

$$p(s) \equiv equal(s,y)$$

and calling

$$find(x).$$

returns one of two results, either *NONE*, meaning y is not reachable from x, or y, meaning it is, but the method of transforming x to y is not returned. Since *find* only returns a state, the way around this minor difficulty is obvious: we must encode in the state not only the orientation of the object but also the sequence of operations applied (to x) in order to reach this orientation. For example, if we start the tetrahedron in orientation $(A \ B \ C \ D)$ and apply the operations R, F and C in that order, we reach the orientation $(D\ A\ B\ C)$. We can record this sequence of transformations in the states

$$((A\ B\ C\ D)\ NIL)$$
$$((C\ A\ B\ D)\ (R))$$
$$((D\ B\ A\ C)\ (F\ R))$$
$$((D\ \ A\ \ B\ \ C)\ (C\ \ F\ \ R))$$

where we have made the state a pair (i.e. a 2-list) consisting of the list of faces and a list of the operations applied to the initial orientation in order to reach this one. For convenience (it hardly matters) we have listed the operations in reverse order of application.

First, let us define in (3.14) a function $ap(op,s)$ which takes as arguments an atom, being R, F or C, and a state and applies the appropriate operation to the state.

$ap(op,s) \equiv$
  {**let** *orientation* $=$ $car(s)$
  and *transform* $=$ $car(cdr(s))$
    {**let** a $=$ $car(orientation)$
    and b $=$ $car(cdr(orientation))$ (3.14)
    and c $=$ $car(cdr(cdr(orientation)))$
    and d $=$ $car(cdr(cdr(cdr(orientation))))$
    if op $=$ R **then** $twolist(fourlist(c,a,b,d),cons(op,transform))$
  else if op $=$ F **then** $twolist(fourlist(d,c,b,a),cons(op,transform))$
                else $twolist(fourlist(a,c,b,d),cons(op,transform))$}}

We see that the new orientation is built using the functions *twolist* and *fourlist*, which have the obvious definitions

$$twolist(x,y) \equiv cons(x,cons(y,NIL))$$
$$fourlist(w,x,y,z) \equiv cons(w,cons(x,cons(y,cons(z,NIL))))$$

and that, by declaring local variables a,b,c and d to name the parts of the original orientation, the three operations are clearly denoted correctly in the program.

Using this function we can define $suc(s)$ very trivially. It is simply a three-element list of the states resulting from applying operations R, F and C, repectively. However, we must also take into account that $suc(s)$ for the tetrahedron builds an infinite tree and it must be artificially pruned by some means. We simply truncate the tree after a certain depth which we will call *maxdepth* (6 would be an appropriate value for the tetrahedron). We have, for the successor function

$$suc(s) \equiv \textbf{if } length(car(cdr(s))) \geqslant maxdepth \textbf{ then } NIL \textbf{ else}$$
$$threelist(ap(R,s),ap(F,s),ap(C,s))$$

The length of the transformation part of the state is taken as the measure of current depth. If it is equal to (or greater than) the maximum depth allowed, then *suc*(*s*) returns no successor.

Finally, we must define the predicate *p* which will be satisfied by the state we are looking for. This is trivial: we simply ask if the orientation part of the state is equal to the orientation we seek

$$p(s) \equiv equal(car(s),y)$$

Now we can put the whole design together to form a program which we define as the function

$$search(x,y,maxdepth),$$

where the user of the program is expected to supply the initial and final orientations *x* and *y* and the limit upon the depth of the search tree. Since the initial orientation is *x*, the initial state is *twolist*(*x*,*NIL*) and thus we have the definition

$$search(x,y,maxdepth) \equiv find(twolist(x,NIL))$$

Clearly, which version of *find* we choose will determine which results we get, for the breadth-first search will find a shortest possible sequence of transformations while the depth-first search will be biased toward applications of the operation *R*, since we have arbitrarily selected this as the first-to-be-applied operation. When asked to find, from (*A B C D*), the orientation (*C B D A*) with depth bound of 6, these algorithms return respectively (*F R R*) and (*R R R F R R*). The breadth-first result ensures that there is no sequence of less than three operations transforming (*A B C D*) to (*C B D A*). The depth-first result, much cheaper to obtain, has no such significance. However, the results which are found and the relative efficiencies of the two searches do not interest us here. Let us return to the discussion of the structure of the program.

When programming the search we defined the functions *find*(*s*) and *findlist*(*S*). These were defined in terms of the successor function *suc*(*s*) and the completion predicate $p(s)$. However, when we came to define particular successor and completion functions for the tetrahedron problem, we did so in terms of the variables *maxdepth* and *y* respectively. These variables are not parameters of the functions *suc* and *p*, they are global to them. They are in fact parameters of the main function *search(x,y,maxdepth)* since their values are supplied to control each search. In order to give *suc* and *p* access to the variables *maxdepth* and *y*, they must be declared local to the function *search*. That is, we must have the program structure given in (3.15) or some

{*search* **whererec** *search* $= \lambda(x,y,maxdepth)$
　　　{ *find(twolist(x,NIL))*
　　　　　whererec *find* $= \ldots$
　　　　　　and *findlist* $= \ldots$
　　　　　　and *suc* $= \ldots maxdepth \ldots$
　　　　　　and *p* $= \ldots y \ldots$　　　　　　(3.15)
　　　　　　and *ap* $= \ldots$ }
　　and *length* $= \ldots$
　　and *append* $= \ldots$
　　and *twolist* $= \ldots$
　　and *threelist* $= \ldots$
　　and *fourlist* $= \ldots$
　　and *equal* $= \ldots$ }

equivalent structure. Note that the references to *maxdepth* and *y* from the functions *suc* and *p* respectively are the only references to these variables in the whole program.

This structure for the program does not clearly delineate the general-purpose searching functions *find* and *findlist* from the special-purpose *suc*, *p* and *ap* which are used to implement the state representation for the tetrahedron problem. We can remedy this by revising the definition of *search* as shown in (3.16).

search $= \lambda(x,y,maxdepth)$
　　{{ *find(twolist(x,NIL))*
　　　　whererec *find* $= \ldots$
　　　　　and *findlist* $= \ldots$ }
　　whererec *suc* $= \ldots maxdepth \ldots$　　　　　(3.16)
　　　and *p* $= \ldots y \ldots$
　　　and *ap* $= \ldots$ }

This organization, while giving, for example, the access from *find* to *suc* and from *suc* to *maxdepth*, required by the logic of the program, clearly states that the only calls of *find* and *findlist* are from the innermost block and that none of the application-oriented functions such as *ap* call them. This was not apparent from the earlier organization.

Another kind of access is, however, not apparently barred by this second organization. This is the fact that *find* and *findlist* could access not only *suc* and *p* but also *ap*. That they do not and should not can be denoted by reorganizing again, this time so that this subsidiary function appears locally to the function which uses it as in (3.17).

$$
\begin{aligned}
search &= \lambda(x,y,maxdepth) \\
&\{\{find(twolist(x,NIL)) \\
&\qquad\qquad \textbf{whererec } find = \ldots \\
&\qquad\qquad\qquad \textbf{and } findlist = \ldots \quad \} \\
&\qquad \textbf{where } suc = \{\ldots maxdepth \ldots \\
&\qquad\qquad\qquad \textbf{where } ap = \ldots \quad \} \\
&\quad \textbf{and } p = \ldots y \ldots \quad \}
\end{aligned}
$$

(3.17)

This organization seems very elaborate. In its favor, apart from the explicitness about lack of certain kinds of access, is the fact that we have been able to use **where** where in the previous organization **whererec** had been necessary to allow accesses to the function *ap*, now local, which was declared at the same level as *suc*. It seems to be bad style to use **whererec**, suggesting a set of functions are mutually recursive, when it can be avoided. However, the price we have paid is a more deeply nested program. Neither is such a transformation always so simple. It is merely fortuitous here that the functions *p* and *suc* have no subfunction in common. If, for example, *p* had also used *ap* we would have had to either duplicate it or take it to a new outer block in order that both could access it.

If we were to carry further this philosophy of making functions only accessible to those other functions which call them, we could end up with a very deeply nested program indeed. Even though the functions *length*, *append* and so on are not called by *find* and *findlist*, having made them accessible to *find* and *findlist* has not made it any harder to understand those functions. This last remark requires a little explanation. When trying to understand a program written by someone else, we first have to delineate those parts of a program which are independent. As authors of a program, to make it understandable to others, we should try to make this task of delineation as simple as possible. We should therefore not give functions unnecessary access to variables and other functions. Now, following that philosophy leads us to a very deeply nested programs. If we place general purpose functions, such as *length*, in an outer block, it is no longer trivial to determine the fact that, for example, *find* does not call *length*. Indeed, the only way to determine this fact is to investigate the text of *find* and *findlist*. Because of this, the question of whether to place a function like *length* one or more blocks further out than strictly necessary is a matter of style. An argument in favor of doing so is that such a function, being very simple and also general purpose, since it could be called from anywhere (and it is indeed only fortuitous that it is not) should be placed in an outermost block. This is in fact what we have done for *length*, *append*, *equal*, *twolist*, *threelist* and *fourlist*.

A final, somewhat different, transformation of our program leads to an alternative structure. We build an intermediate function in (3.18), much the same as *find*, but which is explicit about the fact that *find* and *findlist* use *p* and *suc*, by having them as parameters.

$$
\begin{aligned}
search = \;& \lambda(x,y,maxdepth) \\
& \{lookfor(twolist(x,NIL),p,suc) \\
& \quad \textbf{where } p = \ldots \\
& \quad \textbf{and } suc = \ldots \\
& \quad \textbf{and } lookfor = \lambda(s,p,suc) \\
& \qquad \{find(s) \\
& \qquad \textbf{whererec } find = \ldots \\
& \qquad \textbf{and } findlist = \ldots \quad \}\}
\end{aligned}
\tag{3.18}
$$

Now we seem to have achieved the separation we were looking for in that the definitions of *p*, *suc* and *lookfor*, being on arms of a **where** clause, clearly do not refer to each other, and *find*, being local to *lookfor*, is clearly not accessed by any other function. Now, if *lookfor* is moved out to the same block as *search* we prevent it from being able to access the parameters of *search*, in particular *y* and *maxdepth*. Since it does not require such access, this is clearly an improvement.

This discussion has shown how the global organization of a functional program can be varied almost arbitrarily, and the effect this might have on the understandability of the program. While we have suggested that the organization of the program developed here has been successively improved by the transformations applied to it, we have not meant to suggest that these particular transformations will improve every program. Program organization is still a very subjective area. The options available in our notation for functional programs are no less than in any other language, and hence good judgement is still needed in order to organize the text of the program to aid its understandability.

3.3 THE SINGLETONS PROGRAM

In this section, we tackle a problem which has been presented already in a series of exercises in Chapter 2 (see Exercises 2.9 and 2.10). The problem is that of determining, for a general S-expression, the set of atoms which occur in that expression exactly once. We shall call this function *singletons(s)*. Our main purpose, apart from again showing the general techniques of functional programming and comparing alternative solutions to a problem, is to show how a function can be used to replace a data structure and to discuss the merits of doing this. The reader who has tried the exercises will be aware that there are many ways to tackle this problem, and some particular diffi-culties to be overcome. In order to keep this presentation reasonably short, we shall not discuss all these difficulties, but only those which are novel to this problem. The function we wish to define will have the values given in Table 3.3.

Table 3.3

s	*singletons(s)*
(*A B C A B*)	(*C NIL*)
((*A B*)(*A C*))	(*B C*)
((*A B*)(*A B*))	*NIL*

The result is considered to be a set and therefore we are indifferent to the order of the values appearing in it. Note, however, that since the argument is considered to be a general S-expression, the *NIL* at the end of a list may appear in the result, as in the first example above. Supposing we begin to define *singletons(s)* directly, using our usual case analysis, we get the following cases.

case (i)   *s* is an atom $singletons(s) \equiv cons(s, NIL)$
case (ii)   *s* is not an atom
  suppose *singletons(car(s))* = *A*
  and *singletons(cdr(s))* = *B*
  then *singletons(s)* = ?

The first case, when *s* is an atom, is trivial. The set of atoms occurring in *s* is just the unit set with *s* as its only member. In the second case, when *s* is not an atom, we assume that the set of singletons from the *car* and *cdr* can be respectively computed to be *A* and *B*. But what is *singletons(s)*? It is not the union of *A* and *B*, for if they have a common member then that member occurs at least twice. Neither is it the exclusive union of *A* and *B* (the set of elements in either *A* or *B* but not in both—see Exercise 2.8). To see this we have only to consider an atom which occurs once in *car(s)* and hence appears in *A* but which occurs twice in *cdr(s)* and hence does not appear in *B*. Since this atom occurs three times in the argument as a whole, it should not appear in *singletons(s)*, but we cannot determine this from *A* and *B* alone. In fact, to compute *singletons(s)* we need to take those elements from *A* which do not occur in *cdr(s)* and those elements from *B* which do not occur in *car(s)*.

This is going to be a very inefficient program, but we should not let that observation at this stage prevent us from completing this design. For doing so will give us some insight into the problem and will probably improve our next attempt just because of the experience gained on this one. This program, if completed, may be of invaluable assistance in convincing us that any more efficient version is correct. If the more efficient version is more complex, as it probably will be, it may be easier to see that it is equivalent to the less efficient version than that it is correct in its own right. If the less efficient version is more easily seen to be correct, then it forms an essential part of the documentation of this program.

To complete this design, we assume the existence of three functions. The set of atoms occurring in the S-expression *s* is computed by *set(s)*. If *x* and *y* are lists representing sets of atoms, then *union(x,y)* is a list representing the set of atoms in both *x* and *y*, and *difference(x,y)* is a list representing the set of atoms in *x* but not in *y*. With these functions we can repeat the second case of our design, as in (3.19).

---

case (ii) *s* is not an atom
    suppose *singletons(car(s))* = *A*
    and *singletons(cdr(s))* = *B*
    and *set(car(s))* = *C*   (3.19)
    and *set(cdr(s))* = *D*
    then *singletons(s)* =
        union(difference(A,D),difference(B,C))

Note that, since every atom in *A* must also be in *C* and similarly that every atom in **B** must also be in *D*, the sets *difference(A,D)* and *difference(B,C)* can have no common member. Hence it is not necessary to form the exclusive union of them, although that would have the same result. The function we have designed is the following:

$$singletons(s) \equiv \textbf{if } atom(s) \textbf{ then } cons(s,NIL) \textbf{ else}$$
$$union(difference(singletons(car(s)),set(cdr(s))),$$
$$difference(singletons(cdr(s)),set(car(s))))$$

The subsidiary functions need to be designed but we shall not do that here. We shall, however, include definitions of them, just in order to be able to discuss the efficiency of this program. Suitable definitions would be (3.20)–(3.23).

$$set(s) \equiv \textbf{if } atom(s) \textbf{ then } cons(s,NIL) \textbf{ else} \qquad\qquad (3.20)$$
$$union(set(car(s)),set(cdr(s)))$$

$$union(x,y) \equiv \textbf{if } x = NIL \textbf{ then } y \textbf{ else}$$
$$\{\textbf{let } z = union(cdr(x),y) \qquad\qquad (3.21)$$
$$\textbf{if } member(car(x),z) \textbf{ then } z \textbf{ else}$$
$$cons(car(x),z)\}$$

$$difference(x,y) \equiv \textbf{if } x = NIL \textbf{ then } NIL \textbf{ else}$$
$$\{\textbf{let } z = difference(cdr(x),y) \qquad\qquad (3.22)$$
$$\textbf{if } member(car(x),y) \textbf{ then } z \textbf{ else}$$
$$cons(car(x),z)\}$$

$$member(a,x) \equiv \textbf{if } x = NIL \textbf{ then } F \textbf{ else}$$
$$\textbf{if } eq(a,car(x)) \textbf{ then } T \textbf{ else} \qquad\qquad (3.23)$$
$$member(a,cdr(x))$$

This program displays a number of kinds of inefficiency. If we could assume that the sets generated during evaluation of the function were small, that is, that the same atoms occur again and again and that singletons are unusual, we might excuse this use of the basic set-manipulation functions. However, our use of the function $set(s)$ cannot be excused on this basis, for its efficiency is entirely dependent on the size of the S-expression being analyzed. The problem lies not in the way that $set(s)$ itself is programmed but in the way it is called from $singletons(s)$. The inefficiency arises in a particular way which we can illustrate by looking at the subexpression

$$union(difference(singletons(car(s)),set(cdr(s))),$$
$$difference(singletons(cdr(s)),set(car(s)))),$$

Consider the case when this expression is evaluated with s not an atom. If we investigate the call $singletons(car(s))$ we see that this in turn would cause evaluation of $set(cdr(car(s)))$ and $set(car(car(s)))$. Similarly, if we consider the call of $set(car(s))$, we see that this also evaluates $set(cdr(car(s)))$ and $set(car(car(s)))$. That is, the same lengthy computations are carried out twice. Of course, if we consider the entire evaluation, we can see that the $set(s)$ function will be evaluated many times for the same argument, depending upon how deeply nested is the substructure to which it is applied.

We overcome this inefficiency by the use of accumulating parameters. We shall define the function $sing(s,a,b)$, which has additional parameters to accumulate the sets which we require. In fact, the parameter a will be used to accumulate the set of atoms which have been encountered more than once and b to accumulate the set of atoms which have been encountered exactly once. The value of $sing(s,a,b)$ will be a pair of sets. The first of these returned sets will contain atoms encountered more than once and the second atoms encountered exactly once.

We design $sing(s,a,b)$ in (3.24) by the familiar kind of case analysis, this time, however, choosing rather more problem-oriented cases. Let us consider

---

case (i) s is an atom
   case (i.i) s is a member of a $sing(s,a,b) = cons(a,b)$
   case (i.ii) s is not a member of a
   case (i.ii.i) s is a member of b
$$sing(s,a,b) = cons(cons(s,a),$$
$$remove(s,b)) \qquad (3.24)$$
   case (i.ii.ii) s is not a member of b
$$sing(s,a,b) = cons(a,cons(s,b))$$
case (ii) s is not an atom
   suppose $(c.d) = sing(car(s),a,b)$
   then $sing(s,a,b) = sing(cdr(s),c,d)$

---

the subcases in order. Case (i.i) is when we encounter an atom s which we have seen many times before. We ignore it, for a already records the fact that we are not interested in it. Case (i.ii.i) is when we encounter an atom for the second time. We must remove it from set b and add it to set a. Case (i.ii.ii) is when we encounter an atom for the first time. We add it to the set b. Case (ii) deals with processing a non-atomic structure. We use $sing(car(s),a,b)$ to accumulate the sets of singly and multiply occurring atoms in $car(s)$ and add them to sets b and a respectively, constructing sets d and c. Then we call $sing(cdr(s),c,d)$ in the obvious way. Thus we have defined the set of functions shown in (3.25). We have given an obvious definition of *remove* and assumed the usual definition of *member* (see Section 2.5).

$$singletons(s) \equiv cdr(sing(s,NIL,NIL))$$

$sing(s,a,b) \equiv$ **if** $atom(s)$ **then**
   if $member(s,a)$ **then** $cons(a,b)$ **else**
   if $member(s,b)$ **then** $cons(cons(s,a),remove(s,b))$
   else $cons(a,cons(s,b))$ **else**   (3.25)
   {**let** $p = sing(car(s),a,b)$
    $sing(cdr(s),car(p),cdr(p))$}

$remove(x,y) \equiv$ **if** $eq(x,car(y))$ **then** $cdr(y)$ **else**
                  $cons(car(y),remove(x,cdr(y)))$

$member(x,y) \equiv \ldots$

We can now, for completeness, give a formal definition of the value returned by $sing(s,a,b)$. The pair $(c.d)$ returned as value of this function consists of two sets c and d. The set c contains

1. all members of a
2. all multiply occurring atoms in s
3. all singly occurring atoms in s which are also in b.

The set d contains

1. all singly occurring atoms in s which are not in a or b
2. all members of b which do not occur in s.

Thus we can see that the call $sing(s,NIL,NIL)$ returns the pair consisting of the sets $c =$ all multiply occurring atoms in s and $d =$ all singly occurring atoms in s. Thus the definition

$$singletons(s) \equiv cdr(sing(s,NIL,NIL))$$

is correct.

Now look at the use of the sets a and b in the definition of $sing(s,a,b)$. The set a is searched using *member* and extended using *cons*. The set b is similarly searched and extended, but also sometimes diminished using *remove*. Ultimately it is only the set *b* in which we are interested, the set *a* being used only as an internal device to facilitate the computation of *b*. This point is reflected in the fact that we return *cdr(sing(s,NIL,NIL))*, finally discarding the set of multiples. Because of this, we are free to alter the representation of the set *a*, without any effect on the user of the function *singletons(s)*. Considering the operations which we apply to *s*, we might consider if there is some representation which makes these operations more efficient. The particular choice of representation we shall look at is one which is not open to us in most programming languages. It is to represent the set by a function.

Previously we have represented a set of atoms by a list without repetitions. Suppose *s* is such a list representing a set. We can define a function *f* which has the property that

$$f(x) = member(x,s)$$

and use *f* to represent the set, instead of *s*. Of course it will not be possible to carry out all set operations on *f*, but we can do some of them. For the set *s*, when we want to add a new member *x*, which we already know not to be a member of *s*, we simply use *cons(x,s)*. When using *f* to represent the set, however, we must construct a new function value which behaves like a member function for the extended set. The appropriate expression to use is

$$\lambda(y) \text{ if } eq(y,x) \text{ then } T \text{ else } f(y)$$

Let us consider why this is so. This lambda expression denotes a function which, if applied to an argument *y*, returns *T* if either *y* is equal to *x* or *f(y)* is true. That is to say, it returns *T* if *y* is either *x* or a member of the set represented by *f*. Hence the lambda expression represents the set obtained by extending the set represented by *f*, by the addition of the new member *x*. The empty set would be represented by the function

$$\lambda(y)F$$

because no atom is a member of the empty set. We can modify the definition of *sing(s,a,b)* very easily to use this functional representation of *a*, as in (3.26).

$singletons(s) \equiv cdr(sing(s,\{\lambda(y)F\},NIL))$
$sing(s,a,b) \equiv$
    if $atom(s)$ **then**
        if $a(s)$ **then** $cons(a,b)$ **else**   (3.26)
        if $member(s,b)$ **then** $cons(\{\lambda(y)$ **if** $eq(y,s)$ **then** T **else** $a(y)\}$,
                                    $remove(s,b))$ **else**
    $cons(a,cons(s,b))$ **else**
    $\{$**let** $p = sing(car(s),a,b)$
     $sing(cdr(s),car(p),cdr(p))\}$

There were only three changes required. The empty set *NIL* was replaced by the function $\lambda(y)F$, the call of $member(s,a)$ was replaced by the call $a(s)$ and the call $cons(s,a)$ by $\lambda(y)$ **if** $eq(y,s)$ **then** T **else** $a(y)$. The pair, returned as value of $sing(s,a,b)$, now has as its first member a function. This ability to embed functions in data structures and to use them instead of data structures is a very powerful feature of functional programming.

Suppose that a set, represented by a function, is initially empty and is progressively extended by the addition of the atoms A,B,C. Then the sequence of function values used to represent these sets is as follows:

$$a_1 = \lambda(y)F$$
$$a_2 = \lambda(y) \text{ if } eq(y,A) \text{ then } T \text{ else } a_1\,(y)$$
$$a_3 = \lambda(y) \text{ if } eq(y,B) \text{ then } T \text{ else } a_2(y)$$
$$a_4 = \lambda(y) \text{ if } eq(y,C) \text{ then } T \text{ else } a_3(y)$$

We can see, for example, that the call $a_4(A)$ generates the call $a_3(A)$ which generates the call $a_2(A)$ which generates T. Similarly, we can see that the call $a_4(D)$ generates calls of $a_3(D)$, $a_2(D)$ and $a_1(D)$, which finally returns F. Thus we see that a_4 behaves as we expect for a function representing the set with members A, B and C. In Chapter 6 we shall return to a discussion of this use of functions, and there we shall observe that this particular use of a function is a little more efficient in execution speed than the use of a list and the *member* function.

EXERCISES

3.1 Consider logical expressions built from variables and the operators **and, or** and **not**. Design an S-expression representation of logical expressions and define a function which will evaluate such an expression given an association list associating each variable in the expression with a logical value.

3.2 Design a function *findseq(s)* which, like *find(s)*, locates a state *s'* satisfying $p(s')$ in a tree defined by *suc(s)*, but which returns the list of states (s_1 ... s_k), where $s_1 = s$ and $s_k = s'$, and for each *i* in 2 to *k*, s_1 is a member of $suc(s_{i-1})$. That is, it returns the list of states joining *s* to *s'*. Show how this can be used to solve the tetrahedron problem without having to store the transformation in the state. Which is the better approach?

3.3 Design a representation of the orientations of a cube. What would be a suitable depth bound for the tree of the cube?

3.4 Reprogram the breadth-first search given in this section to avoid the use of *append*. Determine how many times *cons* is called by those programs which use *append* and those which do not, taking the worst case, when the result is *NONE*, and assuming *n* successors at each level and a depth bound of *d*.

3.5 Consider the program to analyze the dimensions of an algebraic formula given in Section 3.1. Discuss the scope of variables occurring in that program and determine an organization of the function declarations to form a program.

3.6 Consider the function

$$map\ (x,f) \equiv \textbf{if } x = NIL \textbf{ then } NIL \textbf{ else}$$
$$cons\ (f(car(x)),map(cdr(x),f))$$

Show how this can be rewritten to avoid the constant "passing on" of the parameter *f*. Discuss the structure of this modified definition from the points of view of efficiency and readability.

3.7 Redesign the first version of *singletons(s)*, not using accumulating parameters, but such that your program returns a pair consisting respectively of the set of singletons and the set of all atoms occurring in *s*. Call this function *singset(s)*. Then we would have

$$singset(s) = cons(singletons(s),set(s))$$
$$singletons(s) = car(singset(s))$$

Does this resolve the inefficiency over calls of *set(s)* referred to in condemnation of the first program?

3.8 Define a function *followers(x,y)* which, for an atom *x* and a list of atoms *y*, returns the set of all atoms in *y* which directly follow occurrences of *x* in *y*.

3.9 Define a function *follow(x,y)* which, for an atom *x* and a general S-expression *y*, returns the set of all atoms in *y* which follow occurrences of *x* in *y*, ignoring parentheses. That is

$$follow(x,y) = followers(x,flatten(y))$$

3.10 Define a function *add(x,f)* which, for an atom *x* and a function *f* representing a set of atoms *S*, returns a function which represents the set *S* extended by *x*.

3.11   Define *rem*(*x*,*f*) which returns the function representing the set *remove*(*x*,*S*), where *x* and *f* are as in the previous exercise.

3.12   Show how a set *S* can be represented by a function *f* with the property that $f(0) = n$ is the size of the set, and $f(1), \ldots, f(n)$ are its members. Show how the set can be extended and how membership can be determined. Discuss the relative merits of this representation and the one used in the main section.

4 THE REPRESENTATION AND INTERPRETATION OF PROGRAMS

This chapter is the beginning of our exploration of the semantics of programming languages. It is largely devoted to a description of an interpreter for a variant of the programming language Lisp. The basic operations of the Lisp language—*car, cdr, cons, atom* and *eq* were introduced in Chapter 2, and you should now be very familiar with them. In general, a Lisp program is a set of functions, defined in terms of these basic operations, but the actual form in which it is presented to the machine differs from the way in which we have chosen to represent programs in this book. Lisp programs are written as S-expressions in order to facilitate machine processing. Just as we transliterated arithmetic formulas to S-expressions: for example,

$$x \times y + z \quad \rightarrow \quad (ADD\,(MUL\; X\; Y)\, Z)$$

in order to make functional programs which process them simpler to write, so we will embed Lisp programs in S-expressions to facilitate their interpretation. In fact, we shall give rules for transliterating into the S-expression form the whole of the purely functional language which we introduced in Chapter 2 and will use throughout the remainder of the book. This will give us a variant of Lisp, very similar in appearance and meaning to real Lisp but somewhat simpler, differing in many minor details from that language. The language described here is called Lispkit Lisp, in order to distinguish it from real Lisp. We shall use the term "Lisp" on its own however, for brevity, except in cases where distinction between Lispkit Lisp and real Lisp is particularly important. Full details of real Lisp would make our simple points here a good deal more complex. The interested reader is referred to the bibliography for texts which deal with real Lisp.

When we refer to a program "written in Lisp", we shall mean, in particular, the program in its S-expression representation. The following expression is a definition of the familiar append function in our purely functional notation:

$$\{append \ \textbf{whererec}$$
$$append = \lambda(x,y) \ \textbf{if} \ x = NIL \ \textbf{then} \ y \ \textbf{else}$$
$$cons(car(x), append(cdr(x),y)) \ \}$$

Writing this in Lispkit Lisp, that is in its S-expression representation, renders it in the form (4.1).

$$(LETREC \ APPEND$$
$$(APPEND \ LAMBDA \ (X \ Y)$$
$$(IF \ (EQ \ X \ (QUOTE \ NIL)) \ Y \qquad\qquad (4.1)$$
$$(CONS \ (CAR \ X)$$
$$(APPEND \ (CDR \ X) \ Y)))))$$

We shall occasionally refer to the former representation as the *abstract form* and the latter representation as the *concrete form* of the append program. The next section is devoted to the simple, and obvious, set of rules used to transform the abstract form to the concrete form.

The concrete representation of a Lisp program as an S-expression enables us to write functional programs which have concrete programs as their arguments. In particular we can write simple analysis programs: for example, to determine the set of variables used in the program. The way in which this could be done should be obvious after the studies we have made in the previous chapter. Less obvious, perhaps, is the fact that we can write functional programs which act as compilers and interpreters of Lisp. A compiler would translate Lisp to another language while an interpreter would determine for a particular function definition and particular arguments, the result of applying that function to those arguments. The third and final section of this chapter is devoted to such an interpreter. A compiler, translating our variant of Lisp into the machine language of a special-purpose machine, is described in Chapter 6.

Consider for a moment a functional program defining a function $apply(f,x)$, where f is the S-expression form of a Lisp program defining a function, such as the *append* program given above, and x is the S-expression representation (a list) of the actual arguments for that function. Then $apply(f,x)$ will be the S-expression representation of the result of applying the function which f represents to the arguments which x represents. Some examples are shown in Table 4.1.

Table 4.1

f	x	$apply\ (f,x)$
	$((A\ B\ C)\ (D\ E\ F))$	$(A\ B\ C\ D\ E\ F)$
the concrete form of the *append* program (4.1)	$((A\ B\ C)\ NIL)$	$(A\ B\ C)$
	$(((A\ B))\ ((C\ D)))$	$((A\ B)\ (C\ D))$

The function *apply(f,x)* will of course have to analyze the structure of the program *f* in order to compute the value of *f* applied to *x*, and it is for this reason that it is called an interpreter (or interpreting function). In a very real sense this interpreter specifies the semantics of the language (Lisp) in which *f* is written. The real sense is clear when we realize that these semantics can be changed by very simple adjustments to the definition of *apply*. We shall return to the discussion of quite what is and what is not specified by an interpreter, when we have completed the definition of *apply(f,x)*.

Before we begin that process, however, there are two fundamentally important ideas which remain to be introduced. We shall be at pains in the next section to describe the transformation between abstract and concrete forms of our functional programs. The interpreter will be written in abstract form, as are the remainder of programs in this book, while the Lispkit Lisp programs being interpreted will be written as S-expressions. Since we shall be able to transform freely between the two representations. however, this allows the following two simple observations.

1. We have not only specified the semantics of Lisp but also of our abstract functional notation.
2. Since the definition of *apply* can be transliterated into Lisp, we have written a Lisp interpreter in Lisp itself.

The reader who feels a little uneasy at the apparent circularity of the two observations is justified in that feeling, for there will be some limitations to what we have specified. Nevertheless, the power of functional programming to make concise formal specifications of the semantics of programming languages is clearly demonstrated in this chapter. In the next chapter we go on to apply these techniques to Algol-like languages with similar success.

4.1 ABSTRACT AND CONCRETE FORMS OF PROGRAMS

We have to show how all the programs of our complete programming language can be represented as S-expressions. The method of doing this is to identify what we shall call the well-formed expressions of the programming language. For Lispkit Lisp, the well-formed expressions are just those sub-expressions of a program which are intended to have a value associated with them. If we consider the kind of expressions we have written in our function definitions, then the following are examples of well-formed expressions:

$$x$$
$$x+1$$
$$car(cdr(s))$$
$$\textbf{if } x = 0 \textbf{ then } 1 \textbf{ else } x \times f(x-1)$$

Each of these is complete, in the sense that if we know suitable values for those variables occurring free in the expression, then we know the intended value of the entire expression. On the other hand, the following subexpressions are *not* well-formed, simply because they are incomplete.

$$x+$$
$$car(cdr$$
$$\textbf{if } x = 0 \textbf{ then } 1$$

Even if we know the values of the variables occurring in each of these sub-expressions, we do not intend the subexpression to have a value. For example, what is the value of the third subexpression in the case $x \neq 0$?

Every functional program which we have written can be considered to be built from nested well-formed expressions. As we have seen in Section 2.8, the program itself can be written as a single well-formed expression, a function-valued expression. It is always possible to break a compound well-formed expression down into a principal operator and a set of operands each of which is a well-formed expression. Thus, for example,

$$\textbf{if } x = 0 \textbf{ then } 1 \textbf{ else } x \times f(x-1)$$

has **if** . . . **then** . . . **else** as its principal operator and the well-formed expressions

$$x = 0$$
$$1$$
$$x \times f(x-1)$$

as its operands. The second of these operands is not compound and does not break down further. However, $x = 0$ has $=$ as its operator and x and 0 as its operands, both well-formed. Similarly, $x \times f(x-1)$ has $\times$ as its operator and x and $f(x-1)$ as its operands, both well-formed. And so on.

We shall identify each of the well-formed expressions in our abstract, purely functional language and give for each a corresponding S–expression. This S–expression, which we shall call the *concrete form*, inherits the property of well-formedness and so, when we refer to a well-formed expression we may mean either the abstract or the concrete form. In order to show how this is accomplished we will deal with each of the different kinds of well-formed expression we have used when making function definitions. Recall that, we are transforming function definitions into S-expressions and that these are easily distinguished in these pages because the latter always appears entirely in upper-case characters.

The most elementary kinds of well-formed expression we have used in function definitions are constants and variables. Variables will be represented by symbolic atoms, thus we will represent x, y and z by X, Y and Z respectively. In order that constants can always be distinguished from variables however, they will be quoted. That is, a 2-list will be formed whose first element is the keyword *QUOTE* and whose second element is the constant. Hence the constants 127, *NIL*, *(A B)* and *X* will be represented by the S-expressions *(QUOTE 127)*, *(QUOTE NIL)*, *(QUOTE (A B))* and *(QUOTE X)* respectively. There is no exception to this rule: variables are *never* quoted, constants are *always* quoted. Indeed this is how the interpreter tells them apart.

In general, a well-formed expression is represented in concrete form as a list with an atom in the first position acting as a keyword. *QUOTE* is a first example of this. Function calls are dealt with similarly. The call

$$f(e_1, \ldots, e_k)$$

is transformed into

$$(f \quad e_1 \quad \quad e_k)$$

that is, a list of $k+1$ elements, the first of which is the function being called and the remainder of which are its parameters suitably transformed. Thus the call

$$car(x)$$

is transformed into

$$(CAR \ X)$$

and the call

$$cons(car(x),append(cdr(x),y))$$

into

$$(CONS\ (CAR\ X)\ (APPEND\ (CDR\ X)\ Y))$$

The unusual feature here is that the function being called appears inside the parentheses, not outside them. S-expressions, being extremely sensitive to the placing of parentheses, allow for no variation of this syntax. It is this rule which gives Lisp its characteristic appearance. All the basic functions (and indeed all user-defined functions) are transformed in this way. To make you certain exactly which are the basic functions and what keywords are adopted for them we list all of them in (4.2).

$car(e)$	$(CAR\ e)$	$e_1 - e_2$	$(SUB\ e_1\ e_2)$	
$cdr(e)$	$(CDR\ e)$	$e_1 \times e_2$	$(MUL\ e_1\ e_2)$	
$cons(e_1,e_2)$	$(CONS\ e_1\ e_2)$	$e_1 \div e_2$	$(DIV\ e_1\ e_2)$	(4.2)
$atom\ (e)$	$(ATOM\ e)$	$e_1\ \text{rem}\ e_2$	$(REM\ e_1\ e_2)$	
$eq(e_1,e_2)$	$(EQ\ e_1\ e_2)$	$e_1 \leqslant e_2$	$(LEQ\ e_1\ e_2)$	
$e_1 + e_2$	$(ADD\ e_1\ e_2)$			

Further examples of applying the rules we have described so far are shown in Table 4.2.

Table 4.2

Function definition form	Concrete form
$car(x)$	$(CAR\ X)$
$car(cdr(x))$	$(CAR\ (CDR\ X))$
$x + 1$	$(ADD\ X\ (QUOTE\ 1))$
$cons\ (x,\ NIL)$	$(CONS\ X\ (QUOTE\ NIL))$

Neither the conditional form nor the lambda expression have surprising appearance in concrete form. What we would write as

if e_1 then e_2 else e_3

in a function definition, we will write as

$$(IF\quad e_1\quad e_2\quad e_3)$$

in a program. That is a 4-list in which the first element is the keyword atom *IF*. Thus

$$\textbf{if } i \leqslant 0 \textbf{ then } cons(0-i, \; NIL) \textbf{ else } cons(i, \; NIL)$$

becomes

$$(IF \; (LEQ \; I \; (QUOTE \; 0))$$
$$(CONS \; (SUB \; (QUOTE \; 0) \; I) \; (QUOTE \; NIL))$$
$$(CONS \; I \; (QUOTE \; NIL)))$$

The lambda expression

$$\lambda(x_1, \ldots, x_k)e$$

is transformed into

$$(LAMBDA \; (x_1 \; \ldots \; x_k) \; e)$$

which is a threelist consisting of the keyword *LAMBDA*, a list of the parameter names and the expression used to compute the value of the function. For example

$$\lambda(x,y)cons(x,cons(y,NIL))$$

becomes

$$(LAMBDA \; (X \; Y) \; (CONS \; X \; (CONS \; Y \; (QUOTE \; NIL))))$$

Now we can see how the lambda expression defining *append*, which appears as

$$\lambda(x,y) \textbf{ if } eq(x,NIL) \textbf{ then } y \textbf{ else}$$
$$cons(car(x),append(cdr(x),y))$$

in the definition, is transformed to

$$(LAMBDA \; (X \; Y)$$
$$(IF \; (EQ \; X \; (QUOTE \; NIL)) \; Y$$
$$(CONS \; (CAR \; X)$$
$$(APPEND \; (CDR \; X) \; Y))))$$

We come finally to the use of *let* and *where* blocks and their recursive forms. In concrete form we allow only one arrangement of the local definitions which is in fact a hybrid of the **let** and **where** forms as we have used them so far. We shall use the keywords *LET* and *LETREC* but have the qualified expression appear before the definitions as in the usual **where** form. Either of the expressions (4.3) is transformed into (4.4).

$$
\{e \qquad\qquad\qquad \{\textbf{let } x_1 = e_1
$$
$$
\textbf{where } x_1 = e_1 \qquad\qquad \textbf{and } x_2 = e_2
$$
$$
\textbf{and } x_2 = e_2 \quad \text{or} \qquad \vdots \qquad\qquad\qquad (4.3)
$$
$$
\vdots \qquad\qquad\qquad \textbf{and } x_k = e_k
$$
$$
\textbf{and } x_k = e_k\} \qquad\qquad e\}
$$

$$
(LET\ e
$$
$$
(x_1.e_1)
$$
$$
(x_2.e_2) \qquad\qquad\qquad\qquad\qquad (4.4)
$$
$$
\vdots
$$
$$
(x_k.e_k))
$$

Similarly the expressions (4.5) appear as (4.6).

$$
\{e \qquad\qquad\qquad \{\textbf{letrec } x_1 = e_1
$$
$$
\textbf{whererec } x_1 = e_1 \qquad\qquad \textbf{and } x_2 = e_2
$$
$$
\textbf{and } x_2 = e_2 \quad \text{or} \qquad \vdots \qquad\qquad\qquad (4.5)
$$
$$
\vdots \qquad\qquad\qquad \textbf{and } x_k = e_k
$$
$$
\textbf{and } x_k = e_k\} \qquad\qquad e\}
$$

$$
(LETREC\ e
$$
$$
(x_1.e_1)
$$
$$
(x_2.e_2) \qquad\qquad\qquad\qquad\qquad (4.6)
$$
$$
\vdots
$$
$$
(x_k.e_k))
$$

Thus a block with k definitions is presented as a $k+2$ list, the first member of which is the keyword, the second member of which is the qualified expression and the remaining members of which are the local definitions. Each local definition appears as a *dotted* pair. Usually the value assigned to the local variable is an expression with parentheses and thus in practice the dot is dropped along with these parentheses. Thus, while a literal application of these rules renders

$$
\{\textbf{let } s = car(z)
$$
$$
\textbf{and } p = car(cdr(z))
$$
$$
twolist(s+n,p \times n)\}
$$

as

```
(LET (TWOLIST (ADD S N) (MUL P N))
 (S.(CAR  Z))
 (P.(CAR (CDR Z))))
```

it is better to write this without the dots as

```
(LET (TWOLIST (ADD S N) (MUL P N))
 (S CAR Z)
 (P CAR (CDR Z)))
```

This explains why, in the definition of *append* at the beginning of the section, there is no parenthesis before the *LAMBDA*. That is, the definition has the form

```
(APPEND   LAMBDA (X Y) ... )
```

As a complete example, transforming the differentiation program given at the very end of Section 2.7, we obtain the concrete form (4.7).

```
(LETREC DIFF
 (DIFF LAMBDA (E)
  (IF (ATOM E) (IF (EQ E (QUOTE X)) (QUOTE 1)
              (QUOTE 0))
  (IF (EQ (CAR E) (QUOTE ADD))
   (LET (SUM (DIFF E1) (DIFF E2))
    (E1 CAR (CDR E))
    (E2 CAR (CDR (CDR E))))
  (IF (EQ (CAR E) (QUOTE MUL))                    (4.7)
   (LET (SUM (PROD E1 (DIFF E2))
             (PROD (DIFF E1) E2))
    (E1 CAR (CDR E))
    (E2 CAR (CDR (CDR E))))
  (QUOTE ERROR)))))
 (SUM LAMBDA (U V)
  (CONS (QUOTE ADD)
       (CONS U (CONS V (QUOTE NIL)))))
 (PROD LAMBDA (U V)
  (CONS (QUOTE MUL)
       (CONS U (CONS V (QUOTE NIL))))))
```

Thus, all of the following S-expressions are well-formed expressions for Lispkit Lisp programs, where $x, x_1, \ldots, x_k$ are atoms and $e, e_1, \ldots, e_k$ are nested well-formed expressions. The identifier s denotes any S-expression.

x	a variable
$(QUOTE\ s)$	a constant
$(ADD\ e_1\ e_2)$	
$(SUB\ e_1\ e_2)$	
$(MUL\ e_1\ e_2)$	arithmetic expressions
$(DIV\ e_1\ e_2)$	
$(REM\ e_1\ e_2)$	
$(EQ\ e_1\ e_2)$	relational expressions
$(LEQ\ e_1\ e_2)$	
$(CAR\ e)$	
$(CDR\ e)$	structural expressions
$(CONS\ e_1\ e_2)$	
$(ATOM\ e)$	
$(IF\ e_1\ e_2\ e_3)$	conditional form
$(LAMBDA\ (x_1 \ldots x_k)\ e)$	lambda expression
$(e\ e_1 \ldots e_k)$	function call
$(LET\ e\ (x_1 \boldsymbol{.} e_1) \ldots (x_k \boldsymbol{.} e_k))$	simple block
$(LETREC\ e\ (x_1 \boldsymbol{.} e_1) \ldots (x_k \boldsymbol{.} e_k))$	recursive block

Each of the well-formed expressions, except the variable and the constant, has nested within it other well-formed expressions. For example, the conditional form has three nested well-formed expressions corresponding to the *test* and the *true* and *false* alternatives. The only unusual well-formed expression in this list is the function call. Of the $k+1$ nested, well-formed expressions, the first is expected to be a function-valued expression, while the remainder are the actual parameters of this function. Thus

$$((DOT\ REVERSE\ INCLIST)\ (QUOTE\ (1\ 2\ 3)))$$

is well formed. It is a 2-list, matching a function call, with function

$$(DOT\ REVERSE\ INCLIST)$$

and single argument

$$(QUOTE\ (1\ 2\ 3))$$

both of which are well formed. The form

$$(DOT\ REVERSE\ INCLIST)$$

is well formed, again matching a function call. In all the above well-formed skeletons we allow k to be 0. In general, this reduces to a degenerate case, such as a block with no definitions or a function with no parameters, but it is nevertheless well formed.

In Section 4.3 we shall define an interpreter for Lispkit Lisp in the form of a function $apply(f,x)$ which expects f to be a well-formed expression with a function value and x to be a list of arguments for this function. During interpretation, each well-formed subexpression of f is identified and evaluated, often more than once. Indeed, it is only the well-formed expressions which are given values, for only those have defined values, and hence the structure of the entire interpreter is dictated by the set of well-formed expressions listed in this section. The interpreter turns out to be just a case analysis of the well-formed subexpressions of a program.

4.2 BINDING

In Chapter 2 we discussed informally the way in which values are associated with variables in a purely functional language. In general, this is straightforward and reflects our intuition about the role of parameters in function definitions. Some subtlety, however, arises when we allow function definitions to have free (or global) variables occurring in them and in relation to variables introduced, not as parameters but locally, using **where** or **let** blocks. To explain the binding rules, we introduce the concept of a *context*. Every expression in a functional program is evaluated with respect to a context (or in a certain context). A context is just an association between variables and values (which are usually S-expressions).

We shall write a binding in the form

$$variable \rightarrow value$$

and thus a context will just be a set of such bindings, usually displayed as a table.

For example,

$$x \rightarrow (A.B)$$
$$y \rightarrow (C\ D)$$
$$z \rightarrow 127$$

is a context. In this context the expressions listed in Table 4.3 have the values listed with them.

Table 4.3

Expression	Value
car(x)	A
cons(x,y)	((A.B) C D)
z+1	128
y	(C D)
X	X

The **let** and **where** blocks are used to establish new bindings. Such a block always appears nested in some context. The expressions defining the values of the new local variables are evaluated in this context. The qualified expression is then evaluated in the context obtained by extending the outer context by the addition of the new bindings, binding each local to its corresponding value. Thus, if the expression

$$\{\textbf{let } u = car(x)$$
$$\textbf{and } v = z+1$$
$$cons(u,cons(v,y))\}$$

occurs in the above context, the expressions $car(x)$ and $z+1$ are evaluated as shown to A and 128 respectively; thus, the qualified expression

$$cons(u,cons(v,y))$$

is evaluated in the extended context

$$x \rightarrow (A.B) \qquad u \rightarrow A$$
$$y \rightarrow (C\ D) \qquad v \rightarrow 128$$
$$z \rightarrow 127$$

and thus yields the value $(A\ 128\ C\ D)$.

When local variables have the same name as variables in the context in which the block is evaluated, then the new bindings override the old. Thus, if we were to evaluate

$$\{\textbf{let } x = car(y)$$
$$cons(x,NIL)\}$$

in the environment

$$x \rightarrow (A \ B)$$
$$y \rightarrow (C \ D)$$

then the new binding for x would be

$$x \rightarrow C$$

and hence the environment in which the qualified expression is evaluated is

$$x \rightarrow C$$
$$y \rightarrow (C \ D)$$

and thus the value computed is (C). The binding $x \rightarrow (A \ B)$ is completely masked from the qualified expression.

Now, this rule gives us a well-defined meaning for local definitions in which the same variable name appears on both the left-hand and right-hand sides of the definition. For example, the expression

$$\{\textbf{let } x = x+1$$
$$x \div 2\}$$

This is only meaningful in a context in which x is already bound to a numeric value. For example, in the context

$$x \rightarrow 127$$

the above expression has the value 64. This is consistent with the notion of localness of the new variables introduced by a **let** or **where** block. Since the names are local to the block, we do not change the meaning (value) of the block by substituting some different names, just as long as this name is not the same as any of the others occurring in the block. Of course, the replacement of a variable name by another must be done consistently, in that every occurrence must be changed. In the above block, it means that changing the expression to

$$\{\textbf{let } y = x+1$$
$$y \div 2\}$$

does not change its value. Its value is more obvious from this rewriting, but nevertheless we must be able to define the value of the earlier form.

To discuss binding in the context of functions, let us begin by dealing with functions which have no free (or global) variables in their bodies. Functions are usually introduced by lambda expressions, and function values are bound to variables using blocks as above. For example, in

$$\{ \mathbf{let}\, f = \lambda(x,y)2 \times x + y$$
$$f(2,3)\}$$

a function which computes a particular arithmetic function of two variables is introduced and bound to the variable f. When the function is called, the actual parameters are evaluated and then each value is bound to the corresponding formal parameter. Thus the body of the function is evaluated in a context which includes bindings for each of its parameters, binding them to the actual parameter values. In the above example, the body

$$2 \times x + y$$

is evaluated in the context

$$x \rightarrow 2$$
$$y \rightarrow 3$$

yielding 7. More generally, if we have

$$\{ \mathbf{let}\, f = \lambda(x,y)2 \times x + y$$
$$f(2,3) + f(3,2)\}$$

where the function is called twice, then the body is evaluated twice, each time with different bindings, once as above and once with

$$x \rightarrow 3$$
$$y \rightarrow 2$$

to yield 8. Hence the entire expression evaluates to 15.

When a function is defined as above, using the block mechanism to give it a name, this name is then bound to a function value. Now, we must be explicit about what a function value is. In the cases described above, where the function body contains no global variables, the lambda expression itself would serve as an appropriate value. When the lambda expression contains free variables, however, this would not be correct, since occurrences of these variables in the body of the function must be considered bound to the value they had when the lambda expression was evaluated to produce the function value. One way around this is to use, as a function value, a lambda expression modified so that free variables are replaced by their values. Thus, if the expression

$$\{\textbf{let } f = \lambda(x)2 \times x + y$$
$$\{\textbf{let } y = 4$$
$$f(2)\}\}$$

is evaluated in the environment

$$y \rightarrow 3$$

then first f is bound to

$$\lambda(x)2 \times x + 3$$

and then y is bound to 4, producing the environment

$$f \rightarrow \lambda(x)2 \times x + 3$$
$$y \rightarrow 4$$

for the evaluation of $f(2)$, yielding 7.

An equivalent way of describing a function value is to use the notion of a *closure*. Instead of substituting in the body of the function we form a composite object called a closure which contains both the lambda expression and the context defining the values of the global variables. For the above evaluation, when we encountered the call $f(2)$, we would have the context

$$f \rightarrow [\lambda(x)2 \times x + y, \{y \rightarrow 3\}]$$
$$y \rightarrow 4$$

where we have denoted the closure by the construction

[lambda expression, context]

Now, we interpret function calls as follows. Evaluate the actual parameters in the context of the call, then augment the context from the closure (the defining context) by binding each formal parameter to its corresponding actual parameter value, and evaluate the body of the function in this environment. Thus, in the above example, the body $2 \times x + y$ is evaluated in the context

$$x \to 2$$
$$y \to 3$$

despite the binding of y to 4 at the place of call.

There is a very simple and instructive equivalence between **let** blocks and lambda expressions. Consider the most general form of the function call

$$e(e_1, \ldots, e_k)$$

where the function to be called is given as the value of the expression e, which may be as simple as a variable, or may be a more general expression. The parameters supplied to this function are $e_1, \ldots, e_k$. For example, in Chapter 2 we met the function $inc(n)$ which had the definition

$$inc(n) \equiv \lambda(z)z + n$$

and yielded as its result the function which incremented its argument by n. Using the general form of call we could write

$$(inc(1))(x)$$

which applies the function value yielded by $inc(1)$ to the argument x.

The particular use we wish to make of this most general form is when the function being called is given by a lambda expression. Hence the call is

$$\{\lambda(x_1, \ldots, x_k)e\}(e_1, \ldots, e_k)$$

where the function $\lambda(x, \ldots, x_k)e$ is being applied directly to the arguments $e_1, \ldots, e_k$. In this form it has exactly the same value as (4.8).

$$\begin{aligned} &\{\textbf{let } x_1 = e_1 \\ &\textbf{ and } x_2 = e_2 \\ &\quad \vdots \\ &\textbf{ and } x_k = e_k \\ &e\} \end{aligned} \qquad (4.8)$$

This is the equivalence we wish to demonstrate. It should help clarify some of the rules of binding. As an equivalence it shows that **let** blocks are not a necessary semantic feature of the language. However, the separation of formal and actual parameters in the lambda form of this expression makes the **let** form much easier to use in practice.

We come now to the more difficult concept of a **letrec** or **whererec** block. That is, a block in which the definitions are mutually recursive. With the form (4.9), we have the semantic condition that, unlike the simpler **let** and

$$
\begin{aligned}
&\{\textbf{letrec } x_1 = e_1 \\
&\textbf{ and } x_2 = e_2 \\
&\quad \vdots \\
&\textbf{ and } x_k = e_k \\
&e\}
\end{aligned}
\tag{4.9}
$$

where blocks, occurrences of $x_1, \ldots, x_k$ throughout $e_1, \ldots, e_k$ are interpreted as occurrences of the local variable. Hence the statement that $x_1, \ldots, x_k$ are defined by mutual recursion. The difficulty with this form of block is that $e_1, \ldots, e_k$ have to be evaluated in an environment in which $x_1, \ldots, x_k$ are bound. But the values to which these variables must be bound are the values of $e_1, \ldots, e_k$ themselves. In general, we do not wish to define such a block unless each of the expressions $e_1, \ldots, e_k$ is a lambda expression. Then the value of each e_i is a closure

$$[e_i, \alpha]$$

where α is the context in which each of $x_1, \ldots, x_k$ is bound to the value of $e_1, \ldots, e_k$. That is,

$$
\begin{aligned}
\alpha \equiv \{ x_1 &\to [e_1, \alpha] \\
&\vdots \\
x_k &\to [e_k, \alpha] \}
\end{aligned}
$$

Note that this assumes that each e_i is a lambda expression. This strangely recursive context is in fact quite easy for humans to deal with, but a little harder for machines. We simply take note of the fact that the context has a name, α, and do not worry about the fact that it is embedded in values within itself. When, during evaluation of e (or any of the $e_1, \ldots, e_k$) we come across a reference to the variable x_i, we take as its value the closure $[e_i, \alpha]$. That is, subsequent occurrences of $x_1, \ldots, x_k$ in e_i will be taken to have their α values, as we intend.

To see how this works, consider the definition

$$\{\textbf{letrec } f = \lambda(x) \textbf{ if } atom(x) \textbf{ then } x \textbf{ else } f(cdr(x))$$
$$f(z)\}$$

evaluated in the context

$$z \to (A \ B.C)$$

For the evaluation of $f(z)$ we set up the context

$$\alpha \equiv \{f \to [\lambda(x) \textbf{ if } atom(x) \textbf{ then } x \textbf{ else } f(cdr(x)), \ \alpha]$$
$$z \to (A \ B.C)\}$$

Hence the call $f(z)$ causes us to enter the function with the context

$$x \to (A \ B.C)$$
$$f \to [\lambda(x) \textbf{ if } atom(x) \textbf{ then } x \textbf{ else } f(cdr(x)), \ \alpha]$$
$$z \to (A \ B.C)$$

Now, since x is not an atom, a recursive call is made with the expression $f(cdr(z))$.

The value of f is as before and hence α is augmented with the new association from the actual parameter of $f(cdr(x))$. Thus we re-enter the function with the context

$$x \to (B.C)$$
$$f \to [\lambda(x) \textbf{ if } atom(x) \textbf{ then } x \textbf{ else } f(cdr(x)), \ \alpha]$$
$$z \to (A \ B.C)$$

Thus we are in much the same state as before and we can see that the recursion is working out properly. In the next section we shall study a particular implementation of these rules for binding, when we define an interpreter for Lispkit Lisp.

4.3 AN INTERPRETER FOR THE LISP VARIANT

A remarkable property of Lisp is the ease with which it can be used to express its own interpreter. Indeed this has been one of its principal design goals. In this section we will describe such an interpreter for Lispkit Lisp.

This is only one of many possible interpreters and a great deal can be learned about Lisp by considering some of the alternatives. In particular, having read this section it is worthwhile looking at some of the published interpreters, particularly the original one by McCarthy (1960) and its subsequent revision (McCarthy *et al.*, 1962). Such a study will convince you that the semantics of a programming language can be very subtle, and, moreover, that it is very difficult to capture the various nuances of a language in an implementation. Our main purpose in this section, however, is to demonstrate the basic technique of direct interpretation of the source of a Lispkit Lisp program, and we shall only briefly touch on the extent to which the semantics of the language are properly represented in this interpreter.

The cases which we analyze are just the set of well-formed expressions from which a Lispkit Lisp program can be composed. There are 18 different forms, listed in Section 4.1. If *e* is a well-formed expression, then we wish to define a function *eval* which returns the value of this expression *e*. Now *e* may have free occurrences of variables in it and hence its value is defined only if we have a context which associates a value with each freely occurring variable in *e*. We used such a device when we explained binding in the previous section. The association list which we used in Section 3.1 is a possible implementation of such a context. Indeed, this is the implementation used by McCarthy in the original Lisp interpreter. Here, however, we shall use a slightly more elaborate implementation which is consistent with the concepts used to implement the compiler which we shall describe in Chapter 6.

We construct a namelist in which the variables of the program are recorded. The namelist has the structure of a list of lists of atoms, each atom being the name of a variable. For example

$$((X \ Y Z) (A \ X) (FN))$$

is a namelist. In a Lispkit Lisp program, every well-formed subexpression occurs in a context in which certain variables are valid, in the sense that the expression is within the scope of these variables. These accessible variables are arranged in the namelist in such a way that more local variables are nearer the front than more global ones. In the interpreter we will need not only the namelist but a congruent list of values. For example, the valuelist

$$((1 \ (A \ B) -127) ((C.D) \ 3) (((LAMBDA \ ...))))$$

is congruent to (has the same shape as) the namelist given above, and thus these two lists taken together represent the context

$$X \rightarrow 1$$
$$Y \rightarrow (A\ B)$$
$$Z \rightarrow -127$$
$$A \rightarrow (C.D)$$
$$FN \rightarrow ((LAMBDA\ \ldots))$$

To access the valuelist using the namelist, we define in (4.10) a function $assoc(x,n,v)$ which takes the atom x to be the name of a variable occurring in the namelist n and returns the value in the corresponding position in the congruent valuelist v.

$assoc(x,n,v) \equiv$
    if $member(x,car(n))$ **then** $locate(x,car(n),car(v))$
        else $assoc(x,cdr(n),cdr(v))$
$locate\ (x,l,m) \equiv$
    if $eq(x,car(l))$ **then** $car(m)$ **else**   (4.10)
        $locate(x,cdr(l),cdr(m))$
$member(x,l) \equiv$
    if $eq(l,NIL)$ **then** F **else**
    if $eq(x,car(l))$ **then** T **else** $member(x,cdr(l))$

We see that *assoc* inspects each sublist of n in turn to determine if x is a member of that sublist. On finding the appropriate sublist, *locate* is used to access the corresponding sublist of v. Note that *assoc* assumes that x occurs somewhere in n. If x does not occur in n, then the result of *assoc* is undefined. We shall avoid the complexity of dealing explicitly with error situations such as this. We shall be content that, in cases in which an error could be detected, the function which could detect the error does not do so, but instead has no defined value.

Now we can begin to define the function $eval(e,n,v)$. This function, which will determine the value of a well-formed expression, will have as its parameters, e the well-formed expression, n the namelist and v the valuelist, which together make up the context in which evaluation is to take place. That is, we require to design a function with a definition of the form

$$eval(e,n,v) \equiv \ldots$$

We shall do this by means of a case analysis on the structure of the well-formed expression e. In order to make the description of this design more easily understood we shall write down each case in the form of an equation. The form we shall use to denote the result of applying *eval* to the arguments *e*, *n* and *v* will be

$$eval[e,n,v]$$

where the square brackets are to avoid confusion with the parentheses in S-expressions. Thus for example we could write the equation

$$eval[(CAR\ X),((X)),(((A.B)))] = A$$

to indicate the value of $(CAR\ X)$ in a context which associates the value $(A.B)$ with the variable X. We shall of course usually write more schematic equations than this where mathematical variables, written as lower-case letters, denote arbitrary S-expressions. For example, the following equation defines the value of $(CAR\ e)$ for any well-formed expression e:

$$\text{if } eval[e,n,v] = (a.b)$$
$$\text{then } eval[(CAR\ e),n,v] = a$$

Also to assist readability we will choose the names of mathematical variables carefully, to suggest their type. We will use $e, e_1, e_2, \ldots$ for well-formed expressions; $x, x_1, x_2, \ldots$ for atoms used as variables in well-formed expressions; $n, n_1, n_2, \ldots$ for namelists and $v, v_1, v_2, \ldots$ for valuelists; finally, other letters but usually a, b and s will be used to denote arbitrary S-expressions. This is consistent with our use of these names in the list of well-formed expressions given in Section 4.1. Let us consider each of these well-formed expressions in turn. We shall omit the arithmetic expressions since they contribute no new insight.

The value of the variable x is just that value we find for it when we look it up in the namelist/valuelist structure. That is

$$eval[x,n,v] = assoc(x,n,v)$$

The value of the well-formed expression $(QUOTE\ s)$ is just s, regardless of the context in which evaluation takes place. Hence

$$eval[(QUOTE\ s),n,v] = s$$

Consider now the basic functions CAR, CDR, $CONS$, $ATOM$ and EQ. Each of these has a certain number of arguments, and the value of a well-formed expression whose principal operator is one of these basic functions is defined in terms of the value of these arguments. For example:

$$\text{if } eval[e_1,n,v]=a$$
$$\text{and } eval[e_2,n,v]=b$$
$$\text{then } eval[(CONS\ e_1\ e_2),n,v]=cons(a,b)$$

Here we have done little more than define $CONS$ in terms of $cons$. We have, however, indicated that the arguments are evaluated and that the function $cons$ is then applied to the values. Clearly, each of the basic functions can be defined by a similar equation. The rule for $(CAR\ e)$ is

$$\text{if } eval[e,n,v]=a$$
$$\text{then } eval[(CAR\ e),n,v]=car(a)$$

and the rules for CDR and $ATOM$ are similar. The rule for EQ is similar to that for $CONS$.

The conditional form $(IF\ e_1\ e_2\ e_3)$ requires a little more thought. It is not intended that the components e_2 and e_3 shall both be evaluated, therefore we cannot evaluate them until after e_1 has been evaluated. We could write the rule as

$$\text{if } eval[e_1,n,v]=a$$
$$\text{then } eval[(IF\ e_1\ e_2\ e_3),n,v]$$
$$= \textbf{if } a \textbf{ then } eval[e_2,n,v] \textbf{ else } eval[e_3,n,v]$$

which is consistent with the way in which the basic functions were defined. Here, the fact that only one of e_2 or e_3 is evaluated is dependent on the fact that **if**...**then**...**else** has that property. If instead we were to write the rule as

$$\text{if } eval[e_1,n,v]=a$$
$$\text{then } eval[(IF\ e_1\ e_2\ e_3),n,v]$$
$$= eval[\textbf{if } a \textbf{ then } e_2 \textbf{ else } e_3,n,v]$$

it is more obvious that only one evaluation, of either e_2 or e_3, takes place and indeed this form of the rule is not dependent on **if**...**then**...**else** having the same property. Either of these definitions will, however, serve us in our interpreter.

The lambda expression $(LAMBDA\ (x_1\ \ldots\ x_k)\ e)$ is a little more difficult and a little more interesting. In the previous section we explained how a function value had to be considered to have its global (free) variables bound to the values they had at function-definition time. Two alternative ways of dealing with this are either to substitute in e for all variables other than $x_1, \ldots, x_k$ the value which they have in the current context, or to construct a composite value, called a *closure*, to represent the function. We choose the latter alternative here. We choose to represent the closure by a simple combination of the lambda expression and the context.

The closure must contain not only the body of the lambda expression but also the names of the bound variables and the context in which the body is to be evaluated. We will choose the following arbitrary structure for this information.

$$eval[(LAMBDA \ y \ e),n,v]$$
$$= cons(cons(y,e),cons(n,v))$$

where y is a list of bound variables of the form $(x_1 \ \ldots \ x_k)$. We shall see the significance of saving all this information when we deal with the function call.

The function call is denoted by the well-formed expression $(e \ e_1 \ldots e_k)$, where e is an expression which evaluates to a function value (closure) and $e_1, \ldots, e_k$ are evaluated to determine the argument values for this function. To evaluate the arguments we define the function

$$evlis(l,n,v) \equiv \textbf{if} \ l = NIL \ \textbf{then} \ NIL \ \textbf{else}$$
$$cons(eval(car(l),n,v),evlis(cdr(l),n,v))$$

and adopt the same convention of using square brackets to avoid confusion when mixing calls of *evlis* with S-expressions. Now we can write the definition of function call as:

$$\textbf{if} \ eval[e,n,v] = ((y.e').(n'.v'))$$
$$\text{and} \ evlis[(e_1 \ \ldots \ e_k),n,v] = z$$
$$\textbf{then}$$
$$eval[(e \ e_1 \ \ldots \ e_k),n,v] = eval[e',(y.n'),(z.v')]$$

This clearly requires some explanation. First we have assumed that e will evaluate to a closure, which will have the structure shown in Fig 4.1, and that the arguments $(e_1 \ \ldots \ e_k)$ will evaluate to the list of values z. That is, z will be a k element list, congruent to the list y of bound variables. With these values we can define the value of the function call $(e \ e_1 \ \ldots \ e_k)$ as that value obtained by evaluating the body of the function in the context whose namelist is $(y.n')$ and whose valuelist is $(z.v')$. This is clearly the way we usually imagine that a function call is done, that the body of the function

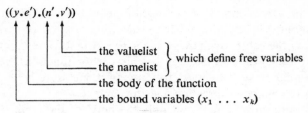

Fig. 4.1

is evaluated with the value of each actual parameter associated with the name of the corresponding formal and with all other variables having the values they had when the function was defined.

As we might expect, the simple *LET* block is very similar to the function call

$$\text{if } evlis[(e_1 \quad \dots \quad e_k), n, v] = z$$
$$\text{then } eval[(LET \ e \ (x_1.e_1)\dots(x_k.e_k)), n, v]$$
$$= eval[e, ((x_1\dots x_k).n), (z.v)]$$

Here we see that the definitions $(e_1 \ \dots \ e_k)$ are grouped together and evaluated by *evlis*. This is merely a convenience. The resulting list of values, z, is then installed in the valuelist in positions corresponding to the list of defined variables $(x_1 \ \dots \ x_k)$. In this extended context, the body of the block e is evaluated. It should be obvious that this rule establishes the equivalence

$$(LET \ e \ (x_1.e_1)\dots(x_k.e_k))$$
$$\cong \ ((LAMBDA \ (x_1\dots x_k) \ e) \ e_1\dots e_k)$$

in the sense that they both evaluate to the same value in any context.

We come now, finally, to the recursive block

$$(LETREC \ e \ (x_1.e_1)\dots(x_k.e_k)).$$

As we would expect, this is going to cause a little difficulty because the definitions $e_1,\dots,e_k$ must be evaluated in an environment in which the values of the defined variables $x_1,\dots,x_k$ are accessible. In fact, we shall make a very restricted, but largely adequate, interpretation of the recursive block here, leaving a fuller interpretation until Chapter 8. We make use of a pseudo-function, usually available in Lisp, but defined here in a restricted way. The pseudofunction $rplaca(x,y)$, so-called because it is called for its effect as well as its value, is used to replace the *car* of x by y. When $rplaca(x,y)$ is called, the *car* of *x* must be a special value Ω, which we shall refer to as "pending". We use *rplaca* to replace Ω by its intended value when it is computed. The result of *rplaca(x,y)* is the value of *x*, except that the value Ω in its *car* has been replaced by its intended value *y*. We simply consider the pending value always to stand for the value which will ultimately replace it. If a program tries to access the pending value before it has been replaced, then the effect of the program is undefined.

Consider

$$\{\textbf{let } b = cons \ (\Omega,B)$$
$$rplaca(b,A)\}$$

then the value of this expression is $(A.B)$. In this sense *rplaca(x,y)* has exactly the same value as *cons(y,cdr(x))*. However, *rplaca* has one important capability which we shall exploit. It can build "circular" structures. Consider

$$\{\textbf{let } b = cons(\Omega,B)$$
$$rplaca(b,b)\}$$

Certainly the value of this expression is an S-expression whose *cdr* is *B*. However, the *car* of the S-expression is the S-expression itself. That is, we have built the structure α whose value is $(\alpha.B)$. Thus for example, if $x = (\alpha.B)$

$$cdr(car(car(car(x)))) = B$$

and in fact, no matter how many times we take the car of *x*, we get the value α. The way in which *rplaca* works can only be understood in terms of the way S-expressions are usually represented in a machine. In practice a *cons* function generates a record with two pointers in it, one pointing to a structure for the car and one to a structure for the *cdr*. The S-expression is then represented by a pointer to this *cons* record. When we first invoke *cons* with *cons(Ω,B)* we build the record shown in Fig. 4.2, and then, when we sub-

$$\alpha \longrightarrow \boxed{\ \Omega\ |\ B\ }$$

Fig. 4.2

sequently call *rplaca* with this value α as its two arguments, we simply replace Ω by α (Fig. 4.3). If, between establishing the record α with Ω in it and

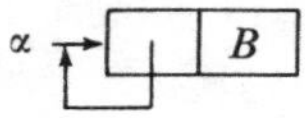

Fig. 4.3

replacing the Ω, copies of α are made, since only the pointer is copied and not the record, the replacement is still effective. For example, the list

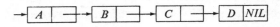

Fig. 4.4

$(A\ B\ C\ D)$ can be represented by Fig 4.4, and hence the expression

$$\{\textbf{let }b = cons(\Omega, NIL)$$
$$rplaca(b, append((A\ B\ C\ D), b))\}$$

generates the structure shown in Fig. 4.5, which can be denoted by the

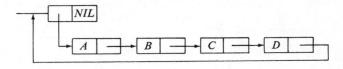

Fig. 4.5

infinitely long S-expression

$$((A\ B\ C\ D\ (A\ B\ C\ D\ (A\ B\ C\ D\ (\ \ldots\ ))))))$$

We use this ability to build circular structures to interpret the recursive block. When evaluating the defining expressions $e_1, \ldots, e_k$ we do so with a valuelist which has the values of $x_1, \ldots, x_k$ still pending. Thus, the restriction we must place on the use of $e_1, \ldots, e_k$ in a *LETREC* block is that their evaluation does not require immediate access to $x_1, \ldots, x_k$. We have the following rule:

$$\text{if } v' = (\Omega.v) \text{ and } n' = ((x_1\ \ldots\ x_k).n)$$
$$\text{and } evlis[(e_1\ \ldots\ e_k), n', v'] = z$$
$$\text{then } eval[(LETREC\ e\ (x_1.e_1)\ldots(x_k.e_k)), n, v]$$
$$= eval[e, n', rplaca[v', z]]$$

We have introduced the dummy valuelist v', congruent to the namelist $n' = ((x_1\ \ldots\ x_k).n)$ except that in its first place it has the pending value Ω, which will eventually be replaced by the list of values of $e_1, \ldots, e_k$. We have used this dummy environment when evaluating the list of definitions $(e_1\ \ldots\ e_k)$ so that when any particular e_i is a lambda expression, the value determined for it will be a closure containing v'. Before we evaluate the body

of the block as we did for *LET*, we replace the car of v' by z, the list of values
of the definitions.

For example, with this rule, when we come to evaluate the well-formed
expression

> (*LETREC e*
>   (*F LAMBDA* y_1 e_1)
>   (*G LAMBDA* y_2 e_2))

we build first the valuelist shown in Fig. 4.6, and then construct the two

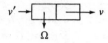

Fig. 4.6

closures for *F* and *G* (Fig. 4.7). Note how they both point at v'. When we

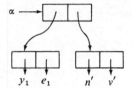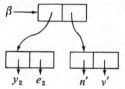

Fig. 4.7

come to evaluate e, the Ω value in v' has been replaced, and now v' has the
value shown in Fig. 4.8.

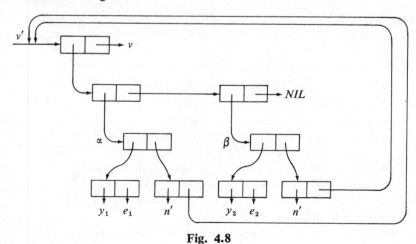

Fig. 4.8

Following this through, we see how references from within e to F or G yield the values of α and β respectively. Similarly, when the bodies of F and G, that is e_1 or e_2, are being interpreted, the context which has been constructed has been built from v' and hence references to F and G from within these expressions also yield α and β. That this interpretation works relies on the fact that the value of a lambda expression does not require evaluation of its body. That is left until the function is called.

Now it is possible to define the evaluation of a *LETREC* block without using *rplaca* and, from a mathematical point of view, this would be a more satisfactory thing to do. However, it is not simple to understand and to some extent would defeat the purpose here of giving a precise but intuitive description of the semantics of this feature. In Chapter 8 we will return to the problem of making a fuller implementation of a *LETREC* block when we discuss delayed evaluation.

We have in fact completed the design of an interpreting function, it remains only to write it out as a conventional function definition. We require to use the functions *vars(d)* and *exprs(d)* which respectively strip a list of variables and definitions $((x_1 \cdot e_1) \ \ldots \ (x_k \cdot e_k))$ to form a list of variables $(x_1 \ \ldots \ x_k)$ and a list of definitions $(e_1 \ \ldots \ e_k)$. These functions are trivial in comparison with the kind of programs we have written previously, but for completeness we include them here.

$$vars(d) \equiv \textbf{if } d = NIL \textbf{ then } NIL \textbf{ else}$$
$$cons(car(car(d)), vars(cdr(d)))$$
$$exprs(d) \equiv \textbf{if } d = NIL \textbf{ then } NIL \textbf{ else}$$
$$cons(cdr(car(d)), exprs(cdr(d)))$$

Using these functions we can write out the definition of $eval(e,n,v)$ simply by rewriting each of the equations defined above, as in (4.11).

$eval(e,n,v) \equiv$
    if $atom(e)$ **then** $assoc(e,n,v)$ **else**
    if $car(e) = QUOTE$ **then** $car(cdr(e))$ **else**
    if $car(e) = CAR$ **then** $car(eval(car(cdr(e)),n,v))$ **else**
    if $car(e) = CDR$ **then** $cdr(eval(car(cdr(e)),n,v))$ **else**
    if $car(e) = ATOM$ **then** $atom(eval(car(cdr(e)),n,v))$ **else**
    if $car(e) = CONS$ **then** $cons(eval(car(cdr(e)),n,v),$
                                     $eval(car(cdr(cdr(e))),n,v))$ **else**
      if $car(e) = EQ$ **then** $eq(eval(car(cdr(e)),n,v),$
                                $eval(car(cdr(cdr(e))),n,v))$ **else**

if $car(e) = IF$ **then**
$\{eval$ (**if** $eval(e1,n,v)$ **then** $e2$ **else** $e3,n,v)$
  where $e1 = car(cdr(e))$
    and $e2 = car(cdr(cdr(e)))$
    and $e3 = car(cdr(cdr(cdr(e))))\}$ **else**
if $car(e) = LAMBDA$ **then**   (4.11)
  $cons(cons(car(cdr(e)),car(cdr(cdr(e)))), cons(n,v))$ **else**
if $car(e) = LET$ **then**
$\{eval(car(cdr(e)),cons(y,n),cons(z,v))$
   where $y = vars(cdr(cdr(e)))$
       $z = evlis(exprs(cdr(cdr(e))),n,v)\}$ **else**
if $car(e) = LETREC$ **then**
$\{\{eval(car(cdr(e)),cons(y,n),rplaca(v',z))$
      where $z = evlis(exprs(cdr(cdr(e))),cons(y,n),v')\}$
    where $y = vars(cdr(cdr(e)))$
      and $v' = cons(PENDING,v)\}$ **else**
$\{eval(cdr(car(c)),cons(car(car(c)),car(cdr(c))),cons(z,cdr(cdr(c))))$
  where $c = eval(car(e),n,v)$
      $z = evlis(cdr(e),n,v)\}$

A careful comparison of this definition with each of the equations derived during its design will confirm that it is a faithful reproduction of those design decisions. The important feature of this rewriting is that it is now clearly in a form in which it can be interpreted by a machine.

In order to make it compatible with the way we would expect to use such an interpreter, we require to define a function which will, rather than evaluate an expression, apply a function to some arguments. A Lispkit Lisp program is a well-formed expression f whose value is a function and we usually require to apply this function to a list of arguments a. This mode of operation is characterized in Section 4.1 by the expression $apply(f,x)$.

We define $apply(f,x)$ so that

$$apply(f,x) \equiv \{eval(cdr(car(c)),cons(car(car(c)),car(cdr(c))), cons(x,cdr(cdr(c))))$$
$$\textbf{where } c = eval(f,NIL,NIL)\}$$

That is to say, f is evaluated to produce a closure $c = ((y.e).(n.v))$, and then we compute the value of

$$eval[e,(y.n),(x.v)].$$

Only a brief discussion of what is specified by such an interpreter, and the extent to which it is a semantic definition of the language, is given here. The first thing we must notice is that the meaning attributed by the interpreter to the basic functions *CONS, CAR, CDR, ATOM* and *EQ* is not specified by the interpreter but by our preconceived understanding of the meaning of *cons, car, cdr, atom* and *eq*. What is specified is that these operations in the source program are applied to their evaluated arguments and not to their literal arguments. Of course, since the basic functions *cons, car, cdr, atom* and *eq* are used in other roles throughout the interpreter it would probably be meaningless to ascribe to them definitions other than those we have given. But, if we extend the source language briefly by the inclusion of the well-formed expression (NULL *e*) and extend the interpreter by the inclusion of the clause

$$\ldots \textbf{if } eq(car(e),NULL) \textbf{ then } null(eval(car(cdr(e)),n,v)) \textbf{ else } \ldots$$

we can ask the question: what is the meaning of this well-formed expression? The answer is that *NULL* means whatever *null* means, and we can choose that to be whatever we want it to be.

We observed a similar phenomenon with the well-formed *IF* expression, in that the only reason why the first form of the rule which we gave had the required property, namely that one of the two arms of the conditional was evaluated, was that that property was possessed also by the **if**...**then**...**else** which we used to define it. In this case, however, we were able to find a form wherein this interdependence of properties was not relied upon. This form is to be preferred, for it is more explicit.

Clearly it would be simple to write alternative interpreters for Lisp intended to give the same meaning to all the constructs of the language and to experiment with changes to these meanings and extensions to the language. Similarly, it is possible to write interpreters for completely different languages, even imperative ones like Algol, although to do this one must tolerate the usual transliteration of the language being interpreted to S-expression form. Since this kind of implementation would be of little practical use, because of inefficiency, it is easy to tolerate this transliteration. The first section of Chapter 5 is devoted to such a semantic specification. In Chapter 6, we will give an alternative definition of Lisp to the one given here—in some senses a more satisfactory one and so we postpone further discussion of the semantics of Lisp until then. In Chapter 8 we will return to the problem of giving a more complete definition to the recursive block structure.

EXERCISES

4.1 Consider the concept of binding in the context of higher-order functions.

in particular, consider *map* as defined in Section 2.8. Show that, with the concept of context as described here, no confusion can arise when, for example, the functional argument of *map* contains a free variable, as in the call $map(y,\lambda(z)z + x)$.

4.2 An alternative to proper binding, as described here, is so-called *fluid binding*. In fluid binding, free variables of functions are not bound when the function is defined. That is to say the value of a function is just the verbatim lambda expression. Hence, when a function is called, free variables take the values of variables with the same name in the context of the call. Determine a simple example of when this binding rule differs from the rule of proper binding. Show that, with the definition of *map* given in Section 2.8, the call of Exercise 4.1 goes wrong because of the confusion of x's.

4.3 The factorial function is written

    fac **whererec**
        $fac = \lambda(n)$ **if** $eq(n,0)$ **then** 1 **else** $n \times fac(n-1)$

It can be rewritten so that it has an extra parameter which is the function to be applied to $n-1$ instead of *fac*. Now, if it is called with itself as its extra actual parameter it should have the same effect. Rewrite *fac* in this way and show that **whererec** is unnecessary. Can this transformation be generalized to the case in which **whererec** introduces many new variables?

4.4 Extend the interpreter given in this section to include an interpretation for the standard conditional form from Lisp, whose keyword is *COND* and which satisfies the following equivalence:
$$(COND\,(p_1\,e_1)\,\ldots\,(p_k\,e_k))$$
$$\cong\,(IF\,p_1\,e_1\,(IF\,p_2\,e_2\,(IF\,\ldots\,(IF\,p_k\,e_k\,\Omega\,))))$$
where Ω is some expression whose value is undefined.

4.5 Modify the interpreter given in this section so that the value of a function is represented, not by a closure, but simply by the *LAMBDA* expression. That is implement fluid binding as described in Exercise 4.2.

4.6 Rewrite the interpreter given in this section so that, instead of having an explicitly held context represented by a namelist and a valuelist, whenever a function is called (or a block entered) the body is modified by substituting values (probably *QUOTE*d) for formal parameters. Hence *eval* will never be required to evaluate an expression with free variables. *LETREC* is of course much harder than anything else here and maybe ought to be avoided at a first attempt.

4.7 Consider the following extension to the language interpreted by $eval(e,n,v)$. The well-formed expression $(VALOF\,e)$ is given a meaning by extending *eval* with

    $\ldots$ **if** $eq(car(e),VALOF)$ **then**
        $assoc(eval(car(cdr(e)),n,v),n,v)$ **else** $\ldots$

What does *VALOF* do? How can it be used? Do you consider it a desirable feature of an extended Lisp?

4.8 By allowing the namelist and the valuelist to have a more general structure, so that they are effectively a tree of names and a congruent tree of values, it is possible to support more general parameter list structures than just a list of variables. Make such an extension and discuss its merits.

4.9 The equational form of the interpreter was much easier to design and understand than the executable form. We could define a version of Lisp which allowed us to write programs more akin to the equational form. The basic idea is to allow a pattern-matching form of conditional such as

> **case** *e* **of**
>   *(QUOTE a)*: . . .
>   *(CAR e′)*: . . .
>   *(LAMBDA y e′)*: . . .
> **esac**

Here the expression *e* is evaluated, and then its shape is compared directly to each of the case-statement labels. If a match is found that case is chosen, and an association between variables in the label and components of the value of *e* is established.

Define such an extension to Lisp and write an interpreter for it.

4.10 Design an interpreting function for the following simple language. The only expressions in the language are logical expressions. The well-formed expressions are of seven kinds (Table 4.4).

Table 4.4

Kind	Form
logical constants	$(QUOTE\ T)$ $(QUOTE\ F)$
variables	atoms
conjunction	$(AND\ e_1\ e_2)$
disjunction	$(OR\ e_1\ e_2)$
negation	$(NOT\ e)$
universal quantifier	$(ALL\ x\ e)$
existential quantifier	$(SOME\ x\ e)$

The universal and existential forms are like lambda expressions in that they each introduce a variable *x* and for a well-formed expression to be interpretable it must have no free variables in it. Examples of interpretable well-formed expressions are:

> *(ALL P (OR P (NOT P)))*
> *(SOME P (AND (ALL Q (OR P Q)) P))*
> *(OR (SOME P P) (ALL P P))*

Such expressions can always be evaluated to a value *T* or value *F*. Normal evaluation of logical expressions is used for *AND*, *OR* and *NOT* of course. *ALL* is evaluated by evaluating the bound expression *e* with the bound variable *x* having the values *T* and *F* respectively, and then *AND*ing the results. Similarly *SOME* is evaluated by evaluating the bound expression *e* with *x* having the values *T* and *F* and *OR*ing the results. This interpreter is evaluating a form of the propositional calculus. For a good description of the propositional calculus and this form of evaluation, see Manna (1974), Chapter 2.

4.11 Design a program to analyze a well-formed Lispkit Lisp expression, checking the "arity" (see the following definition) of the variables appearing in it (see p. 102 for a list of well-formed expressions). The *arity* of a variable is the number of arguments it expects. Hence a simple variable has arity 0, the "variables" *CAR*, *CDR* etc., have arity 1, *CONS* has arity 2 and so on. To begin with, do not consider the well-formed expressions constructed using *LAMBDA*, *LET* and *LETREC*, since these introduce their own particular difficulties. Eventually you should try to extend your program to cope with at least simple uses of these.

4.12 Design a program to analyze a well-formed Lispkit Lisp expression, checking the type of each subexpression. Assume every variable in the well-formed expression is associated with a type t where t is

1. *ATOM*, indicating the associated variable has an atomic value
2. *SEXP*, indicating the associated variable has an unknown structure.
3. (*CONS* t_1 t_2) where t_1, t_2 are type expressions, indicating the associated variable has a composite value, composed of values of types t_1 and t_2 respectively.

Do not consider the lambda expression or block constructs, at least to begin with. If the variable X is associated with the type (*CONS SEXP* (*CONS SEXP ATOM*)) then (*CAR X*), (*CAR* (*CDR X*)) and (*CDR* (*CDR X*)) are all type correct, but (*CAR* (*CAR X*)) is not (since a *SEXP* may be an atom) and neither is (*CAR* (*CDR* (*CDR X*))). Extend the basic type domain to include the ability to distinguish symbolic from numeric atoms, and to distinguish the atom *NIL*.

5 CORRESPONDENCE BETWEEN FUNCTIONAL PROGRAMS AND IMPERATIVE PROGRAMS

This chapter is devoted to an informal introduction to the methods of semantic specification of programming languages and analysis of programs. Our approach is to show the strong relationships between these methods and those of functional programming which we have already studied. Indeed, we shall show a number of direct correspondences between an Algol-like programming language and the purely functional language used in this book.

We shall use the term imperative to describe a program or programming language which computes by effect rather than value. Let us repeat the explanation of value and effect given in Chapter 1. The principal characteristic of writing a program in Algol is that variables are considered to possess a value which can be changed by assignment. The way in which one computes in Algol is to make a sequence of changes to the values of the variables, determining the new value for each variable as a function of the current values of some or all of the program variables, including possibly itself. Thus an Algol program consists of a sequence of imperative statements, each of which effects a simple or composite change in the values of the program variables. As we explained in Chapter 1, it is the absence of this ability to effect changes to values of variables which characterizes purely functional languages.

In Section 5.1 we will introduce a fragment of an Algol-like language which will be used throughout the chapter as the essence of an imperative language. We will give a precise formal specification of the semantics of our fragment by defining an interpreter for it. In Section 5.1 also we introduce the very important notion of abstract syntax. In Section 5.2 we develop from the interpreter a more concise and powerful way of specifying the semantics of each construct in our Algol fragment. Here we associate a function with each construct and claim that the function specifies, in a certain sense, what the construct computes. This is the basis for the now very well established field of mathematical semantics. However, we give only the briefest introduction to that field and recommend other sources of study to the interested reader. Instead, we go on in Section 5.3 to review the ways in which imperative programs can be transformed into functional programs. In a sense, this is a repetition of the development given in Section 5.2, but in a more intuitive style, and it helps to establish a strong correspondence between certain types of imperative program and certain types of functional program. In particular, we show that the usual way in which a **while** loop is used corresponds to the kind of functional program usually written with accumulating parameters.

To conclude this chapter and set the scene for the next, in Section 5.4 we discuss the way in which expressions, the basis of functional programs, are evaluated by using a stack. In a sense this completes the picture of correspondences between imperative and functional programs, showing how to specify the semantics of a functional language using an imperative one. The whole of Chapter 6 is devoted to an imperative language and to a translator from Lisp to that language, and so here we give only a brief introduction to the basis of this translation.

5.1 AN INTERPRETER FOR AN IMPERATIVE LANGUAGE

We shall use an Algol-like notation for our imperative language. (5.1) is a simple imperative program, written in this notation, to compute the quotient q and remainder r on division of y by x. It does this by successive subtraction.

$$r := y; \; q := 0;$$
while $r \geqslant x$ **do**
$$\quad\quad r := r - x; \tag{5.1}$$
$$\quad\quad q := q + 1$$
od

As you see, we allow arithmetic and logical expressions, sequences of assignment statements and simple loops. In addition, we shall allow a dummy statement and a conditional statement.

First, let us enumerate the *well-formed expressions* in our fragment. We shall only illustrate one arithmetic and one logical operator, since the others are very similar. A variable (written as an identifier) is a well-formed expression. A constant (written as an integer value or as T or F) is a well-formed expression. If e_1 and e_2 are well-formed expressions, then so are e_1+e_2, $e_1=e_2$ etc. These are, respectively, an arithmetic expression and a logical expression. When defining the interpreter we shall need to give a function which yields the value of any well-formed expression. There is a slight difficulty with the way we have enumerated these well-formed expressions, however, which we must clear up. It is most easily illustrated if we use the subtraction operator. The expression $x-y-z$ is well-formed in two different ways corresponding to the expressions $(x-y)-z$ and $x-(y-z)$. Since we have not indicated which of these is intended by $x-y-z$ we have what is called a *syntactic ambiguity*. To avoid this problem we shall always add sufficient parentheses to a well-formed expression to make it unambiguous.

Now let us enumerate the *well-formed statements* in our fragment. The dummy statement **skip** is well-formed. Execution of this statement will have no effect. The assignment statement $x:=e$ is well-formed if x is a variable and e is a well-formed expression. Execution of this statement causes evaluation of e and then causes the current value of x to be changed (updated) to be that value of e. If S_1 and S_2 are well-formed statements, then $S_1;S_2$ is a well-formed statement. The effect of executing $S_1;S_2$ is to execute S_1 and then execute S_2. Again, we have a syntactic ambiguity with the composite form $S_1;S_2;S_3$ but, since both analyses of this form will lead to the same result, we ignore the ambiguity. If e is a well-formed expression and S_1 and S_2 are well-formed statements, then **if** e **then** S_1 **else** S_2 **fi** is a well-formed statement. The effect of executing **if** e **then** S_1 **else** S_2 **fi** is to evaluate e and then to execute either S_1 or S_2 according to whether e yields T or F. Similarly, if e is a well-formed expression and S is a well-formed statement, then **while** e **do** S **od** is a well-formed statement. The effect of executing **while** e **do** S **od** is to evaluate e and, if this yields T, to execute S then repeat the whole statement again. If the evaluation of e yields F, the effect is null. Thus **while** e **do** S **od** will cause zero or more repeated executions of S, until such time as e yields F.

We come now to a very useful technique for dealing with programming languages, the notion of *abstract syntax*. For each kind of well-formed expression we introduce a predicate which will be true when applied to an expression of that kind and false when applied to any other well-formed expression. Then, for each composite well-formed expression, we introduce selector functions which select the well-formed components of that expression. For our fragment we choose the predicates and selectors shown in Table 5.1, where e is a well-formed expression. Using these, we can write, for example,

Table 5.1

e	Predicates	Selectors
variable	$isvar(e)$	$name(e)$
constant	$isconst(e)$	$number(e)$
$e_1 + e_2$	$issum(e)$	$operand1(e)$ yields e_1
		$operand2(e)$ yields e_2
$e_1 = e_2$	$iseq(e)$	$operand1(e)$ yields e_1
		$operand2(e)$ yields e_2

the following simple function, which evaluates arithmetic expressions containing only additions and constants:

$$simplevalue(e) \equiv \textbf{if } isconst(e) \textbf{ then } number(e) \textbf{ else}$$
$$\textbf{if } issum(e) \textbf{ then}$$
$$simplevalue(operand1(e)) + simplevalue(operand2(e))$$
$$\textbf{else } \text{ERROR}$$

Similarly, for well-formed statements we introduce the predicates and selectors shown in Table 5.2, and these allow us to deal with the syntax of the Algol fragment with the minimum of reliance upon its actual representation. However, to fix these ideas more firmly in our minds it is useful to consider briefly one possible representation for the syntax of the Algol fragment and then to define the predicates and selectors for this representation. Of course, we choose to represent the fragment as S-expressions. For the

Table 5.2

S	Predicates	Selectors
skip	$isnull(S)$	none
$x := e$	$isassignment(S)$	$lhs(S)$ yields x
		$rhs(S)$ yields e
$S_1 ; S_2$	$issequence(S)$	$first(S)$ yields S_1
		$second(S)$ yields S_2
if e **then** S_1 **else** S_2 **fi**	$isconditional(S)$	$iftest(S)$ yields e
		$then(S)$ yields S_1
		$else(S)$ yields S_2
while e **do** S' **od**	$isloop(S)$	$wtest(S)$ yields e
		$wbody(S)$ yields S'

well-formed expressions of the fragment we could choose lists with key
atoms in their first place:

$$
\begin{array}{ll}
x & (VAR\ x) \\
c & (QUOTE\ c) \\
e_1 + e_2 & (ADD\ e_1\ e_2) \\
e_1 = e_2 & (EQ\ e_1\ e_2)
\end{array}
$$

We would then have

$$
\begin{aligned}
&isvar(e) \equiv eq(car(e), VAR) \\
&name(e) \equiv car(cdr(e)) \\
&isconst(e) \equiv eq(car(e),\ QUOTE) \\
&number(e) \equiv car(cdr(e))
\end{aligned}
$$

and so on. For the well-formed statements of the fragment we could choose
the following representations:

$$
\begin{array}{ll}
\textbf{skip} & (SKIP) \\
x := e & (ASSIGN\ x\ e) \\
S_1 ; S_2 & (SEQ\ S_1\ S_2) \\
\textbf{if } e \textbf{ then } S_1 \textbf{ else } S_2 \textbf{ fi} & (IF\ e\ S_1\ S_2) \\
\textbf{while } e \textbf{ do } S \textbf{ od} & (WHILE\ e\ S)
\end{array}
$$

Then we would have the following definitions:

$$
\begin{aligned}
&isnull(S) \equiv eq(car(S), SKIP) \\
&isassignment(S) \equiv eq(car(S),\ ASSIGN) \\
&lhs(S) \equiv car(cdr(S)) \\
&rhs(S) \equiv car(cdr(cdr(S)))
\end{aligned}
$$

and so on. The reader can easily complete this list for himself. Note that
we have chosen particular partial function definitions and may need to
exhibit some care if we are actually to use them. For example, it is necessary
first to apply the predicate for a particular form in order to ensure that the
selectors for that form are defined.

The next step in defining an interpreter is to decide how to represent
the environment, that is the context which gives values to all the variables.
We could choose an association list as we did for the dimensions problem
in Section 3.1 or the namelist/valuelist structure used for the Lisp interpreter
in Chapter 4 or many other possibilities. The particular choice we make here

is ideal for our purpose in that it is both simple and serves us unchanged in the next section. It is similar to the namelist/valuelist structure used in the Lisp interpreter, but has only a single level of names and values. We make a list of all the variables occurring in the program being interpreted, call this the namelist, and then make a congruent list of the values of each of these variables. Using S-expression notation and our usual convention of writing variables as atoms (that is in upper-case letters), a namelist and valuelist for the sample program given at the beginning of this section could be

$$(X \quad Y \quad Q \quad R) \qquad (3 \quad 7 \quad 1 \quad 4)$$

at a particular point in the execution of the program.

We need two functions to manipulate an environment represented in this way. The first, $assoc(x,n,v)$, finds the value in the valuelist v corresponding to the variable x which is assumed to occur in the namelist n:

$$assoc(x,n,v) \equiv \textbf{if } eq(car(n),x) \textbf{ then } car(v) \textbf{ else}$$
$$assoc(x,cdr(n),cdr(v))$$

Altogether a very trivial function, reminiscent of functions with the same name used in Sections 3.1 and 4.3. The other function which we need is used to update (that is, replace) the value corresponding to a variable x with a new value y.

$$update(n,v,x,y) \equiv \textbf{if } eq(car(n),x) \textbf{ then } cons(y,cdr(v)) \textbf{ else}$$
$$cons(car(v),update(cdr(n),cdr(v),x,y))$$

Again, this kind of function is very familiar. We see that it assumes x occurs somewhere in n, that n and v are of the same length and returns a list identical to v except that the value corresponding to the name x has been replaced by the value y. With the above values for n and v the call $update(n,v,Q,2)$ would yield the value (3 7 2 4).

Now we are in a position to write out the interpreter for our Algol fragment. It takes the form of two functions. The first, $val(e,n,v)$, yields the value of the well-formed expression e in the environment represented by the namelist n and the valuelist v, as shown in (5.2).

This is very straightforward, being similar to the interpreter for Lisp. We see that if e is a variable, we find its value in v; if e is a constant, then it is its own value; if e is a sum, we evaluate each of the operands, then add the results. Similarly, if e is an equality comparison, we evaluate each of the operands and compare their values. The other operators of the fragemnt can be dealt with in the same way.

$$val(e,n,v) \equiv \textbf{if } isvar(e) \textbf{ then } assoc(name(e),n,v) \textbf{ else}$$
$$\textbf{if } isconst(e) \textbf{ then } number(e) \textbf{ else}$$
$$\textbf{if } issum(e) \textbf{ then}$$
$$\{x+y \textbf{ where } x = val(operand1(e),n,v) \tag{5.2}$$
$$\textbf{and } y = val(operand2(e),n,v)\} \textbf{ else}$$
$$\textbf{if } iseq(e) \textbf{ then}$$
$$\{eq(x,y)$$
$$\textbf{where } x = val(operand1(e),n,v)$$
$$\textbf{and } y = val(operand2(e),n,v)\} \textbf{ else } \ldots$$

The other function which we require is *effect(S,n,v)*. The result of this, which is shown in (5.3), is a valuelist of the same length as *v*, which reflects the result of executing the well-formed statement *S* in the initial environment represented by *n* and *v*.

$$effect(S,n,v) \equiv \textbf{if } isnull(S) \textbf{ then } v \textbf{ else}$$
$$\textbf{if } isassignment(S) \textbf{ then } update(n,v,lhs(S),val(rhs(S),n,v)) \textbf{ else}$$
$$\textbf{if } issequence(S) \textbf{ then } effect(second(S),n,effect(first(S),n,v)) \textbf{ else}$$
$$\textbf{if } isconditional(S) \textbf{ then} \tag{5.3}$$
$$effect(\textbf{if } val(iftest(S),n,v) \textbf{ then } then(S) \textbf{ else } else(S),n,v) \textbf{ else}$$
$$\textbf{if } isloop(S) \textbf{ then}$$
$$\{w(v) \textbf{ whererec } w = \lambda(v) \textbf{ if } val (wtest(S),n,v) \textbf{ then}$$
$$w(effect(wbody(S),n,v)) \textbf{ else } v\} \textbf{ else}$$
$$\text{ERROR}$$

This function requires a little explanation. We see that it deals with each of the five kinds of well-formed statement in turn. In the case of the dummy statement **skip**, the value returned is just *v*, since no change to *v* is required. In the case of the assignment statement we evaluate the right-hand side using *val(rhs(S),n,v)* and then update the environment, so that the position corresponding to the variable on the left-hand side will now be associated with the value computed for the right-hand side of the assignment. Next, the sequence is dealt with. Here we see that *effect(first(S),n,v)* is evaluated to obtain the valuelist *v'* updated by the first of the two statements in the sequence. Then, *effect(second(S),n,v')* is evaluated, thus determining the effect of executing the second statement *after* the first. Note that the semantic definition is quite precise about this order of evaluation. In the case of the conditional statement, one of the arms of the conditional is chosen, either *then(S)* or *else(S)* according to whether the *iftest(S)* yields the value true or not. Finally we deal with the case of a loop statement. Here we state that the result is $w(v)$, where w is a locally defined recursive function. In fact $w(v)$ is defined in such a way that if $wtest(S)$ yields false then v is returned and if $wtest(S)$ yields true then $w(effect(wbody(S),n,w))$ is called. That is, a single execution of the body of the loop is effected and the resulting valuelist is resubmitted to w. A little consideration will persuade you that this definition has the semantics intended for the **while** loop.

To complete this section, let us illustrate an alternative way of writing out the interpreter. We write it as a form of equation (see (5.4)), similar to the way we did for the Lisp interpreter when we designed it. This form has the advantage that we avoid the explicit names for the predicates and selectors of the abstract syntax. Nevertheless we are still dealing with the syntax in the same abstract way. We use x to denote a variable, c to denote a constant, $e,e_1,e_2,\ldots$ to denote well-formed expressions and $S,S_1,S_2,\ldots$ to denote well-formed statements. We enclose Algol fragment text in braces $\{\ \}$ so as to distinguish it clearly from the remainder of the equation.

$$
\begin{aligned}
&val(\{x\},n,v) = assoc(x,n,v) \\
&val(\{c\},n,v) = c \\
&val(\{e_1+e_2\},n,v) = val(\{e_1\},n,v)+val(\{e_2\},n,v) \\
&val(\{e_1=e_2\},n,v) = eq(val(\{e_1\},n,v),val(\{e_2\},n,v)) \\
&effect(\{\textbf{skip}\},n,v) = v \\
&effect(\{x:=e\},n,v) = update(n,v,x,val(\{e\},n,v)) \\
&effect(\{S_1;S_2\},n,v) = effect(\{S_2\},n,effect(\{S_1\},n,v)) \\
&effect(\{\textbf{if } e \textbf{ then } S_1 \textbf{ else } S_2 \textbf{ fi}\},n,v) \\
&\qquad = effect(\textbf{if } val(\{e\},n,v) \textbf{ then } \{S_1\} \textbf{ else } \{S_2\},n,v) \\
&effect(\{\textbf{while } e \textbf{ do } S \textbf{ od}\},n,v) = w(v) \\
&\qquad \textbf{whererec } w = \lambda(v) \textbf{ if } val(\{e\},n,v) \textbf{ then} \\
&\qquad\qquad w(effect(\{S\},n,v)) \textbf{ else } v
\end{aligned}
$$

(5.4)

This way of writing down the interpreter can often be more easily understood than the full function definition. To help make some of the connections, it is useful to think of the text written in braces as standing for the S-expression form of the syntax, then these equations can be seen as just a simple re-writing of an executable functional program—the interpreter.

5.2 FUNCTIONAL EQUIVALENTS OF IMPERATIVE PROGRAMS

In this section we will show how each well-formed expression and well-formed statement can be associated with a function. If we say that this function defines the value of the expression or effect of the statement, then we can take it to be a definition of the semantics of that construct. The functional equivalent of each construct is closely related to the part of the interpreter dealing with that construct. The function which we derive is also closely related to the functional program which we shall discuss in the next section, and so the present section forms a useful bridge. If the reader prefers to pass on to the next section without reading this one, however, it is possible for him to do so.

Let us consider first, the well-formed expressions. The simplest well-formed expression is the constant. We will associate with each well-formed expression a function which, if applied to the valuelist part of the environment, will produce the value of that expression in that environment. Thus the function associated with the constant expression c is just

$$\lambda(v)c$$

This is just what we would expect; it is the function which, when applied to any valuelist v, yields the constant value c. Similarly, the well-formed expression which is the variable x is associated with the following function, in an environment whose namelist part is n:

$$\lambda(v)assoc(x,n,v)$$

This function is interesting. It already has the values of x and n resolved and therefore will always select a fixed position in the list provided to it as argument. This is of course the meaning we usually give to a variable, a certain position in the valuelist part of the environment.

For any well-formed expression e, we will write $e{\dagger}n$ for the function associated with it for a given namelist n. We shall not enclose well-formed expressions in braces unless they are composite. Thus, although we shall write $\{e_1+e_2\}{\dagger}n$ we shall not write $\{e_1\}{\dagger}n$, since with the simpler form $e_1{\dagger}n$ it is clear that the left-hand operand of $\dagger$ must be a well-formed expression. This omission of braces aids legibility a little but, if you find it confusing, simply add braces to the left-hand operand of each occurrence of $\dagger$ where they have been omitted. We already have

$$c{\dagger}n = \lambda(v)c$$
$$x{\dagger}n = \lambda(v)assoc(x,n,v)$$

Note that the form $e{\dagger}n$ is used to indicate that the functional equivalent of e

is determined not only by e but also by n. Let us consider the composite well-formed expression e_1+e_2. We have

$$\{e_1+e_2\}\dagger n \ = \ \lambda(v) \ e_1\dagger n(v)+e_2\dagger n(v)$$

That is, the functional equivalent of e_1+e_2 is that function of v which applies the functional equivalents of e_1 and e_2 to v and then adds their results. Similarly, we have

$$\{e_1=e_2\}\dagger n=\lambda(v)eq(e_1\dagger n(v),e_2\dagger n(v))$$

In reading equations of this form, remember that $e\dagger n$ is a function, and hence the $e\dagger n(v)$ is the result of that function applied to v.

Let us turn to the well-formed statements. Again we shall use $S\dagger n$ to denote the functional equivalent of the well-formed statement S. Trivially we have

$$\mathbf{skip}\dagger n \ = \ \lambda(v)v$$

That is, the functional equivalent of the null statement **skip** is just the identity function. For the assignment statement we have

$$\{x:=e\}\dagger n \ = \ \lambda(v)update(n,v,x,e\dagger n(v))$$

The function defined here returns a valuelist which has been changed in the xth position to a value computed from e. Thus, for example, the function $\{y:=y+1\}\dagger n$ will return a valuelist whose yth element has been increased by one. The statement sequence form is very trivially deduced.

$$\{S_1;S_2\}\dagger n \ = \ \lambda(v) \ S_2\dagger n(S_1\dagger n(v))$$

In fact this form of function composition is the usual function dot product discussed at the end of Section 2.8 and thus we can write

$$\{S_1;S_2\}\dagger n \ = \ dot(S_2\dagger n,S_1\dagger n)$$

This semantic definition confirms that the effect of $S_1;S_2$ is to execute S_2 in the environment produced by excuting S_1.

We come at last to the two composite control statements. Firstly, the conditional statement has the following semantic definition.

$$\{\mathbf{if} \ e \ \mathbf{then} \ S_1 \ \mathbf{else} \ S_2 \ \mathbf{fi}\}\dagger n \ = \ \lambda(v) \ (\mathbf{if} \ e\dagger n(v) \ \mathbf{then} \ S_1\dagger n \ \mathbf{else} \ S_2\dagger n)(v)$$

That is, the equivalent function selects between $S_1 {\dagger} n$ and $S_2 {\dagger} n$ depending on the value of $e{\dagger}n(v)$. Similarly, for the loop statement we have the following definition:

$$\{\textbf{while } e \textbf{ do } S \textbf{ od}\}{\dagger}n = w$$
$$\textbf{whererec } w = \lambda(v) \textbf{ if } e{\dagger}n(v) \textbf{ then } w(S{\dagger}n(v)) \textbf{ else } v$$

This is very close to the form given in the interpreter. The function w, which corresponds to the well-formed statement **while** e **do** S **od**, is recursively defined. If the value $e{\dagger}n(v)$ is false, then $w(v)$ is just v, whereas if $e{\dagger}n(v)$ is true we compute $v' = S{\dagger}n(v)$, and then $w(v)$ is computed to be $w(v')$. This specifies that the valuelist $w(v)$ is computed from v by zero or more applications of the function $S{\dagger}n$ until such time as $e{\dagger}n$ yields the value false. Exactly the semantics we intend for **while** statements.

Thus we have derived, for each well-formed expression and statement in our fragment, an equivalent function. We can claim that the semantics of our fragment is specified by these functions, in the sense that each well-formed entity has the value defined by this function for any particular argument. Of course, we have only shifted the burden of understanding what a program means to understanding what the equivalent function means. The reader will have noticed that it is the rules themselves which convey information about the semantics of the fragment, rather than the functions which would be obtained if these rules were applied to a particular program. Nevertheless, in order to familiarize himself with these rules the reader is encouraged to derive the function equivalent to a simple program.

The method of associating a function with every well-formed construct in a programming language is called *mathematical semantics* (or denotational semantics). We have only made the smallest beginning here in a study of that topic. Students of mathematical semantics concern themselves with the very important problems of establishing that the mathematical domain in which they are working, that is the set of functions which their rules produce, is well-defined. The appropriate mathematics is very sophisticated modern algebra (hence this is sometimes also referred to as the algebraic approach). Nevertheless, the area is one of some importance to the computer scientist. When work in that field has been more advanced it may well be that useable, formal semantic specifications of entire programming languages, based on this method, become as common as BNF descriptions of syntax.

5.3 TRANSFORMING IMPERATIVE PROGRAMS INTO FUNCTIONAL PROGRAMS

In the previous section we saw how each imperative program could be

related to a particular function which, if applied to an appropriate environment, would produce an environment reflecting the effect of executing that
program. In this section we will repeat that exercise in a more intuitive way,
deriving functional programs which correspond in a very direct way to
imperative programs. Temporarily we turn our attention to flow diagrams,
for this is the way in which the transformation we wish to discuss is most
easily described. Later we will give the rules of transformation in terms of the
Algol fragment.

Consider first flow diagrams with a single variable x. We assume all
assignments to x are of the form shown in Fig. 5.1, and all tests of the form

Fig. 5.1

shown in Fig. 5.2, where $f(x)$ and $p(x)$ are simple functions. For example,

Fig. 5.2

the program shown in Fig 5.3 repeatedly doubles x until it is greater than 100.

We will determine the function of x which is computed (in x) between
the entrance and the exit to Fig. 5.3. We do this by progressively labeling the
edges in the flow diagram, with the function computed between that edge and

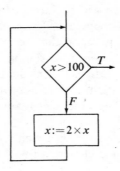

Fig. 5.3

the exit to the diagram. Clearly we label the exit edge with the identity
function (Fig. 5.4).

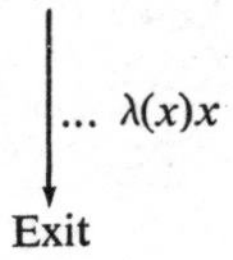

Fig. 5.4

Suppose that the edge leading out of the assignment $x:=f(x)$ is labeled
with the function g. Then we label the edge leading into the assignment
with $\lambda(x)g(f(x))$ (Fig. 5.5).

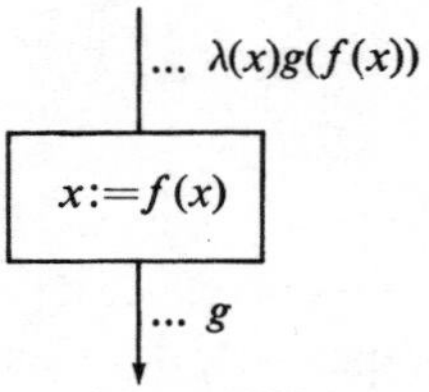

$$\vdots\ \lambda(x)g(f(x))$$

$$x:=f(x)$$

$$\vdots\ g$$

Fig. 5.5

Similarly, if the edges leading out of the test $p(x)$ are labeled g and h, respectively, we label the edge leading in as shown in Fig. 5.6.

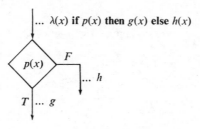

Fig. 5.6

Now, because our programs have loops in them, this process would go on forever, unless we cut the loops in some way. We do this by choosing some point on each loop and selecting a name for the function computed between this point and the exit. Forcing this named function back around the loop will lead to the named edge being labeled with some function-valued expression e. We then make the definition

$$w \equiv e,$$

where w is the name chosen for the cut point, thus embodying the loop in a recursive function. Let us apply his process to our simple example above, choosing to cut the loop just before the test. Denote by q the function computed from that point to the exit (Fig. 5.7). Note that cutting the loop has

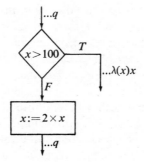

Fig. 5.7

led to a flow diagram with a shape which is in general a tree, each of the edges leading out of the diagram now being labeled. If we complete the labeling as suggested above, we arrive at Fig. 5.8.

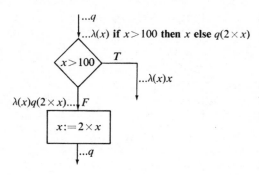

Fig. 5.8

Thus we have the definition

$$q(x) \equiv \textbf{if } x > 100 \textbf{ then } x \textbf{ else } q(2 \times x)$$

which, since q labels also the entrance to the entire diagram, is the function computed between the entrance and exit of the diagram. It is clearly also a functional program which computes that value which x will have after executing the imperative program.

Now this method of tranforming an imperative program to determine an equivalent functional one clearly extends to programs with more than one variable. We simply construct functions with all the program variables as parameters. If we assume that we are interested in the values of all the program variables at the exit to the flow diagram, then we label this edge with a function which simply forms a list of their values. However, if we are interested in just a subset of the program variables, we can omit those in which we are not interested. An example will serve to demonstrate this process. The program shown in Fig. 5.9 is that with which we began the chapter, written as a flow diagram.

We have labeled the exit with a function, indicating our interest in the values of all the program variables (*fourlist* simply forms a list of the values of all its arguments) and have cut the loop just above the test by deciding to call the function computed from that edge w. Thus we expect to derive a definition of w, of the form

$$w(y,x,q,r) \equiv \ldots$$

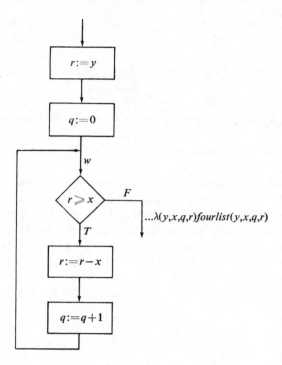

Fig. 5.9

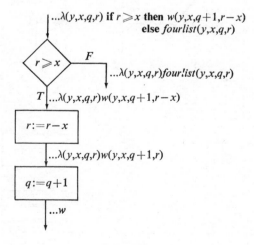

Fig. 5.10

142   FUNCTIONAL AND IMPERATIVE PROGRAMS

Performing the labeling leads to Fig. 5.10, and hence to the recursive function definition

$$w(y,x,q,r) \equiv \textbf{if } r \geqslant x \textbf{ then } w(y,x,q+1,r-x)$$
$$\textbf{else } fourlist(y,x,q,r)$$

Similarly we can determine that the entire program computes the function

$$\lambda(y,x,q,r)w(y,x,0,y)$$

Now our very simple expedient of listing all the program variables as parameters to each of these functions has led to the strange and unnecessary appearance of q and r in this last definition. In the definition of w, y need not be a parameter if we make w local to the main function. These are matters we shall return to. First, let us transform a program with more than one loop.

The program shown in Fig. 5.11 computes the highest common factor of x and y, leaving the result in x.

The subprogram shown in the dashed box in Fig 5.11 computes the

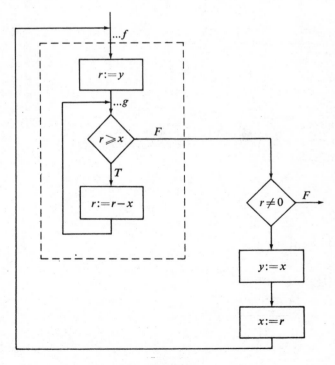

Fig. 5.11

remainder of y divided by x, leaving the result in r. The outer loop is just the Euclidean algorithm (Fig. 5.12) for determining the highest common factor

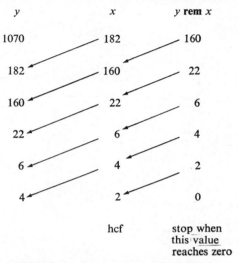

Fig. 5.12   The Euclidean Algorithm

of x and y successively replacing y and x by x and y **rem** x respectively. For this program, we choose as cut points those edges labeled f and g on the diagram. We can choose as many cut points as we wish, just as long as every loop contains at least one.

We arrive at the following function definitions, by applying the process of labeling each edge with the function computed between it and the exit. We assume every function has arguments y, x and r, and that on exit we are interested only in the value of x. Thus the exit is labeled $\lambda(y,x,r)x$ (Fig 5.13). The function definitions are

$$f(y,x,r) \equiv g(y,x,y)$$
$$g(y,x,r) \equiv \textbf{if } r > x \textbf{ then } g(y,x,r-x)$$
$$\textbf{else if } r \neq 0 \textbf{ then } f(x,r,r)$$
$$\textbf{else } x$$

Not very natural functions, but nevertheless they serve to illustrate the process of transformation.

The use of a name to identify the function computed from the cut point of a loop is analogous to the use of a label in an imperative language. The recursive calls of f and g behave exactly like **goto** statements, causing a transfer to the body of the function with that name. The analogy becomes complete if we note that the pair of functions given above are such that they

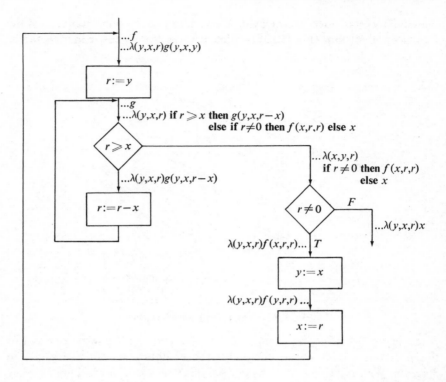

Fig. 5.13

successively call each other until eventually g returns (the value x), whereupon all the previously nested function calls return, without applying any other function.

To conclude this section and make it consistent with the others, we will develop these rules of transformation for the Algol fragment. We do this using the following technique. If S is a well-formed statement from the fragment and e is a well-formed expression from either the fragment or the purely functional language, then we construct

$$S \textbf{ result } e$$

as a well-formed expression in a temporarily extended functional language. The intention is that the effect of executing the statement S within the expression S **result** e is entirely local to the expression. The value of S **result** e is the value of e in the context produced by executing S. Thus, for example, the value of

$$\{x := x+1;\; y := y+1\} \textbf{ result } x \times y$$

is just the same as the value of the expression $(x+1) \times (y+1)$.

We can take any well-formed statement from the fragment and form it into an expression by appending **result** e for some arbitrary choice of e, which reflects our interest in the outcome of S. For example, with the simple quotient and remainder dealt with earlier in this section, we might append **result** $fourlist(y,x,q,r,)$, giving (5.5).

$$\{r:=y;\ q:=0;$$
$$\textbf{while } r \geqslant x \textbf{ do}$$
$$r:=r-x;$$
$$q:=q+1$$
$$\textbf{od}\}\ \textbf{result } fourlist(y,x,q,r)$$

(5.5)

Now, we give the rules of transformation by showing how to progressively remove expressions of the form S **result** e from functional programs which contain them. We will write

$$e \rightarrow e'$$

to mean e can be replaced by e', where e contains a subexpression of the form S **result** e'' and e' either contains no such expression or contains only shorter expressions of this kind. Hence repeated application of these transformation rules will drive **result** expressions out of the program.

The simplest transformation rule deals with the null statement:

$$\textbf{skip result } e \rightarrow e$$

The assignment statement can be dealt with in two ways. We can use a **where** clause, giving

$$\{x:=e\}\ \textbf{result } e' \rightarrow e' \textbf{ where } x=e$$

which preserves the occurrence of the expression e and the variable x. Alternatively, we can substitute e for every occurrence of x in e'. This we write as

$$\{x:=e\}\ \textbf{result } e' \rightarrow e'\Big|_{x}^{e}$$

Thus, for example $\{x:=2\times x+1\}$ **result** $x\times y$ can be transformed to either

$$x\times y \text{ where } x=2\times x+1$$

or

$$(2\times x+1)\times y.$$

Note that we have had to add parentheses to preserve the correct order of evaluation in the second case. We assume the substitution process is sophisticated enough to do this.

The sequence $\{S_1;S_2\}$ has the following rule of transformation.

$$\{S_1;S_2\} \text{ result } e \;\rightarrow\; S_1 \text{ result } \{S_2 \text{ result } e\}$$

Thus, S_2 **result** e can be transformed to an expression e' and then S_1 **result** e' transformed in turn. An example is given in (5.6).

$$
\begin{aligned}
&\{x:=x+1;\; y:=y+1\} \text{ result } x\times y \\
&\rightarrow x:=x+1 \text{ result } \{y:=y+1 \text{ result } x\times y\} \\
&\rightarrow x:=x+1 \text{ result } x\times(y+1) \\
&\rightarrow (x+1)\times(y+1)
\end{aligned}
\tag{5.6}
$$

The conditional form is extremely simple, as shown in (5.7), with an example in (5.8).

$$
\begin{aligned}
&\{\textbf{if } e \textbf{ then } S_1 \textbf{ else } S_2 \textbf{ fi}\} \text{ result } e' \\
&\rightarrow \textbf{if } e \textbf{ then } \{S_1 \text{ result } e'\} \textbf{ else } \{S_2 \text{ result } e'\}
\end{aligned}
\tag{5.7}
$$

$$
\begin{aligned}
&\{\textbf{if } x\geqslant 0 \textbf{ then skip else } x:=-x \textbf{ fi}\} \text{ result } x \\
&\rightarrow \textbf{if } x\geqslant 0 \textbf{ then } \{\textbf{skip result } x\} \textbf{ else } \{x:=-x \text{ result } x\} \\
&\rightarrow \textbf{if } x\geqslant 0 \textbf{ then } x \textbf{ else } -x
\end{aligned}
\tag{5.8}
$$

Finally, we come to the most interesting case, the loop statement. Let us first write the rule of transformation as (5.9), and then discuss it.

$$
\begin{aligned}
&\{\textbf{while } e \textbf{ do } S \textbf{ od}\} \text{ result } e' \\
&\rightarrow w(x_1,\ldots,x_k) \textbf{ whererec} \\
&\qquad w=\lambda(x_1,\ldots,x_k) \textbf{ if } e \textbf{ then } w(S \text{ result } x_1,\ldots,S \text{ result } x_k) \\
&\qquad\qquad \textbf{ else } e'
\end{aligned}
\tag{5.9}
$$

This rule is quite complex but has an obvious ancestry in the rules given for loops in previous sections. We have made a recursive definition of a function called w, although what we call it is entirely immaterial. This function has as parameters the variables $x_1, \ldots, x_k$. For the time being, let us assume they are all the variables used in the statement **while** e **do** S **od**, for that will be satisfactory. The body of the function w evaluates e. If the value is false, then e' is evaluated as the result; if e evaluates to true, however a recursive call of w is made, each of the parameters being replaced by the value which will be assigned to it by S. As an example, consider (5.10)

$\{$**while** $r > x$ **do** $r := r - x$ **od**$\}$ **result** r
$\rightarrow w(r,x)$ **whererec**
$\quad w = \lambda(r,x)$ **if** $r > x$ **then** $w(r := r - x$ **result** r,
$\qquad\qquad\qquad\qquad\qquad\qquad\quad r := r - x$ **result** $x)$ $\qquad$ (5.10)
$\qquad\qquad\qquad$ **else** r
$\rightarrow w(r,x)$ **whererec**
$\quad w = \lambda(r,x)$ **if** $r > x$ **then** $w(r - x, x)$ **else** r

---

The choice of parameters for the function w need not be so wide as to include all those used in **while** e **do** S **od**, but need only include those assigned in S. When this is done, care must be taken to nest definitions properly. On the other hand, there is no harm in including any other variable in the parameter list. Determining the smallest possible set of parameters to w is left as an exercise for the reader.

The process of transforming an imperative program into a functional one is now complete. For the imperative program S, first choose an expression e which expresses the outcome of S, then construct S **result** e and use the rules of transformation to drive out **result**, deriving the equivalent expression e'. Finally, construct the function

$$\lambda(x_1, \ldots, x_k)e'$$

where $x_1, \ldots, x_k$ are just the variables free in e'. As a final example of this process, let us transform the simple factorial program (5.11).

$\{f := 1; i := 1;$
$\quad$**while** $i \leqslant n$ **do**
$\qquad f := f \times i;$ $\qquad\qquad\qquad\qquad\qquad\qquad\qquad$ (5.11)
$\qquad i := i + 1$
$\quad$**od**$\}$ **result** f

First, consider only the loop, which is transformed as in (5.12). Note,

---

while $i \leqslant n$ **do** $f := f \times i$; $i := i+1$ **od result** f
  $\rightarrow$ $w(i,f)$ **whererec**
    $w = \lambda(i,f)$ **if** $i \leqslant n$ **then** $w(\{f := f \times i$; $i := i+1\}$ **result** i,
                                   $\{f := f \times i$; $i := i+1\}$ **result** f)
        else f (5.12)
  $\rightarrow$ $w(i,f)$ **whererec**
    $w = \lambda(i,f)$ **if** $i \leqslant n$ **then** $w(i+1, f \times i)$ **else** f

---

the last expression in (5.12) has to be "pushed back" through the assignment statements $f := 1$; $i := 1$ which will substitute 1 for the free occurrences of f and i, which are just those in the body of the **whererec** block. Thus we obtain (5.13).

$\{f := 1$; $i := 1$; **while** $i \leqslant n$ **do** $f := f \times i$; $i := i+1$ **od**$\}$ **result** f
  $\rightarrow$ $\{f := 1$; $i := 1\}$ **result** $\{w(i,f)$ **whererec**   (5.13)
                          $w = \lambda(i,f)$ **if** $i \leqslant n$ **then** $w(i+1, f \times i)$
                                                   else $f\}$
  $\rightarrow$ $w(1,1)$ **whererec**
    $w = \lambda(i,f)$ **if** $i \leqslant n$ **then** $w(i+1, f \times i)$ **else** f

---

Finally, we must make this expression into a function of the variables which occur free in it, which is just n. Hence we arrive at the equivalent functional program (5.14).

$\lambda(n) w(1,1)$
  whererec $w = \lambda(i,f)$ **if** $i \leqslant n$ **then** $w(i+1, f \times i)$ (5.14)
               else f

In this functional program, derived from what could be called a standard imperative program for computing the factorial, we can observe that the parameter f is being used as an accumulating parameter. The usual use of a while statement is to iteratively assign values to a set of variables, and the corresponding style in functional programming is the use of accumulating parameters. Consider the above definition of the function $w(i,f)$. This function computes the value

$$f \times i \times (i+1) \times \cdots \times (n-1) \times n$$

and this is why $w(1,1) = n! = 1 \times 2 \times \cdots \times n$. Another way of expressing this property of w is to observe that every call of w satisfies the following constraint. The call $w(i,f)$ is such that $f = 1 \times 2 \times \cdots \times (i-1)$ and hence $w(i,f)$ computes $n!$ for all i and f with this property. In particular, $w(1,1)$ computes $n!$ The fact that this program also works for $n = 0$ can be confirmed by inspection.

Let us conclude with a review of what we have achieved. In the earlier sections we used functional programs to define the semantics of imperative programs, firstly by deriving an interpreter which explicitly identifies each construct in an imperative program and gives a rule for executing it to determine its effect, and secondly by deriving a function formally equivalent to each construct in the imperative language. The emphasis in these sections was on giving a formal semantic specification of each well-formed construct in the imperative language. Hence, in those sections it was the semantic rules which were intended to be studied. In this section, we have concentrated on deriving a more intuitive functional program from an imperative one, and so here the emphasis has not been on the individual language constructs, but on complete programs. It is fair to say that the techniques of these three sections are closely inter-related: the first two concentrate on the semantics of the language; this third section concentrates on the semantics of programs.

5.4 SUPPORTING FUNCTIONAL PROGRAMS ON CONVENTIONAL MACHINES

As a preliminary study, before embarking on a complete machine architecture for functional programs, and as a complementary study to the other correspondences between functional and imperative programs, we review here the basic way in which a stack is used to evaluate expressions and recursive functions. In Section 5.2 we discussed how to transform an imperative program into an equivalent functional one. The question arises, can we transform an arbitrary functional program into an equivalent imperative one? Before we can answer this question we must clarify it, for the answer is negative if we interpret the question in one way and positive if we interpret it in another. Ultimately we will show that it is possible to derive, from a functional program, an equivalent imperative program which unfortunately is far from readable in its own right. This is the basis upon which an implementation of a functional programming language can be made for a conventional computer. The next chapter is devoted to a full description of such an implementation. The lack of readability in these programs will not concern us, for we are concerned only with the formal correspondence. That is, it is the rules of transformation from functional to imperative form which convey information about the semantics of the functional form, rather than the transformed program.

We might begin by asking why the rules of transformation used in Section 5.3 cannot just be applied backwards. This is because the functional programs which can be derived from imperative programs using the rules given there have a very particular form. If we consider the transformation process applied to flow diagrams where each loop is cut by introducing a new function name, the set of function definitions derived have the property that each call of the defined functions is outermost. We say that a call of the function f is outermost in an expression if the expression is of the form $f(e_1,\ldots,e_k)$ or if the expression is a conditional **if** e **then** e' **else** e'' and the call of f is outermost in e' or e'', that is on one or other arms of the conditional. A functional program which consists of a set of function definitions and which is such that all calls of these defined functions are outermost is said to be in *iterative* form. Such a functional program can be transformed to an imperative one simply by applying the rules of Section 5.3 in reverse.

However, not all functional programs are in iterative form. The factorial program

$$fact(n) \equiv \textbf{if } n=0 \textbf{ then } 1 \textbf{ else } n \times fact(n-1)$$

is not in iterative form because the call of $fact(n-1)$ is nested as an operand of multiplication. It can be transformed to iterative form and hence to an imperative program.

$$fact(n) \equiv f(n,1)$$
$$f(n,m) \equiv \textbf{if } n=0 \textbf{ then } m \textbf{ else } f(n-1,m \times n)$$

This transformation has made use of the accumulating parameter technique. There are other ways of transforming functional programs in non-iterative form to equivalent imperative programs by the addition of such things as extra integer variables to count the depth of recursive nesting. Despite all these techniques there are nevertheless functional programs which cannot be transformed to imperative ones without the addition of an indeterminate number of variables. For a full discussion of this topic see Manna (1974), Chapter 4. In practice, then, we have to admit the need for a device allowing the use of an unspecified number of additional variables. Such a device, and an adequate and natural one for this purpose, is the *stack*.

To describe the way in which a stack is employed for the evaluation of purely functional programs, we will make use of a particular stack implementation, using an array *st* and a pointer (index) *top* (see Fig 5.14). We will assume that elements in array positions $st[1],st[2],\ldots,st[top]$ are those that

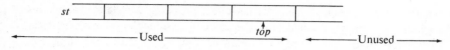

Fig. 5.14

have been pushed onto the stack and this is the order in which they were pushed. Hence, the operation of pushing a new element x onto the stack is

$$top := top + 1; \; st[top] := x$$

Conversely, the operation of popping an element from the stack is

$$x := st[top]; \; top := top - 1$$

Strictly speaking, a pure stack allows only these two operations upon it and is said to be used in a last-in–first-out discipline. These operations are then more naturally used if embedded in procedure calls, say, $push(x)$ and $pop(x)$. Here, however, we shall have occasion to access elements further down the stack than the top element, not to remove or change them, just to determine their values. Also, we shall have occasion to recompute the value of top, thus moving it down many places, effecting many pops. While we could restrict ourselves to using just the $push$ and pop operations, it is a little clearer to always show the operations in their full form, for the reader will be closely concerned with, in particular, the value of top. We shall not worry about overflow or underflow of the stack, nor with initializing it, all trivial points which distract from the simplicity of the presentation.

We will describe, for each well-formed expression of the functional language, a sequence of statements manipulating the stack, which have the property that, when executed, they leave the value of the expression on top of the stack. This will be a very important property of the imperative program and so we give it a name—the *net-effect property*.

The net-effect property The sequence of statements derived from a well-formed expression will, if executed, leave a single value on top of the stack, and otherwise leave unchanged that part of the stack in use before those statements were executed. The single value thus pushed onto the stack will be the value computed for the well-formed expression.

The very simplest of well-formed expressions is a constant c. The equivalent statements are

$$top := top + 1; \; st[top] := c$$

which are easily seen to have the net-effect property. Similarly, the values of variables are simply pushed onto the stack. Consider the typical well-formed expression built using a binary operator, say $e_1 + e_2$, where e_1 and e_2 are well-formed expressions. For this we generate the following statements:

$$e_1^*; \; e_2^*; \; st[top-1] := st[top-1] + st[top]; \; top := top-1$$

The appearance of e_1^* and e_2^* in this sequence is used to denote the corresponding sequence of statements obtained from the corresponding well-formed subexpression. So, for example, the expression $x+y$ will translate to the composite sequence of statements

$$top := top+1; \; st[top] := x;$$
$$top := top+1; \; st[top] := y;$$
$$st[top-1] := st[top-1] + st[top]; \; top := top-1$$

where the first line has been obtained from the subexpression x and the second line from the subexpression y. That the general form of statement sequence obtained from $e_1 + e_2$ has the net-effect property follows from the following reasoning. The subexpression e_1, being well-formed, yields statements with the net-effect property; hence after execution the value of e_1 appears on top of the stack and the stack is otherwise unchanged. Similarly, the statements e_2^* corresponding to e_2, when executed, leave the value of e_2 on top of the stack. Thus the top two elements are the values of e_1 and e_2, respectively and, apart from these two additional values, the stack is unchanged (Fig 5.15).

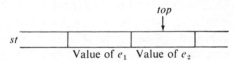

Fig. 5.15

Now, by adding these two top values together, putting the result in $st[top-1]$ and reducing top by 1, we guarantee that the sequence of statements corresponding to $e_1 + e_2$ has the net-effect property. This is simple enough and clearly the same kind of rule can be used for each binary operator. Care must be taken with operators such as minus, for which the order of the operands is important (the operator is not *commutative*, in mathematical terminology).

We can deal with conditional expressions equally simply. The well-formed expression **if** e_1 **then** e_2 **else** e_3 has three well-formed sub-expressions. Using e_1^*, e_2^* and e_3^* respectively to denote the sequences of statements derived from them, we can derive for the conditional expression the following sequence:

$$e_1^*; \textbf{if } st[top] = T \textbf{ then } top := top-1; e_2^* \textbf{ else}$$
$$top := top-1; e_3^* \textbf{ fi}$$

This sequence has the net-effect property because whichever branch of the conditional statement is chosen the statement $top := top-1$ removes the value of the test left on top of the stack by the statements derived from e_1. Then, of course, only one of e_2 or e_3 is computed and its value left on top of the stack. Since none of e_1^*, e_2^* or e_3^* have any other effect, the sequence of statements corresponding to the conditional expression does indeed have the net-effect property. Now we can deal with arbitrarily nested expressions built from simple operators and conditional expressions. It remains to show how function definition and function call are dealt with.

We confine our attention to a simple type of recursive-function definition. We assume we are dealing with a set of mutually recursive functions, each defined by an equation of the form

$$f(x_1, \ldots, x_n) \equiv e,$$

where the defining expression e refers only to the variables $x_1, \ldots, x_n$ and calls, apart from primitive functions, only other functions defined by these equations. Thus, in particular, we avoid functions which refer to global (i.e. non-parametric) values and the passing of functions as parameters. The principal problem, as the reader surely anticipates, is to deal with recursive calls of defined functions. If none of the defined functions were called recursively, that is, entered while an outstanding call was incomplete, then we could allocate one variable to each parameter of each function and proceed with a call as follows. On entry, each of the variables representing a parameter of the function to be called would be assigned the value of the corresponding actual parameter. The body of the function, being a well-formed expression, is represented by a sequence of statements with the net-effect property; hence, when executed, by referring to these variables it computes the appropriate value, leaving it on top of the stack. The problem would arise if, during execution of this sequence of statements, the same function were re-entered either directly or indirectly, that is via one or more other function calls. For then the values of the variables used to hold the parameters would be overwritten, and thus undefined upon return to the earlier execution of the body. The obvious way to overcome this problem is to provide a distinct set of variables to represent the parameters of each call of a function. In turn, the obvious way to implement these variables is to use the stack.

Accordingly, we shall contrive to arrange it so that, when we are executing the statements corresponding to a function body, a portion of the stack, somewhat below the top of the stack, has been· set aside to hold the values of the parameters. The portion of the stack will be identified by a pointer *act* (Fig. 5.16).

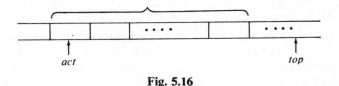

Fig. 5.16

Stack locations $st[act]$, $st[act+1]$,. . .,$st[act+k-1]$ will be used to hold the values of the parameters of a function with k parameter positions. The segment of the stack which contains these parameters, and certain other values which we shall explain, is called the *activation record*, for the particular activation of the function whose body is currently being executed. Hence the use of the particular acronym *act* (for "active"). Thus, when executing the statements derived from the body of the definition

$$f(x_1,\ldots,x_k) \equiv e$$

we refer to the variable x_i by accessing $st[act+i-1]$. Thus the well-formed expression x_i generates the statement sequence

$$top := top+1; \quad st[top] := st[act+i-1]$$

Note that this simple device only gives us access to a single activation record; hence the restriction on the form of function definition with which we can deal.

Let us deal with the function call. The expression

$$f(e_1,\ldots,e_k)$$

is well-formed if f is the name of a function and $e_1,\ldots,e_k$ are well-formed expressions providing parameter values. The sequence of statements

$$e_1^*; e_2^*;\ldots;e_k^*$$

will, since each parameter is well-formed, increase the stack by k values, being the values of each of the expressions in order. Thus, for the call given above, we generate the statement sequence (5.15).

$$e_1^*;e_2^*;\ldots;e_k^*$$
$$top := top+1; st[top] := r;$$
$$\mathbf{goto}\ f;$$
$$r: top := top-k-1;$$
$$st[top] := st[top+k+1]$$

(5.15)

We see that this sequence first places the k parameter values on the stack, then pushes the value r (a label) representing the point to which the function f must return upon completion. Then the statement **goto** f is used to branch to the statement sequence generated from the body of the function f, which we shall encounter a little later. If the statement sequence generated from the body of the definition of f has the net-effect property, it will leave the value of the call on top of the stack. Thus, when it returns control to r, the state of the stack will be as shown in Fig 5.17.

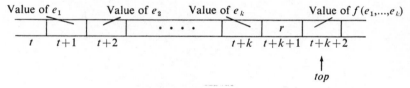

Fig. 5.17

We have chosen to denote the stack positions by $t,t+1,\ldots$ etc., where t denotes the original location of top before the call was commenced. The above sequence places the return address r at location $st[t+k+1]$ and then, as a result of execution of the (sequence of statements corresponding to the) body of f, leaves the value of $f(e_1,\ldots,e_k)$ at location $st[t+k+2]$. Thus the statements at label r, that is $top := top-k-1$, leaves top with the value $t+1$ and then the assignment $st[top] := st[top+k+1]$ moves the value of $f(e_1,\ldots,e_k)$ down to location $st[t+1]$. The result is that the original stack has been unchanged, except for the addition of a single value on top of its previously existing values; thus the net-effect property has been established.

Consider now the sequence of statements generated for the body of the function whose definition is

$$f(x_1,\ldots,x_k) \equiv e$$

This sequence must have the net-effect property and must also correctly set and reset the value of the pointer *act* for the duration of the call. The sequence (5.16) is satisfactory.

$$f: top := top+1; st[top] := act; act := top-k-1;$$
$$e^*;$$
$$top := top-1; act := st[top]; st[top] := st[top+1];$$
$$\textbf{goto } st[top-1]$$

(5.16)

The sequence (5.16) is labeled with the name of the function, to correspond to the **goto** *f* statement in the call sequence. On entry at *f*, the current value of *act* is pushed onto the stack and then *act* set to point to the first parameter. The shape of the stack, using the same indexing as before, is as shown in Fig 5.18.

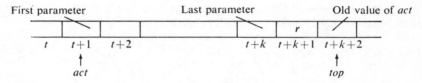

Fig. 5.18

Now, execution of the statement sequence e^* will leave the value of e in location $st[t+k+3]$ and *top* will have the value $t+k+3$, because of the net-effect property of e^*. The subsequent $top := top-1; act := st[top]$ therefore restores the old value of *act*, and then the statement $st[top] := st[top+1]$ copies the value of $f(e_1, \ldots, e_k)$ down one place. This establishes the stack format expected at the label r; thus we can go there immediately, which we do with the statement **goto** $st[top-1]$, intended to indicate that the label value to which a jump must be made is taken from this position on the stack.

The reader will find it useful to consider a simple example of a recursive function and derive its equivalent imperative program. This will establish firmly his understanding of the net-effect property and the way in which it contributes to the correct evaluation of the function. In particular, the reader should consider how the values of the parameters of a procedure are preserved when a recursive call is made from the body of that procedure, and restored when that call returns.

EXERCISES

5.1 Consider the following programming language. It is identical to the Algol fragment used here except that in addition to being able to access the current value of every variable, it is also possible to access its previous value. If a variable is prefixed with **prev**, the value it had before the previous assignment is retrieved. Thus **prev** x is a well-formed expression, where x is a variable. For example,

$$x := y; \quad y := \textbf{prev } x$$

will exchange the values of x and y. Give an interpreter for this language.

5.2 Define *assoc* and *update* for the following alternative representation of the environment. The environment σ is a function which, given a variable x, returns the value of that variable. Show that a simple translation of the equations given at the end of Section 5.1, omitting the variable n and replacing v with σ, defines a perfectly satisfactory interpreter (cf. the *singletons* program, Section 3.3).

5.3 Consider a more realistic model of the environment in which variables are associated with addresses and addresses with values. This can be modeled very simply by having a pair of congruent lists associating variables with addresses and a further pair associating addresses with values. Revise the interpreter given in Section 5.1 to use such an environment, and then define the semantics of the well-formed statement $x := -y$, where x and y are variables, which means give x the same address as y.

5.4 The logical expression e_1 **and** e_2 has the value true only if both e_1 and e_2 have the value true. It has the value false only if both e_1 and e_2 are defined and one of them has the value false. That is to say, both e_1 and e_2 are evaluated. We use the form e_1 **cand** e_2 to express the form of *and* where, if e_1 is false, e_2 is not evaluated. Thus e_1 **cand** e_2 is true only if both e_1 and e_2 yield true. However, e_1 **cand** e_2 is false if either e_1 yields false or e_1 yields true and e_2 yields false. Give an interpretive semantic definition of these two operators, to show this distinction clearly.

5.5 Define abstract syntax and extend the interpreting function of Section 5.1 to give semantics for the well-formed statement

do S_1 **while** e; S_2 **od**

which has the control structure shown in Fig. 5.19.

5.6 Consider how you might give a formal interpretive definition of the semantics of the following pair of well-formed statements.

1. **recbegin** S **end** is a well-formed statement which establishes the well-formed statement S as "recursively re-enterable".
2. **recur** is a well-formed statement which causes "recursive re-entry" of the **recbegin** block in which it occurs.

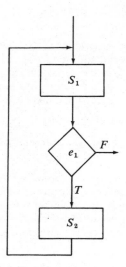

Fig. 5.19

Thus, factorial can be written as in (5.17).

$$
\begin{aligned}
&i := n; \\
&\textbf{recbegin} \\
&\quad \textbf{if } i = 0 \textbf{ then } f := 1 \\
&\qquad \textbf{else } i := i - 1; \\
&\qquad\quad \textbf{recur}; \\
&\qquad\quad i := i + 1; \\
&\qquad\quad f := f \times i \\
&\quad \textbf{fi} \\
&\textbf{end}
\end{aligned}
\tag{5.17}
$$

The semantics of **recbegin/recur** can be informally specified by saying that **recur**, when encountered, behaves exactly as if the entire enclosing **recbegin** block were copied to replace **recur**.

5.7 Derive the function equivalent to the well-formed statement (5.18). The appropriate environment will be a 2-list.

$$
\begin{aligned}
&\textbf{while } i > 1 \textbf{ do} \\
&\quad \textbf{begin } i := i - 1; \\
&\qquad\quad f := f \times i \\
&\textbf{end}
\end{aligned}
\tag{5.18}
$$

5.8   Write $q\uparrow n$ as an executable functional program *dagger* (q,n), where q is either a well-formed expression or a well-formed statement. Now since

$$(dagger(e,n))(v)=val(e,n,v)$$

and

$$(dagger(S,n))(v)=effect(S,n,v)$$

it follows that *dagger*(q,n) is an alternative to the interpreter. In fact, since *dagger*(q,n) is independent of the valuelist to which it is applied, it is more akin to a compiler than an interpreter. Discuss this last point.

5.9   Attach suitable functions to the edges of the flow diagram shown in Fig. 5.20 and so derive a corresponding functional program.

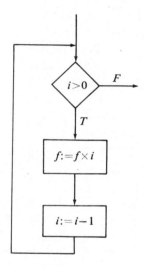

Fig. 5.20

5.10   Do the same for the flow diagram in Fig. 5.21, where the inner box is being used to compute $m:=f\times i$ by successive addition.

5.11   Use the rules given for removing **result** to transform the program given in Section 5.3 for the Euclidean algorithm. In order to write this program using **while** statements, it is necessary to repeat the part which finds the remainder. Suppose we denote this repeated program part by *REM*; then we have the program (5.19).

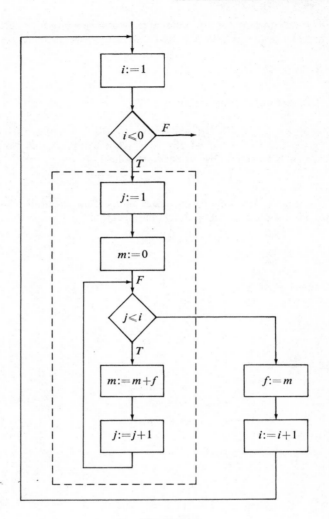

Fig. 5.21

$REM;$
while $r \neq 0$ **do**
  $y := x;$
  $x := r;$
  REM
od   (5.19)

where

$REM ::$ $r := y;$
         $|$**while** $r \geqslant x$ **do** $r := r - x$ **od**

5.12 Rewrite the program of Exercise 5.9 in the Algol fragment and transform it to a functional program. Compare the program derived in this exercise and in Exercise 5.9.

5.13 A problem which arises from the rules for removing **result**, and will have arisen in the previous exercise, occurs because of nested **while** loops. The rules as stated will construct separate functions for the effect of a nested loop on each variable which it updates. Rules which avoid this problem can be expressed if we extend the functional language to allow an expression list to be a well-formed construct. Suppose $(e_1, \ldots, e_k)$ is an expression list; then we have to give rules for each well-formed statement S, so that **result** can be removed from

$$S \text{ result } (e_1, \ldots, e_k)$$

Derive such rules. Show that in general, use of the transformation

$$S \text{ result } (e_1, \ldots, e_k) \to (S \text{ result } e_1, \ldots, S \text{ result } e_k)$$

will lead to the same functions as derived by the rules given in the main section.

5.14 Having extended the functional language as required by Exercise 5.13, extend the imperative language to allow the parallel assignment

$$x_1, \ldots, x_k := e_1, \ldots, e_k$$

which evaluates each of e_1 through e_k and assigns the resulting value to the corresponding member of x_1 through x_k. Derive a transformation rule for this extension to the fragment.

5.15 Show that every statement in the Algol fragment can be transformed to a single, parallel assignment.

5.16 When we gave the rule for *sequence* we described it as meaning that first S_2 **result** e was transformed, and then the resulting expression "pushed back" through S_1. Alternatively, we could have pushed back S_2 **result** e without first transforming it. Do we always eventually arrive at the same functional program, whichever of these interpretations of the rule we use?

5.17 What is the smallest set of variables which must be made parameters of the recursive function introduced by the transformation of the **while** statement?

5.18 Show that the stack pointer *top* is not strictly necessary and that its value at any point in the statement sequence can be determined to be a fixed displacement from the value of *act*.

5.19 Define a statement sequence with the net-effect property for the block expression

$$\textbf{let } x_1 = e_1 \textbf{ and } \ldots \textbf{ and } x_k = e_k \quad e$$

so that the *only* variables accessible in e are $x_1, \ldots, x_k$. Now consider how the rules of accessing can be relaxed so that when block expressions are nested within each other, or within functions, access can be made from nested expressions to variables in outer blocks.

6 A MACHINE ARCHITECTURE FOR FUNCTIONAL PROGRAMS

6.1 OVERVIEW OF THE MACHINE

In Chapter 4 we gave an interpreter for a variant of the Lisp language in the form of a function *apply(f,a)*. Here, *f* was the S-expression representation of a Lisp program and *a* the representation of its list of arguments by an S-expression. For example, *f* might be the program for *append*

```
(LETREC APPEND
    (APPEND LAMBDA (X Y)
        (IF (EQ X (QUOTE NIL)) Y
            (CONS (CAR X)
                (APPEND (CDR X) Y)))))
```

and then a possible value for *a* would be

$$((A\ B\ C\ D)\ (E\ F\ G\ H))$$

that is, a list of values respectively taken to be the value of the parameter *X* and the parameter *Y*. The value of *apply(f,a)* is then the S-expression representation of the result of applying *f* to *a*. In the above example, the result is

$$(A\ B\ C\ D\ E\ F\ G\ H)$$

Thus we can take *apply(f,a)* to be a formal specification of the semantics of the Lisp language, since it determines for us the value of any Lisp program for any given set of arguments. It may be that some properties which we wished to define for the language were not defined, or not defined correctly, or that we have given arbitrary meanings to some constructs which we would prefer to leave undefined. We can sweep such considerations aside by *defining* the interpreter *apply(f,a)* as the semantics of the language, so that every meaning which it ascribes to a program, or fails to ascribe, is entirely intentional and correct. Even if we do this, however, the definition is unsatisfactory in some senses. The principal criticism which can be justifiably leveled at it, and which we discussed briefly at the end of Section 4.3, is that the meaning of the language being defined (in this case Lispkit Lisp) depends on our understanding of the language used to write the interpreter (in this case our purely functional language). Of course this will always be so, but the criticism is the more pertinent here because of the semantic closeness of the defined and the defining languages.

As long as we have a correct understanding of our purely functional language, we can agree that the interpreter of Chapter 4 gives valid meanings to the well-formed expressions of the Lisp language. If, however, our understanding of the purely functional language were slightly flawed, but in such a way that the interpreter gave a plausible meaning to each Lisp construct, how would we ever know that our understanding of Lisp was also flawed? Similarly, if there is some aspect of the purely functional language which we do not understand, can we turn to the interpreter for a definition of the equivalent aspect of Lisp? The answer is often that we cannot, for almost every aspect of the purely functional language is used to make the definition. For example, suppose we wish to determine whether actual parameters are evaluated before function entry or only when needed (that is, are they called by value or by name—but more of that in Chapter 8). Suppose we consider the function

$$(LAMBDA\ (X)\ (QUOTE\ 1))$$

This function, if called with an actual parameter which is undefined, such as $(CAR\ (QUOTE\ 2))$ would be undefined in one case and yet return the value 1 in the other. We could understand the interpreter of Chapter 4 to give either of these meanings. The problem arises because the level of the defining language is too high and therefore itself open to many different interpretations. In this chapter we shall define a transformation from Lisp to programs in a much lower-level language, close to a conventional machine language, in an attempt to overcome these difficulties. As a final remark, in defense of the interpreter however, it must be said that it has great semantic value in defining some of the more esoteric or high-level features of Lisp. For example it gives a clear meaning to the idea of a function as a parameter to, or as a result of, another function (so-called higher-order functions) without making use of these features in the interpreter itself. Similarly, the complete binding rules of the language are explicitly set out in the interpreter, so that the most complex usage can be analyzed, yet the interpreter itself only makes the simplest kind of use of variable scope. So if one has a valid understanding of functional programs to a certain level, sufficient to give a correct understanding of the interpreter, then the interpreter can indeed extend that understanding.

The definition given in this chapter has two parts. We define an abstract machine which essentially operates a stack in the same way as we used it to evaluate functional programs in Section 5. Then we define a translator (compiler) which translates Lisp into programs which run on this machine. The abstract machine, which is the subject of the next section, is called the SECD machine (for a reason which will be explained) and was invented by Landin. The particular form in which this machine is given here makes use of our concrete data representation, that is, S-expressions. In particular, a program for this machine is an S-expression. For example, when translated, the *append* program given at the beginning of this section has the form:

$$(DUM\ LDC\ NIL\ LDF\ (LD\ (0.0)\ LDC\ NIL\ \ldots)\ \ldots)$$

Altogether, about 60 atoms appear. Each of the atoms appearing in this S-expression is either a machine instruction or an operand for a machine instruction. The SECD machine can be envisaged as a function *exec* which takes a compiled version of a function f, call it f^* (which is an S-expression such as that given above), and the S-expression representation of the arguments a, and produces the S-expression representation of the result of applying f to a. Thus

$$exec(f^*,a) = apply(f,a)$$

That is, in some way the SECD machine, given the S-expression representations of the compiled function (a machine-language program) and its arguments, executes the machine-language program to compute the result of applying that function to those arguments.

After defining the machine, we will define the compiler. That is, we will define a function *compile*(f) with the property that

$$compile(f) = f^*$$

In fact, both $exec(f^*,a)$ and *compile*(f) will be given by sets of rules, rather than by the usual kind of function definition. However, by turning the rules for *compile*(f) into a program in the purely functional language, we are then in a position to transliterate that into a Lisp program. From this we can generate *compile**, a machine-language program with the property that

$$exec(compile^*,f) = f^*$$

for all f. This will be the basis for the kit described in Chapters 11 and 12, and indeed the S-expression representation of *compile* and *compile** which form the essential basis for this kit are listed in Appendix 2.

The function $exec(f*,a)$ is implemented in such a way that it operates a stack for the evaluation of function calls, much as we have described that process in Chapter 5. Since the program $f*$ is an S-expression and since the data with which it computes are S-expressions, the natural notation for expressing the state of this stack machine is the S-expression notation. We can implement a stack structure as an S-expression, simply by using a list of the stacked elements and pushing and popping values from the left-hand end of that list. Thus, for example,

$$(A\ B\ C\ D)$$

could represent a stack of exactly 4 items. We will make a great deal of use of dot notation (see Section 2.9), in order to exhibit the structure of the stack. Thus, if we wish to denote the stack in such a way that its top item is clearly exhibited, we will write, for example,

$$(x.s)$$

Then we can use x to denote the top item and s the remaining items. With the above example we would take x to be A and s to be $(B\ C\ D)$. Similarly, if we wish to exhibit the top two items of an arbitrary stack, we will write, for example

$$(x\ y.s)$$

With the same stack as before we now have that x is A, y is B and s is $(C\ D)$. Thus, for example, we can describe the sum of two arbitrary values on top of the stack by saying that a stack with the form $(x\ y.s)$ is changed into a stack with the form $(x+y.s)$.

The way in which the stack was used in Section 5.5 required that, upon each function call, a new area of the stack was set up to hold the parameters for that call. We called it the activation record. During evaluation, intermediate values would be placed on the stack and if, as is usually the case, this evaluation required another function call, a new area of stack was begun. The way in which this arrangement is implemented in the SECD machine is to operate two stacks. One stack is used to hold intermediate values. The other (called the dump) is used to save values of the first stack and the other information which amounts to the suspended activation record. The reader will easily recognize the use of the stack as an evaluation mechanism in the description of the SECD machine. The precise relationship between the SECD machine and the abstract machine of Section 5.5 is left as an exercise for the reader.

The form of the function $exec(f^*,a)$ is such that the values of f^* and a are loaded into the registers of the SECD machine in order to initialize it. Then, by analyzing the program f^*, the SECD machine operates in such a way that the state of the machine is transformed according to the semantics of each machine instruction which is encountered in the program. Ultimately the value of $exec(f^*,a)$ is computed and, because of a property similar to the net-effect property, is to be found on top of one of the stacks. The next section is devoted to a description of the machine transitions for each of the SECD machine instructions. In Section 6.5 we return to a discussion of how $exec(f^*,a)$ is precisely realized by this machine.

6.2 THE SECD MACHINE

The SECD machine, which in its original form was invented by Landin, derives its name from the designation of its four principal registers:

s	the stack	used to hold intermediate results when computing the values of expressions
e	the environment	used to hold the values bound to variables during evaluation
c	the control list	used to hold the machine-language program being executed
d	the dump	used as a stack to save values of other registers on calling a new function.

Each of the registers will hold an S-expression. As we shall see in Chapter 11 when we come to emulate the SECD machine, the register will contain a pointer to a data structure which represents the S-expression. For our purpose in this chapter, however, it is more convenient if we think of the entire S-expression as contained in the register.

The entire state of the machine can be denoted by giving the content of its four registers. Thus, each instruction in the machine can be described by giving the state of the machine before and after its execution. We call this a *machine transition*. We will write it in the form

$$s\ e\ c\ d \rightarrow s'\ e'\ c'\ d'$$

that is, four S-expressions on the right of the arrow giving the before state and four S-expressions on the left giving the after state. When we wish to indicate that part of an S-expression in the before state is repeated in the after state, when we shall use the same lower-case variable in both S-expressions. For example, the transition for the load constant instruction (*LDC*) is as shown in Fig. 6.1.

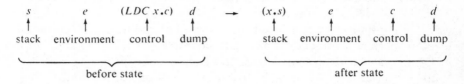

Fig. 6.1

The control before execution of the instruction has the form

$$(LDC\ x.c)$$

That is, we identify three separate parts of the control list. The operation code *LDC* given here as a mnemonic will in practice be a numeric atom, but this need not concern us until Chapter 11. The next item in the control list is the operand of the *LDC* instruction, the constant to be "loaded". The variable *c* identifies the rest of the control list, hence the use of the dot. Thus if the control list were actually

$$(LDC\ (A.B)\ CAR\ LDC\ A\ EQ\ RTN)$$

then *x* would match (*A.B*) and *c* would match (*CAR LDC A EQ RTN*). In the after state we see that only this tail part of the control is left in the control register and thus the execution of the *LDC* instruction involves skipping past the instruction and its operand. The operand has been pushed onto the stack as is indicated by the S-expression

$$(x.s)$$

showing that all the previous stack entries are still available but that *x* has been placed in front of them. Other than this the transition defines that the environment and the dump are unchanged by the transition. Hence if, for example, the machine is in the state

$$((A.B)\ 127)\quad ((3\ (C)))\quad (LDC\ 17\ RTN)\quad NIL$$

then after execution of the *LDC* instruction it will be in the state

$$(17 \ (A.B) \ 127) \quad ((3 \ (C))) \quad (RTN) \quad NIL$$

The machine will be so organized that the program in its control register is always a list with an instruction code in its first position. This instruction code determines which transition will be invoked. The machine then executes its program by going through the sequence of transitions invoked by the instructions in the control. Since various instructions cause the control to be reloaded, effecting a subprogram call, this sequence can be very long, even though at any time the control may be quite short. Execution terminates when the instruction *STOP* is encountered. We indicate this formally by the transition

$$s \ e \ (STOP) \ d \ \rightarrow \ s \ e \ (STOP) \ d$$

which clearly, once encountered, prevents further execution. The complete set of instructions with their mnemonics is as follows.

LD	load
LDC	load constant
LDF	load function
AP	apply function
RTN	return
DUM	create dummy environment
RAP	recursive apply
SEL	select subcontrol
JOIN	rejoin main control
CAR	take *car* of item on top of stack
CDR	take *cdr* of item on top of stack
ATOM	apply *atom* predicate to top stack item
CONS	form *cons* of top two stack items
EQ	apply *eq* predicate to top two stack items
ADD	⎫
SUB	⎪
MUL	⎬ apply arithmetic operation to top two stack items
DIV	⎪
REM	⎪
LEQ	⎭
STOP	stop

In the remainder of this section we give the transitions for each of these instructions with some examples of their use.

First, let us give transitions for each of the arithmetic operations. The transition for *ADD* is

$$(a\ b.s)\ e\ (ADD.c)\ d \to (b+a.s)\ e\ c\ d$$

Here, (*a b.s*) denotes that the stack has at least two members and the form (*b+a.s*) that these two members (which should be numbers) are replaced by their sum. Thus in particular, if the machine is in the state

$$(7\ 6.s)\ e\ (A\dot{D}D.c)\ d$$

then it will, at the next step, go into the state

$$(13.s)\ e\ c\ d$$

The rule for each of the arithmetic operations has exactly the same form as that for *ADD*. They are as follows:

$$
\begin{array}{lll}
(a\ b.s)\ e\ (SUB.c) & d \to (b-a.s) & e\ c\ d \\
(a\ b.s)\ e\ (MUL.c) & d \to (b\times a.s) & e\ c\ d \\
(a\ b.s)\ e\ (DIV.c) & d \to (b\div a.s) & e\ c\ d \\
(a\ b.s)\ e\ (REM.c) & d \to (b\ \textbf{rem}\ a.s) & e\ c\ d \\
(a\ b.s)\ e\ (EQ.c) & d \to (b=a.s) & e\ c\ d \\
(a\ b.s)\ e\ (LEQ.c) & d \to (b\leqslant a.s) & e\ c\ d \\
\end{array}
$$

In the last two cases, the logical value which replaces the arithmetic values on the stack will be one of the atoms *T* or *F* used to denote true or false repectively.

Now we can demonstrate the sequence of machine states which are reached in turn as a longer program is executed. In the following display (Table 6.1), each line represents a machine state and each is derived from its predecessor by the application of one of the previously given transition rules. Note that the code used here would be that compiled from the expression $1-2\times3=4$ or, more specifically, from (*EQ* (*SUB* (*QUOTE* 1) (*MUL* (*QUOTE* 2) (*QUOTE* 3))) (*QUOTE* 4)). Thus we see clearly how the stack

Table 6.1

s	e		d
	e	(*LDC* 1 *LDC* 2 *LDC* 3 *MUL SUB LDC* 4 *EQ*)	*d*
(1.s)	*e*	(*LDC* 2 *LDC* 3 *MUL SUB LDC* 4 *EQ*)	*d*
(2 1.s)	*e*	(*LDC* 3 *MUL SUB LDC* 4 *EQ*)	*d*
(3 2 1.s)	*e*	(*MUL SUB LDC* 4 *EQ*)	*d*
(6 1.s)	*e*	(*SUB LDC* 4 *EQ*)	*d*
(−5.s)	*e*	(*LDC* 4 *EQ*)	*d*
(4 −5.s)	*e*	(*EQ*)	*d*
(F.s)	*e*	NIL	*d*

and control are used in this machine. The control holds a machine-language program, the head item of which is always a machine instruction. The state transition to be used is determined solely by this instruction. The stack is used in a conventional way to hold partial results during expression evaluation.

There are machine instructions for each of the primitive operations on S-expressions, *CAR*, *CDR* and *CONS*. These operate on values at the top of the stack and leave their results at the top of the stack as we might expect. Their transitions are

$$(a\ b.s)\quad e\ (CONS.c)\ d \to ((a.b).s)\quad e\ c\ d$$
$$((a.b).s)\ e\ (CAR.c)\quad d \to (a.s)\qquad e\ c\ d$$
$$((a.b).s)\ e\ (CDR.c)\quad d \to (b.s)\qquad e\ c\ d$$

Here, by denoting a composite value (*a.b*) at the top of the stack, we are able to show exactly the effect of each of the instructions. There is of course a similar transition for the predicate, which tests whether a value is atomic or not, a machine instruction which we have called *ATOM*.

$$(a.s)\ e\ (ATOM.c)\ d \to (t.s)\ e\ c\ d$$

where $t = T$ if a is an atom and $t = F$ if a is not an atom.

Now this particular SECD machine was designed just so that Lispkit Lisp could be compiled for it. The remaining instructions are very specific to the structure of that language. The first of these that we must consider allows the SECD machine to access values corresponding to variables in the Lisp program. In order to describe this instruction it is necessary to define the structure of the environment component of the SECD machine state and how this structure will relate to the scope of variables in the Lisp program.

The environment component of the SECD machine has the same structure as the valuelist used to define the interpreter in Chapter 4. That is, it is a list of lists. For example,

$$((3\ 17)\ ((A\ B)\ (C\ D)))$$

is a possible environment. The environment will be accessed by an *LD* instruction which has as an operand a pair of integers, called an index pair. The sublists of the environment are numbered 0,1,2,... and each element of each sublist is also numbered 0,1,2,.... The index pair (*i.j*) selects the *jth* member of the *ith* sublist. Thus the above environment can be indexed by (0.0),(0.1),(1.0) and (1.1) to select each of its values (Table 6.2).

Table 6.2

Index pair	Value selected
(0.0)	3
(0.1)	17
(1.0)	$(A\ B)$
(1.1)	$(C\ D)$

We can define a function which returns the *nth* ($\geqslant 0$) member of a list *s*. considering the members to be numbered from 0 upwards.

$$index(n,s) \equiv \textbf{if } eq(n,0) \textbf{ then } car(s) \textbf{ else}$$
$$index(n-1,\ cdr(s))$$

and with this we can define a function which determines for an index pair $i = (b.n)$ the corresponding value in the environment *e*.

$$locate(i,e) \equiv$$
$$\{index(n,index(b,e))$$
$$\textbf{where } b = car(i)$$
$$\textbf{and } n = cdr(i)\}$$

Finally, with this we can define the transition for the load instruction *LD* which has one parameter, an index pair, and copies the value corresponding to this index pair to the top of the stack:

$$s\ e\ (LD\ i.c)\ d\ \rightarrow\ (x.s)\ e\ c\ d\quad \textbf{where } x = locate(i,e)$$

To be specific, observe the following sequence of transitions:

$$NIL\ ((3\ 7)\ (2\ 0))\ (LD\ (0.1)\ LD\ (1.0)\ ADD)\quad d$$
$$(7)\quad ((3\ 7)\ (2\ 0))\ (LD\ (1.0)\ ADD)\quad d$$
$$(2\ 7)\ ((3\ 7)\ (2\ 0))\ (ADD)\quad d$$
$$(9)\quad ((3\ 7)\ (2\ 0))\ NIL\quad d$$

Here we have obtained two values from the environment and added them together.

The *LD* instructions will be used to access values bound to variables in the Lisp program. Each variable will be associated with a location in the environment. In fact, the 0th sublist of the environment will correspond to the declarations in the block (or function) immediately enclosing the variable, the 1st sublist to those of the block enclosing that, and so on. We shall deal with these accessing schemes more completely when we describe the compiler in the next section.

We have two instructions used to implement conditional forms. *SEL* selects a sublist of the control based on the value at the top of the stack and *JOIN* is used to rejoin the main control. Thus, in practice, we expect the control to have the form

$$(\ldots SEL (\ldots JOIN) (\ldots JOIN) \ldots)$$
$$\uparrow \qquad\quad \uparrow \qquad\quad \uparrow$$
$$c_T \qquad\quad c_F \qquad\quad c$$

and either c_T or c_F is executed according to whether *SEL* finds T or F on top of the stack. After c_T or c_F has been selected, *JOIN* causes control to revert to c. This is accomplished by the following transitions for *SEL* and *JOIN*:

$$(x.s) \; e \; (SEL \; c_T \; c_F.c) \; d \rightarrow s \; e \; c_x \; (c.d)$$
$$s \quad e \; (JOIN) \; (c.d) \qquad \rightarrow s \; e \; c \quad d$$

Here we see that *SEL* inspects the top value on the stack x and selects the appropriate sublist (c_T or c_F according to whether $x = T$ or $x = F$). The remainder of the control c is pushed onto the dump. If the selected sublist is well formed, in the sense that it leaves the dump as it found it, then when the *JOIN* instruction is encountered, the top item on the dump is the remainder of the original control. *JOIN* reinstates this and so computation proceeds. Consider the control list

$$(LD \; (0.0) \; SEL \; (LD \; (0.1) \; JOIN)$$
$$(LD \; (0.2) \; JOIN) \; STOP)$$

If executed with an environment which has values in positions (0.0), (0.1) and (0.2), it will result in the value at position (0.1) or (0.2) being loaded onto the stack, depending upon whether the value at position (0.0) is T or F.

The instructions which we use to evaluate function calls are somewhat more complex. In fact these instructions will be generated also when **let** blocks are compiled. The *AP* instruction is particularly important. It is the principal way in which values are established in the environment. We shall see that when a user-defined function is applied to its arguments, the values of those arguments are placed in the environment as a sublist so that they can be accessed by the code for the function body using *LD* instructions. First, however, we must consider the run-time representation of a function value. In Section 4.2 we used the notion of a context to discuss the binding rules of Lispkit Lisp. There we determined that a function value should be represented by a closure which consisted of the lambda expression defining the function and a copy of the context in which the definition was made. The SECD machine equivalent of the context is the environment and the equivalent of an expression to be evaluated is a control list. Thus a closure at run time is represented by a pair consisting of a control list and an environment. Such a pair is built by the *LDF* instruction, which has the control list as operand. The transition for *LDF* is

$$s \ e \ (LDF \ c'.c) \ d \ \rightarrow \ ((c'.e).s) \ e \ c \ d$$

Thus the closure is $(c'.e)$, simply a *cons* of the control list operand of *LDF* and the environment. For example, if the machine is in the state

$$(0) \quad ((3 \ 7) \ (A)) \quad (LDF \ (LD \ (1.1) \ RTN) \ LD \ (0.1)) \quad NIL$$

then, applying the above transition gets us to the state

$$(((LD \ (1.1) \ RTN).((3 \ 7) \ (A))) \ 0) \quad ((3 \ 7)(A)) \quad (LD \ (0.1)) \quad NIL$$

where the closure is $((LD \ (1.1) \ RTN).((3 \ 7)(A)))$. In general, a closure will, once created, not be applied immediately, but will find its way into the environment and be recalled a number of times, using an *LD* instruction so that it can be applied to different arguments.

When it is recalled and applied using an *AP* instruction, it must appear on the stack directly above a list of actual parameters. The *AP* instruction installs these in the environment and installs the code from the closure in the control register to be executed. The dump is used to save all the existing register contents so that they can be restored by the *RTN* instruction at the end of the code from the closure. The *AP* instruction has the transition

$$((c'.e') \ v.s) \ e \ (AP.c) \ d \ \rightarrow \ NIL \ (v.e') \ c' \ (s \ e \ c.d)$$

This is the most elaborate transition we have had so far. *AP* expects the top stack item to be a closure $(c'.e')$ and the second item on the stack to be a list v of values for the parameters for the function represented by the closure. The evaluation of the function is begun by installing the code c' in the control and building the environment $(v.e')$. This form for the environment means that the parameters of the function will be accessed at position (0.0), (0.1), (0.2), etc., whereas the free variables will be accessed at positions $(1.0), (1.1), \ldots, (2.0), (2.1), \ldots$ etc. For execution of the code from the closure we begin with an empty stack. The form of the dump immediately after the *AP* instruction is $(s \ e \ c.d)$, showing that the entire state before execution has been saved. As an example of the execution of an *AP* instruction, consider the machine state

$$(((LD\ (1.1)\ LD\ (0.0)\ ADD\ RTN).((3\ 7)(A)))\ (6)\ 0)\quad((2\ B))\quad(AP\ STOP)\quad d$$

which, applying the above transition, leads to

$$NIL\ ((6)\ (3\ 7)\ (A))\quad(LD\ (1.1)\ LD\ (0.0)\ ADD\ RTN)\quad((0)\ ((2\ B))\ (STOP).d)$$

Looking at the code which has been installed in the control register, we see that it accesses position (0.0), finding 6 the first (only) actual parameter and position (1.1), finding 7 a global value not available at the point of call but acquired from the closure.

The *RTN* instruction complements the *AP* instruction in the sense that it restores the state saved in the dump. The code loaded into the control register by the *AP* instruction should therefore end with a *RTN* instruction. The transition for *RTN* is

$$(x)\ e'\ (RTN)\ (s\ e\ c.d) \rightarrow (x.s)\ e\ c\ d$$

We see that *RTN* expects to find a single value x on the stack. It returns this to the calling environment by pushing in onto the restored stack s. For example, after executing the *LD*s and *ADD* in the above state, we arrive at

$$(13)\quad((6)\ (3\ 7)\ (A))\quad(RTN)\quad((0)\ ((2\ B))\ (STOP).d)$$

to which the *RTN* transition is applicable, leading to

$$(13\ 0)\ ((2\ B))\ (STOP)\ d$$

and the value 13 is returned on top of the stack as a result of the function call.

In order to define the remaining two SECD machine instructions, *DUM* and *RAP*, we again need to make use of the Lisp pseudofunction $rplaca(x,y)$. This pseudofunction, which we discussed in Section 4.3, means replace the *car* of x by y. It is evaluated for its effect, rather than its value. It does have a value however. Its value is x except that the *car* of x has been replaced by y. Recall that we made the restriction that it is only allowed to replace the *car* of x if the *car* has previously been set to a special value Ω which we call *pending*.

We will use *rplaca* to implement recursive **letrec** blocks, where it is necessary for the local definitions to be evaluated in a context which includes their own values. We will do this by creating a dummy environment with the local definitions pending, evaluating the definitions using this dummy environment and then subsequently replacing the pending part of the environment by the values of the definitions. Thus the dummy environment will be incorporated in any closures generated when evaluating the definitions. After replacement of the pending part, these closures will become circular, each containing an environment which contains the closures themselves as values. All this, which we will explain fully at the end of the next section, is accomplished by just the *DUM* and *RAP* instructions.

The *DUM* instruction creates a dummy environment with Ω as its first sublist. Hence any attempts to access values in this sublist will be undefined until the Ω has been replaced. The transition for *DUM* is simple:

$$s \; e \; (DUM.c) \; d \; \to \; s \; (\Omega.e) \; c \; d$$

The *RAP* instruction is almost identical to *AP* except that, rather than *cons*ing the actual parameter values into the environment, it uses *rplaca* to replace the Ω set by *DUM*:

$$((c'.e') \; v.s) \; (\Omega.e) \; (RAP.c) \; d \; \to \; NIL \; rplaca(e',v) \; c' \; (s \; e \; c.d)$$

At first sight this seems a little unusual. *RAP* will always be used in a state where $e' = (\Omega.e)$. That is, the closure on top of the stack contains an environment identical to the current environment. Otherwise, *RAP* behaves much like *AP*. It installs the code c' from the closure in the control and the environment e' in the environment register, having replaced its *car* by the list of values v. The stack, environment and control are dumped. In the case of the environment, since it has been expanded by a *DUM* instruction, only its *cdr* is saved. Comparing the transition for *AP* with that for *RAP* and bearing in mind that when *RAP* is executed, the environment has already been extended by Ω, it is easy to see that they are consistent. The use of these later instructions should be clearer when we have studied the code which we get from the compiler of the next section.

6.3 A COMPILER FOR THE LISP VARIANT

In order to define a compiler for our variant of Lisp, we consider separately each well-formed expression of the Lisp language, as we defined them in Section 4.1. For each well-formed expression, we will generate a list of SECD machine instructions with the following property.

Net-effect property of well-formed expressions   The code compiled for a well-formed expression is such that, if loaded into the control of the SECD machine and executed, it will leave the value of the expression on top of the stack. It expects the environment to have been loaded with a structure containing, in appropriate positions, values for the free variables of the expression. It leaves the stack unchanged apart from the pushing of the value of the expression. The environment and the dump have the same values before and after execution of the code.

––––––––––––––

To summarize this property, we have that if c is the code generated from a well-formed expression and e is an environment containing the values of the variables in the well-formed expression, then, for any stack s and any dump d, executing the code c according to the rules of the previous section results in the state change

$$s\ e\ c\ d \rightarrow (x.s)\ e\ NIL\ d$$

where x is the value computed by c. We use "$\rightarrow$" to indicate that one or more of the transitions of the previous section has been applied. More generally, if we denote by

$$c_1 \mid c_2$$

the result of appending the control lists c_1 and c_2, we have

$$s\ \ e\ \ c|c'\ \ d \rightarrow (x.s)\ e\ c'\ d$$

For example, if

$$c = (LDC\ 1)$$
$$c' = (RTN)$$

then

$$c \mid c' = (LDC\ 1\ RTN)$$

and we have

$$s\ e\ (LDC\ 1\ RTN)\ d \rightarrow (1.s)\ e\ (RTN)\ d$$

From this rule, we can determine that if both c_1 and c_2 are generated from well-formed expressions and they compute the value x_1 and x_2 respectively, then

$$s \quad e \quad c_1 \,|\, c_2 \,|\, c' \quad d \rightarrow (x_2 \; x_1.s) \; e \; c' \; d$$

That is to say, executing the code from two well-formed expressions in sequence results in the values of these expressions appearing on the stack, the code disappearing from the control and the rest of the machine otherwise being left unchanged.

We shall make a great deal of use of the abbreviation for appending two lists in this section, and therefore it is as well to understand it now. In fact $x \,|\, y$ is nothing more than $append(x,y)$ written in a shorter form. However, we make use of the fact that

$$append(x,append(y,z)) = append(append(x,y),z)$$

to allow ourselves to write

$$x \,|\, y \,|\, z$$

rather than

$$\{x \,|\, y\} \,|\, z \quad \text{or} \quad x \,|\, \{y \,|\, z\}$$

Thus, for example,

$$(LDC \; NIL) \,|\, (LDC \; 1) \,|\, (CONS)$$

simplifies to

$$(LDC \; NIL \; LDC \; 1 \; CONS)$$

and therefore

$$(LDC \; NIL) \,|\, c \,|\, (CONS)$$

is one way of denoting the code that computes the value $cons(x,NIL)$ (that is, the singleton list) if c computes (on top of the stack) the value x.

As we analyze each well-formed expression we shall build up a list of the variables declared in lambda expressions and blocks within it. This list will have a form congruent to the form of the environment at run time. That is to say it will be a list of lists. As we did in the interpreter, we call this list of lists the *namelist*.

$$((A) \, (X \, Y) \, (APPEND \, REV \, DUP))$$

is an example of a name list. Whenever we enter a new block or function, the variables declared there will be added to the namelist as a new first sublist. The above namelist suggests that we are three blocks deep in the nesting. For example, it might have been generated by the program structure (6.1) when analyzing the expression at the program location marked by an

---

$$
\begin{array}{ll}
(LETREC \text{———————} & \\
\quad (APPEND \, LAMBDA \, (X \, Y) & \\
\qquad (LET \text{—————————} \leftarrow\!\!\text{———} & \qquad (6.1) \\
\qquad\quad (A \text{———————————}))) & \\
\quad (REV \text{——————————}) & \\
\quad (DUP \text{——————————})) &
\end{array}
$$

---

arrow. Given such a name list we can determine the index pair used to access each variable by numbering the sublists 0,1,... and the members of each sublist 0,1,.... Hence the above namelist has the following indexes:

$$
\begin{array}{cccccc}
((A) & (X & Y) & (APPEND & REV & DUP)) \\
\uparrow & \uparrow & \uparrow & \uparrow & \uparrow & \uparrow \\
(0.0) & (1.0) & (1.1) & (2.0) & (2.1) & (2.2)
\end{array}
$$

These index pairs are easily computed using the function *location*(x,n), where x is the variable we are looking for and n is the namelist. First we define the function *position*(x,a) which, given a list of atoms a (a sublist of n), returns the index of x in a, assuming it is there.

$$position(x,a) \equiv \textbf{if } eq(x,car(a)) \textbf{ then } 0 \textbf{ else } 1+position(x,cdr(a))$$

Now, the function *location* can be defined as follows:

$$
\begin{aligned}
&location(x,n) \equiv \\
&\quad \textbf{if } member(x,car(n)) \textbf{ then } cons(0,position(x,car(n))) \textbf{ else} \\
&\quad \{cons(car(z)+1,cdr(z)) \\
&\qquad\qquad \textbf{where } z = location(x,cdr(n)))\}
\end{aligned}
$$

using the function *member*, as defined in Section 2.5. Here we see that *location* returns $(0.q)$ if the variable x occurs in the first sublist at position q. If, however, it does not occur in the first sublist, then *location* is called recursively with the $cdr(n)$ and the index pair $(p.q)$ determined. The appropriate value to return is then $(p+1.q)$. The function $location(x,n)$ is undefined if s does not occur anywhere in n, but for our purposes here we shall ignore this eventuality.

Now we begin to describe the code which is generated for each well-formed expression. If e is a well-formed expression and n is a namelist, then we shall denote by

$$e*n$$

the code which is generated when e is compiled with respect to the namelist n. The code for the two most elementary well-formed expressions, the variable and the constant, is trivial:

$$x*n = (LD\ i)\ \textbf{where}\ i = location(x,n)$$
$$(QUOTE\ s)*n = (LDC\ s)$$

Both of these generate a single instruction whose effect is to load a value onto the stack. In the case of the variable, the appropriate instruction is the LD instruction which retrieves the value of the variable from the environment. In the case of a constant, the appropriate instruction is the LDC instruction which simply loads its operand onto the stack. It is easily seen that both these code sequences satisfy the net-effect property of well-formed expressions.

Consider now the well-formed expression

$$(ADD\ e_1\ e_2)$$

If we compile e_1 and e_2 and obtain the code c_1 and c_2 respectively, then the code we require for the arithmetic expression is

$$c_1\ |\ c_2\ |\ (ADD)$$

for this will have the net-effect property. First the value of e_1 will be computed by c_1 and left on the stack, then the value of e_2 will be computed by c_2 and left on the stack and finally the ADD instruction will add these two values together with the net effect of leaving a single value, the value of $(ADD\ e_1\ e_2)$, on the stack. Writing this as a single rule, we have

$$(ADD\ e_1\ e_2)*n = e_1*n\ |\ e_2*n\ |\ (ADD)$$

When writing such rules we take the $*$ as more binding than the $|$. However, it is usually the case that only one sensible meaning can be attached to such a rule. Here, for example, the append operation is clearly only sensible between code lists and the $*$ operation between well-formed expressions and namelists. It is therefore possible, without remembering which operator binds more strongly, to ascertain the correct meaning for this rule.

The remaining rules for simple arithmetic, relational and structural expressions, are entirely equivalent to the rule for ADD. They are

$$(SUB\ e_1\ e_2)*n = e_1*n\ |\ e_2*n\ |\ (SUB)$$
$$(MUL\ e_1\ e_2)*n = e_1*n\ |\ e_2*n\ |\ (MUL)$$
$$(DIV\ e_1\ e_2)*n = e_1*n\ |\ e_2*n\ |\ (DIV)$$
$$(REM\ e_1\ e_2)*n = e_1*n\ |\ e_2*n\ |\ (REM)$$
$$(EQ\ e_1\ e_2)*n = e_1*n\ |\ e_2*n\ |\ (EQ)$$
$$(LEQ\ e_1\ e_2)*n = e_1*n\ |\ e_2*n\ |\ (LEQ)$$
$$(CAR\ e)*n = e*n\ |\ (CAR)$$
$$(CDR\ e)*n = e*n\ |\ (CDR)$$
$$(CONS\ e_1\ e_2)*n = e_2*n\ |\ e_1*n\ |\ (CONS)$$
$$(ATOM\ e)*n = e*n\ |\ (ATOM)$$

Because of the way the SECD machine was defined, the $CONS$ instruction expects its operands in the "wrong" order. This presents no difficulty and has no special significance.

To consolidate these rules, consider the compilation (6.2). This form of

---

$$(ADD\ (CAR\ X)\ (QUOTE\ 1))*((X\ Y))$$
$$=\ (CAR\ X)*((X\ Y))\ |\ (QUOTE\ 1)*((X\ Y))\ |\ (ADD)$$
$$=\ X*((X\ Y))\ |\ (CAR)\ |\ (LDC\ 1)\ |\ (ADD) \qquad (6.2)$$
$$=\ (LD\ (0.0))\ |\ (CAR)\ |\ (LDC\ 1)\ |\ (ADD)$$
$$=\ (LD\ (0.0)\ CAR\ LDC\ 1\ ADD)$$

---

evaluation of arithmetic expression, where the operands are computed and placed on a stack before the operator is applied, is quite conventional. When the operator appears, as it does here, after the code for the operands, the code is said to be in postfix or reverse form. It is exactly as we used it in Section 5.4.

Now we come to the code to be generated for the conditional form. The conditional form is

$$(IF\ e_1\ e_2\ e_3)$$

and so, of course, we must compile each of e_1, e_2 and e_3. The code lists we obtain from e_2 and e_3 must have a *JOIN* instruction appended to them. That is we must construct, for e_2

$$e_2*n \mid (JOIN)$$

and similarly for e_3. Hence the entire code for the conditional form is

$$(IF\ e_1\ e_2\ e_3)*n = e_1*n \mid (SEL \quad e_2*n \mid (JOIN) \quad e_3*n \mid (JOIN))$$

Here we see that the code lists for e_2 and e_3 are properly nested as the operands of *SEL*, whereas the code for e_1 precedes *SEL*. The code can be seen to have the net-effect property, by the following reasoning. After executing the code for e_1 the value of this expression is on top of the stack, the *SEL* instruction pops this value and selects one of the sublists to execute. Since both these sublists are terminated by *JOIN*, the net effect, as explained when *SEL* and *JOIN* were defined, is to leave the value of e_2 or e_3 on the stack and the machine state otherwise unchanged. As an example, consider

$$(ADD\ Y\ (IF\ (LEQ\ X\ Y)\ X\ (QUOTE\ 1)))*((X\ Y))$$

which generates the following code (the code for the conditional expression is marked by arrows):

$$\begin{array}{c} \downarrow \\ (LD\ (0.1)\ LD\ (0.0)\ LD\ (0.1)\ LEQ\ SEL \\ (LD\ (0.0)\ JOIN) \\ (LDC\ 1\ JOIN)\ ADD) \\ \uparrow \end{array}$$

Following this code through execution, we see that, after the *LEQ* instruction the machine state is such that either T or F is on top of the stack. *SEL* then selects one of the sublists following it and either the value in position (0.0), corresponding to X, or the constant 1 is loaded onto the stack, and the *JOIN* restores the control state of the machine so that the *ADD* instruction can be executed. The net effect of the conditional form, which is the bit between the arrows, has thus been to leave a single value on the stack, the second operand of *ADD*.

The lambda expression presents us with some new problems with regard to its compilation. In particular, since it introduces new variables, we must adjust the namelist. Consider the compilation, with respect to the namelist n, of the lambda expression

$$(LAMBDA\ (x_1 \ldots x_k)\ e)$$

Clearly, we must compile e but not with respect to n. We must augment n with the parameters $(x_1 \ldots x_k)$. The appropriate form for the namelist is

$$((x_1 \ldots x_k).n)$$

This means that variables in n will now be referred to by an index pair whose first element is one higher. This is exactly what we require, for when we come to apply the function, we will use an AP instruction, which will install the actual parameter values in the environment in positions with indexes of the form $(0.j)$, and hence global variables will be in this more displaced position. Now, when we have generated the code

$$c = e*((x_1 \ldots x_k).n)$$

we must append an RTN instruction to it and then make it the parameter of an LDF instruction. Thus the entire code for the lambda expression is

$$(LDF \ c \mid (RTN))$$

The complete rule is

$$(LAMBDA \ (x_1 \ldots x_k) \ e)*n = (LDF \ e*((x_1 \ldots x_k).n) \mid (RTN))$$

For example,

$$(LAMBDA \ (X) \ (ADD \ X \ Y))*((X \ Y)) =$$
$$(LDF \ (LD \ (0.0) \ LD \ (1.1) \ ADD \ RTN))$$

The result of executing the code for a λ-expression is therefore just to put a closure containing the code for its body on top of the stack. The net-effect rule is then trivially satisfied.

The well-formed expression

$$(e \ e_1 \ldots e_k)$$

is interpreted as a function call. Each of its components is compiled to generate the code lists $c, c_1, \ldots, c_k$. It is necessary to combine these code lists so that we build on the stack at run time a list of the values computed by $c_1, \ldots, c_k$ and the closure computed by c. The list of values can be obtained using the code

$$(LDC \ NIL) \mid c_k \mid (CONS) \mid c_{k-1} \mid (CONS) \mid \ldots \mid c_1 \mid (CONS)$$

where, by computation of the values in reverse order, the list is built up in the correct order. If $c_1, \ldots, c_k$ compute the values $v_1, \ldots, v_k$ leaving each of them, since each $e_1, \ldots, e_k$ is a well-formed expression, on top of the stack, then the above list-constructing code leaves the value

$$(v_1 \ldots v_k)$$

on top of the stack. Since the code $c = e*n$ will leave the closure for the function to be called on top of the stack, we have the following code for a function call:

$$(e\, e_1 \ldots e_k)*n = (LDC\ NIL) \mid e_k*n \mid (CONS) \mid \ldots \mid e_1*n \mid$$
$$(CONS) \mid e*n \mid (AP)$$

The net effect of this code must take into account the well-formedness of the body of the function, compiled to produce the code in the closure, and the effect of the *RTN* instruction. As explained above, the code, when executed, first constructs the list of actual parameter values on the stack and then places a closure on top of this. This is exactly the form of stack expected by the *AP* instruction, which saves the state of the machine (excluding the closure and parameter values) on the dump. The code from the closure is then executed but, since this has been compiled from a well-formed expression, its net effect is to place its value on the stack. The *RTN* instruction is such that the dumped state, which corresponds to that before the code for the call was begun, is restored with the single value of the body of the function added to the stack. Hence the net-effect property is satisfied by the code for function call.

As an example, consider the call

$$(INC\ (QUOTE\ 1))$$

compiled in a context where *INC* is the only variable and its value has been obtained from the lambda expression

$$(LAMBDA\ (X)\ (ADD\ X\ (QUOTE\ 1)))$$

The closure which represents this lambda expression at run time is

$$\beta = ((LD\ (0.0)\ LDC\ 1\ ADD\ RTN).\ NIL)$$

$$\hspace{2.2cm}\uparrow \hspace{4.2cm}\uparrow$$

$$\hspace{1.8cm}\text{code part} \hspace{2.5cm}\text{environment part}$$

The call compiles to produce

$$(INC \ (QUOTE \ 1))*((INC))$$
$$= (LDC \ NIL) \mid (LDC \ 1) \mid (CONS) \mid (LD \ (0,0)) \mid (AP)$$
$$= (LDC \ NIL \ LDC \ 1 \ CONS \ LD \ (0,0) \ AP)$$

Therefore, we execute this code with an environment containing the closure as shown in Table 6.3.

Table 6.3

s	$((\beta))$	$(LDC \ NIL \ LDC \ 1 \ CONS \ LD \ (0,0) \ AP)$	d
$(NIL.s)$	$((\beta))$	$(LDC \ 1 \ CONS \ LD \ (0,0) \ AP)$	d
$(1 \ NIL.s)$	$((\beta))$	$(CONS \ LD \ (0,0) \ AP)$	d
$((1).s)$	$((\beta))$	$(LD \ (0,0) \ AP)$	d
$(\beta \ (1).s)$	$((\beta))$	(AP)	d
NIL	$((1))$	$(LD \ (0,0) \ LDC \ 1 \ ADD \ RTN)$	$(s \ ((\beta)) \ NIL.d)$
(1)	$((1))$	$(LDC \ 1 \ ADD \ RTN)$	$(s \ ((\beta)) \ NIL.d)$
$(1 \ 1)$	$((1))$	$(ADD \ RTN)$	$(s \ ((\beta)) \ NIL.d)$
(2)	$((1))$	(RTN)	$(s \ ((\beta)) \ NIL.d)$
$(2.s)$	$((\beta))$	NIL	d

Each of the lines in the sequence of machine states shown in Table 6.3 has been obtained from the previous line by applying one of the rules of the previous section. It demonstrates quite clearly the net-effect property of the code.

Now the compilation of simple *LET* blocks is straightforward, for we recognize the equivalence, investigated in Section 4.3, between such blocks and function calls. We have

$$(LET \ e \ (x_1.e_1) \ldots (x_k.e_k)) \cong ((LAMBDA \ (x_1 \ldots x_k) \ e) \ e_1 \ldots e_k)$$

and hence we generate the same code for the *LET* block as if we had written it in this way. That is

$$(LET \ e \ (x_1.e_1) \ldots (x_k.e_k))*n =$$
$$(LDC \ NIL) \mid e_k*n \mid (CONS) \mid \ldots \mid e_1*n \mid (CONS) \mid$$
$$(LDF \ e*m \mid (RTN) \ AP)$$
$$\textbf{where } m = ((x_1 \ldots x_k).n)$$

The important thing to note here is that, whereas the qualified expression e is compiled with respect to the namelist augmented by the locally defined variables, the expressions defining values for these local variables are compiled with respect to the unaugmented namelist. Consistently, the code is such that, when the values of $e_1, \ldots, e_k$ are computed, the environment is such that positions for $x_1, \ldots, x_k$ have not been established. These are only established by the *AP* instruction, for the evaluation of the qualified expression. Since this code is the same as for the composite of lambda definition and function call, the net-effect property is clearly satisfied.

We come finally to the recursive block. The code we generate is very similar to that for the simple block, with two small changes. First, the expressions defining the values of local variables are compiled with respect to the augmented namelist, rather than the unaugmented one as above. Second, to be consistent with this, when the code for these expressions is executed, this is done with a dummy environment created by *DUM*. Accordingly, instead of *AP* we use the *RAP* instruction. We have

$$(LETREC\ e\ (x_1.e_1)\ \ldots\ (x_k.e_k))*n =$$
$$(DUM\ LDC\ NIL)\ |\ e_k*m\ |\ (CONS)\ |\ \ldots\ |\ e_1*m\ |\ (CONS)\ |$$
$$(LDF\ e*m\ |\ (RTN)\ RAP)$$
where $m = ((x_1\ \ldots\ x_k).n)$

That this code has the net-effect property which we require of it follows from the argument we gave for the simple block and the reasoning given about *DUM* and *RAP* in the last section. In order to demonstrate this code in action, however, we consider the simple case of one recursive definition.

Consider the well-formed expression

$$(LETREC\ (FAC\ (QUOTE\ 6))$$
$$(FAC\ LAMBDA\ (X) \text{------}))$$

where *FAC* is defined in the usual way to be the factorial function. Compiling this with respect to the namelist *NIL* gives us the code

$$(DUM\ LDC\ NIL\ LDF\ c\ CONS$$
$$LDF\ (LDC\ NIL\ LDC\ 6\ CONS$$
$$LD\ (0.0)\ AP\ RTN)\ RAP)$$

where *c* is the code for the body of the function definition. If we load the registers of our SECD machine with the above code in the control and the other registers all *NIL*, we get the following sequence of states:

$$NIL\quad NIL\quad (DUM \ldots RAP)\quad NIL$$
$$NIL\quad \alpha\quad (LDC\ NIL \ldots RAP)\quad NIL$$

where the dummy environment α has the structure

$$\alpha = (\Omega.NIL)$$

Execution continues

(NIL)	α	$(LDF\ c \ldots RAP)$	NIL
$((c.\alpha)NIL)$	α	$(CONS \ldots RAP)$	NIL
$(((c.\alpha)))$	α	$(LDF\ (LDC\ NIL \ldots RTN)\ RAP)$	NIL
$(((LDC\ NIL\ldots RTN).\alpha)((c.\alpha)))$	α	(RAP)	NIL

Now we have on the top of the stack a closure for the qualified expression in the block. Below it is a list of the values defined in this block, in this case just one value, a closure representing the function FAC. Both closures contain the dummy environment. Now when we apply RAP, this dummy environment gets updated so that its *car* contains the list of defined values That is, the machine goes into the state

$$NIL \quad \alpha \quad (LDC\ NIL \ldots RTN) \quad (NIL\ NIL\ NIL.NIL)$$

where now, because of the *rplaca*, α satisfies

$$\alpha = (((c.\alpha)).NIL)$$

That is, α is an environment with only one value position (0.0) where the value $(c.\alpha)$ is stored. Hence, when we encounter LD (0.0) in the control list, the correct closure for FAC will be loaded, and when recursive calls are made from within the code list c, by LD (1.0), this closure will again be retrieved because α is correctly contained in the environment part of that closure.

   This concludes our description of the SECD machine instructions which are generated for each well-formed Lisp expression. In the next section we will show how a function can be written which takes as argument a well-formed expression and produces as its result the corresponding code list.

6.4 PROGRAMMING THE COMPILER

We wish to define a function *compile(e)* which, given a well-formed expression e, computes the code defined for e in the previous section. We could simply define a function which implements $*$ as defined in the previous section, say

$$comp1(e,n) = e*n$$

and then we would have

$$compile(e) = comp1(e,NIL)$$

However, such a function uses *append* a great deal, and we can avoid that by using an accumulating parameter c into which the code is collected. Thus we define $comp(e,n,c)$ in such a way that

$$comp(e,n,c) = e*n \mid c$$

That is, if $comp(e,n,c)$ is called with a well-formed expression e, a namelist n and a code list c, it generates a list containing the instructions for e with the instructions in c following them. We can then define

$$compile(e) \equiv comp(e,NIL,NIL)$$

The function *comp* is used in a particular way. For example, since

$$(ADD\ e_1\ e_2)*n = e_1*n \mid e_2*n \mid (ADD)$$

then, if e has the form $(ADD\ e_1\ e_2)$, the value of $comp(e,n,c)$ is

$$comp(e_1,n,comp(e_2,n,cons(ADD,c)))$$

Note how the instructions ADD and e_2*n and e_1*n are built up in front of the code list c. In order to define *comp* we make use of some subsidiary functions. First, the composite selectors

$$cadr(x) \equiv car(cdr(x)) \qquad\qquad caar(x) \equiv car(car(x))$$
$$cddr(x) \equiv cdr(cdr(x)) \qquad\qquad caddr(x) \equiv car(cdr(cdr(x)))$$
$$cdar(x) \equiv cdr(car(x)) \qquad\qquad cadddr(x) \equiv car(cdr(cdr(cdr(x))))$$

Then, we have functions which allow us to select from a list of definitions

$$((x_1.e_1) \ldots (x_k.e_k))$$

respectively the variables $(x_1 \ldots x_k)$ and the expressions $(e_1 \ldots e_k)$. We have

$$vars(d) \equiv \textbf{if}\ eq(d,NIL)\ \textbf{then}\ NIL\ \textbf{else}$$
$$cons(caar(d),vars(cdr(d)))$$

$$exprs(d) \equiv \textbf{if}\ eq(d,NIL)\ \textbf{then}\ NIL\ \textbf{else}$$
$$cons(cdar(d),exprs(cdr(d)))$$

These functions were used in the interpreter of Chapter 4. Finally, we use the function $complis(e,n,c)$ to compile a list of expressions $e = (e_1 \ldots e_k)$ and generate the code

$$(LDC\ NIL)\ |\ e_k*n\ |\ (CONS)\ |\ \ldots\ |\ e_1*n\ |\ (CONS)\ |\ c$$

As in the rest of this chapter, we continue to use symbolic atoms for the instructions of the SECD machine. When the compiler is put in input form (see Appendix 2) these will be replaced by the appropriate numeric instruction codes:

$$complis(e,n,c) \equiv \textbf{if } eq(e,NIL) \textbf{ then } cons(LDC,cons(NIL,c)) \textbf{ else}$$
$$complis(cdr(e),n,comp(car(e),n,cons(CONS,c)))$$

In terms of these subsidiary functions, the programming of the function *comp* is quite straightforward, as shown in (6.3)

$comp(e,n,c) \equiv$
    if $atom(e)$ **then** $cons(LD, cons\ (location(e,n),c))$ **else**
    if $eq(car(e),QUOTE)$ **then** $cons(LDC,\ cons(cadr(e),c))$ **else**
    if $eq(car(e),ADD)$ **then**
        $comp(cadr(e),n,\ comp(caddr(e),n,cons(ADD,c)))$ **else**
            ... similarly for $SUB,\ MUL,\ DIV,\ REM,\ EQ,\ LEQ,...$
    if $eq(car(e),CAR)$ **then**
        $comp(cadr(e),cons(CAR,c))$ **else**
            ... similarly for $CDR,\ ATOM,...$
    if $eq(car(e),CONS)$ **then**
        $comp(caddr(e),n,comp(cadr(e),n,cons(CONS,c)))$ **else**   (6.3)
    if $eq(car(e),IF)$ **then**
      $\{comp(cadr(e),n,cons(SEL,cons(thenpt,cons(elsept,c))))$
        where $thenpt = comp(caddr(e),n,(JOIN))$
          and $elsept = comp(cadddr(e),n,(JOIN))\}$ **else**
    if $eq(car(e),LAMBDA)$ **then**
      $\{cons\ (LDF,cons(body,\ c))$
        where $body = comp(caddr(e),cons(cadr(e),n),(RTN))\}$ **else**
    if $eq(car(e),LET)$ **then**
      $\{\{complis(args,n,cons(LDF,cons(body,cons(AP,c))))$
              where $body = comp(cadr(e),m,(RTN))\}$
        where $m = cons(vars(cddr(e)),n)$
          and $args = exprs(cddr(e))\}$ **else**

if *eq*(*car*(*e*), *LETREC*) **then**
  {{*cons*(*DUM*, *complis*(*args*,*m*,
    cons(*LDF*,*cons*(*body*,*cons*(*RAP*,*c*)))))
                where *body* = *comp*(*cadr*(*e*),*m*,(*RTN*))}
        where *m* = *cons*(*vars*(*cddr*(*e*)),*n*)
      and *args* = *exprs*(*cddr*(*e*))} **else**
complis(*cdr*(*e*),*n*,*comp*(*car*(*e*),*n*,*cons*(*AP*,*c*)))

The complete compiler can be defined as a single expression by writing it in the form

        compile
        whererec *compile* = λ(*e*) *comp*(*e*,*NIL*,(*AP STOP*))
        and *comp* = λ(*e*,*n*,*c*) . . .
        and *complis* = λ(*e*,*n*,*c*) . . .
        and *exprs* = λ(*d*) . . .
        and *vars* = λ(*d*) . . .
        and *location* = λ(*x*,*n*) . . .   etc.

The need for (*AP STOP*) is explained in the next section. Finally, this compiler can be transformed into input form according to the rules of Chapter 4. A compiler in this form appears in Appendix 2 and forms an essential part of the Lispkit system described in Chapters 11 and 12.

6.5 COMPLETING THE SEMANTIC DESCRIPTION

In the preceding sections of this chapter we have given a formal definition of an abstract machine, the SECD machine, and a function which compiles Lisp programs to run on that machine. We have defined exactly what value is yielded by any well-formed expression in the Lisp language. Hence we have given a formal description of the semantics of the language. The question arises, have we defined everything that we should have defined and have all the well-formed expressions been assigned the meaning we would wish them to have? The answer to both these questions is negative. In this section we will discuss the limitations of the definition given here and analyze the reasons why a stronger definition has not been given.

    Let us summarize what we have defined. The function *compile*(*e*) takes a well-formed expression *e*, that is a Lisp program in input form, and produces as result a list *c*. The expression *e* which is compiled by *compile*(*e*) is a function-valued expression and the form of *c* is

        (. . .*code to load closure for function*. . .*AP STOP*)

that is, code which when executed loads a closure on the stack and applies it. This code expects to find on the stack a suitable list of actual parameter values for the function e. Thus, if we start the SECD machine in the state

$$(v) \quad NIL \quad c \quad NIL$$

and allow it to operate by applying successive machine transitions, the effect will be to apply the function c to the values v and, because of the net-effect rule, to leave the result of this application on the stack. That is, the final state of the machine will be

$$(x) \quad NIL \quad (STOP) \quad NIL$$

and x is the result of the function application. For example, if we compile the append function as given in Section 6.1, we obtain code in the above form. If this code is loaded into a machine whose stack is

$$(((A \ B \ C \ D) \ (E \ F \ G \ H))),$$

the machine will execute and terminate with the stack

$$((A \ B \ C \ D \ E \ F \ G \ H))$$

This process of executing the compiled code can be encapsulated in the function $exec(c,v)$ in such a way that c and v are used to construct the initial machine state, as defined above, and the result of the function is given by the top stack value after execution terminates. That is,

$$exec(c,v) = x$$

With this, we can define the semantics of any well-formed Lisp program. A Lisp program is a function. The result of applying this function f to the list of arguments a is the value

$$exec(compile(f),a)$$

as discussed in Section 6.1. In other words, if the SECD machine terminates and produces a value on top of the stack, that value is the result of the application of f to a.

There are some points which we must note in relation to this definition if we take it literally. In particular, as suggested in the opening paragraph of this section, we must investigate some of the more esoteric areas of this semantic definition. We shall only give examples here, rather than attempt a complete catalog of the good and bad points of this definition, the purpose being to illuminate rather than analyze the technique. We shall give examples of four specific points.

1. The definition is precise about important features of the language. For example, the parameter mechanism defined is what is usually referred to as *call-by-value*.
2. Many well-formed expressions are given a meaning where none is intended. For example, function calls with too many actual parameters.
3. Some well-formed expressions are not given a meaning where one is possible. For example, the partial definition of *LETREC*.
4. Some special cases of well-formed expressions, whose meaning we might not consider intuitive, are given a reasonable or acceptable meaning by this definition. For example, a function with no parameters.

Many other examples are of course possible under these four headings. The four we have chosen lead on to material in later chapters and of course there is an opportunity for the reader to investigate the definition further in the exercises at the end of the chapter.

Consider the definition given for function call:

$$(e\ e_1 \ldots e_k)*n = (LDC\ NIL) \mid e_k*n \mid (CONS) \mid \ldots$$
$$\mid e_1*n \mid (CONS) \mid e*n \mid (AP)$$

Each of the actual parameters $e_1, \ldots, e_k$ is evaluated before entry to the function. The formal parameters of the function behave as local variables whose values are the values of the corresponding actual parameters. This is the mechanism in Algol which is termed *call-by-value*. The use of "call by" here is unfortunate, but traditional. It is used to refer to the method in which actual parameters are passed to a function or procedure. The phrase "pass-by" would be better, but here we continue with conventional usage. Call-by-value can be contrasted to an alternative method, *call-by-name*. In call-by-name the actual parameter expression is considered to be substituted for the formal parameter. There is a problem here with free variables in the actual parameter expression, in that the context in which the function body needs to be evaluated may not contain values for these variables, or even worse, may contain values for local variables with the same names, a so-called *name clash*. We shall not consider that problem.

The classic example of the difference in meaning between call-by-value and call-by-name is the following function definition:

$$badif\ (a,b,c) \equiv \textbf{if } a \textbf{ then } b \textbf{ else } c$$

Consider the calls

$$badif(atom(x),x,car(x))$$
$$badif(eq(y,0),1,100 \div y)$$

If these were interpreted by Lispkit according to the semantics given here, each of the actual parameters of *badif* would be evaluated before entry to the function. Thus, if *x* were an atom, we should attempt to take its *car* with undefined results. Similarly, even when *y* is *zero*, we shall attempt to compute $100 \div y$ with a similar undefined result. However, if call-by-name were used, because of the substitution of the unevaluated actual parameter expression for the corresponding formal parameter, the two function calls would have the same values as the expressions

if *atom(x)* **then** *x* **else** *car(x)*
if *eq(y,0)* **then** 1 **else** $100 \div y$

both of which are perfectly well defined. There is, however, no failure of the definition here. The mechanism which has been defined is call-by-value and that is the mechanism which was intended. For functional programming, the call-by-value mechanism is by far the most useful and generally used. We shall, however, return to parameter mechanisms in Chapter 8 where more powerful, if less generally useful, mechanisms will be discussed.

A serious failing of our definition is its indifference to erroneous Lispkit programs. There are many cases in which a check, either in the compiler or in the SECD machine, could make undefined a case where no meaning was intended. Our only reason for omitting such checks was to shorten the definition. The consequence is that we have given meanings to some very unusual constructions. For example, the following expression has value *A*:

$$(LET\ (FN\ (QUOTE\ A)\ (QUOTE\ B))$$
$$(FN\ LAMBDA\ (X)\ X))$$

An extra actual parameter has been supplied to the (identity) function *FN* and will go completely undetected. Throughout this definition and the eventual implementation of Lispkit, we shall take a completely cavalier approach to erroneous programs. While recognizing that this is an important issue—since the user of a system should be able to expect that system to take a sensible approach and to detect errors when it can—we nevertheless concentrate on the issue of giving correct meanings to valid expressions, and largely ignore the meanings of invalid ones.

The definition of *LETREC* is partial. Since the code given for the compilation of $(LETREC\ e\ (x_1.e_1)...(x_k.e_k))$ evaluates each of the defining expressions $e_1,...,e_k$ in the dummy environment $(\Omega.—)$, any defining expression which, on evaluation, accesses any of $x_1,...,x_k$ will cause an error. This is because, until Ω has been replaced, LD $(0.i)$ cannot be executed. Hence, the only valid forms for the $e_1,...,e_k$ are those that mention the $x_1,...,x_k$ inside a lambda expression, which is not entered until after the qualified expression has begun evaluation. Thus, simple cases like

> (LETREC Y
>   (Y CAR X)
>   (X QUOTE (A B C D))

yield undefined results. A simple rule, which hardly restricts Lispkit Lisp and guarantees that all *LETREC* blocks at least begin evaluation of their qualified expression, is that every defining expression should be a lambda expression. That is, all local variables introduced by a *LETREC* block should have function values. For this restricted form of Lispkit our semantic definition is correct. Consider, however, the block

> (LETREC ————————
>   (B APPEND (QUOTE (1 2 3)) B))

That is, we want to create an environment in which the variable B is bound to the circular list shown in Fig. 6.2. It seems a shame that *LETREC* will not

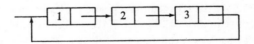

Fig. 6.2

implement this correctly. We shall consider later how to enhance Lisp so that this is possible.

    To end on a happier note, we consider those cases where our definition yields a meaning for an expression which we not only consider sensible but will find useful. Consider the case of a function with no parameters. The syntax of the language allows us to write such a thing. For example

> (LET ————————
>   (FN LAMBDA NIL ————————))

is perfectly acceptable, and calls of *FN* inside the qualified expression are accomplished by

(*FN*)

which is also syntactically acceptable. When we consider the code which is compiled and its execution, we see that when the function is called, an appropriately empty list of actual parameter values is established in the environment and then, when the body is evaluated, the global variables are correctly accessed in positions (*i.i*), where $i \geqslant 1$. Although a function with no parameters may not seem very useful, we can use it on occasion to delay evaluation of an expression, when evaluation may be costly but unnecessary. This is again a feature to which we shall return both in the exercises and in a later chapter. As a simple example of another way of using a function with no parameters, suppose we required Lispkit to evaluate an expression *e* for us, and that this expression were not in the form of a function: then we could instead compile

(*LAMBDA NIL e*)

and the compiled code would operate correctly if supplied with the actual parameter list *NIL*. That is, the value of the expression *e* is given by

exec(*compile*((*LAMBDA NIL e*)),*NIL*)

The most important feature of the definition of Lisp given in this chapter is that it forms a very precise specification of any implementation made to support Lispkit. Indeed, the implementation given in Chapter 11 faithfully reproduces the semantics defined here. Of course, the particular form of this definition has been made with that objective in mind, and in fact is already an abstract version of an implementation. For this reason a description such as this one is said to be *operational*. A more mathematical definition, in which the meaning of each Lisp expression is some mathematically more respectable object than an SECD machine-language program, might have the advantage of being simpler or more intuitive. It would certainly have the property of being a sounder basis upon which to base proofs of correctness, either of Lisp programs or of a Lispkit implementation. It would probably lead to certain insights which the details of this definition have masked from us. However, the overriding benefit afforded by this definition is that it has resolved many design issues with respect to Lisp implementation, and this outweighs the advantages of a more mathematical definition for our eventual purposes. The definition appeals to the intuition of a computer scientist precisely because it is operational, whereas a mathematician might well find another type of definition more intuitive.

EXERCISES

6.1 Design a machine instruction $AP0$ which applies a function of no arguments. It expects only a closure on the stack. Show that (code to load closure $AP0$) has the same effect as (LDC NIL code to load closure AP).

6.2 Design a machine instruction $AP1$ which applies a function of a single argument. It expects the closure and the argument to appear, but the argument has not been built into a one-element list. What is an equivalent sequence to

(code to load argument   code to load closure $AP1$)

using the AP instruction?

6.3 Design a machine in which the roles of the stack and the dump are combined, using only a single register t. The design of this machine constitutes a proof that the stack and the dump behave in a synchronized fashion that allows them to be implemented as a single stack. The design requires that you implement the same instructions as are available for the SECD machine.

6.4 Suppose that the instructions $AP0$ and $AP1$ defined in Exercises 6.1 and 6.2 are available. Define the code lists produced for the special cases of calling functions with zero and one argument, using these instructions.

6.5 Extend Lisp to include the well-formed expression ($CAND$ e_1 e_2) with the property that its value is the logical "and" of e_1 and e_2, that is T only if both e_1 and e_2 are T, but with the property that if e_1 is F then e_2 is never evaluated. What code would be generated for this expression? That is, what is ($CAND$ e_1 e_2)$*n$? Similarly, define the code for (COR e_1 e_2) which is F only if both e_1 and e_2 are F and is such that e_2 is not evaluated if e_1 is T (cf. Exercise 5.4).

6.6 How is the instruction sequence AP RTN sometimes generated? Why is it redundant? Design an instruction to replace it. When could such an instruction be generated?

6.7 Suppose we extend Lispkit Lisp to include the construction ($LABEL$ x e) which has the same meaning as ($LETREC$ x ($x.e$)), where x is a variable and e a well-formed expression. Determine ($LABEL$ x e) $*n$ and the net effect of executing that code on the SECD machine.

6.8 Call-by-name can be simulated in Lisp by making parameters which require this mechanism into functions and calling them each time they are required in the function body. That is, the evaluation of the actual parameter is delayed by wrapping it in a lambda expression. Show that $badif$ can be redefined to give a function $goodif(a,b,c)$, such that calls similar to those given in this section have values whenever they would have with a call-by-name parameter mechanism.

6.9 Consider the definition of factorial using *badif* as follows:

$$badfac(n) \equiv badif\,(n=0,\ 1,\ n \times badfac(n-1))$$

What is wrong with it? Why will it not produce the factorial values we expect?

6.10 Define a factorial function *goodfac(n)* which uses *goodif* from Exercise 6.8 in just the way that *badfac* uses *badif* in Exercise 6.9. Consider how the value of factorial 6 is arrived at by the *SECD* machine interpreting *goodfac(6)*. How many times is the *SUB* operator, compiled from the expression $n-1$, executed?

7 NON-DETERMINISTIC PRIMITIVES AND BACKTRACK PROGRAMS

In this chapter we begin a study, continued in the next two chapters, which leads us to discover more expressive forms for certain types of program. That is to say, we will define new primitives for our purely functional language, or new methods of using existing primitives, such that programs which would otherwise be long and difficult to understand become shorter and relatively easy to understand. The intention is to demonstrate that the definition of suitable primitive operations can greatly simplify problems in particular areas of application of computers. However, we shall also illustrate the power of the operational definition given in Chapter 6, to define precise semantics for these small extensions. That is to say, we will give corresponding extensions to the SECD machine which make precise and intuitive the meanings of each of the new primitives added to our purely functional language.

7.1 NON-DETERMINISTIC PRIMITIVES

Consider the problem of inserting an item into a list. If the list is of length n, then there are $n+1$ different positions in which we can insert the item. Suppose we wish to define a function which, given an item and a list, inserts the item into an arbitrary position and returns the resulting list. We would be quite satisfied whichever of the $n+1$ possible results was returned. Such a function—call it $insert(x,a)$, where x is the item and a is the list—is easily defined. If $a = NIL$, then the only possible result is $cons(x,NIL)$. However, if $a \neq NIL$, then we can return either $cons(x,a)$ or $cons(car(a),insert(x,cdr(a)))$. That is to say, we can either place x in the first position, or we can use $insert$ recursively to place x arbitrarily in the list $cdr(a)$ and then replace $car(a)$. In order to write such a function definition, however, we need to be able to denote the arbitrary choice which can be made between these two alternatives. If we denote by

$$e_1 \text{ or } e_2$$

a well-formed expression whose result is either the value of e_1 or the value of e_2, but we cannot say which, then the definition of *insert*(x,a) may be written

$$insert(x,a) \equiv \text{if } eq(a,NIL) \text{ then } cons(x,NIL) \text{ else}$$
$$\{cons(x,a) \text{ or } cons(car(a),insert(x,cdr(a)))\}$$

To illustrate the use of such a function consider how an arbitrary permutation of a list might be generated. The following function will, when called, return a permutation of the list given to it as argument.

$$perm(b) \equiv \text{if } eq(b,NIL) \text{ then } NIL \text{ else}$$
$$insert(car(b),perm(cdr(b)))$$

Clearly, if b is an empty list, then the only possible permutation is the empty list. When b is not empty, we generate an arbitrary permutation of *cdr*(b) and then insert *car*(b) into an arbitrary place in that permutation.

A similar example is the following function, which yields an arbitrary integer result in the range 1 to n.

$$choice(n) \equiv \text{if } n = 1 \text{ then } 1 \text{ else}$$
$$\{choice\ (n-1) \text{ or } n\}$$

This rather simple function allows us to illustrate a particularly unpleasant feature which we have introduced by this extension of our purely functional language. The function *pair*(n) defined below generates an arbitrary pair of integers, by calling *choice*(n) twice:

$$pair(n) \equiv cons(choice(n),choice(n))$$

The question arises, are the values which are the respective components of this pair equal or not? Up till now, in our purely functional language, whenever we have had the same subexpression occurring twice in the same context we have been able to assume that it will yield the same value at each place. Thus we could extract it and make it the value of a locally defined variable without changing the meaning of the program as a whole. If we are to retain that property, we must ensure that both calls of *choice*(n) in the definition of *pair(n)* yield the same result. Then we could have written

$$pair(n) \equiv \{\textbf{let } x = choice(n)$$
$$cons(x,x)\}$$

as an alternative to the above definition. That is to say, *pair(n)* returns a pair of numbers, both of which are the same.

This question leads us to a dilemma. How can we define a function which returns an arbitrary pair of values, from the set of all n^2 possibilities? Well, of course, we could go back to first principles and define it directly in terms of **or**, for example:

$$pair(n) \equiv \textbf{if } n = 1 \textbf{ then } cons(1,1) \textbf{ else}$$
$$\{\textbf{let } p = pair(n-1)$$
$$p \textbf{ or } cons(car(p),n) \textbf{ or } cons(n,cdr(p)) \textbf{ or } cons(n,n)\}$$

This definition is unwieldy and far less satisfying than our original.

We have always assumed that substituting a defining expression (*e* in **let** $x = e\ e'$) for each occurrence of the variable (*x*) to which it is assigned will not alter the meaning of a program. If we are to retain this property of substitutivity then we must accept some such definition as this unwieldy second version of *pair(n)*. Rather than do that, for the remainder of this chapter we shall use an interpretation of

$$e_1 \textbf{ or } e_2$$

which is such that, whichever value is chosen is truly indeterminate in the sense that knowing the values of e_1 and e_2 is not sufficient to determine what the value of e_1 **or** e_2 will be, other than that it will be one of these values. This fact is of course the source of our dilemma. The value of an expression in our purely functional language has, until this point, always been determined only by the values of its constituent expressions. Now we depart from that property, but for this chapter alone. A useful way to think of the evaluation of e_1 **or** e_2 is that both e_1 and e_2 are evaluated and then a coin is tossed to decide which value to select. Thus, for example, the evaluation of

$$\{1 \textbf{ or } 2\} - \{1 \textbf{ or } 2\}$$

will require two tosses of the coin and there can be no guarantee that the result will be zero. The decision to choose this interpretation means that we lose the property of substitutivity for the entire extended language, for we can never be certain that any expression will not invoke the coin-tossing requirement. This is a severe loss, and we shall return, at the end of the chapter, to a discussion of whether the language extension justifies it.

Let us return to the problem of generating an arbitrary permutation. Suppose we wish to restrict the class of permutations we are prepared to accept. For example, we may wish only to accept the result returned by *perm(a)* if it satisfies some predicate *p*. We could write a function which tests *perm(a)* and if it does not satisfy *p*, calls *perm(a)* again in the hope that the coin tossing used to evaluate **or** may be more favorable. However, because of the arbitrary nature of this coin-tossing exercise, there can be no guarantee that a permutation satisfying *p* will ever be found by such a process. We must extend our functional language yet again to overcome this small difficulty.

We add to our functional language the well-formed expression

none

which has the following meaning. If, during evaluation of an entire program, there is a sequence of choices which avoids evaluation of all subexpressions of the form **none**, then such a sequence of choices will be made. That is to say, whilst the result of each toss of the coin required to determine the value of e_1 **or** e_2 is arbitrary, the net effect over the whole program will be such that the outcome of these tosses avoids the need to ever evaluate **none**. With this device we can write our function for restricted perms as follows:

$$restrictedperm(a) \equiv \textbf{let } b = perm(a)$$
$$\textbf{if } p(b) \textbf{ then } b \textbf{ else none}$$

This is a very unusual program. By our definition of **none**, we have that if there is a value of *perm(a)* which satisfies *p*, then such a value will be returned.

To better understand the use of **none** in conjunction with **or**, consider the following possible way of interpreting a program which uses them. Suppose that we have an abstract machine which is responsible for evaluating such a functional program. When this machine encounters e_1 **or** e_2, it generates a copy of itself with exactly the same state except that the first machine proceeds as if e_1 had been encountered and the second machine proceeds as if e_2 had been encountered. In this way, as the evaluation proceeds, the number of machines multiplies. If any machine should encounter **none** to be evaluated, then that machine is discarded, for the sequence of choices which led to its creation and its subsequent computation was not a satisfactory one. If any machine completes its evaluation, then that machine has determined a possible result for the whole program, and this can be taken as *the* result and all the other machines discarded. Of course it is entirely possible that no machine will ever terminate in this way, in which case the program is a meaningless one.

As a simple application of these non-deterministic primitives, consider the generation of permutations with the property that consecutive elements of the permutation satisfy the predicate $q(x,y)$. We could use the function *restrictedperm(a)* by defining the function $p(b)$ as in (7.1).

$$
\begin{aligned}
p(b) \equiv\ &\textbf{if } eq(b,NIL) \textbf{ then } T \textbf{ else}\\
&\textbf{if } eq(cdr(b),NIL) \textbf{ then } T \textbf{ else}\\
&\textbf{if } q(car(b),car(cdr(b))) \textbf{ then } p(cdr(b))\\
&\qquad\qquad \textbf{else } F
\end{aligned}
\tag{7.1}
$$

However, another way of doing it, which tests each consecutive pair of values as they are chosen, is illustrative of an important feature of the use of non-deterministic primitives, that **none** can be embedded arbitrarily deeply in the expression being evaluated. We redefine our functions as in (7.2).

$$
\begin{aligned}
restrictedperm(b) \equiv\ &\textbf{if } eq(b,NIL) \textbf{ then } NIL \textbf{ else}\\
&restrictedinsert(car(b),restrictedperm(cdr(b)))\\
restrictedinsert(x,a) \equiv\ &\textbf{if } eq(a,NIL) \textbf{ then } cons(x,NIL) \textbf{ else}\\
&\{build(x,a) \textbf{ or } build(car(a),restrictedinsert(x,cdr(a)))\}\\
build(x,y) \equiv\ &\textbf{if } q(x,car(y)) \textbf{ then } cons(x,y) \textbf{ else none}
\end{aligned}
\tag{7.2}
$$

Here we see that *restrictedperm(b)* and *restrictedinsert(x,a)* have the same form as our original *perm(b)* and *insert(x,a)*, except that they call *build(x,y)* rather than *cons(x,y)* to construct the permutation. Now *build(x,y)* can rely upon the fact that y will not be the empty list and thus simply determine that $q(x,car(y))$ is satisfied. If this condition is not satisfied, then **none** will be evaluated. Our rules for **or** and **none** are such that this eventuality will be avoided if this is possible, and thus a restricted permutation will be generated if one exists. The point to note in this example is that we can be nested quite deeply, in terms of recursive invocations of functions when **none** is encountered (thinking in terms of the interpretation by separate machines). The rules we have given of course allow this: indeed, it would be a fairly sterile extension if they did not. We must be careful when, in the next section, we come to give a precise specification of the meaning of **or** and **none**, to see that we take account of this possibility.

7.2 INTERPRETATION OF NON-DETERMINISTIC PRIMITIVES

We can give a very precise interpretation to the non-deterministic primitives described in the previous section, by embedding them in Lispkit Lisp and then extending the SECD machine so that it can execute the compiled programs. Let us choose the obvious syntactic forms for this extension of Lispkit Lisp; that is, the following now become well-formed expressions

$$(OR\ e_1\ e_2)$$
$$(NONE)$$

As usual, the subexpressions of the OR form are expected to be well-formed. Now, it is necessary to add two more instructions to the SECD machine which will be the machine-language counterparts of these two source-language forms. The two instructions are given the mnemonics SOR and NON, the S being used to suggest that the SOR operator is similar to SEL and to clearly distinguish the machine form (SOR) from the source form (OR).

As usual, the interpretation process is a two-stage one of giving rules for compiling the source language into SECD machine instructions and rules for the state transitions for these two new instructions. It will not be possible to explain clearly what is happening until both halves of this interpretation have been given. First, consider the rules of compilation

$$(OR\ e_1\ e_2)*n = (SOR\ \ e_1*n\ |\ (JOIN)\ \ e_2*n\ |\ (JOIN))$$
$$(NONE)*n = (NON)$$

Here we see that compilation of the well-formed expression $(OR\ e_1\ e_2)$ with respect to the namelist n generates a control list of the form $(SOR\ c_1\ c_2)$ where c_1 and c_2 are properly nested control lists, one for each of the possible choices. Each of these sublists is terminated by a $JOIN$ instruction; it is in this way that SOR resembles SEL. The compilation of the well-formed expression $(NONE)$ is trivial, generating a one-instruction control list containing the other new instruction.

The SECD machine must now be extended by the addition of a new register, which we call **r** and refer to as the resumption register. This register will be used, like the dump, to save entire machine states. In fact, the purpose which it serves is to save the state of the machine when a choice is made by the SOR instruction, in case this choice should lead to NON. When this happens the machine state can be restored from **r** and the other choice made by SOR. The addition of this new register does not affect the rules for the other machine instructions, except to note that they leave it unchanged.

Formally, where previously we had a rule of the form

$$s\ e\ c\ d \to s'\ e'\ c'\ d'$$

we must replace this by the rule

$$s\ e\ c\ d\ r \to s'\ e'\ c'\ d'\ r$$

to indicate that the value in r is left intact.

Now we may give the rules for our new instructions. First, consider SOR:

$$s\ e\ (SOR\ c_1\ c_2.c)\ d\ r \to s\ e\ c_1\ (c.d)\ (s\ e\ c_2\ (c.d).r)$$

When SOR is encountered in a well-formed SECD machine-language program, the structure of the entire control list is $(SOR\ c_1\ c_2.c)$. That is, SOR has as operands two control lists c_1 and c_2 and the remainder of the program is represented by c. If we were to make an arbitrary choice between c_1 and c_2 and then continue, then we would set the s,e,c and d registers to one of the states

$$s\ e\ c_1\ (c.d)$$

or

$$s\ e\ c_2\ (c.d)$$

We have so contrived it that c_1 and c_2 both end in a $JOIN$ instruction, and thus by pushing c onto the front of the dump, when this $JOIN$ is encountered, execution will continue with c, as required. Now, since we cannot be certain that the choice of c_1 will not lead to NON, we must save the state which includes c_2, in order that we can resume that execution if NON is indeed encountered. Thus SOR establishes the machine state

$$s\ e\ c_1\ (c.d)\ (s\ e\ c_2\ (c.d).r)$$

which implies that it will continue with c_1 but could, if necessary, restore the machine to the same state and then choose c_2.

If all the choices made in this way eventually lead to execution of the $STOP$ instruction, then the machine halts with its result on top of the stack. We must consider what the machine does if it reaches instead a NON instruction. On encountering a NON instruction it will normally be the case that there is a previously stored state waiting in the resumption list. In this case we have the transition

$$s \ e \ (NON) \ d \ (s' \ e' \ c' \ d'.r) \rightarrow s' \ e' \ c' \ d' \ r$$

This indicates that the entire state of the **s**, **e**, **c** and **d** registers is discarded when *NON* is encountered. The values s', e', c' and d' which are reinstated from **r** will have been put there by a *SOR* instruction and thus represent a previously achieved state of the machine with an alternative control list. When a *NON* instruction is encountered and the resumption **r** is empty, then the machine stops with no result. We indicate this fact by the transition

$$s \ e \ (NON) \ d \ NIL \rightarrow NIL \ e \ (NON) \ d \ NIL$$

which is similar to the transition for *STOP*, except that it discards the stack.

Consider now the way in which the extended SECD machine interprets the well-formed expression $(OR \ e_1 \ e_2)$. Its behavior is based on the process described in the previous section, that of generating separate abstract machines to execute each possibility, and stopping when one of them reaches a successful conclusion. However, the extended SECD machine will actually simulate the execution of these abstract machines in a specific order, and we shall see later that that is a restriction on the meaning of our non-deterministic primitives. In evaluating $(OR \ e_1 \ e_2)$ the SECD machine behaves as if e_1 had been encountered in place of $(OR \ e_1 \ e_2)$. If this leads to a successful termination of the program then that is the end of the story. If, however, this choice of e_1 leads to an evaluation of $(NONE)$, then the behavior of the SECD machine is as if e_1 had not been chosen and e_2 had been chosen instead. Of course, this may in turn lead to an evaluation of (NON) and the program may as a consequence yield no result.

The difference between the actual behavior of the SECD machine described in this section and that of the multiplicity of abstract machines described in the previous section arises when we consider non-terminating programs. If a non-deterministic program is such that a certain $(OR \ e_1 \ e_2)$ occurring in it has the property that the choice of e_1 will lead to an infinite execution of the SECD machine, then the rules given here will lead to non-termination. It may well be that the choice of e_2 would have yielded a satisfactory result. Had we been able to follow the rules of the previous section and generate separate machines, one with e_1, the other with e_2 in place of $(OR \ e_1 \ e_2)$, then the machine with e_2 would have halted and the machine with e_1 would have been discarded. Giving a set of rules which implement this wider interpretation is not difficult, but it is a lengthy process and so has been left as an exercise for the reader (Exercise 7.8).

7.3 BACKTRACK PROGRAMS

The process described in the previous section, of saving the state of an entire computation, when a choice has to be made, in order that it can be restored when it is subsequently found that that choice was made incorrectly, is a well-known programming technique called *backtrack programming*. It is usually used to program searches. The non-deterministic primitives which were introduced in Section 7.1 provide a particularly natural way of writing backtrack programs. In this section we shall illustrate this by tackling a typical problem for the technique of backtrack programming. This problem is a very famous one, known as the problem of the eight queens. In chess, queens attack each other in any direction along the rows, columns or diagonals of a chessboard. The problem is to determine whether there is a placement of 8 queens on an 8×8 chessboard such that no two queens are attacking each other. It turns out that there are 12 different solutions (excluding symmetric solutions obtained by rotating or flipping the board) so our search will not be a barren one. Since it does not add to the difficulty, we shall in fact solve the problem for n queens on an n by n board. The solution we will give is a version of what one might call the standard solution in that it is well known to many people and will usually be discovered by any programmer who tackles the problem. It does not require much explanation.

First we consider that the rows and columns of the chessboard are numbered 1 to n. Then we note that the sum of the row and column numbers is constant down the NE–SW diagonals and the difference of the row and column numbers is constant down the NW–SE diagonals. This is shown in Fig. 7.1 for the case $n = 5$. This fact gives us a simple method of determining

	1	2	3	4	5
1	2	3	4	5	6
2	3	4	5	6	7
3	4	5	6	7	8
4	5	6	7	8	9
5	6	7	8	9	10

row + column

	1	2	3	4	5
1	0	−1	−2	−3	−4
2	1	0	−1	−2	−3
3	2	1	0	−1	−2
4	3	2	1	0	−1
5	4	3	2	1	0

row − column

Fig. 7.1

whether two squares are on the same diagonal. We can represent the placement of queens on the chessboard by a list of pairs of numbers, where each pair is a row number and a column number. Thus the partial placement shown in Fig 7.2 is represented by the list

$$((1.2) \; (2.4) \; (3.1) \; (4.3))$$

Of course, the order in which the pairs occur in this list is immaterial.

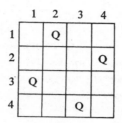

Fig. 7.2

With such a representation we can easily define a predicate *attacks* $(i, j, place)$ which is true only if the square whose row number is i and whose column number is j, is attacked by the queens in the placement *place*. This predicate is as shown in (7.3).

> $attacks(i, j, place) \equiv$
>   **if** $eq(place, NIL)$ **then** F **else**
>   {**let** $i' = car(car(place))$
>   **and** $j' = cdr(car(place))$ (7.3)
>   **if** $i = i'$ **then** T **else**
>   **if** $j = j'$ **then** T **else**
>   **if** $i+j = i'+j'$ **then** T **else**
>   **if** $i-j = i'-j'$ **then** T **else** $attacks(i, j, cdr(place))$}

Here we see that, if the placement is empty, then the i, j square is not attacked. Otherwise we inspect the first queen (on i', j') given in the placement. If it is in the same row, column, NE–SW diagonal or NW–SE diagonal, then $attacks(i, i, place)$ returns T. If it is not attacked by the first queen then we call $attacks(i, i, cdr(place))$ to inspect the remaining queens.

Now we can define a function $addqueen(i, n, place)$ which, given a placement of $i-1$ queens on an $n \times n$ board, attempts to add a queen in the ith row. We do this in a very simple manner. First we choose an arbitrary column position for the queen in the ith row, using the function $choice(n)$

defined in Section 7.1. If the queens already on the board attack this square, then we must use **none** to indicate that at least one of the choices which led to this selection was incorrect. If the square is not attacked, we place a queen on it and, unless we are in the final (*n*th) row, we proceed to add a queen in the next row. This function is therefore defined as in (7.4).

$$addqueen(i,n,place) \equiv$$
$$\{\textbf{let } j = choice(n)$$
$$\textbf{if } attacks(i,j,place) \textbf{ then none else}$$
$$\{\textbf{if } i = n \textbf{ then } newplace \textbf{ else} \qquad\qquad (7.4)$$
$$addqueen(i+1,n,newplace)$$
$$\textbf{where } newplace = cons(cons(i,j),place)\}\}$$

Consider the definition of *choice(n)*.

$$choice(n) \equiv \textbf{if } n = 1 \textbf{ then } 1 \textbf{ else}$$
$$\{choice(n-1) \textbf{ or } n\}$$

This is the place in this program where non-determinism is introduced. We see that any choice of the integers 1 to *n* is possible and thus, if there is a solution to the $n \times n$ problem, one will be found by this program, according to the rules we have given for our primitives. The program can be completed by the addition of the principal function

$$queensoln(n) \equiv addqueen(1,n,NIL)$$

which simply begins the search with an empty placement by attempting to add a queen to the first row. Hence the call *queensoln(8)* will return a solution to the 8×8 problem.

Now this program which we have written is a fairly natural one. One may almost say it is *the* natural program. Insofar as our functional language is capable of it, we have expressed the algorithm very directly. The algorithm is simple enough, it is to place one queen in each row, for each of the *n* rows in turn, so that no two queens attack each other. Of course, arbitrary choices for the positions of each queen will in general not be satisfactory. The program invokes a systematic process of searching for a suitable placement by what is called a backtracking procedure. The SECD machine performs the backtracking in a simple and obvious way. A new queen is placed on the board in positions where it is not attacked by queens already on the board. If it is found to be impossible to so place a queen, then an earlier placement of a queen is revoked and that queen and all subsequent queens replaced. If you consider the way we have described the interpretation of **or** by the SECD machine you will see that if the particular value returned by *choice(n)* is *j* and this leads to **none**, then *j*+1 will be chosen. Thus, when a series of placements of queens can lead to no solution, the most recently placed queen which can be moved to the right is so moved, and then the placement of all subsequent queens is recomputed. The question arises, is the program as we have it a simpler description of this process than could be obtained using the purely functional language without the addition of non-deterministic primitives? To answer that question we must construct such a program.

This program will explicitly encode the backtracking search. It is only one of many possible ways of encoding that search, but is (the author believes) as simple as any of those other programs. First, we note that it is *addqueen(i,n,place)* which must be replaced, since this function invokes the use of the non-deterministic primitives. We shall in fact redefine this without using those primitives and leave the remainder of the program intact. The function

$$tryqueen(i,j,n,place) \equiv$$
$$\textbf{if } attacks(i,j,place) \textbf{ then } NIL \textbf{ else}$$
$$\{\textbf{if } i=n \textbf{ then } newplace \textbf{ else } addqueen(i+1,n,newplace)$$
$$\textbf{where } newplace = cons(cons(i,i),place)\}$$

differs from the definition of *addqueen(i,n,place)* only in two respects. Firstly, whereas *addqueen* selects a value for *j* internally, *tryqueen* expects to receive it as a parameter. Secondly, whereas *addqueen* invokes **none** when no solution is possible, *tryqueen* returns *NIL*. Now, this function will only try one position in the *i*th row and so we need a function which will try each in turn. The function *anyqueen(i, j,n,place)* does just that.

$$anyqueen(i,j,n,place) \equiv$$
$$\{\textbf{let } newplace = tryqueen(i,j,n,place)$$
$$\textbf{if } newplace \neq NIL \textbf{ then } newplace \textbf{ else}$$
$$\textbf{if } j=n \textbf{ then } NIL \textbf{ else } anyqueen(i, j+1,n,place)\}$$

Here we see that the *j*th position is tried. If no solution is obtained, indicated by *NIL* being returned by *tryqueen*, then we must consider whether the *j*+1st position is possible. If *j*=*n*, we cannot use this position and so *anyqueen* returns *NIL* to indicate that fact, otherwise it calls itself recursively to try position *j*+1. Now, with this definition we can very simply redefine *addqueen(i,n,place)* as follows:

$$addqueen(i,n,place) \equiv anyqueen(i,1,n,place)$$

That is to say, we can add a queen in the ith row by trying each of the positions from 1 to n. Note that the call of *addqueen* from within *tryqueen* makes these three functions mutually recursive. A consideration of their behavior will persuade the reader that they explicitly encode the process of backtracking described at the end of the previous paragraph.

There are other ways in which the backtrack process could be programmed. Common ways are to use functions which return sets of results or to recover previous states from the data structure representing the placement of queens. An interesting alternative to our program arises because it is possible to abstract from it a general-purpose function (which could be used for other problems). This function is used simply to try each of a sequence of values between j and n as arguments for a function f, until a non-*NIL* result is obtained, if possible.

$$any(j,n,f) \equiv$$
$$\{\textbf{let } s = f(j)$$
$$\textbf{if } s \neq NIL \textbf{ then } s \textbf{ else}$$
$$\textbf{if } j = n \textbf{ then } NIL \textbf{ else } any(j+1,n,f)\}$$

Now, using this *anyqueen(i,j,n,place)* can be redefined:

$$anyqueen(i,j,n,place) \equiv any(j,n,\lambda(j)tryqueen(i,j,n,place))$$

The original non-deterministic form is more strictly comparable with this form, $any(j,n,f)$ corresponding closely to *choice(n)*.

Comparison of the two types of program, with and without non-deterministic primitives, is of course a matter of subjective judgement and the reader must come to his own decision. The fact is that the non-deterministic form avoids one level of recursive definition as is illustrated by

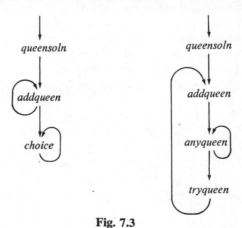

Fig. 7.3

the call diagrams shown in Fig. 7.3. However, if one considers $any(j,n,f)$ as being given and comparable (in difficulty of understanding) with $choice(n)$, this argument all but disappears, for one would write the call diagram as in Fig. 7.4.

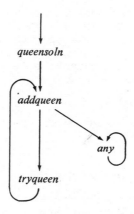

Fig. 7.4

Of course, the problem of the 8 queens is a very simple one as far as backtrack programming is concerned. In this case there is only one source of non-determinism, in the definition of $choice(n)$. In more complex problems, where the non-determinism is introduced in many places, the direct formulation in terms of non-deterministic primitives will have a substantial advantage over the explicit programming of backtracking. The advantage derives from the ability to think in terms of arbitrary choice but to know that the most advantageous choice will be made. This is a powerful paradigm and one which is easily forgotten when one has to program the necessary searches oneself.

The price we pay for this greater expressive power is, as we discussed in the first section of this chapter, the important property of substitutivity. Since expressions in the functional language may now invoke arbitrary choice we can, for example, no longer be certain that some such expression as $f(x)-f(x)$ will be zero. Thus, reasoning about such programs requires a different set of premises from those used for purely deterministic programs. Whether this price is too great, and that the apparently simpler expression of algorithms is in fact just an illusion which may trap us into false reasoning and then incorrect designs, can only be judged in the light of the reader's own experience.

EXERCISES

7.1   Define a function *monotonic*(x) which is true only if the list of integers x is an increasing sequence. Now, define a function which generates an arbitrary monotonic permutation.

7.2   Define a function *tree*(x) which takes as argument a list of atoms. Its result will be an arbitrary binary tree with the atoms of x occurring as the leaves of the tree and each atom occurring exactly once. Recall that a binary tree can be represented by an *atom* or a *cons* of two binary trees. The leaves of the tree should occur (left to right) in the order in which the atoms are listed in x. Hence, *flatten* (*tree*(x)) = x where *flatten* is as defined in Exercise 2.14.

7.3   Show that

$$(e_1 \text{ or none}) \text{ or } (\text{none or } e_2)$$

is the same as

$$e_1 \text{ or } e_2$$

(*Hint:* consider the generation of abstract machines.)

7.4   Define a function *subset*(x) which takes as argument a list of atoms representing a set (that is, there are no repetitions and the order of occurrence of the atoms is immaterial) and generates an arbitrary subset of x.

7.5   Extend the interpreter of Chapter 4 to give the same meaning to ($OR\ e_1\ e_2$) and (*NONE*) as we have given in this section. This can be done in two ways and both should be attempted. Either you can assume that the language in which the interpreter is written already has **or** and **none** or you can assume that it has neither.

7.6   In this section the rules given for *SOR* and *NON* are such that as soon as *STOP* is encountered the machine stops and thus presents the result at the top of its stack. It would be possible, by giving a new rule for *STOP*, to continue with the remaining states of the resumption list and thus to generate *all* results possible for the non-deterministic program. Give such a rule for *STOP*, presuming that there is some way of dumping each result as it is found.

7.7   The interpretation we have given to programs which use **or** and **none** is that some choice will be made at each evaluation of **or** such that, if possible, no **none** will ever be evaluated. An expression e whose evaluation requires such choices can be considered to have a set of possible values, all those values for which suitable determination of the choices in evaluating e avoids evaluation of **none**. For example,

$$1 \text{ or } 2 \text{ or } 3 \text{ or } 4$$

in an expression whose value is a member of the set $\{1,2,3,4\}$. Suppose we further extend our functional language so that **all** e is a well-formed expression whose value is the set of all values which e could yield by this means. Give a corresponding extension of Lispkit Lisp, rules for its compilation, and relevant extensions to the SECD machine to precisely define this concept. What is the value of

all *perm*(b)

where *perm*(b) is as defined at the beginning of Section 7.1?

7.8 In order to be able to generate a result for a non-deterministic program where some choices might lead to non-termination, we require to *implement* the notion of a multiplicity of machines. An example of a functional program with termination problems is the following definition of factorial:

$$fac(n) \equiv (fac(n-1)*n) \text{ or (if } n=0 \text{ then 1 else none)}$$

There is a sequence of choices in the above program which leads to the factorial result, all other choices either leading to **none** or to non-termination. To make an implementation of the notion of multiplicity of machines, it is necessary only to construct a list of SECD machines. Each machine on the list is advanced by one instruction in turn. *SOR* leads to extension of the list by one new machine, *NON* leads to its diminution by one machine. Make a formulation of the SECD machine which works in this way.

7.9 Design a function *restrictedperms(a)* with the same specification as the function of that name given in Section 7.1, but avoiding the use of **or** and **none** by programming the backtrack process explicitly.

7.10 Design a function *allperms(a)* which generates the set of all permutations of the elements in the list *a*. Compare this function with the non-deterministic program which generates an arbitrary permutation.

7.11 Design a function *syllables(w)* which takes as argument a list of letters *w*, representing an English word, and generates an arbitrary syllable structure for that word, according to the following rules. If *c* represents a sequence of consonants and *v* a sequence of vowels, then syllables of the following structure only are acceptable: *cv, vc, cvc*.

8

DELAYED EVALUATION—A FUNCTIONAL APPROACH TO PARALLELISM

This chapter is devoted to the study of a small extension to our purely functional language which helps expose some of the inherently parallel nature of such languages. We extend the language to allow expression evaluation to be explicitly delayed. Expressions so delayed yield values which must be explicitly forced to complete their evaluation. This facility leads, as we shall see, to a mode of function evaluation which is such that each function executes a little and is then delayed whilst another executes a little. Eventually each function is resumed and execution proceeds in a quasi-parallel interleaving of the function bodies. In fact, the language extension which is introduced in this chapter is a functional equivalent of the notion of a coroutine. As we did with the non-deterministic primitives we will give a precise meaning to our extension by extending the operational definition of the SECD machine.

With delayed evaluation it is possible to write functional programs which process infinite structures, in particular infinite lists, just as long as we are careful to explore only a finite part of them. Most of the examples in this chapter are designed to illustrate this phenomenon and show that it is often simpler than processing the corresponding finite structure. By delaying almost every expression in a program and driving execution by repeatedly forcing the unevaluated result to resume evaluation, we develop a mode of interpretation of functional languages which is called *lazy evaluation*. We show that many otherwise difficult programming problems are simply solved when lazy evaluation is used. In particular we show that lazy evaluation gives a more general, and generally more acceptable, interpretation to **letrec.** Finally, we tackle some interesting computational problems, in particular the generation of the sequence of all primes. In so doing we introduce a notation for networks of processes which clearly illustrates the relationship between delayed evaluation and processes which execute in parallel.

8.1 DELAYED EVALUATION

Consider the simple program (8.1).

$$sumints(n) \equiv sum(integersbetween(1,n))$$
$$sum(x) \equiv \textbf{if } eq(x,NIL) \textbf{ then } 0 \textbf{ else}$$
$$car(x)+sum(cdr(x)) \qquad\qquad (8.1)$$
$$integersbetween(m,n) \equiv \textbf{if } m > n \textbf{ then } NIL \textbf{ else}$$
$$cons(m,integersbetween(m+1,n))$$

The call *sumints(n)* computes $1+2+\ldots+n$, the sum of the first *n* natural numbers, by using subsidiary functions to construct a list of these numbers and to sum a list of numbers. Ordinarily we think of the behavior of this program as being to construct the entire list $(1\ 2\ 3 \ldots n)$, and then to apply *sum(x)* to it. We could however conceive the computation taking place in a different way, so that the function *integersbetween(m,n)* constructs only part of the intermediate list of numbers which is then consumed by the function *sum(x)*. This is possible because of the fact that *integersbetween(m,n)* produces the list elements exactly in the order in which *sum(x)* requires them. The computation might proceed as follows. The initial call of *sumints(n)* causes *integersbetween(1,n)* to be called. Assuming $n \geqslant 1$, the function *integersbetween* can construct *cons(1,integersbetween(2,n))* as its result. By delaying the evaluation of *integersbetween(2,n)* this value can be returned immediately as the result of *integersbetween(1,n)*. It is then taken as argument to *sum(x)* and, since it is not *NIL*, is used to evaluate $car(x)+sum(cdr(x))$, yielding

$$1+sum(integersbetween(2,n))$$

This requires that the delayed evaluation of *integersbetween(2,n)* be resumed, but as we can foresee, this will simply result in *integersbetween(3,n)* being delayed until it is necessary to evaluate

$$1+2+sum(integersbetween(3,n))$$

and so the computation proceeds. It is not necessary for us to consider the intermediate list of numbers as ever actually existing as a whole at any stage of the computation.

The process of delaying evaluation is most easily explained if we make it explicit. That is to say, by introducing new operators into our purely functional language, which allow the explicit delaying and resumption of expression evaluation. If *e* is a well-formed expression, then **delay** *e* is also a well-formed expression. The value of **delay** e is a closure-like object which we shall call a *recipe*. It incorporates in some way the unevaluated expression e and the environment required for its evaluation. If e' is a well-formed expression then **force** e' is also a well-formed expression. The value of e' must be a recipe, in which case the value of **force** e' is that value obtained by evaluating the expression encapsulated by the recipe. Thus, for all well-formed expressions e, **force**(**delay** e) always has the same value as e. Here is a simple example:

$$adjust(a,b) \equiv \textbf{if } a < 0 \textbf{ then } a \textbf{ else } a + \textbf{force } b$$

This simple function expects its second argument b to be delayed. Thus we use some such call as

$$adjust(g(x), \textbf{delay } f(x))$$

This use of **delay** and **force** will avoid evaluation of $f(x)$ in just the case when this is unnecessary, when $g(x) < 0$. Although it is not possible to avoid the evaluation of $g(x)$, since $adjust(a,b)$ must inspect its value, if we **delay**ed the first argument to $adjust(a,b)$ we would have to **force** all occurrences of a in the definition of $adjust(a,b)$

$$adjust(a,b) \equiv \textbf{if } (\textbf{force } a) < 0 \textbf{ then } (\textbf{force } a) \textbf{ else } (\textbf{force } a) + (\textbf{force } b)$$

Then the corresponding call would be

$$adjust(\textbf{delay } g(x), \textbf{delay } f(x))$$

Now, it would appear that, while we may have avoided evaluation of $f(x)$, we have actually caused the evaluation of $g(x)$ to take place twice, whether or not it is less than zero. This is not, however, the case, as we shall now explain.

In describing delayed evaluation we introduced the notion of a recipe and it is the nature of this recipe which requires further explanation. The recipe constructed as the value of **delay** e represents the value of the expression e in the sense that the value obtained by forcing the recipe is just the value of e. There is no way we can alter the value which will be obtained as a result of the force. Thus, when a recipe is forced, we can replace the contents of the recipe by the value obtained as a result of this force just as long as we mark the recipe as having been evaluated. Subsequent forces can thus avoid re-evaluation when they find the recipe so marked. Note that it is only the representation of the value of the recipe which has changed. The object, which began as a recipe embodying the unevaluated expression e, has ended as a recipe embodying the value of e. It is still a recipe and must still be forced in order to yield its value.

Consider how we might use **delay** and **force** to effect the computation of *sumints(n)* which avoids constructing the entire intermediate list of n numbers. We will represent this intermediate list by a structure whose *car* is a number and whose *cdr* is a recipe. Thus we modify *integersbetween(m,n)* to the following definition:

$$integersbetween(m,n) \equiv \textbf{if } m > n \textbf{ then } NIL \textbf{ else}$$
$$cons(m, \textbf{delay } integersbetween(m+1,n))$$

Now we must make a corresponding modification to *sum(x)* to take account of the fact that x is no longer a simple list but a list whose *cdr* has been delayed. This is straightforward:

$$sum(x) \equiv \textbf{if } eq(x,NIL) \textbf{ then } 0 \textbf{ else}$$
$$car(x) + sum(\textbf{force } cdr(x))$$

Now the definition of *sumints(n)* requires no modification. Look at how the computation proceeds: the function *sum(x)*, by evaluating **force** *cdr(x)* resumes evaluation of *integersbetween(m+1,n)* which again returns an object whose *cdr* has been delayed. The effect is that the intermediate list of numbers is built on demand only as required by *sum(x)*.

This effect can be seen more clearly if we consider the call

$$first(k, integersbetween(1,n))$$

where we have the following definition of *first(k,x)*.

$$first(k,x) \equiv \textbf{if } k = 0 \textbf{ then } NIL \textbf{ else}$$
$$cons(car(x), first(k-1, \textbf{force } cdr(x)))$$

This function returns a list of the first k elements of x and hence *first(k, integersbetween(1,n))* is the list (1 2 3 ... k), assuming $k \leq n$. However, the part of the list from $k+1$ onward is never constructed. Each time *integersbetween(m,n)* is called it returns a list whose *cdr* has been delayed. Thus, the initial call of *integersbetween(1,n)* returns $cons(1,\delta)$, where δ is a recipe representing *integersbetween(2,n)*. Now we evaluate *first(k,cons(1,δ))* which, assuming $k > 0$, will force δ. The result of forcing δ is $cons(2,\delta')$, where δ' is a recipe representing *integersbetween(3,n)*. The evaluation of *first(k,cons(1,δ))* is now resumed, with the embedded call *first(k-1,cons(2,δ'))*. Now δ' will be forced and so we see that evaluation proceeds, now in *first*, now in *integersbetween* and so on, back and forth between the two, extending the intermediate data structure, the list (1 2 3 ... n), only as far as is required.

In the next section we will see that this is a functional analog of coroutine execution.

The fact that by delaying the *cdr* of a list we can avoid evaluation of it altogether if only a short initial segment of it is required means that we can in fact process potentially infinite lists, just as long as we only actually require a finite initial segment of such a list. Consider the function definition

$$integersfrom(m) \equiv cons(m, \textbf{delay } integersfrom(m+1))$$

The result of this function is the list of integers from *m* onward: that is, it is an infinite list. It would be meaningless to evaluate *sum(integersfrom(1))*, for the computation could never terminate. However, *first(k,integersfrom(1))* is perfectly well defined, it is the list (1 2 3 ... *k*). The fact that the result of *integersfrom(1)* is potentially infinite causes no problem, that part of the list from *k*+1 onward never being evaluated.

It will transpire, in the last section of this chapter, that the use of potentially infinite lists is a powerful and lucid technique for writing many types of program. As a foretaste of this technique, consider the following program for computing a list of the first *k* sums of natural numbers, that is a list whose members are 1, 1+2, 1+2+3, ..., 1+2+...+*k*:

$$firstsums(k) \equiv first(k, sums(0, integersfrom(1)))$$
$$sums(a,x) \equiv cons(a + car(x), \textbf{delay } sums(a + car(x), \textbf{force } cdr(x)))$$

The functions *integersfrom(m)* and *first(k,x)* are as before. Note that *sums(a,x)* expects a list *x* whose *cdr* has been delayed. It also returns a list of this form. The argument *a* to sums(*a,x*) is used to accumulate the sum of the elements of *x*. Thus *sums(0,integersfrom(1))* is the infinite list (1 3 6 10 15 ...). An interesting feature of this program is the way we have defined the process of generating the sequences of natural numbers and of partial sums of natural numbers without consideration of how this process is to be terminated. Termination of the program as a whole is specified entirely by the behavior of the function *first(k,x)*. This, then, is a simpler program than the corresponding program which builds finite lists. However, in the final section of this chapter we shall see an even simpler version.

8.2 INTERPRETATION OF DELAY AND FORCE

First let us observe that, aside from considerations of efficiency, there is no need for us to extend the purely functional language with which we have been dealing in order to implement **delay** and **force**. We hinted at this possibility at the end of Chapter 6, when we discussed the notion of a function with no parameters. Making an expression *e* into a function of no parameters $\lambda()e$ simply has the effect of postponing its evaluation. Before we could properly use the value, we should have to call the function with a corresponding empty list of actual parameters. Thus, from a program using **delay** and **force** we can derive an equivalent program using parameterless functions simply by using the replacements

$$\textbf{delay } e \rightarrow \lambda(\,)e$$
$$\textbf{force } e \rightarrow e(\,)$$

Doing this for the function $first(k,x)$ and $integersfrom(m)$ of the previous section gives us

$$first(k,x) \equiv \textbf{if } k=0 \textbf{ then } NIL \textbf{ else}$$
$$cons(car(x), first(k-1,(cdr(x))(\,)))$$
$$integersfrom(m) \equiv cons(m,\lambda(\,)integersfrom(m+1))$$

The corresponding calls of these functions are unchanged. Thus $first(k, integersfrom(m))$ will quite satisfactorily produce the list whose members are the numbers $m,m+1,\ldots,m+k-1$. We see that $integersfrom(m)$ returns a *cons* whose *car* is a number and whose *cdr* is a parameterless function. The function $first(k,x)$ expects such a *cons* as its second argument and properly accesses the *cdr* by means of the call $(cdr(x))(\,)$. In this simple program, each parameterless function is called at most once. However, if the list obtained from $integersfrom(m)$ were required twice, as for example in

$$\{\textbf{let } x = integersfrom(m) \quad cons(first(k,x), first(l,x))\}$$

this implementation using parameterless functions would cause us to evaluate it twice. This is not the effect we had required from **delay** and **force**.

Nevertheless, this study of parameterless functions leads us directly to a satisfactory implementation for **delay** and **force**. First, we note that a parameterless function of the form $\lambda(\,)e$ will always yield the same value when called, because of the nature of the proper binding rules which we have adopted. Thus, when that value is defined, that is when the evaluation of e is neither erroneous nor non-terminating, an equally good representation of the function is just to store the value of e. Thus, when the computation first requires that we call $\lambda(\,)e$, we cannot proceed without doing so, and having done so successfully, we may as well replace the closure by the value which we obtain. That is to say, the value of **delay** e can be represented by a closure and when this closure, which will initially contain e, is forced, it can be updated to contain the value of e instead.

In order to make this method of evaluation precise, we shall embed the **delay** and **force** concepts in our Lispkit Lisp language and then extend the SECD machine in order to give them a meaning. Consistently with the rest of Lispkit Lisp, we shall denote the respective well-formed expressions by $(DELAY\ e)$ and $(FORCE\ e)$. Now, we shall require three new SECD machine-language instructions in order to compile these well-formed expressions. The names and implementations of these three new instructions will bear a very strong resemblance to the instructions used to implement functions. They are *LDE* (load expression), *AP0* (apply parameterless function) and *UPD* (return and update). They are generated by *DELAY* and *FORCE* as follows:

$$(DELAY\ e)*n = (LDE\ \ e*n\ |\ (UPD))$$
$$(FORCE\ e)*n = e*n\ |\ (AP0)$$

Here we see that (*DELAY e*) is compiled to a control list of the form (*LDE c*), where c is a control list obtained by compiling e, and where the final instruction of c is *UPD*. The code for (*FORCE e*) is simply the list of instructions for e followed by the instruction *AP0*.

To complete our definition we must give the SECD machine transitions for the new instructions. To do this it is necessary to denote a new type of structure. Since a delayed expression will be represented by a closure which, when forced, will be updated to contain the value, it is necessary to mark the closure as to whether or not it has been evaluated. Recall in Chapter 6 that we represented a closure by a pair (*c.e*), where c was the control list compiled from the function body and e the environment containing the values of global variables. Here we shall use an object with a similar structure, which we shall distinguish with the name recipe. A recipe may be denoted by

$$[F\ (c.e)]$$

in which case (*c.e*) is the closure part and F is a flag to indicate that the recipe has not been evaluated. Alternatively, a recipe may be denoted by

$$[T\ x]$$

in which case x is the value and T is a flag indicating that the recipe has been evaluated. The square brackets are a convenience which assist the eye in deciphering the transition rules. It is fair to think of a recipe as simply being a *cons* whose *car* and *cdr* are both updated as a result of forced evaluation.

Now to enumerate the transitions. Referring back to the corresponding transitions for *LDF*, *AP* and *RTN* will explain much of the structure of these transitions (see also Exercise 8.6). First, the transition for *LDE*, which is straightforward:

$$s\ e\ (LDE\ c.c')\ d\ \rightarrow\ ([F\ (c.e)].s)\ e\ c'\ d$$

Here we see that *LDE c* simply builds the recipe [*F* (*c.e*)] and pushes it on top of the stack. Execution continues with the remainder of the program

c', execution of c having been delayed. Consider next the transition for $AP0$. It must find a recipe on top of the stack. Either the recipe has been evaluated, or it has not. We deal with each case separately:

$$([T\ x].s)\ e\ (AP0.c)\ d\ \to\ (x.s)\ e\ c\ d$$

In case the recipe has been evaluated, we simply remove its value. However, if the recipe has not been evaluated we must contrive to commence its evaluation.

$$([F\ (c.e)].s)\ e'\ (AP0.c')\ d$$
$$\to\ NIL\ e\ c\ (((F\ (c.e)].s)\ e'\ c'.d)$$

This is a little complicated. What we have done is to push the entire stack, recipe and all $([F\ (c.e)].s)$ onto the dump d along with the environment e' and the remainder of the control string c'. The reason for saving the recipe as well as the remainder of the stack is so that we shall have it available when it becomes necessary to update it. This situation arises when we have reached the final instruction UPD of the control list c which was embedded in the recipe. The relevant transition is as follows:

$$(x)\ e\ (UPD)\ (((F\ (c.e)].s)\ e'\ c'.d)\ \to\ (x.s)\ e'\ c'\ d$$
$$\text{and}\ [F\ (c.e)]\ \to\ [T\ x]$$

The transition itself is straightforward. It simply indicates that, when execution of c is completed, its value x is returned to the calling environment and execution in that environment resumed, exactly as if RTN had been used. However, our transition also has the side effect (a benevolent one) of updating the contents of the recipe so that the flag is now T, indicating that the recipe has been evaluated, and that the value x, rather than the closure $(c.e)$, is saved. Clearly it is not semantically necessary to implement this "update in place" but for the sake of efficiency it is very desirable. It is desirable further that every occurrence of the recipe is so updated. It is usually possible to contrive that recipes never get copied, only pointers to them, and so the symbolic entity $[F\ (c.e)]$ in this transition effectively stands for all occurrences (in practice *the single* occurrence) of the recipe. Thus the "update in place" affects all subsequent accesses to the recipe.

For a moment, let us consider how this SECD machine extension evaluates the program which we had in the previous section for *first*(k,*integersfrom*-(m)). The first essential part of that program which we must consider is the expression in the definition of *integersfrom*(m) which generates a list with delayed *cdr*. This expression is

$$cons(m,\textbf{delay}\ integersfrom(m+1))$$

The other essential part is the expression in *first*(*k*,*x*) which causes the delayed *cdr* to be evaluated. This expression is

force *cdr*(*x*)

At the instant when **force** *cdr*(*x*) is evaluated, we can consider *x* as bound to the value of *cons*(*m*,**delay** *integersfrom*(*m*+1)). According to our definition for the evaluation of **delay** by the SECD machine, this value will have the structure shown in Fig. 8.1. Here the first record is a normal *cons* type record, the second is a recipe. Now **force** *cdr*(*x*) generates code which puts this value

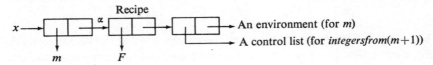

Fig. 8.1

of *x* on the stack, takes its *cdr*, which is the recipe, and then executes the operation *AP*0. This causes the recipe to be evaluated, since the *F* flag indicates this has not been done. Since the recipe is for an expression of the form *integersfrom*(*m*+1), the result of this evaluation will be a list with the same structure as *x*, as shown in Fig. 8.2.

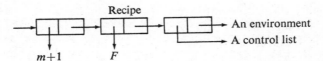

Fig. 8.2

Now, the code generated by *delay* is terminated by an *UPD* operation, and this results in the recipe which is the *cdr* of *x* above (it is marked α) to have its fields updated to indicate that evaluation has taken place, and the list for *x* then has the form of Fig. 8.3.

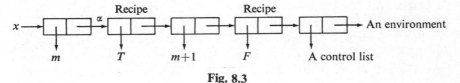

Fig. 8.3

Thus a subsequent evaluation of **force** *cdr*(*x*) (there would be none in the simple program which we have considered) would not require to evaluate the recipe, only to skip over it. In a practical implementation it is possible to avoid these intermediate records, but that should not concern us here (but see Exercise 8.7).

There is a different way of looking at the behavior of a program which uses delayed evaluation, and it is instructive. For *first(k,integersfrom(m))*, the program is such that the code which is generated for it executes in a way which is more usually associated with coroutines than subroutines. That is to say, the code for *integersfrom(m)* executes only partially and is then suspended. The code for *first(k,x)* is then entered and after a brief execution it is itself suspended and the code for *integersfrom(m)* resumed. This in turn suspends itself, and again resumes *first(k,x)* where it was previously suspended. Thus execution of the code generated for each of the functions skips between them alternately, progressing first a little way in the one, then a little way in the other, then back to the first and so on. This contrasts with the orderly way in which we have previously thought of the execution of code generated from functions. The code for functions not using **delay** or **force** is exactly what we normally call a subroutine. It is entered at the beginning, exited at the end and only suspended between these times to call other subroutines in a fully nested fashion. It is precisely because of this fully nested phenomenon that we find it difficult to process finite parts of infinite structures. Without the **delay** in *integersfrom(m)* the code for that function would, once entered, never return or otherwise suspend itself.

Coroutines are a very simple form of quasi-parallelism. We can see why they are considered thus if we imagine the following interpretation of **delay** and **force**. When, during evaluation of a function, we encounter **delay** *e*, we do not consider that it means *suspend* computation, but that it means establish a separate, independent, parallel computation. That is to say, *e* is to be evaluated in parallel with the expression in which it is embedded. The recipe which is returned as the intermediate result of **delay** *e* is marked by *F* to indicate that *it is being* evaluated. The process in which **delay** *e* is embedded, when it requires access to the value of this recipe, inspects the flag using **force**. If the flag is *F*, that process waits until it is set to *T*. Thus we can consider each recipe whose flag is *F* as representing a process in execution. There will be a number of other processes waiting for its completion. If we have an infinite number of processors, then we can simply set each recipe to be evaluated on a separate processor as it is created. If we have a finite number of processors, we must continue to multiprogram the evaluation. The details of this are left as an exercise for the reader (Exercise 8.9).

8.3 LAZY EVALUATION

In Algol there are two distinct mechanisms for handing parameters to procedures. They are referred to as call-by-value and call-by-name. The mechanism we have used in our purely functional language is call-by-value. That is, each argument of a function is evaluated before the function body is evaluated. The evaluation of the body takes place with the value of the actual parameter bound to the formal parameter name. Consider now the use of the call-by-name mechanism in a purely functional language. A parameter which is called-by-name in Algol is not evaluated until a reference to it is encountered in the execution of the procedure body. Moreover, each time the formal parameter is encountered in the execution of the procedure body the corresponding actual parameter is re-evaluated. We can simulate this mechanism in our purely functional language by delaying an actual parameter which we wish to call-by-name and forcing the corresponding formal parameter. Consider, for example, the function

$$f(a,b) \equiv \textbf{if } a > 0 \textbf{ then } a \textbf{ else } b$$

and the call of it

$$f(g(x),h(x))$$

The evaluation of $h(x)$ can be avoided when $g(x) > 0$ by using call-by-name for parameter b, illustrated by the following definition:

$$f(a,b) \equiv \textbf{if } a > 0 \textbf{ then } a \textbf{ else force } b$$

where the corresponding call must be

$$f(g(x),\textbf{delay } h(x))$$

So we see that, in our purely functional language, call-by-name (simulated here) can be a useful mechanism.

Another example was introduced in Section 6.5 (p. 192) with the function

$$\cdot \ badif(a,b,c) \equiv \textbf{if } a \textbf{ then } b \textbf{ else } c$$

Here, in order to make $badif(a,b,c)$ behave semantically like **if** a **then** b **else** c we must call b and c by name, to avoid evaluating whichever one is not chosen (see also Exercise 6.8). However, call-by-name has a disadvantage not possessed by this simulation of it. The disadvantage arises because of the fact that a parameter called-by-name which is accessed more than once will be evaluated on each access. Thus, for example, with the (unusually contrived) function

$$f(a,b) \equiv \textbf{if } a > 0 \textbf{ then } a \textbf{ else } b+b$$

if b is called-by-name in the call

$$f(g(x),h(x))$$

then the computation invoked to evaluate $h(x)$ will be done twice. However, because of the updating associated with the recipe generated by **delay**, re-evaluation does not take place when we simulate call-by-name. Consider for example,

$$f(a,b) \equiv \textbf{if } a > 0 \textbf{ then } a \textbf{ else } (\textbf{force } b) + (\textbf{force } b)$$

and the associated call

$$f(g(x), \textbf{delay } h(x))$$

Whichever occurrence of (**force** b) is first evaluated will require the computation of $h(x)$, but the other evaluation will find the value of $h(x)$ already computed in b. This form of parameter mechanism, which enjoys the advantages of both call-by-value and call-by-name, has been appropriately termed call-by-need. It has the advantage of call-by-name, that actual parameters whose values are not required are not evaluated, and the advantage of call-by-value, that those whose values are required are evaluated once only. A parameter called-by-need is evaluated only when its value is actually required.

We could consider that the way we were using *cons* in Section 8.1, delaying its *cdr*, was tantamount to calling its second parameter by name. But there is a subtle difference. In our description of call-by-need we have assumed that the function either evaluates a call-by-need parameter or discards it. The function *cons* does neither of these things. It returns a value in which the unevaluated parameter is embedded, still unevaluated. Both features, that of *cons* having a delayed *cdr* and the call-by-need mechanism, provide us with useful computational capability. That is to say, there are occasions when we wish to delay the parameters of a user-defined function and there are occasions when we wish to delay the parameters of *cons*. Now it is perfectly possible to define a variant of our purely functional language in which all parameters are called-by-need, and equally it is possible to define a variant in which one or both of the arguments of *cons* are delayed and the corresponding result from *car* and/or *cdr* automatically forced. In these variants the delaying and forcing would be implicit. What we shall do however is to define a variant which has both facilities together.

The reason that it is not sufficient just to delay the arguments of *cons* is illustrated by the following program:

$$triangle(n) \equiv append(integersbetween(1,n), triangle(n+1))$$
$$append(x,y) \equiv \textbf{if } eq(x,NIL) \textbf{ then } y \textbf{ else}$$
$$cons(car(x), \textbf{delay } append(\textbf{force } cdr(x), y))$$

The function *triangle(n)* is intended to return a list (with delayed *cdr*) composed by appending each of the sublists

$$(1\ 2\ \ldots\ n)$$
$$(1\ 2\ \ldots\ n+1)$$
$$(1\ 2\ \ldots\ n+2)\ \ldots$$

to each other. Unfortunately, with a call-by-value mechanism for the arguments of *append(x,y)*, the program runs forever. The fault lies in the definition of *triangle(n)* where, because of the call-by-value on the second argument of *append*, *triangle* is again called before *append* is entered, leading to an infinite recursion. It is easy to see how delaying the second parameter to *append(x,y)* will solve this problem.

The process of delaying both the arguments to user-defined functions and the arguments to *cons* we shall call *lazy evaluation*. Now we must consider when the corresponding forces have to be applied. The solution we shall adopt is to force the arguments of primitive functions (such as *car*, *cdr*, +, etc.). The rationale behind this decision is that this is the last possible point, beyond which evaluation cannot be further delayed. For example, we cannot proceed further with the addition if the arguments of + have been delayed. It will be necessary in fact to force any arguments of a primitive function repeatedly in order to guarantee that the value of the argument is evaluated. For this purpose we shall introduce the operator **rf** (repeatedly force) with the property that, for any well-formed expression *e*, the expression **rf** *e* is well-formed and its value is not an unevaluated recipe. That is to say, if we introduce the predicate *isrecipe(x)*, true only if its argument is an unevaluated recipe, then **rf** *e* satisfies the equation

$$\textbf{rf } e = \textbf{if } isrecipe(e) \textbf{ then rf(force } e) \textbf{ else } e$$

Equivalently, we can say that **rf** *e* has the same value as *e* or **force** *e* or **force** (**force** *e*) ... etc., whichever is the first of these values which is not an unevaluated recipe. We see that we can apply **rf** to any expression, in particular when its value has not been delayed, and obtain a value which is an evaluated recipe.

Now we can give a precise definition to what we mean by lazy evaluation. In a purely functional program, usually without any explicit **delays** or **forces**, we make the following changes throughout the entire program;

1. delay all arguments to user-defined functions;
2. delay all arguments to *cons*;
3. delay all definitions in both **let** and **letrec** blocks;

4. repeatedly force all arguments to primitive functions (other than *cons*);
5. repeatedly force the test in conditional expressions;
6. repeatedly force the function in a function application.

These rules can be written as a series of program transformations, as in (8.2), where we understand that each of the $e, e_1, \ldots, e_k$ are well-formed expressions and "$\rightarrow$" means "is replaced by".

$$e(e_1, \ldots, e_k) \rightarrow (\textbf{rf } e)(\textbf{delay } e_1, \ldots, \textbf{delay } e_k)$$
$$cons(e_1, e_2) \rightarrow cons(\textbf{delay } e_1, \textbf{delay } e_2)$$
$$car(e) \rightarrow car(\textbf{rf } e) \text{ etc.}$$
$$\textbf{if } e_1 \textbf{ then } e_2 \textbf{ else } e_3 \rightarrow \textbf{if rf } e \textbf{ then } e_1 \textbf{ else } e_2 \qquad (8.2)$$

$$\left.\begin{array}{l} \{\textbf{let } x_1 = e_1 \\ \quad \vdots \\ \textbf{and } x_k = e_k \\ e\} \end{array}\right\} \rightarrow \left\{\begin{array}{l} \{\textbf{let } x_1 = \textbf{delay } e_1 \\ \quad \vdots \\ \textbf{and } x_k = \textbf{delay } e_k \\ e\} \end{array}\right.$$

(similarly for **letrec**)

It will be necessary in any actual implementation of lazy evaluation either to ensure that the selection functions (*car* and *cdr*) in the routine used to print the final answer actually repeatedly force their arguments, or to do something equivalent.

The decision to delay the definitions in the **let** and **letrec** blocks is essentially one of symmetry, based on the previously discussed correspondence between blocks and function application. We do not want to lose that correspondence. We shall see, however, that it is a particularly fortunate decision in the case of **letrec** blocks. In addition to repeatedly forcing the arguments of primitive functions it was also necessary to repeatedly force the test in the conditional expression and the function in the function call, because their values are needed before the computation can proceed. That the power of **rf** may be needed can be seen from the above transformations when we realize that a parameter which is simply handed on by a function to one of its subsidiary functions will come to be delayed twice (or more). A final point to note is that we have now delayed both arguments to *cons*. This will allow us to deal with potentially infinite trees of which the potentially infinite lists of the earlier sections were only an example.

It is easy to see that the rules of transformation which we have given will result in the construction of many recipes by the transformed program. If we write programs which process (finite portions) of infinite structures, but write such programs without explicit **delays** and **forces** the transformed program will have the necessary **delays** and **forces**. Consider, for example, the program which allows us to compute $first(n, integersfrom(1))$ using the function definitions

$$first(k,x) \equiv \textbf{if } eq(k,0) \textbf{ then } NIL \textbf{ else}$$
$$cons(car(x), first(k-1, cdr(x)))$$
$$integersfrom(m) \equiv cons(m, integersfrom(m+1))$$

Assume that it has been transformed according to the rules given above. Had we written it out properly, using **letrec** to introduce the function definitions, we should have had to repeatedly force all the user-defined functions in the calls. We omit this level of detail, leaving it to an exercise (Exercise 8.5). The function $integersfrom(m)$ returns a $cons$ of two recipes. The function $first(k,x)$ returns either NIL or a $cons$ of two recipes. Thus the principal call $first(n, integersfrom(1))$, assuming $n > 0$, returns a $cons$ of two unevaluated recipes. Note that $integersfrom(1)$ has not been called. This would be the end of the story unless we required to inspect (for example, print) the value of $first(n, integersfrom(1))$. Assuming we request its car, this will force the evaluation of $integersfrom(1)$, as far as the $cons$ of two unevaluated recipes. Repeatedly forcing the car will yield the value 1. The cdr, which will ultimately come to yield the numbers 2 onwards, has not yet been disturbed. In the next section we shall adopt this device of writing programs without explicit delays and forces, relying upon this transformation to a form in which they can be evaluated. We shall also refer to the process of carrying out this transformation followed by lazy evaluation as *lazy evaluation*, and hope this is not confusing.

Before we do that, however, consider the simple program

> **letrec** $x = cons(1,x)$
> $car(cdr(x))$

Under normal evaluation rules this would not be well defined. However, under lazy evaluation rules it has a perfectly acceptable meaning. The list x is an infinite list of 1's. Then $car(cdr(x))$ is of course 1. It is worth looking at the evaluation of this expression in some detail, since it illustrates many points. The transformation rules produce the following equivalent expression:

> **letrec** $x = $ **delay** $cons($**delay** $1,$**delay** $x)$
> $car($**rf** $cdr($**rf** $x))$

Evaluation proceeds as follows. A recipe is built as the value to be bound to x (Fig. 8.4). Next, evaluation of $car(\textbf{rf }cdr(\textbf{rf }x))$ causes x to be forced. Thus it becomes a *cons* of two recipes (Fig. 8.5).

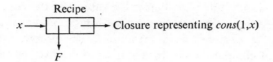

Fig. 8.4

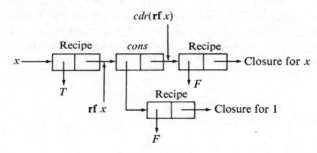

Fig. 8.5

The value of **rf** x is a *cons* record and thus the *cdr* of this record is forced. The *cdr* is a recipe with a closure representing x. On forcing this recipe we obtain Fig. 8.6.

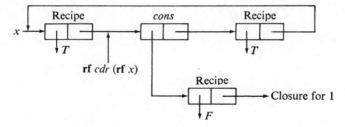

Fig. 8.6

The value of **rf** $cdr(\textbf{rf }x)$ is the same *cons* record. Thus the value of $car(\textbf{rf }cdr(\textbf{rf }x))$ is the recipe which contains a closure for 1. That is the value we expected. Note that we could have gone as far down the list for x as we wished without constructing any more records to represent it. Note also that the two **delays** in the recursive equation defining x have left us with two recipes in its representation. This is an example of the need for repeated forces. We conclude that lazy evaluation allows a proper interpretation of **letrec** blocks wherein recursive equations defining infinite data structures can be expressed and evaluated. This is the subject of the next section.

To conclude this section let us consider a more practical application of lazy evaluation to ordinary finite structures. The problem (introduced in Exercise 2.15) of comparing two binary trees to discover whether they have the same fringe when read from left to right has been considered to be an unnatural problem for functional programs using conventional recursive functions, in the sense that programs written in such a language are unusually contorted or inefficient. The problem arises because the two binary trees may be of completely different shapes. In Fig. 8.7, for example, trees (1), (2) and (4) are considered to be the same, while (3) and (5) are not the same as any of the others.

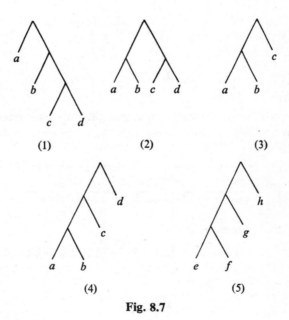

Fig. 8.7

The simplest program one can write for this problem is one which *flattens* the two trees to be compared, constructing lists of their leaves and then compares the resulting lists. This program is given in (8.3).

$$samefringe(t1,t2) \equiv eqlis(flatten(t1),flatten(t2))$$

$$flatten(t) \equiv \textbf{if } atom(t) \textbf{ then } cons(t,NIL) \textbf{ else}$$
$$append(flatten(car(t)),flatten(cdr(t)))$$

$$append(x,y) \equiv \textbf{if } eq(x,NIL) \textbf{ then } y \textbf{ else}$$
$$cons(car(x),append(cdr(x),y)) \qquad (8.3)$$

$$eqlis(x,y) \equiv \textbf{if } eq(x,NIL) \textbf{ then } eq(y,NIL) \textbf{ else}$$
$$\textbf{if } eq(y,NIL) \textbf{ then } F \textbf{ else}$$
$$\textbf{if } eq(car(x),car(y)) \textbf{ then } eqlis(cdr(x),cdr(y))$$
$$\textbf{else } F$$

If run under normal evaluation this program will construct two lists and compare them. If they differ in the first place, as they would if comparing trees (1) and (5) above, much of this work would have been wasted. However, with lazy evaluation, the computation would be driven by $eqlis(x,y)$, which would require the construction of only that prefix of each list which was needed until a mismatch was encountered. Of course, if the lists were equal this would not be a saving (indeed all the delays and forces would increase the computation time). However, if one of the trees to be compared was huge and the result of the comparison was false, the lazy evaluation scheme avoids constructing much of that huge tree.

8.4 NETWORKS OF COMMUNICATING PROCESSES

In this section we shall make considerable use of the power of lazy evaluation to allow the processing of potentially infinite structures and to properly interpret mutually recursive equations defined by the **letrec** construction. Everything we shall do can be done with explicit delays and forces, and the reader is recommended to convince himself of this fact, since such an exercise greatly aids the understanding of how these lazy computations proceed. However, the sets of equations which we shall construct for each example in this section can be understood by themselves, without knowing precisely how they are evaluated, and thus we avoid the time-consuming effort of repeating each example with explicit delays and forces, In fact, although we shall write each example as a functional program, we shall also depict it as a set of processes communicating by streams of values. These processes can be thought of as executing in parallel, reading data from their input streams and sending data to their output streams, Synchronization of these activities will not be a problem, but we must ensure that progress is made by the system as a whole.

Our first example concerns the construction of the list of all integers. Assume we have the function definition

$$add1(x) \equiv cons(car(x)+1,add1(cdr(x)))$$

which, given an infinite list x, returns the infinite list obtained by increasing all the values in x by 1. We shall adopt this mode of referring to infinite lists as if they were completely processed, even though we know they cannot be, now that we are thoroughly familiar with the way they are represented as having their unaccessed parts delayed. The list of all integers is then defined by the expression

$$integers \textbf{ whererec } integers = cons(1,add1(integers))$$

That is to say, the list of all integers begins with 1, which is followed by the result of applying $add1$ to the entire list itself. This is a strange way to define it. The definition $integersfrom(1)$ seemed more natural. However, we can illustrate this definition in a way which makes it seem more obvious. In Fig. 8.8, the defined function $add1(x)$ has become what we shall call a process.

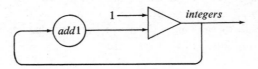

Fig. 8.8

The ingoing arrow denotes its argument and the outgoing arrow its result. The triangle on its side is used to depict the *cons* operation, hence its two arguments and one result (Fig. 8.9).

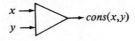

Fig. 8.9

The fork in the arrow labeled *integers* in Fig. 8.8 illustrates the fact that this value is used twice, as output to the entire network and as feedback to the $add1$ process. The correspondence between this network and the definition of integers should be obvious.

The network can be considered to compute the list of all integers in one of two distinct ways. It can be driven by demand for its output or it can be driven by availability of its inputs. We shall refer to these two modes of working as *demand mode* and *availability mode* respectively. Demand mode corresponds to lazy evaluation. If we require the first value on the list *integers* we can evaluate that list as far as the value 1, without demanding any activity from the *add*1 process. When we demand the second value on the list *integers*, this causes *add*1 to demand the first value on that list, which of course has already been computed, and so the chain of demands is finite and the second value is obtained. Clearly demanding the nth value on the list will result in the $(n-1)$th being demanded if it has not been previously constructed, and so on. Conversely, we can think of the above network as a process, working independently, producing the integers at its own speed. The first value 1 is available, so it is output and fed back. This makes the second value 2 available and so we do the same with this, and so on. Both modes of evaluation require us to consider values as queueing up on edges in the network, and at forks in the arrows we must consider that all values go both ways. We shall never use a join of arrows. That is, we allow fan out but not fan in. The power of this network notation will appear when we use it the other way round: first drawing the network, then deriving the corresponding functional program.

Let us try to do this for the example with which we began the chapter. To generate a list of all the partial sums of natural numbers we require the following function:

$$addlist(x,y) \equiv cons(car(x)+car(y),addlist(cdr(x),cdr(y)))$$

Then we can construct a network which generates the list *sums* of all partial sums, where the nth element of sums is $\Sigma_{i=1}^{n} i$, by observing that $addlist(integers,sums)$ is almost equal to *sums*. In fact, its value is just $cdr(sums)$. The network which we construct is shown in Fig. 8.10.

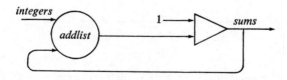

Fig. 8.10

The input *integers* is obtained from the earlier network. The output *sums* is fed back and added, element by element, to the list of integers. The output from *addlist* will be the sequence 2,3,4,... etc., and hence the need for the *cons* element to insert the missing 1. This network proceeds through its computation exactly like the network for integers; the equivalent functional program is

$$sums \textbf{ whererec } sums = cons(1, addlist(integers, sums))$$

Combining the two networks we obtain the program illustrated both as a

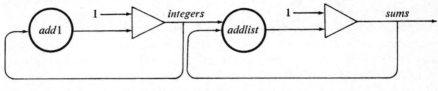

Fig. 8.11

network in Fig. 8.11 and in functional form as (8.4).

$$sums \textbf{ whererec } sums = cons(1, addlist(integers, sums))$$
$$\textbf{and } integers = cons(1, add1(integers)) \qquad (8.4)$$

In order to guarantee that this network defines a program which makes progress, we have had to take care in its construction. It would not have been satisfactory, for example, to generate the list 1,2,3,... from 2,3,4,... by subtracting 1 from each member (see Exercise 8.17).

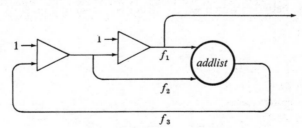

Fig. 8.12

A slightly more elaborate example is the network shown in Fig. 8.12 for generating the Fibonacci sequence. The rationale behind this network is that the Fibonacci sequence from the first element onwards, when added element by element to the sequence from the second element onwards, gives us the sequence from the third element onwards. These three sequences have been denoted f_1, f_2 and f_3 in the network. Having generated f_3, we can use it to generate the necessary values of f_1 and f_2 simply by *cons*ing the two initial values (both 1) onto the front of it. That is, the Fibonacci sequence is defined by

$$x_1 = 1$$
$$x_2 = 1$$
$$x_i = x_{i-1} + x_{i-2} \qquad i > 2$$

and the sequences f_1, f_2, f_3 by

$$f_1 = x_1, x_2, x_3, \ldots = x_1, f_2$$
$$f_2 = x_2, x_3, x_4, \ldots = x_2, f_3$$
$$f_3 = x_3, x_4, x_5, \ldots$$

The Fibonacci program can now be constructed in functional form from the network shown in Fig. 8.10:

$$f_1 \textbf{ whererec } f_1 = cons(1, f_2)$$
$$\textbf{and } f_2 = cons(1, f_3)$$
$$\textbf{and } f_3 = addlist(f_1, f_2)$$

Quite a remarkable program, and well worth the effort of adding explicit delays and forces in order to understand how the lazy method of evaluation gives it a valid meaning.

The next problem which we tackle is attributed by Dijkstra (1976) to Hamming. The problem is to generate a sequence which satisfies the following three properties:

1. The value 1 is in the sequence.
2. If x is in the sequence, so are $2 \times x$, $3 \times x$ and $5 \times x$.
3. The sequence contains no other values than those that belong to it on account of (1) and (2).

Further, we must generate this sequence in ascending order. In order to do it we shall make use of a process, embodying the function $merge(x, y)$ which merges two ascending sequences of numbers x and y, omitting duplicates.

$$merge(x,y) \equiv \textbf{if } eq(car(x),car(y)) \textbf{ then } merge(cdr(x),y) \textbf{ else}$$
$$\textbf{if } car(x) < car(y) \textbf{ then}$$
$$cons(car(x),merge(cdr(x),y)) \textbf{ else}$$
$$cons(car(y),merge(x,cdr(y)))$$

Our method will be to assume we have generated the sequence x, called for by rules $(1)-(3)$ above, to multiply it by 2, 3 and 5 and to merge the resulting sequences. When fed back, this merged sequence can be used as the previously assumed x. The network we obtain is shown in Fig. 8.13.

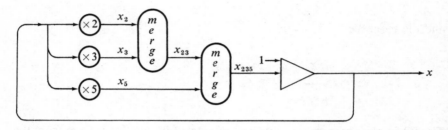

Fig. 8.13

Here the process labeled $\times 2$ embeds the function

$$mul2(x) \equiv cons(car(x) \times 2, mul2(cdr(x)))$$

and $\times 3$, $\times 5$ are similarly defined. The sequence x is multiplied by 2, 3 and 5 respectively to generate the sequences x_2, x_3 and x_5. These are merged pairwise to obtain the sequences x_{23} and x_{235}. The sequence x_{235} contains all the elements of x, except 1, hence the need for *cons*. This description leads us to write the program functionally as in (8.5).

$$x \textbf{ whererec } x = cons(1,x_{235})$$
$$\textbf{and } x_{235} = merge(x_{23},x_5)$$
$$\textbf{and } x_{23} = merge\ (x_2,x_3)$$
$$\textbf{and } x_2 = mul2(x) \qquad\qquad (8.5)$$
$$\textbf{and } x_3 = mul3(x)$$
$$\textbf{and } x_5 = mul5(x)$$

That this program is well defined in the sense that it can make progress is left as an exercise for the reader (Exercise 8.19). Note that this program can also be written

$$x \textbf{ whererec } x = cons(1, merge(merge(mul2(x), mul3(x)), mul5(x)))$$

Finally, let us construct a network which implements the prime sieve of Eratosthenes. This is less trivial, for it contains a properly nested copy of itself. Other prime-number generators are structurally simpler and are set as exercises. We include this one in the text because of its extreme elegance. The original functional program on which this network is based was devised by P. Quarendon. The sieve of Eratosthenes is usually described as follows. Make a list of the integers, commencing at 2. Repeat the following process of marking the numbers in the list.

1. The first unmarked number of the list is prime, call it p.
2. Mark the first unmarked number in the list and each pth number thereafter whether previously marked or not (here you are marking all multiples of p).
3. Repeat from 1.

Usually of course the list of numbers constructed before this process is begun, is finite. We shall not bother with that restriction. The following function can be embedded in a process to carry out rule 2.

$$filter(p,y) \equiv \textbf{if } car(y) \textbf{ rem } p = 0 \textbf{ then } filter(p, cdr(y)) \textbf{ else}$$
$$cons(car(y), filter(p, cdr(y)))$$

Now, we must build a network which, given a list x such as would be presented to the algorithm at rule 1, will generate from it the list of all primes. That is, we want a network which implements the process of Fig. 8.14.

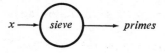

$$x \longrightarrow \text{sieve} \longrightarrow primes$$

Fig. 8.14

If we denote the process of taking the car and cdr of a list by an inverted triangle as in Fig. 8.15, then the network which implements rules 1, 2 and 3 is as shown in Fig. 8.16.

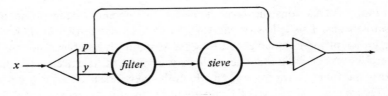

Fig. 8.15

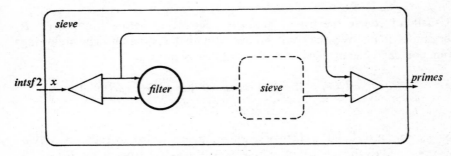

Fig. 8.16

Observe that the input x is split to obtain the two inputs for *filter*(p,y). The results of this filtering process are then handed to another copy of the entire sieve. The list of primes thus produced is then augmented with the prime p. Thus the above network is the entire sieve. We draw it in such a way as to make this obvious in Fig. 8.17.

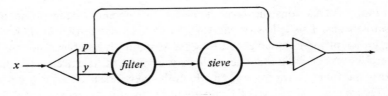

Fig. 8.17

Now, the initial input to the sieve is just the integers from 2 onward, so we can write out this network as the following functional programs

$$primes \text{ whererec } primes = sieve(intsf\,2)$$
$$\text{and } intsf\,2 = cdr(integers)$$
$$\text{and } sieve = \lambda(x)$$
$$cons(car(x),sieve(filter(car(x),cdr(x))))$$

Again, that this program makes progress is left as an exercise for the reader.

In this chapter we have tried to illustrate that funtional languages are a particularly natural form of expression for certain types of parallelism. It is the lack of commitment to the order of evaluation of subexpressions which is particularly important. Should expression evaluation possibly involve side effect, the construction of parallel interpretations of expressions is much more difficult. Lazy evaluation has allowed us to implement a demand-driven form of evaluation without a change to the structure of the programs being interpreted, although it has widened the class of programs to which we can now give a satisfactory meaning. The use of explicit delays and forces remains, however, a powerful device, with which we can experiment with different forms of quasi-parallelism.

EXERCISES

8.1 Infinite lists can be dealt with in another way. Rather than have a delayed *cdr* we can delay the list itself. This means we need to force it in order to inspect its *car*. Thus a list is either *NIL* or it is a delayed *cons*. Rewrite *integersfrom*(m) and *first*(k,x) in this form, using explicit delays and forces.

8.2 Define a function *seq*(a) which generates the infinite sequence (x_1 x_2 ...) defined as follows:

$$x_1 = a$$
$$x_{i+1} = \begin{cases} x_i/2 \text{ if } x_i \text{ is even, } i \geqslant 1 \\ (3x_i+1)/2 \text{ if } x_i \text{ is odd, } i \geqslant 1 \end{cases}$$

8.3 Define a function *truncate*(x,b) which produces the finite list obtained from the infinite list x by truncating it after the occurrence of an element equal to b. Thus *truncate* (*seq*(17),1) will generate

$$(17\ 26\ 13\ 20\ 10\ 5\ 8\ 4\ 2\ 1)$$

8.4 Show that the code generated for **force**(**delay** e) has the same effect as the code for e.

8.5 Consider the code for **delay**(**force** e). Show that in general this is not equivalent in effect to the code for e.

8.6 Construct the code which would be generated when **delay** e is replaced by $\lambda()e$ and **force** e by $e()$. Show that the effect of this code is the same as that for **delay** and **force**.

8.7 The implementation of recipes which we have discussed has the property that, when a list with delayed *cdr*s has been forced, it comes to be represented by a list with alternate *cons* and *recipe* type records. Consider how the concept of a recipe could be implemented so as to avoid this phenomenon and to present the list, once it had been forced, as normal.

8.8   Show, by an analysis of the SECD code, that the expression

$$\{\textbf{letrec } x = cons(1, \textbf{ delay } x)$$
$$first \ (k,x)\}$$

is well defined, in a context in which $first(k,x)$ and k have suitably defined values. In particular, $first(k,x)$ is the function as we have always used it in this chapter. (*Hint*: draw a picture of the data structure constructed for x.)

8.9   Devise a multiprogrammed method of evaluating recipes in which a queue of recipes requiring evaluation is maintained on a first-in–first-out discipline. It is also necessary to queue processes which are waiting for a recipe to complete. Are there programs which have different interpretations under the uniprogrammed interpretation given here and the multiprogrammed one you have just postulated?

8.10   Discuss the following method of evaluation. Delay all arguments to user-defined functions and to *cons* and delay all definitions (rules (1)–(3) of lazy evaluation). Repeatedly force all variables and the results of *car* and *cdr*.

8.11   Show that the operator **cf** *e*, called *conditional force*, which satisfies

$$\textbf{cf } e = \textbf{if } isrecipe(e) \textbf{ then force } e \textbf{ else } e$$

cannot be used in place of any of the uses of **rf** in the transformation rules for lazy evaluation.

8.12   Consider the breadth-first search procedure described in Section 3.2. Use delayed evaluation to avoid the problem of computing the value of any node not inspected by the search.

8.13   Design an interpreter for Lispkit Lisp which evaluates the program under the rules for lazy evaluation. The interpreter itself may or may not be lazily evaluated.

8.14   Construct a network which generates an infinite list *ones* each member of which is the number one.

8.15   Construct a network which generates the infinite list *integers* by doing element-by-element addition on the lists *integers* and *ones*.

8.16   Construct a network for the function *integersfrom*(*m*) (see Section 8.1) and compare it with the network for *integers*.

8.17   Revise the network for sums given in this section so that, instead of using *cons*, it uses *sub*1, where

$$sub1(x) \equiv cons(car(x) - 1, sub1(cdr(x)))$$

Show that the evaluation of *sums* is not well defined.

8.18   Rewrite the functional program for the Fibonacci sequence to include explicit delays and forces rather than relying on lazy evaluation.

8.19 Show that the program given for the Dijkstra–Hamming problem actually does make progress. (*Hint*: show that for any *n*, demanding the *nth* output is well defined.)

8.20 Redefine *filter(p,x)* given for the sieve of Eratosthenes program so that, rather than using **rem** it is more faithful to the description of the algorithm, and omits every *pth* member of *x*.

8.21 An alternative program for primes can be built using the network in Fig. 8.18. The process *remult(intsf3,primes)* removes multiples of elements in the list *primes* from the list *intsf3*. The list *intsf3* is the list of all integers, commencing at 3.

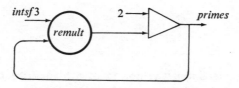

Fig. 8.18

8.22 Another prime-number generator can be based on the fact that a network like that for the Dijkstra–Hamming problem would generate all composite (non-prime) numbers if it had a multiplier for every prime. A process which generates primes from the sequence of composites by noticing which numbers are missing can be used as the source of primes needed to generate the multipliers. This exercise is hard. In particular, in order to ensure progress you will require a slightly modified merge process.

9 HIGHER-ORDER FUNCTIONS

In Chapter 2 we introduced the notion of a higher-order function as one which either takes a function as argument or which returns a function as its result. In this chapter we shall demonstrate that higher-order functions are an extremely powerful programming tool. In particular, we shall illustrate how higher-order functions can give a particularly natural form of expression to certain kinds of computation. For any particular program the design of suitable higher-order functions is far from trivial. However, the fact that the resulting program is often much shorter and its overall structure easier to comprehend, usually amply repays the extra effort involved.

The principal difficulty which we have with higher-order functions, and the one which we tackle in the first section, arises because it is not easy to determine from the form in which a function is written the types of arguments which it may take. Thus, we must be explicit about the types of these arguments, and for this purpose we develop an informal notation. The type of an argument for a higher-order function is denoted by a *type-expression*. The crucial property which these type-expressions have is that, when the argument whose type is being specified is itself a function, then the type-expression contains in turn a specification of the types of the arguments of that function. When we have, as indeed we shall, functions whose arguments are themselves functions of higher order, then the need to be explicit about the types of arguments becomes even greater.

The first example we have chosen for illustration of the power of functional programming is a simple language recognizer. The choice of suitable higher-order functions for this application leads to a form of expression of the recognizer which is directly related to the usual form of syntactic productions. Thus, one can say that the recognizer has been given a natural form of expression. Similarly, in our second example, we produce a natural form of expression for a certain class of geometrical figures. The chosen figures are "brick walls" and we develop, with appropriate higher-order functions, expressions which directly represent the geometric arrangement of the bricks. Evaluation of the expressions however, yields a data structure from which a graph plotter could be driven very directly to draw the corresponding picture.

9.1 ON TYPES OF FUNCTIONS

Suppose we denote by N the set of all integer numbers, positive, zero and negative. The function $f(x)$ given by the definition

$$f(x) \equiv x+1$$

is said to be of type $N \rightarrow N$. The type of its argument x is a number and so is the type of its result. Normally we write this type information as

$$f:N \rightarrow N.$$

The type of the argument is placed to the left of the arrow and the type of the result to the right. The function $g(x)$ given below is of type $N \times N \rightarrow N$

$$g(x,y) \equiv x+y, \qquad g:N \times N \rightarrow N.$$

Here we have listed the type of the arguments to $g(x,y)$ in order, separated by $\times$ signs. In general, then, a function $f(x_1, \ldots, x_n)$ is of type $X_1 \times X_2 \times \ldots \times X_n \rightarrow Y$ if its argument x_1 is of type X_1, x_2 is of type X_2 and so on and its result is of type Y. Let us look at some more interesting functions.

Consider a function which takes as argument a number and a function and produces a number as result:

$$h(x,f) \equiv x+f(x).$$

The type of the argument x is N and the type of the argument f is $N \rightarrow N$. The result is of type N, so we write the type specification of the function h as

$$h:N \times (N \rightarrow N) \rightarrow N$$

Next consider the function

$$twice(f) \equiv \lambda(x)f(f(x))$$

then we would have

$$twice: (N \rightarrow N) \rightarrow (N \rightarrow N)$$

by the following argument. Since x is of type N and f is of type $N \to N$ then $f(x)$ is of type N. Further $f(f(x))$ is of type N and hence $\lambda(x)f(f(x))$ is of type $N \to N$. Thus, *twice* is a function which maps an argument of type $N \to N$ to a result of type $N \to N$.

Thus far in the book we have been somewhat casual in the way we have named a function when writing about it in the body of the text. In the case of a function with a definition such as the usual one for *append(x,y)*:

$$append(x,y) \equiv \ldots$$

when discussing the function we have sometimes referred to it as "the function *append(x,y)*" in conformity with common usage and sometimes as "the function *append*". We can afford this casualness no longer. For now "the function *twice(f)*" and "the function *twice*" are two different things. In fact they are different types of things.

$$twice(f) \colon N \to N$$
$$twice \colon (N \to N) \to (N \to N)$$

We have been able to avoid confusion so far because the results of functions have generally been simple data values and not functions. Thus in "the function *append(x,y)*" it is clear that we do not mean the result of *append(x,y)*, for that is a list and not a function. However, throughout the remainder of this chapter we shall be much more strict about our method of naming functions in the text so that when we write a function with arguments attached, for example *twice(f)*, we are referring to the results of applying *twice* to f and not simply to the function *twice*.

There is another small difficulty with the function *twice*. It is indifferent to the fact that its argument applies to numbers. It would be more correct to state that the type of *twice* is

$$twice \colon (X \to X) \to (X \to X)$$

for any X. To illustrate this indifference, and as a first example of the power of higher-order functions, consider the call *twice(twice)*. Supposing that we denote the type of the argument as $(Y \to Y) \to (Y \to Y)$; then the constraint on the type definition of *twice* has been met. This argument is certainly of the form $X \to X$ if we take $X = (Y \to Y)$. Thus the call

$$(twice(twice))(g)$$

is well defined. In fact, if we inspect the definition we see that this has the same value as

$$twice(twice(g))$$

and eventually that it has the same value as *fourtimes*(g), where

$$fourtimes(g) \equiv \lambda(x) \; g(g(g(g(x))))$$

Note that *fourtimes* is of the same type as twice. The important point is the flexibility which has been achieved by the use of function-producing functions. If we had defined *twice* as a function of two arguments, *twice*(f,x) $\equiv$ $f(f(x))$, we could not have made the call *twice*(*twice*). It will transpire that this form of definition is very powerful, not least in that it allows a definition of the form

$$fourtimes \equiv twice(twice)$$

This is the first of a number of simplifications of expression which higher-order functions allow.

Suppose we denote by *List*(X) the type of a value which is either *NIL* or is a list of values of type X. Then we can specify the types of the basic Lisp primitives:

$$cons: X \times List(X) \to List(X)$$
$$car: List(X) \to X$$
$$cdr: List(X) \to List(X)$$

Often the type of the arguments of a function will be given as a wider domain than those for which the function is actually defined. That is to say, we shall consider our functions to be defined only for some of the values which can be given as arguments according to the type specifications. Above, *car* and *cdr* are functions which are only defined on arguments of type *List*(X) which are not *NIL*. A function which is not defined for some arguments which satisfy the type constraint is said to be *partial*. It will be perfectly satisfactory, from the point of view of our understanding of what our higher-order functions will do, if we specify them as partial functions.

The higher-order function *map* which we met in Chapter 2 has the definition

$$map(x,f) \equiv \textbf{if } eq(x,NIL) \textbf{ then } NIL \textbf{ else}$$
$$cons(f(car(x)), map(cdr(x),f))$$

The type of this function is as follows:

$$map: List(X) \times (X \rightarrow Y) \rightarrow List(Y)$$

That is, *map* expects to be given a list of X's and a function from X to Y. It will produce a List of Y's. We can check that the definition is correct from the point of view of type. We may tabulate our check of the expression $cons(f(car(x)), map(cdr(x),f))$ as in (9.1).

$$
\begin{aligned}
x &: List(X) \\
f &: X \rightarrow Y \\
car(x) &: X \\
cdr(x) &: List(X) \\
f(car(x)) &: Y \\
map(cdr(x),f) &: List(Y) \\
cons(f(car(x)),map(cdr(x),f)) &: List(Y)
\end{aligned}
\tag{9.1}
$$

Here we have begun by tabulating the types of the parameters x and f and then each of the subexpressions. We assume that *map* has the type we are trying to check and hope that we do not encounter some of the paradoxical situations familiar to students of basic mathematics. A more formal treatment of this process is beyond the scope of this book.

Let us redefine *map*, so that it has type

$$map: (X \rightarrow Y) \rightarrow (List(X) \rightarrow List(Y))$$

That is to say, this new *map* expects only one argument, a function of type $X \rightarrow Y$. Its result is a function of type $List(X) \rightarrow List(Y)$. The definition we require is

$$map(f) \equiv \lambda(x) \textbf{ if } eq(x,NIL) \textbf{ then } NIL \textbf{ else}$$
$$cons(f(car(x)),(map(f))(cdr(x)))$$

or perhaps better

$$map(f) \equiv g \textbf{ whererec } g = \lambda(x) \textbf{ if } eq(x,NIL) \textbf{ then } NIL \textbf{ else}$$
$$cons(f(car(x)), g(cdr(x)))$$

This version of *map* is a very powerful function, as we shall demonstrate. Suppose we have f of type $X \rightarrow Y$: then $map(f)$ is of type $List(X) \rightarrow List(Y)$.

Now, a similar construction leads us to conclude that the type of $map(map(f))$ is

$$List(List(X)) \rightarrow List(List(Y)).$$

Thus, $map(map(f))$ is a function which expects as argument a two-level list, and produces a two-level list as result. If we consider what it does, we will see that it constructs from the argument x: $List(List(X))$ a congruent list y: $List(List(Y))$, where each second level element of y is the result of applying f to the corresponding element of x. To be more specific, if $f = \lambda(v) \ v+1$ and we have

$$x = ((1 \ 2 \ 3) \ (4 \ 5) \ (6 \ 7 \ 8)),$$

then

$$(map(map(f)))(x) = ((2 \ 3 \ 4) \ (5 \ 6) \ (7 \ 8 \ 9)).$$

Clearly we can nest the applications of map as deeply as we wish.

Next, let us consider the function $map(map)$. Since we have

$$map: (X \rightarrow Y) \rightarrow (List(X) \rightarrow List(Y))$$

we can conclude that

$$map(map): List(X \rightarrow Y) \rightarrow List(List(X) \rightarrow List(Y))$$

That is to say, $map(map)$ expects to be given as argument a list of functions, each of type $X \rightarrow Y$. It produces as result a list of functions, each of type $List(X) \rightarrow List(Y)$. This also requires an example, which of necessity is quite elaborate. First we define the function

$$aplist(f \ l) = \lambda(x) \ \textbf{if} \ eq(x,NIL) \ \textbf{then} \ NIL \ \textbf{else}$$
$$cons((car(f \ l))(x),(aplist(cdr(f \ l)))(x))$$

This function takes as argument a list of functions. Its result is a function which, if applied to a value x, produces as result a list, congruent to the original list of functions, where each element in the result list is obtained by applying the corresponding function to x. Thus the type of $aplist$ is

$$aplist: List(X \rightarrow Y) \rightarrow (X \rightarrow List(Y))$$

As an example of the application of *aplist*, consider the list *increments* defined as follows:

$$increments \equiv cons(\lambda(v)v+1,cons(\lambda(v)v+2,cons(\lambda(v)v+3,NIL)))$$

That is, *increments* is a list of three functions, which respectively increment their arguments by 1, 2 and 3. Now, we can easily determine the correctness of the statement

$$(aplist(increments))(0) = (1\ 2\ 3)$$

In particular, we can check the types using the method of tabulation

$$increments:\ List(N \to N)$$
$$aplist(increments):\ N \to List(N)$$
$$(aplist(increments))(0):\ List(N)$$

Now, we can return to our consideration of *map(map)*. We can verify that

$$(aplist((map(map))(increments)))(0\ 1\ 2) = ((1\ 2\ 3)(2\ 3\ 4)(3\ 4\ 5))$$

Our understanding of this expression is greatly enhanced by the consideration of types of each subexpression.

$$increments:\ List(N \to N)$$
$$map(map):\ List(X \to Y) \to List(List(X) \to List(Y))$$
$$(map(map))(increments):\ List(List(N) \to List(N))$$
$$aplist((map(map))(increments)):\ List(N) \to List(List(N))$$

from which we deduce that the argument and result structures have the correct type. A closer analysis will convince the reader that the results predicted are indeed those which would be computed.

The reader may have come to suspect that if sufficient functions of the power of *map* were available, then programs might be written which were not only incredibly short, but rarely if ever used the concept of a variable. It is indeed possible to achieve this, at least in particular areas of application, and a most convincing argument of this fact has been made recently by Backus. He introduces many powerful functions and those we have studied here are simple equivalents based on his more general forms. The basis of Backus' method is a result from combinatory logic wherein functions called combinators are studied. This result concerns the fact that, given only a few elementary combinators, all other functions can be built without using lambda expressions. Thus, in theory it is possible to avoid the use of variables altogether, although it is convenient at least to have names for functions. In order to give a flavor of the kind of program one constructs using combinators, let us study just two of the basic ones. The interested reader is referred, not only to Backus' work, but to the relevant books on combinatory logic wherein this beautiful theory can be studied, rather independently of the remainder of mathematical logic. The first combinator we shall study is the equivalent of *dot*, which we introduced in Section 2.8. There we defined

$$dot(f,g) \equiv \lambda(x) f(g(x))$$

and hence, although we were not in a position to state it, we had

$$dot:(Y \to Z) \times (X \to Y) \to (X \to Z)$$

for any types X, Y and Z. The equivalent combinator is usually given the uninspiring name B. The type of B is

$$B: (Y \to Z) \to ((X \to Y) \to (X \to Z))$$

and the definition of B is

$$B \equiv \lambda(f) \{\lambda(g) \{\lambda(x) f(g(x))\}\}.$$

However, it is more usual to present the definition of combinators in terms of the identities which they satisfy. The identity for B is

$$((B(f))(g))(x) = f(g(x))$$

and in the theory of combinatory logic, special effort is made to avoid the profusion of parentheses, which we shall not go into here. It is clear from this that we can define

$$twice(f) \equiv (B(f))(f),$$

but this does not avoid the use of a variable, f. This problem is solved by the introduction of another combinator, usually called W, which satisfies the identity

$$(W(f))(x) = (f(x))(x).$$

From this we see that *twice* can be redefined as

$$twice \equiv W(B)$$

simply by substituting in the identities. This, then, is the basis for programming without variables, in our case without lambda expressions. It is instructive to carry out the type checking of these expressions, but this is left as an exercise for the industrious reader.

Finally, in our excursion into the realm of different types of higher-order function, we come to the notion of a *continuation*. Here, we simply gave an example of the utility of a continuation and a discussion of its general form using our type notation. In the next chapter we will give a more convincing example of its power. A continuation is a function which is passed as a parameter to a second function, and to which this second function supplies its result. In general, everything that is to be done to the result of this second function is bound up in the continuation. The utility in this inverted way of programming is that a function which has a continuation as parameter can, by deciding not to call the continuation, effectively abort part or all of the remainder of the program.

We consider the factorial function which, without a continuation, is usually defined as follows:

$$fac(n) \equiv \textbf{if } n=0 \textbf{ then } 1 \textbf{ else } n \times fac(n-1)$$

Now we add a continuation to this definition by writing it as follows:

$$facc(n,c) \equiv \textbf{if } n=0 \textbf{ then } c(1) \textbf{ else } facc(n-1, \lambda(z)c(n \times z))$$

The continuation is the parameter c.

First note that $fac(k) = facc(k, \lambda(z)z)$. That is, $facc$ can compute the same values as fac, provided we supply an identity function as the initial continuation. We must convince ourselves that $facc$ has the property that it supplies the factorial of n to the continuation c. This is certainly true when $n=0$. If it is assumed to be true when the first parameter has the value $n-1$, then we see that $(n-1)!$ is supplied to $\lambda(z)c(n \times z)$; hence indeed $n!$ is supplied to c. In general, if we have a function of type $X \rightarrow Y$ and we add a continuation to it we get a function of type $X \times (Y \rightarrow Z) \rightarrow Z$ for some Z. That is to say, the type of the result of the continuation determines the type of the result of the extended function. To illustrate this fact consider the call

$$facc(n, \lambda(z) \ cons(z,z))$$

the result of which will be a pair each of whose parts is $n!$

Now, let us illustrate the use of a continuation to effect abortion of part of a program. First we alter the definition of *facc*, to include a test on whether the argument *n* is negative:

$$facc(n,c) \equiv \textbf{if } n < 0 \textbf{ then } cons(NEGATIVE,n) \textbf{ else}$$
$$\textbf{if } n = 0 \textbf{ then } c(1) \textbf{ else } facc(n-1,\lambda(z)c(n \times z))$$

The important point to note here is that, if the call of *facc* does find $n < 0$, then the result is *cons(NEGATIVE,n)* and the continuation is not called. Hence if we make a call such as

$$facc(k, \lambda(z)cons(z \textbf{ div } m, z \textbf{ rem } m))$$

and, if $k \geqslant 0$, then *facc* will indeed compute the factorial and submit it to the continuation which will compute $k!$ **div** m and $k!$ **rem** m. However, if $k < 0$, the result (*NEGATIVE,k*) will be produced and this will *not* be submitted to the ensuing arithmetic operations **div** and **rem**. Clearly, if the ensuing computation had been a lengthier one, then we would willingly say that it had been aborted by the failure to call the continuation. Programming with continuations in a larger program is far from straightforward unless some very simple scheme is adopted, such as that every function has a continuation. It is not really to be recommended, the device having been invented to give formal mathematical semantics for programming language concepts like **goto** rather than as a programming tool. As programmers, we should recognize that programming with a function such as the second version of *facc* will be difficult. The warning signs are clearly seen when we try to specify the type of this function. The result of *facc(n,c)* is either of type Z, where $c:N \rightarrow Z$, or a *cons* of two atoms. Dealing with this hybrid object is not going to make programming very simple. Nevertheless, continuations are an important concept and something more of their utility can be appreciated by devoting some attention to Exercise 9.8.

9.2 DESCRIBING THE SYNTAX OF A LANGUAGE

We come to the first of our two applications of higher-order functions. We address the problem of building a recognizer for a simple context-free language. A context-free language is one whose syntax can be specified by a set of rules, usually called *productions*, such as the following.

$$\langle csequence \rangle ::= C \mid C \langle csequence \rangle$$
$$\langle vsequence \rangle ::= V \mid V \langle vsequence \rangle$$
$$\langle syllable \rangle ::= \langle csequence \rangle \langle vsequence \rangle \mid \langle vsequence \rangle \langle csequence \rangle \mid$$
$$\langle csequence \rangle \langle vsequence \rangle \langle csequence \rangle$$

In this set of productions (called a grammar) the terminal symbols are C and V. The grammar defines a language of strings of C's and V's. There are three types of phrase. $\langle csequence \rangle$ is a sequence of one or more C's. $\langle vsequence \rangle$ is a sequence of one or more V's. $\langle syllable \rangle$ has one of three forms, a sequence of C's followed by a sequence of V's, a sequence of V's followed by a sequence of C's or the more elaborate C's followed by V's followed by C's. The grammar is intended to describe the common forms of syllables in an English word. Here C stands for "consonant" and V for "vowel". We could have made C and V into non-terminals and enumerated their respective 21 and 5 cases, but we shall not do so because that would complicate our example unnecessarily and it is obvious. If we consider the C and V symbols to be the terminal symbols of the above grammar we have the following examples of strings which are valid instances of the phrase $\langle syllable \rangle$

$$CV, \ VC, \ CVC, \ CCV, \ VCC, \ VVC, \ CVVC, \ CCVVVC$$

Of course, there are infinitely many possibilities.

Assume that the string to be recognized is represented as a list of C's and V's. Assume we have defined functions *vowel* and *consonant* such that, if x is a list of atoms, $vowel(x)$ is true only if x is a singleton list and its member is V, otherwise $vowel(x)$ is false. Similarly, $consonant(x)$ is true only if x is a singleton list and its member is C, otherwise it is false. Clearly, if we wanted to we could redefine these two functions to recognize the 21 consonants and 5 vowels of English without any difficulty. If we denote by A the type of an atom and by L the type of a logical value which is either T (true) or F (false), we have

$$vowel: List(A) \rightarrow L$$
$$consonant: List(A) \rightarrow L$$

Now we wish to be able to define functions of type $List(A) \rightarrow L$ such that, when they are given a list whose entire contents represent a string in one of the phrase classes defined by our grammar, they return the value T, and otherwise return the value F. To do this, we define some higher-order functions which allow us to produce predicates (functions of type $X \rightarrow L$, for any X), from predicates.

Consider first the function

$$orp(p,q) \equiv \lambda(x) \ \textbf{if} \ p(x) \ \textbf{then} \ T \ \textbf{else} \ q(x)$$

If we assume that p and q are of type $X \rightarrow L$, then the type of this function is

$$orp: (X \rightarrow L) \times (X \rightarrow L) \rightarrow (X \rightarrow L)$$

Thus $orp(p,q)$ is also of type $X \to L$. In fact $orp(p,q)$ returns true when applied to arguments $x:X$ only where true would be returned by one or other of p or q. For example, $orp(consonant, vowel)$ is a predicate of type $List(A) \to L$, true only when applied to singleton lists whose sole member is either a C or a V. The next function we need is less trivial. It must be able to determine of a list x if it can be split into two parts, the first of which satisfies the predicate p and the second of which satisfies the predicate q. Let us call this function seq and decide that it will have the same type as orp. Consider how we can split a list x into two lists y and z so that $append(y,z) = x$. There are two cases to consider: $x = NIL$ and $x \neq NIL$. In the first case, there is only one possibility:

$$\text{case (i)} \quad x = NIL \quad y = NIL, \quad z = NIL$$

In the second case there are two possibilities, or we shall consider them so:

$$\text{case (ii)} \quad x \neq NIL$$
$$\text{subcase(a)} \quad y = NIL, z = x$$
$$\text{subcase(b)}$$
$$\text{Suppose } append(y_1, z_1) = cdr(x)$$
$$\text{then } y = cons(car(x), y_1), \ z = z_1$$

Subcase(a) allows for the possibility that x is split into y and z in the trivial way of choosing $y = NIL$. Subcase(b) is the most elaborate of the possibilities. Here we split $cdr(x)$ into parts y_1 and z_1 and then choose y to be the part built from y_1 by replacing $car(x)$ and by choosing z to be just z_1.

We can write a definition of seq most economically if we allow ourselves to use the logical connective e_1 **and** e_2 which is true only if both e_1 and e_2 are true. It is false if e_1 is false or if e_1 is true and e_2 is false. That is, we have the following identity:

$$e_1 \text{ and } e_2 = \textbf{if } e_1 \textbf{ then } e_2 \textbf{ else } F$$

Now, we define seq as follows:

$$seq(p,q) \equiv \lambda(x) \textbf{ if } eq(x, NIL) \textbf{ then } p(NIL) \textbf{ and } q(NIL) \textbf{ else}$$
$$\textbf{if } p(NIL) \textbf{ and } q(x) \textbf{ then } T \textbf{ else}$$
$$(seq(\lambda(y)p(cons(car(x),y)),q))(cdr(x))$$

This definition requires some explanation. The three clauses correspond respectively to case(i), case(ii)(a) and case (ii)(b) of our analysis above. When x is NIL the only split we need analyze is into sublists which are both NIL.

Hence we evaluate $p(NIL)$ **and** $q(NIL)$. When x is not NIL we first try $p(NIL)$ **and** $q(x)$ to find if this trivial split satisfies p and q. If it does, we then return true. If it does not, then we must try to split $cdr(x)$. In fact we rely upon the observation that if x can be split into two nontrivial sublists which satisfy p and q respectively, then that means $cdr(x)$ can be split in such a way that it satisfies $\lambda(y)p(cons(car(x),y))$ and q respectively. The first of these two predicates simply takes the first sublist of $cdr(x)$ and, referring to it as y, replaces $car(x)$ before it applies p. The interested reader may like to check that this definition is consistent from the point of view of types according to the types we have given for seq.

Let us look at how seq can be applied. Consider $seq(consonant, vowel)$: it is typewise correct and has type $List(A) \to L$. In fact, it is true only for lists of exactly two elements, the first of which is a C and the second of which is a V. Now consider

$$seq(consonant, orp(consonant, vowel)),$$

again a function of type $List(A) \to L$. This predicate is true only for lists of two elements, the first of which is a consonant and the second of which is either a consonant or a vowel. With these powerful functions, then, we can define recognizers for the phrases of the little language introduced at the beginning of the section. The necessary definitions are

$$csequence \equiv orp(consonant, seq(consonant, csequence))$$
$$vsequence \equiv orp(vowel, seq(vowel, vsequence))$$
$$syllable \equiv orp(seq(csequence, vsequence), orp(seq(vsequence, csequence),$$
$$seq(csequence, seq(vsequence, csequence))))$$

That these are typewise correct is easily checked. That they define the correct recognizers requires a little study. The predicate $csequence$ is true if its argument either satisfies $consonant$ or is a list which splits into sublists satisfying $consonant$ and $csequence$. That is precisely the category of phrase which we referred to as $\langle csequence \rangle$. Similarly, $vsequence$ is a recognizer for phrases of category $\langle vsequence \rangle$. Finally, $syllable$ is true when applied to list x if x has one of three structures, precisely those defined in the rule of syntax given at the beginning of this section.

The important point to note is that the form of the definitions of these functions is a precise transliteration of the form of the rules of syntax. The ability to write our definitions in this form, without the intrusion of any lower-level detail, was afforded by the careful choice of the higher-order functions orp and seq. A recognizer of this kind may not be terribly efficient and it does have some theoretical limitations (it can arbitrarily remove ambiguities from an ambiguous language) but it has the important property that, if our definitions of *orp* and *seq* do indeed correctly implement the equivalent concepts used to write productions, then the above recognizer is correct by inspection. The program could not be a more obvious implementation of the rules of syntax. It effectively *is* the rules of syntax. This is a most convincing demonstration of the power of higher-order functions to give a natural expression to an executable program.

9.3 DESCRIBING THE STRUCTURE OF A PICTURE

We turn now to a thoroughly different kind of application to those we have studied elsewhere in the book. We shall show how suitably chosen higher-order functions can be defined with the property that expressions constructed from them give what would be generally agreed to be succinct descriptions of geometrical patterns. However, the functions will be so defined that their evaluation amounts to a construction of the pattern. The class of patterns, or any picture for that matter, which could be so treated, is unlimited, but we shall concentrate in this section on what we shall refer to as tiling patterns. The principal example we shall use is the pattern made by the regular arrangement of bricks in a brick wall. A quick glance ahead at some of the pictures illustrating this section will familiarize you with the details of such patterns. It is necessary first for us to review some of the properties of the geometrical concept of a vector. We shall only need the most elementary concepts of adding and subtracting vectors and multiplying a vector by a scalar quantity. We shall embed these facilities in our purely functional language, noting that they could easily be implemented in terms of the existing facilities of that language, but we shall not define such an implementation.

In geometry, vectors are used to represent displacements in space. We shall consider only the two-dimensional space of our flat sheet of paper. We shall denote vectors by names such as **a**, **b**, **c**, etc., and draw them in pictures as directed arrows (Fig. 9.1).

Fig. 9.1

The value of **a** is the displacement of the point of the arrow from the tail of the arrow. In general, a two-dimensional vector **a** is thought of as a pair of numbers $\langle a_x, a_y \rangle$ representing the components of the displacement parallel to the x and y axes respectively (Fig. 9.2).

Fig. 9.2

With this representation, we can define the operations of addition and negation of vectors as follows:

$$\mathbf{a} = \langle a_x, a_y \rangle \qquad \mathbf{a}+\mathbf{b} = \langle a_x+b_x, a_y+b_y \rangle$$
$$\mathbf{b} = \langle b_x, b_y \rangle \qquad -\mathbf{a} = \langle -a_x, -a_y \rangle.$$

The addition of vectors satisfies what is called the *parallelogram rule*. It is in this form that it is most easily understood, especially with respect to the application of this section (Fig. 9.3).

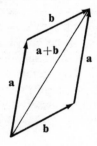

Fig. 9.3

The displacement represented by $\mathbf{a}+\mathbf{b}$ is that displacement one gets by experiencing the displacement $\mathbf{a}$ followed by the displacement $\mathbf{b}$ or vice versa. The reader can easily check this by drawing the x and y projections of the vectors in the parallelogram. The negation of a vector yields a vector of equal magnitude and opposite direction (Fig. 9.4).

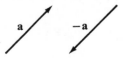

Fig. 9.4

We define subtraction of vectors by

$$\mathbf{a} - \mathbf{b} = \mathbf{a} + (-\mathbf{b}).$$

A vector is not fixed in space, it has simply a direction and a magnitude. We regard $\mathbf{0} = \langle 0,0 \rangle$ as a special case of a vector which has magnitude 0. The fact that it does not have direction causes no problems. Clearly

$$\mathbf{a} + \mathbf{0} = \mathbf{a}.$$

Consider the very simple pattern shown in Fig. 9.5, each of the four

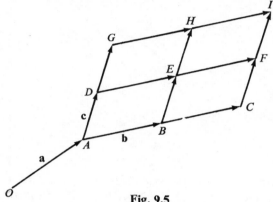

Fig. 9.5

parallelograms being congruent. We can enumerate the displacements from O of some of the points in the figure as in Table 9.1.

Table 9.1

Point	Displacement from O
A	$\mathbf{a}$
B	$\mathbf{a} + \mathbf{b}$
C	$\mathbf{a} + \mathbf{b} + \mathbf{b}$
D	$\mathbf{a} + \mathbf{c}$
E	$\mathbf{a} + \mathbf{b} + \mathbf{c}$
I	$\mathbf{a} + \mathbf{b} + \mathbf{b} + \mathbf{c} + \mathbf{c}$
O	$\mathbf{0}$

One final useful feature of vectors is the fact that they may be multiplied by scalars (numbers). This multiplication is defined by

$$k\,\mathbf{a} = \langle ka_x, kb_x \rangle.$$

Thus, for example, the displacement of I from O in the above figure is re-written as $\mathbf{a}+2\mathbf{b}+2\mathbf{c}$. It is in fact a proven property of vectors that we can manipulate them algebraically, using the operations we have defined, using the same rules (of cancellation etc.) that we use for numbers.

Next we must consider how we are going to describe pictures in such a way that they can be drawn by a mechanical device such as a graph plotter. The method we choose is to build a data structure which contains details of each line in the picture. We assume that pictures are built from short, straight lines. First we must consider how we can define just one line. We must specify its position relative to an origin and its magnitude and direction. This we can do with two vectors (Fig. 9.6). The line AB is specified by the two vectors

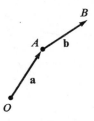

Fig. 9.6

$\mathbf{a}$ and $\mathbf{b}$. The vector $\mathbf{a}$ denotes the position of the point A relative to O and the vector $\mathbf{b}$ the position of point B relative to A. The data structure which we shall use to represent the occurrence of line AB is written as

$$line(\mathbf{a},\mathbf{b})$$

It is best to think of the function *line* as being similar to *cons*. It builds a record which embeds the vectors $\mathbf{a}$ and $\mathbf{b}$ and which is recognizable as a record of that type. That is, when we analyze the data structure representing a picture, we can determine when we have encountered a substructure repre-senting a line. Now, to represent a picture with more than one line in it, we use another *cons*-like function, which we call *picture*, such that if p and q are representations of pictures then *picture*(p,q) is the data-structure obtained by including all the lines of p and all the lines of q.

If we denote by V the type of a vector value and by P the type of a data structure representing a picture, we have the following types for our func-tions:

$$line: V \times V \to P$$
$$picture: P \times P \to P$$

The parallelogram rule can be depicted by drawing the structure represented by

$$picture(line(\mathbf{0},\mathbf{a}),\ picture(line(\mathbf{0},\mathbf{b}),\ picture(line\ (\mathbf{a},\mathbf{b}),$$
$$picture(line(\mathbf{b},\mathbf{a}),\ line(\mathbf{0},\mathbf{a}+\mathbf{b})))))$$

which constructs the picture which we used to illustrate that rule, situated with its lower left-hand corner at the origin. To illustrate how we use these functions to build a picture, consider the following function, which is called *ladder*. When using variables which have vector variables, we shall write them as we usually write variables, that is as *a,b,c,...* reserving the form **a,b,c,...** for vector values.

$$ladder:\ N\times V\times V\ \rightarrow P$$
$$ladder(n,\ a,\ b)\ \equiv\ \textbf{if}\ n=1\ \textbf{then}\ line(a,b)\ \textbf{else}$$
$$picture(line(n\times a,b),ladder(n-1,a,b))$$

This function, if called with arguments *ladder*(7,**a,b**) will build a structure representing Fig. 9.7.

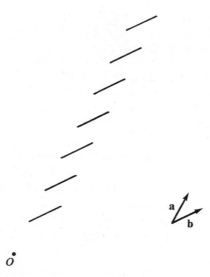

Fig. 9.7

Here we have adopted the convention of drawing the constant vectors, on which the picture is based, off to the side, so that those lines which actually appear in the picture (to the right) are clearly shown. The definition of the function *ladder* is trivially similar to many functions we have used earlier and the reader will easily determine that the call *ladder*(7,**a**,**b**) generates a picture including the lines

$$line(7\mathbf{a},\mathbf{b}), line(6\mathbf{a},\mathbf{b}), \ldots, line(\mathbf{a},\mathbf{b})$$

which are indeed the lines of the ladder in the picture.

If we introduce functions which allow us to compute the projections of a vector on the axes, we can easily define a picture for a box. We define *xproj* and *yproj* so that

$$xproj(\mathbf{a}) = \langle a_x, 0 \rangle \qquad yproj(\mathbf{a}) = \langle 0, a_y \rangle$$

thus *xproj* and *yproj* are both of type $V \rightarrow V$. We can describe a rectangular box by giving the location of one of its corners and the magnitude and direction of its diameter. Our box will always have its sides parallel to the axes:

$$\begin{aligned} box(\mathbf{a},\mathbf{b}) \equiv\ &picture\ (picture(line(\mathbf{a},xproj(\mathbf{b})), line(\mathbf{a},yproj(\mathbf{b}))),\\ &picture(line(\mathbf{a}+\mathbf{b}, -xproj(\mathbf{b})), line(\mathbf{a}+\mathbf{b}, -yproj(\mathbf{b})))) \end{aligned}$$

The reader can easily verify that the box which would be drawn by the call *box*(**a**,**b**) is as shown in Fig. 9.8. Here, **a** gives the location of *A* relative to *O* and **b** the location of *B* relative to *A*.

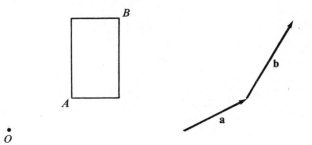

Fig. 9.8

Now we can begin to establish a set of higher-order functions with which to describe pictures. Note that line and box are both of type $V \times V \rightarrow P$. We shall refer to a function of this type as a *skeleton*. We shall be concerned with defining functions which generate skeletons from skeletons. Consider first the function

$$both(p,q) \equiv \lambda(a,b)picture(p(a,b),q(a,b))$$

which has the type

$$both:(V\times V \to P) \times (V\times V \to P) \to (V\times V \to P)$$

That is to say, *both* generates a skeleton from two skeletons. It defines the skeleton *both(p,q)* which includes both pictures which can be generated by skeletons *p* and *q*, at the same place in the picture. Thus the skeleton *both(box,line)* can generate a picture of a box with a diagonal line through it. That is to say the call *(both(box,line))*(**a,b**) would generate the picture in Fig. 9.9.

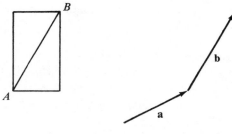

Fig. 9.9

In general, we shall refer to the picture generated by a skeleton, without reference to the vectors to which it is applied. All these vectors can do is to change the location and magnitude of the picture and this is irrelevant to our discussion. Thus we say that the skeleton *both(box,line)* generates the diagonalized box in Fig. 9.9. If we denote the type of a skeleton by S, then *box*, *line* and *both(box,line)* are all of type S and *both* is of type $S\times S \to S$.

Next we define a function of type $N\times S \to S$ which allows us to displace pictures in the x direction.

$$xdisp(k,p) \equiv \lambda(a,b)p(a+k\times xproj(b),b)$$

From this definition we see that *xdisp(k,p)* draws the same picture as that drawn by *p*, but *k* units to the right of where *p* draws it, where a unit is the projection of the vector *b* on the *x*-axis. Thus, for example, the skeleton *both(box,xdisp(3,box))* denotes the picture shown in Fig. 9.10, where the gap is exactly large enough to accommodate two boxes. Two similar functions are *ydisp* and *ddisp* which determine for us the equivalent pictures with displacements in the *y*-direction and diagonally (parallel to *b*). Their definitions are

$$ydisp(k,p) \equiv \lambda(a,b)p(a+k\times yproj(b),b)$$
$$ddisp(k,p) \equiv \lambda(a,b)p(a+k\times b,b)$$

Fig. 9.10

Using these definitions we can define others which allow us to repeat pictures an arbitrary number of times. For example, the following two functions are both of type $N \times S \to S$.

$$row(n,p) \equiv \textbf{if } n=1 \textbf{ then } p \textbf{ else}$$
$$both(p, \, xdisp(1,row(n-1,p)))$$
$$col(n,p) \equiv \textbf{if } n=1 \textbf{ then } p \textbf{ else}$$
$$both(p,ydisp(1,row(n-1,p)))$$

They represent the pictures obtained by n repetitions of p, respectively in the x and y directions. Hence $row(6,box)$ gives us Fig. 9.11 and $col(3,box)$ gives

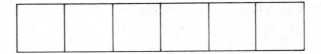

Fig. 9.11

us Fig. 9.12, while $col(3,row(6,box))$ gives us Fig. 9.13, which is almost a

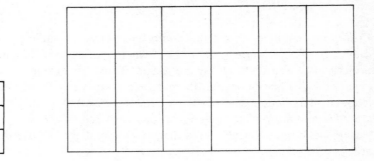

Fig. 9.12   **Fig. 9.13**

brick wall, except for the lapping of bricks. Interestingly, this same picture is denoted by *row*(6, *col*(3,*box*)), the former expression representing its decomposition into 3 layers, this latter its decomposition into 6 piles.

In order to lap bricks in a brick wall we introduce the following function, which is rather like *xdisp*, except that it makes fractional displacements:

$$xfrac(k,p) \equiv \lambda(a,b)p(a+xproj(b)/k,b)$$

Thus, for example, the pictures denoted by *box* and by *both*(*box*,*xfrac*(3,*box*)) are shown in Fig. 9.14.

Fig. 9.14

Now, in order to define a brick wall pattern we want to alternate layers of *row*(*n*,*box*) and *xfrac*(2, *row*(*n*,*box*)). We define a function like *col*, which alternates the pictures in the column:

$$altcol(n,p,q) \equiv \textbf{if } n=1 \textbf{ then } p \textbf{ else } both(p,ydisp(1,altcol(n-1,q,p)))$$

Note how the two skeleton parameters, *p* and *q*, are alternated on the re-

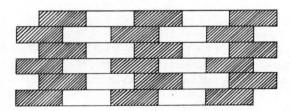

Fig. 9.15

cursive calls. The brick wall of Fig. 9.15 is then

$$altcol(6,row(5,box),xfrac(2,row(5,box)))$$

which describes it as 6 alternating layers of either 5 boxes or 5 boxes shifted right half a box. The corresponding description

$$row(5,altcol(6,box,xfrac(2,box)))$$

describes it as a row of 5 columns of the form shown shaded in Fig. 9.15, each column being 6 bricks high. Each of these functional forms is a concise description of the picture which it denotes. The reader is recommended to convince himself that, when evaluated, they compute a picture which is indeed a brick-wall pattern.

Before leaving this beautiful subject, let us tackle one more pattern. Consider the following function, again of type $N \times S \to S$:

$$cascade(n,p) \equiv \textbf{if } n = 1 \textbf{ then } p \textbf{ else}$$
$$both(p,ydisp(1,xfrac(2,cascade(n-1,p))))$$

A moment's consideration will be enough to discover that this function is based on *row* and *col*. The pictures are stacked up as in *col*, but also fractionally displaced half a picture width in the x direction. Thus for example, the skeleton *cascade*(6,*box*) has the form of Fig. 9.16.

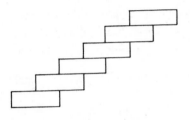

Fig. 9.16

Again, we can define a brick-wall pattern using *row*(n,*cascade*(m,*box*)) or equivalently *cascade*(m,*row*(n,*box*)). In this case, the edges of the walls are sloping. Next we define a function at an even higher level. It will have type

$$N \times (N \times S \to S) \times S \to S$$

where the second parameter has the same type as *row*, *col* and *cascade*. The function *xdimin*(n,s,p) constructs a picture built from s(i,e), where i has all the values between 1 and n.

$$xdimin(n,s,p) \equiv \textbf{if } n = 1 \textbf{ then } s(1,p) \textbf{ else}$$
$$both(s(n,p), xdimin(n-1,s,xdisp(p)))$$

With this definition, for example, we can use *xdimin*(5,*col*,*box*) to describe Fig. 9.17, and *xdimin*(5,*cascade*,*box*) to describe Fig. 9.18. Clearly, equivalent

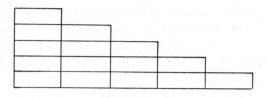

Fig. 9.17

functions for *ydimin* and *ddimin* could be defined and a whole range of brick patterns succinctly described.

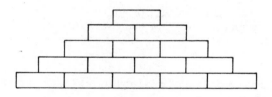

Fig. 9.18

EXERCISES

9.1 The function

$$dot \ (inc(1),rem(2))$$

was used in Section 2.8. Determine its type.

9.2 The function

$$reduce \ (x,g,a) = \textbf{if} \ eq(x,NIL) \ \textbf{then} \ a \ \textbf{else}$$
$$g(car(x),reduce(cdr(x),g,a))$$

was defined in Section 2.8. Determine its type.

9.3 Denote by *Tree*(X) the type of an object which is either of type X or is a *cons* of two objects of type *Tree*(X). Redefine the types of *car*, *cdr* and *cons*. Hence, determine the type of

$$flatten(x) \equiv \textbf{if} \ atom(x) \ \textbf{then} \ cons \ (x,NIL) \ \textbf{else}$$
$$append(flatten(car(x)),flatten(cdr(x)))$$

and, by assuming *append: List*(X) $\times$ *List*(X)$\rightarrow$ *List*(X), tabulate the types of all subexpressions.

9.4 Denote by $Delayed(X)$ the type of an object which is a recipe whose value, when forced, is of type X. We have

delay: $X \rightarrow Delayed(X)$
force: $Delayed(X) \rightarrow X$

Now, determine the type of

$append(x,y) \equiv$ **if** $eq(x,NIL)$ **then** y **else**
$\quad\quad\quad cons(car(x),$**delay**$(append($**force** $cdr(x),y)))$

and check the types of all subexpressions. It will be necessary to introduce a type $Delayedlist(X)$ and to redefine car, cdr and $cons$ for this type.

9.5 What is the type of $dot(map,map)$? Take the definition of dot and map to be

$dot(f,g) \equiv \lambda(x)f(g(x))$
$map(f) \equiv \lambda(x)$ **if** $eq(x,NIL)$ **then** NIL **else** $cons(f(car(x)),(map(f))(cdr(x)))$

as in the text.

9.6 With the above definition of map, what is the type of $map(map(map))$? How could you use such a function?

9.7 Using the definition of B given in the text, what is the type of $B(map)$?

9.8 It is possible to transliterate non-deterministic programs, as described in Chapter 7, to deterministic ones which use continuations as follows. Each function in the program is given two continuations, one to be taken in case of success, the other in case of failure. When **none** is encountered, the failure continuation is called (it has no parameters) otherwise the success continuation is used normally. Devise rules for transforming a non-deterministic program to a deterministic one in this way and transform the program for restricted permutations given in Section 7.1.

9.9 Define a function $andp$ with the same type as orp and the meaning that $andp\,(p,q)$ is true only if the list to which it is applied satisfies both p and q. For what problem of syntax analysis would this function be useful?

9.10 Define a recognizer for the simple arithmetic expression grammar

$\langle term \rangle ::= \langle primary \rangle \,|\, \langle term \rangle - \langle primary \rangle$
$\langle primary \rangle ::= I \,|\, (\langle term \rangle)$

where I stands for some identifier.

9.11 Redefine the functions col, row and $cascade$ to be not of type $N \times S \rightarrow S$ but of type $N \rightarrow (S \rightarrow S)$. Thus the call, for example, $col(6,box)$ would be replaced by $(col(6))(box)$.

9.12 Define a function *dimin* such that, for example,

$$dimin(n,col,xdisp,p) = xdimin(n,col,p)$$

where *col*, *xdisp* and *xdimin* are as defined in the text.

9.13 Hence, or otherwise, write an expression describing Fig. 9.19.

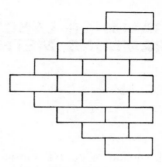

Fig. 9.19

10 PROGRAMMING LANGUAGES AND PROGRAMMING METHODS

Now we return to the discussion of the relationship between conventional programming languages and purely functional languages, which we began in Chapter 1. In that chapter we suggested that conventional programming languages were large and unwieldy as a result of two opposing requirements. They must make reasonably efficient use of conventional computing machines, and they must express as clearly as they can the algorithm which they encode, in order that their validity may be more easily checked. The purely functional language which we have studied since that discussion, whilst being very elementary, has nevertheless illustrated that a higher degree of expressiveness can be obtained by programs in that language than in conventional languages with assignment. Many of these programs can be executed quite efficiently on conventional machines but certainly not as efficiently as equivalent assignment programs. In this chapter, we discuss to what extent this is simply a property of the specific domain of data structures which we have chosen, and illustrate that the choice of many other domains is possible.

First of all, however, we discuss ways in which functional programs can be more clearly expressed in a somewhat more elaborate language than that which we have used in this book. In particular, we address the problem of a function with multiple results, because this has an important and elegant solution. We briefly discuss other possible data domains for functional programming and show that, with an appropriate choice of domain, functional programs can be taken to be specifications of computer components conventionally built in hardware. With this preparation, we turn to the important question of efficiency. In the next chapter we shall study a particular implementation of a functional language, which is the basis for our statement that some functional programs can be efficiently executed on conventional machines. Nevertheless, we must consider the dominant.effect conventional machines have on our programming languages and programming methods, and in particular the influence of the assignment statement upon the structure of our programs. We conclude by arguing that new machine architectures can alter the balance which is currently in favor of the assignment statement, and that developments in this direction are extremely desirable.

10.1 ON CLARITY OF EXPRESSION

In Chapters 7–9 we gave many examples of the effectiveness of functional programs for expressing certain computations in a natural way. This clarity of expression in programs is of paramount importance, in order that we may know that our program is correct. A proof of correctness can only be constructed for a program whose own structure is clearly expressed, for otherwise the proof would be too obscure for us to check. One of the fundamental properties of a programming language which makes it possible to express computations clearly in that language is the simplicity of the semantics underlying its constructs. The great advantage which our purely functional language has had is that there are few concepts in that language and each has a relatively simple semantics. In particular, the semantics of our purely functional language is understood entirely in terms of the values which expressions have and not at all in terms of the effect of their order of evaluation. For practical purposes, however, it would be right to conclude that our purely functional language was in fact very rudimentary, and some very simple extensions would greatly enhance its ability to express clearly certain classes of computation. We ought to distinguish carefully between extensions which are purely syntactic and those which require a revision of the semantics of the language. The latter require greater care, if their inclusion in the language makes it more difficult to understand already valid programs. Purely syntactic changes, which still require careful consideration, cannot, however, interfere with our understanding of already valid programs. That purely syntactic extensions can have great power, in terms of improved clarity of expression, is illustrated by the extension which we now undertake.

We extend our purely functional language to allow functions to return multiple results. This is done in two steps as follows. First, we allow a list of well-formed expressions, enclosed in angle brackets, to be a well-formed expression. Thus $\langle e_1, e_2, \ldots, e_k \rangle$ is well-formed if $e_1, \ldots, e_k$ are well-formed. The other extension is that, where previously the language allowed a simple variable to be placed on the left-hand side of a definition (in a block), we now allow a list of identifiers to appear, again enclosed in angle brackets. The way in which we use these combined extensions is illustrated by the following example:

$$\{\textbf{let } f = \lambda(x,y)\langle x \textbf{ rem } y, x \textbf{ div } y\rangle$$
$$\textbf{let } \langle r,d\rangle = f(u,v) \ldots\}$$

Observe how the result of the function f is a list of values and how the structure of this list exactly matches the list of variables to which it is assigned. Hence, the inner block binds r to the value of u **rem** v and d to the value of u **div** v. It is clear that this extension is a purely syntactic one, for what we have done with angle brackets we could have done with *cons*:

$$\{\textbf{let } f = \lambda(x,y)cons(x \textbf{ rem } y, cons(x \textbf{ div } y, NIL))$$
$$\textbf{let } s = f(u,v)$$
$$\textbf{let } r = car(s) \textbf{ and } d = car(cdr(s)) \ldots\}$$

Just as we have allowed lists of variables to occur in the left-hand sides of definitions, we can usefully allow them to occur in formal parameter lists. Further we can allow nesting of lists of variables in a fairly obvious way, but we shall not go into that here.

To illustrate the increased clarity of expression which we obtain from this extension, consider the following definition of digit-by-digit addition. Suppose we have a function which does modulo m addition on three modulo m digits.

$$add1d(a,b,c) = \langle (a+b+c) \textbf{ div } m,(a+b+c) \textbf{ rem } m\rangle$$

Here we assume that a and b are digits to be added in a digit-by-digit addition and c is the carry digit, carried into that place. The result of *add1d* is a pair of values, respectively the carry out of that place and the sum digit. Now, we can define *addnd* which takes as argument two lists of modulo m digits, each list of the same length, and returns as its result a list of the sum digits and a final carry digit. The definition is straightforward:

$$addnd(\dot{x},y) = \textbf{if } cdr(x) = NIL \textbf{ then } add1d(car(x),car(y),0) \textbf{ else}$$
$$\{\textbf{let } \langle ci,s\rangle = addnd(cdr(x),cdr(y))$$
$$\{\textbf{let } \langle co,d\rangle = add1d(car(x),car(y),ci)$$
$$\langle co,cons(d,s)\rangle\}\}$$

If the lists x and y have only one digit in them then *add1d* can be used with a carry in of 0. Otherwise we use *addnd* to add together all but the top digit, obtaining a carry ci and a sum s. Next we use *add1d* to add the top digits with a carry in of ci and a carry out of co. The resulting top digit is d and hence the result of adding x to y is obtained by *consing* d onto the front of s.

We could of course write this definition without extending the language. Is the function more clearly expressed using the extension than not using it? Let us consider the other ways we have of writing it. Expanding the angle brackets using *cons* is left as an exercise for the reader, who must consider for himself which version of the program he best understands. A second alternative is to implement *addnd* as two separate functions, one which computes the carry, the other which computes the list of sum digits. This is a strong contender for equal clarity of expression. Again it is left to the reader to construct the program (see Exercise 10.3) but this time it is the author's opinion that clarity of expression has been lost. In fact it is not really the same algorithm which is expressed. The computation of the carry appears to recompute the low-order sums and the computation of the sum appears to recompute the low-order carries, in an inefficient way. The effect is that the parallel evaluation of these two parts of the result is not expressed at all; indeed the resulting program suggests that carries are recomputed frequently. This is a different kind of addition process. A third method of avoiding use of the extension is to use the notion of continuation, discussed in Chapter 9. We shall construct this solution.

Each of the functions *add1d* and *addnd* is extended to include an additional parameter, its continuation. The call, for example $addnd(x,y,f)$ then means add the list of digits x to the list of digits y and apply the function f to the results of this addition. The continuation of course will expect two parameters, respectively the carry and the list of sum digits. The new definitions are

$$add1d(a,b,c,f) \equiv f((a+b+c) \textbf{ div } m,(a+b+c) \textbf{ rem } m)$$

$$addnd(x,y,f) \equiv$$
$$\textbf{if } cdr(x) = NIL \textbf{ then } add1d(car(x),car(y),0,f) \textbf{ else}$$
$$addnd \ (cdr(x),cdr(y),\{\lambda(ci,s)$$
$$add1d(car(x),car(y),ci,\{\lambda(co,d)$$
$$f(co,cons(d,s))\})\})$$

This definition has been written in a form which suggests its close syntactic relationship to the form which uses angle brackets. Note how the actual continuations supplied to nested calls of *addnd* and *add1d* have been written as lambda expressions with formal parameters with the same names (indeed the same roles) as the corresponding local variables in the earlier program. Is this program an equally clear expression? Again, it is a strong contender because of the close syntactic relationship to the earlier form, but the use of continuations makes this program, in the author's opinion, less attractive than the earlier form. Without regard to efficiency (in any case, these programs have comparable efficiency) we must conclude that the extension of our functional language to include functions with multiple results adds a great deal of power to the language in terms of clarity of expression.

There are many ways in which the language can be redefined, in particular to give it alternative syntaxes, which may or may not enhance its ability to express computation clearly. For example, a syntax which looks thoroughly different is the syntax of equations. This was what we used when we first defined the compiler for Lispkit Lisp in Chapter 6. Each conditional part of a function definition is written as a separate equation. Thus in the compiler we wrote, for example,

$$(ADD \; e_1 \; e_2)*n = e_1*n \mid e_2*n \mid (ADD)$$

This was just an abbreviation for the form

$$compile(cons(ADD,cons(e_1,cons(e_2,NIL))),n,c)$$
$$= compile(e_1,n,compile(e_2,n,cons(ADD,c)))$$

In such an equation, structures are introduced on the left-hand side only to allow names (here e_1,e_2) to be assigned to their parts. The same name used on the right-hand side indicates inclusion of the corresponding part in the expression. Designing large functional programs, one often adopts this style of writing. The reason we have not used it throughout the book is that it is difficult to define the allowable forms of the left-hand side without appealing to the kind of language one knows how to interpret. Equations of this form are a powerful means of expression, since they combine a parsimonious description (of part of a program) with a close syntactic relationship to the eventual, executable form of the program.

10.2 ON DATA DOMAINS

Our discussion of functional programming has consistently made use of the specific data domain, that is lists or S-expressions, which were introduced at the very beginning of Chapter 2. However, much of the development we have made is not dependent upon that choice and, to put the record straight, we shall discuss some of the alternative domains which we might have used. The extent to which the choice of this domain was essential to, or considerably eased the progress of, our development will also be identified. We shall not be greatly concerned by the fact that the data domain of S-expressions allows, in particular, symbolic data in the form of alphanumeric atoms. Rather, we shall be concerned with the fact that it restricts us to the representation of trees of atoms, which whilst being very general are nevertheless not entirely natural for some applications. Whether the atoms are symbolic or numeric is not so important as whether we can easily combine them into the structures which are natural to the problem we wish to solve.

A number of alternative data domains can easily be enumerated if only we consider the facilities of other programming languages. Instead of lists we could have employed sets or arrays or sequences. However, before we discuss the effect each of these choices would have had on the language which we have developed and the applications to which we have been able to put it, let us recall the various facts which we have learned about functions. We are familiar with the notion that a function may be an argument to another function or the result of a function. We have discussed at length the notion of embedding a function in a data structure. It is only a small step further to the conclusion that we could use the notion of function as our only data structure. Then every data structure which our program manipulated would be a function. In Chapter 3 we saw how a (restricted form of) set could be represented by a function. As another illustration, consider the following definitions of functions car', cdr', and $cons'$.

$$car'(s) \equiv s(CAR)$$
$$cdr'(s) \equiv s(CDR)$$
$$cons'(x,y) \equiv \lambda(z) \text{ if } z = CAR \text{ then } x \text{ else } y$$

They are a set of functions which we could consistently use as replacements for car, cdr and $cons$. An S-expression constructed by $cons'$ is represented by a function which expects to be given the arguments CAR or CDR and which then returns the corresponding part of the structure which it represents. Hence it seems we can indeed, at least theoretically, do without list structures as we have used them.

However, if we look at this proposition a little more carefully, we see that it leaves some questions unanswered. In particular, can functions themselves be implemented without using the notion of a list or something equivalent to it? Our study of the SECD machine has given us the opportunity to learn a great deal about how to support functions in terms of more machine-oriented concepts. There of course we made a great deal of use of the ability to construct arbitrarily complex tree structures. We embedded control lists in closures and environments in closures and eventually embedded closures in environments. Hence, if we were to base an implementation of functions on such a machine, the subsequent implementation of lists using $cons'$ as above would not be avoiding the use of $cons$, but simply hiding it within the machine. In fact, because functions can, once constructed by the run-time machine, exist for an arbitrarily long time (in fact until the end of the program because the function may itself be the result), we are forced to accept that the storage management problem for functions is at least as difficult as it is for lists. Of course it is only just exactly as difficult, because we have shown how to implement functions using lists. Hence we must conclude that using functions as our only data domain buys us nothing other than a parsimony of language and even that saving is very slight. The efficiency of *cons'* and its associated functions is of course another matter. We can hardly expect it to be as efficient as *cons*.

Depending upon the area of application of a functional language, other choices of data domains might be more appropriate. The three which we have mentioned—sets, arrays and sequences—deserve a little discussion. We have, in the examples which we have discussed from time to time, often used sets with such functions as *addtoset* and *member*. This has only illustrated the fact that lists can be used to represent sets. The converse is also true, but not so trivial. However, for applications in which sets are all that is required, a direct use of the usual operations of set algebra is more appropriate than the use of list operations. However, even in such an application we might accidentally make use of lists. This might occur, for example, if we assumed that our functional language could support multiple-valued functions as described in the previous section.

The case of arrays as a data domain really requires more discussion than we can afford to give it. The basic operations on arrays are, like those for lists, construction of an array from subarrays and selection of a subarray from an array. The essential difference is that selection is done by indexing. In the simplest case one selects a 0-dimensional array, a scalar, from a 1-dimensional array, a vector, using an integer value. Conversely, a 0-dimensional array, and a 1-dimensional array can be combined to form a new 1-dimensional array. The advantages of arrays are two-fold. Firstly there are many applications which we (now) think of naturally in terms of indexing, and secondly conventional machines are very good at this precise operation. Section 10.3 is devoted to a study of the relationship between conventional machines and programming, and so in that section we will discuss this point further. The notion of sequence is not very different from that of list. We could well have used it as an alternative. As it is, we leave the study of it as an exercise for the reader (Exercise 10.5).

As an illustration of a thoroughly different data domain for functional programs, we consider the implementation of algorithms in hardware rather than software. The example we choose, of course, is the adder of the previous section. This program is very much simpler than the usual adder of a real machine, but it serves to illustrate the principle. Recall that the function *addnd*(x,y) expects as arguments two lists, each of n digits, say. Rather than consider these *n* digits as available as elements of a list, accessible by successive applications of the function *cdr*, we consider them to be available on *n* adjacent wires. We will deal with this bundle of wires as a whole and depict it by an arrow, labeled with the size of the bundle (Fig. 10.1). The adder is then

Fig. 10.1

represented by a box of the form shown in Fig. 10.2. Similarly, the one digit

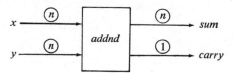

Fig. 10.2

adder is represented by a box of the form shown in Fig. 10.3. Remember, all

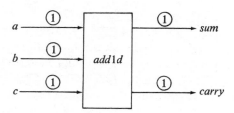

Fig. 10.3

digits are represented in the same base *m*, but we have not stipulated what that is. For real hardware it is normally 2.

The adder described by the function *addnd*(x,y) can now be illustrated in two diagrams. First we deal with the case when the size of x and y is just one digit (Fig. 10.4). Secondly, we deal with the case when the lists x and y are of

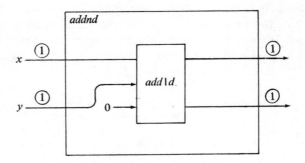

Fig. 10.4

size two or more, in which case we get a nested occurrence of *addnd* (Fig. 10.5).

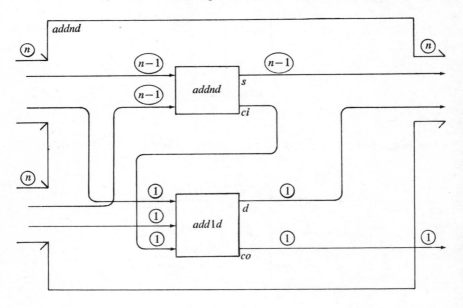

Fig. 10.5

Using these two diagrams we can easily construct the layout for, for example, a four-digit adder. Of course, this is a thoroughly inadequate design as far as hardware is concerned, for it ignores the significant problem of timing.

As a data domain, the use of bundles of wires is interesting. The data values which we ordinarily consider to be in a list, and available as the result of successive applications of *cdr*, have become available on separate wires laid out in space. Thus we have transformed what is essentially a time sequence of values, the list, into a space sequence of values. We ought not to consider this simply as a method of describing hardware components. We ought to consider the use of hardware as an alternative method of implementing our functional programs. Clearly, it would have to be a functional program of significant utility which we committed to hardware, and none of the programs in this book would qualify. The design of a new fast floating-point multiply, for example, could be written as a functional program, and such a program might well be sensibly implemented as hardware.

10.3 THE DOMINANT ASSIGNMENT

It is a principal characteristic of conventional computing machines that they compute by storing data values in memory locations and, not infrequently, replacing the values in those locations by overwriting them. This feature of real machines is reflected in the assignment construct which is fundamental to most programming languages. There is, however, a second aspect of real machines which makes their use with conventional languages so much more efficient than with functional languages, and that is the notion of accessing a data structure by indexing. In this section we shall discuss why it is that these two notions are so closely bound together and why it is that functional languages cannot achieve an equivalent efficiency on conventional machines. There are various ways in which we can interpret this observation. Firstly, we can conclude that unless we are prepared to accept a degree of inefficiency in execution we must avoid functional programming. Secondly, we can conclude that better ways must be discovered of transforming functional programs to run on conventional machines, so that the clarity of expression of these languages can be retained along with acceptable efficiency. Thirdly, we can conclude that we must wait for machines to become a lot faster or we must redesign them to improve their interpretation of functional programs. Each conclusion is a satisfactory one from a particular point of view, and it is these conclusions which we shall now discuss.

The operation of assignment to a simple variable is closly related to the notion of binding a value to a name, as we have used it in our functional language. In Chapter 5, we saw how a program with such assignments could be transformed into an equivalent functional program. The resulting functional program had a characteristic structure and we observed that functional programs written in this restricted form could be compiled into assignment programs simply by reversing the transformation. Therefore we could conclude that functional languages do not exclude the possibility of using conventional machines efficiently, unless we require to use the full generality of those languages. But this observation addresses only part of the problem.

The assignment to simple variables characterized by statements of the form

$$i:=1$$
$$r:=r-x$$

is different from the assignment to components of structures, such as arrays, characterized by statements of the form

$$a[i]:=1$$
$$a[i+1]:=a[i]+1$$

It is this latter use of assignment, to alter only a small part of a larger structure, leaving the remainder of the structure unchanged, which makes the assignment statement such a dominant one in the languages which we use on conventional machines.

In a purely functional language, where we compute values and have no notion of computation by effect, arrays must be handled as entire array values. The principal operators on array values are indexing to obtain a component value, and construction of a new array value from an old one. If a is an array value, i an index and x a value, we write

$$update(a,i,x)$$

for the array value which agrees with a everywhere except in the ith position, where it has the value x. The value of the expression

$$update(update(a,i,a[j]),j,a[i]))$$

is then the array value obtained from a by exchanging the values of the ith and jth elements. This form of expression implies that the new array value, and indeed the intermediate array value $update(a,i,a[j])$ are constructed as independently existing values, for this expression may be used in an environment where further access to the value of a is still required. In general, to determine that $update(a,i,x)$ could be correctly interpreted by overwriting the value of a is a very difficult problem. In the above expression, for example, the nested call generating the intermediate array value could not be so interpreted. That the problem is particularly vicious is easily seen when we realize that the same array value could have more than one name.

Implementation of array values and in particular the update operation on them would involve a great deal of copying of such values, which is avoided by the programmer using the element assignment $a[i]:=x$ precisely because this is a statement of the fact that he has finished with the (*current*) value of *a* and only subsequently requires the value of *update(a,i,x)*. We must ask, is there some representation of array values which might avoid this need to copy either entirely or partially? The problem does not arise with the usual implementation of *cons* (covered in detail in Chapter 12), for the substructures which become the components of *cons* are not copied—only a pointer to them is stored in the structure representing the result of *cons*. It would not be satisfactory to implement array values in this way, however, because doing so loses one of the principal efficiencies of a conventional computer—its ability to index. If an array value is represented in contiguous storage locations, each element is accessible by indexing in the same time, independently of its position in the array. For a linear list, stored with pointers, the time to access the *i*th element is proportional to *i*, its distance from the front of the list. One can use binary trees to represent array values, with the property that for an array value with *n* elements, time to access an element is proportional to $\log_2 n$ and the number of *cons*es required to copy an array value is also proportional to $\log_2 n$. Nevertheless this still compares unfavorably with requirements of unit time to access and zero space for copy required by the elementary update-in-place implied by $a[i] := x$.

Functional languages cannot compete with conventional languages on conventional machines in terms of efficiency if that is an absolute requirement. However, programs written with element-by-element assignment to structured values are very low-level programs. As a consequence, we can expect them to be long and difficult to reason about, and thus difficult to construct correctly. The basic speed of conventional machines is increasing greatly, not least of all because the size of machine one can afford to buy is increasing. Currently, in a computing center one might share a large machine at any point in time between about a hundred users. Soon, machines of equivalent power will be available to individual users simply as a result of advances in microelectronics. Thus, without any advances in machine design, we can expect a hundredfold improvement in the speed of our machines and a hundredfold improvement in available storage. Many applications currently beyond the range to which functional programming can be applied will then come into reach. We might hope that advances in computer architecture, especially memory architecture, which we have principally discussed in this section, will achieve even greater improvements, but it is not within the scope of this book to go into that. Is it too much to hope that eventually we will be able to design machines to fit the languages which we find it natural to use, or must we always have languages which reflect directly the structure of the machines on which they are executed?

EXERCISES

10.1   Define a function which takes as argument a pair of numbers and returns as result their minimum and their maximum. Use the extended language of Section 10.1.

10.2   Hence define a function which takes as argument three numbers and returns three results, the numbers in ascending order.

10.3   Define the digit-by-digit adder of Section 10.1 by separate functions for computing the carry and sum digits. Confirm the observations with respect to the repetition of the carry evaluation.

10.4   Rewrite your digit-by-digit adder as a set of equations. The left-hand sides of these equations will distinguish lists of digits of the form *cons* (*d,NIL*) and of the form *cons(d,s)* where $s \neq NIL$.

10.5   Consider a functional programming language which, instead of lists as its basic data domain, has sequences instead. The operations on sequences are *append*(*s*1, *s*2), which constructs a sequence from two subsequences, and *left*(*s*), *right*(*s*), which return the left and right portions of an arbitrary splitting of the sequence *s*. A sequence *s* of length 1 satisfies the predicate *unitsequence*(*s*) and in that case the value of its single member is *element*(*s*). We have

$$append(left(s),right(s)) = s$$

but neither of the following conditions necessarily holds:

$$left(append(s1,s2)) = s1$$
$$right(append(s1,s2)) = s2$$

Write programs which determine the length of a sequence and the maximum value in a sequence of numbers. Are such programs clearer than the corresponding programs which use lists?

10.6   Design a function which does digit-by-digit multiplication of base *m* numbers. Draw the corresponding multiplier.

10.7   Define a function *sort*(*a,n*) which returns the array value obtained by sorting the *n* elements of the array value *a*. Use any convenient sorting method.

10.8   Define *a*[*i*] and *update* (*a,i,x*) in terms of *car*, *cdr* and *cons* using

        (a) a linear list to represent *a*;
        (b) a binary tree to represent *a*.

Confirm the time and size estimates given in this section with respect to accessing and copying each structure.

11   A FUNCTIONAL PROGRAMMING KIT

At this point we have completed our discussion of functional programming as a technique for building programs. We have also completed our discussion of the semantics of functional programming languages. There remains one important connection which we must establish, that a purely functional language can be efficiently implemented on a conventional computer. Accordingly, this chapter and the next are devoted to a complete description of an implementation of the variant of Lisp which we have used in Chapters 4 and 6 as an example of a concrete programming language. The implementation described here is based on the SECD machine semantics of Chapter 6. This is not by any means the only method of implementing a purely functional language, nor necessarily the best. A major advantage which it does have, however, is that it is reasonably close to the usual methods of implementing high-level languages such as Algol, being complicated only by the need to handle higher-level features such as function-returning functions.

The importance of studying this chapter, even for the reader not intending to implement a purely functional language, cannot be over-emphasized. The details of a full implementation establish important connections between computation with pure functions and the more familiar computation with conventional machines. These connections aid both the reader's understanding of certain uses of functions and his appreciation of the capabilities of conventional machines when suitably organized. As suggested in the Preface, these last two chapters can be read at any time after Chapter 2 has been studied, although a full understanding of them can only be gained after Chapters 4 and 6 have been read. It is hoped that the reader will find himself glancing frequently at these chapters for illumination of the kind that comes from seeing precisely one way of making an implementation.

By repeating the design process described here, the reader will be able to build his own Lispkit system and thus run many of the programs he has devised either as solutions to the exercises or to problems he has invented for himself. The method of description will be to take a traditional top-down structured programming approach to the design, followed by advice on a bottom-up method of testing the program as it is constructed. In describing the design we shall use a *pseudo-code*, that is, a language which is invented for just this descriptive purpose and which, while closely resembling the programming language Algol, is not a programming language for which there exists a compiler. If the reader wishes to actually code the program he will have to transliterate this pseudo-code into his actual programming language. Depending upon the actual programming language chosen for the implementation, this may or may not be a straightforward task.

The advantages of using a pseudo-code over an actual programming language for describing a design are that one both avoids describing the idiosyncrasies of an actual programming language, which are far from relevant to the design and, probably more important, that one also avoids using a language which probably lacks some essential descriptive feature. Pseudo-codes never lack essential features, for one is at liberty to include any features one finds desirable. I shall refer to a program written in pseudo-code as an *abstract program*.

The description of the design is divided into two levels. At the higher level we assume the existence of nice facilities like a record storage area, a string storage area and support for recursive procedures. The next chapter is devoted to the lower-level design, in which we describe the design of such higher-level features for implementation languages which do not have them. It is to be expected that most implementations will need some or all of the features defined in the next chapter. We conclude with a lengthy description of the process of actually building the system once its various components have been transliterated into code. Particular attention is paid to the testing process and a complete test plan is laid out for commissioning new Lispkit systems. Finally, since the implementor of a Lispkit system will undoubtedly wish to make extensions and changes to his system, the process of boot-strapping, whereby this can be done, is described.

11.1 THE LIST SPACE

Symbolic expressions in Lisp are of three kinds: they are either symbolic atoms, numeric atoms or composite items, that is the result of a *cons* operation. The storage structures which represent these symbolic data values will therefore be of three kinds. We can implement them as records (or storage areas) of three types. We shall call these record types respectively *symbol*, *number* and *cons*. When, in our abstract programs (that is our design descriptions in pseudo-code) we wish to refer to a record, we shall do so by means of a **pointer**. A pointer is nothing more than a value which uniquely determines a record. We think of it as pointing at the record. It may be a machine address or an index into an array of records or possibly something a little more complex. If we always think of it as an index into an array of records, that will be perfectly satisfactory, and possibly the simplest conception of it.

A record of type symbol will contain a string, being the alphanumeric atom which that record represents. A new record of this type can be allocated by calling the construction function *symbol*, whose value is a pointer to the newly allocated record. Given a pointer p to a record of type *symbol* we can use the selection function *svalue* to access the string which it contains. Thus, for example, in an abstract program we could write

> **pointer** p; $p := symbol$;
> $svalue(p) := "LAMBDA"$;

to describe the following sequence of events. Declare a pointer variable, allocate a new record of type *symbol* (letting p point to it) and finally set the string field of this new record to point to the string $"LAMBDA"$. We can visualize the outcome of this abstract program as in Fig. 11.1. Here we denote

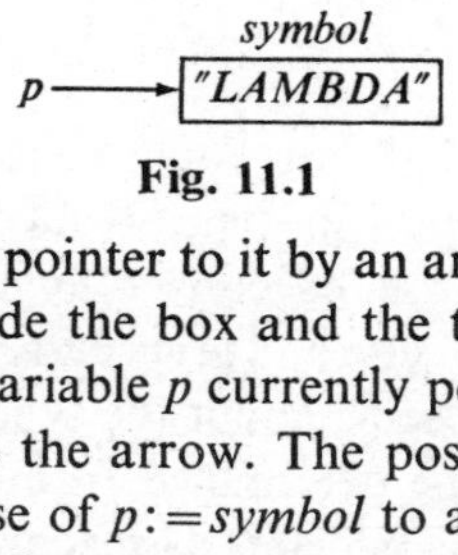

Fig. 11.1

the record by a box and the pointer to it by an arrow. The string value stored in the record is written inside the box and the type of the record is written above it. That the pointer variable p currently points to this record is shown by writing its name next to the arrow. The possibly unusual feature of the above pseudo-code is the use of $p := symbol$ to allocate storage. It is a good idea to think of *symbol* as a function procedure whose result is a pointer.

We use exactly the same ideas for records of type *number*. Here we use *number* as the construction and *ivalue* as the selector function. The value stored in a record of type *number* is an integer, and hence a similar sequence to that given above is

> $p := number$; $ivalue(p) := 127$;

The selector function can also be used simply for retrieving the value stored in a record. Hence we could write, for example,

> $i := ivalue(p)$

to obtain the integer value in the (supposedly) *number* type record pointed to by p. It is possible to discriminate between the record types using additional functions (predicates). The predicate *issymbol* can be applied to a pointer p and will return true or false according to whether the record that p is pointing to is or is not of type symbol. Similarly, *isnumber* can be used

Fig. 11.2

to determine if a record is of type number. If we have the situation of Fig. 11.2, then we would have

$$issymbol(p) = true$$
$$issymbol(q) = false$$
$$isnumber(p) = false$$
$$isnumber(q) = true$$

Now we can give some idea of what an abstract program will look like by introducing the following procedure:

> **procedure** *initialize(p)*;
> **if** *issymbol(p)* **then** *svalue(p)*:=" " **else**
> **if** *isnumber(p)* **then** *ivalue(p)*:=0;

which, if we required it (we shall not) could be used to initialize a record to a standard value depending upon its type. Notice how, in our abstract programming, we have made use of conventional Algol-style programming notions such as **if . . . then . . . else** and **procedure**, while we have taken various liberties such as not being specific about the type of variable used as a parameter, since this can easily be determined from the context. In general, we shall try to write pseudo-code which is as readable as possible by making a judicious compromise between the length of what we write and the redundancy of detail it contains.

Consider now records of type *cons*. These will be used to represent composite values, in particular the result of a *CONS* operation in Lispkit Lisp. Thus they contain two values, both pointers, which respectively represent the *car* and the *cdr* of this composite value (Fig. 11.3).

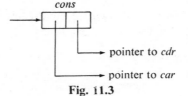

Fig. 11.3

We denote the constructor functions for a record of type *cons*, as before, by *cons* and its selector functions by *car* and *cdr*. Thus the sequence

$$p := cons;$$
$$car(p) := symbol; \; svalue(car(p)) := "LAMBDA";$$
$$cdr(p) := number; \; ivalue(cdr(p)) := 17$$

could be used to build the structure shown in Fig. 11.4,

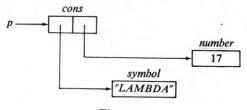

Fig. 11.4

which, as an S-expression, is denoted by

$$(LAMBDA.17)$$

In addition to the constructor and selector functions, we have the predicate *iscons*, which we can use to determine the type of record pointed to by its argument.

It is constructive to look at the structure we obtain for various S-expressions. The structure for the list (A B C) is as shown in Fig. 11.5. The

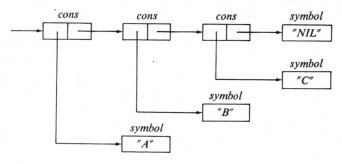

Fig. 11.5

correspondence between the structure and the S-expression can be seen more clearly if we write out the full dot-notation form of it, which is (A.(B.(C.NIL))), where we see that there is a one-to-one correspondence between the *cons* records in the structure and the dots in its S-expression notation. Consider the S-expression $((A.B).(A.B))$. This is equally well represented by the two structures shown in Fig. 11.6. Which of these two structures will actually be

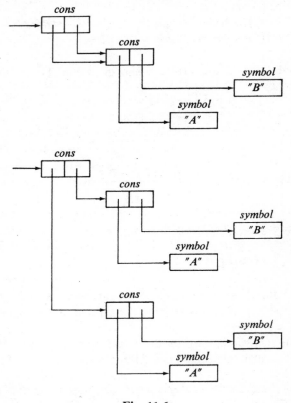

Fig. 11.6

used in any particular instance will depend upon how the value $((A.B).(A.B))$ was constructed. The first could be constructed by

$$(LET (CONS\ X\ X)$$
$$(X\ QUOTE\ (A.B)))$$

and the second by

$$(CONS\ (QUOTE\ (A.B))$$
$$(QUOTE\ (A.B)))$$

The notion of two pointer fields pointing to the same record (that is the pointers have the same value) is called *sharing*. It can present severe difficulties and we shall be at some pains to avoid them. We shall not avoid sharing, however, for it is this precise concept that can make our implementation acceptably efficient not only in storage use but also in use of time, for much copying of structures can be avoided. As an illustration of the difficulty that sharing of storage can introduce, consider the assignment statement

$$car(car(p)):=q$$

where p points to a structure representing the value $((A.B).(A.B))$ and q to a structure representing the value C. According to whether sharing is or is not being used, the effect of this assignment could be to change the value represented by the structure pointed to by p to either $((C.B).(C.B))$ or $((C.B).(A.B))$. Clearly, a definite one of these effects would be intended in any particular circumstance. To avoid such ambiguous possibilities we shall be very cautious about changing the contents of a record which may be pointed to from more than one place.

To avoid cumbersome diagrams in the sequel, we shall drop the convention of drawing symbol and number type records in boxes. The diagram for $(A\ B\ C)$ will then be as shown in Fig. 11.7, where the symbolic atoms are

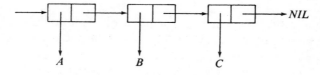

$$A \qquad\qquad B \qquad\qquad C$$

Fig. 11.7

depicted as the item pointed to and where the now redundant record type *cons* has been omitted from the diagram. It must be understood that this diagram is simply an abbreviation of the former, and when at the next level we come to implement these record structures, symbolic and numeric atoms will indeed be represented by records.

Now we are able to collect together all the information about how we will manipulate record structures in Table 11.1. In addition to the functions

Table 11.1

Constructor (returns **pointer**)	Predicate (returns **logical**)	Selector	Selects
symbol	*issymbol* (p)	*svalue(p)*	**string**
number	*isnumber(p)*	*ivalue(p)*	**integer**
cons	*iscons(p)*	*car(p)*	**pointer**
		cdr(p)	**pointer**

shown in Table 11.1 we shall assume the existence of a **pointer** variable called *nil*, declared and initialized as follows:

$$\textbf{pointer } nil; \; nil := symbol; \; svalue(nil) := "NIL";$$

It will be the responsibility of a second-level module to implement the functions described here. For the remainder of the first-level description we shall assume that they are available to us.

11.2 THE PRINCIPAL CONTROL OPERATION

In an earlier section we described how the SECD machine would look to its user. As Fig. 11.8 shows, it expects two inputs, a function in SECD machine

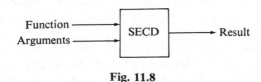

Fig. 11.8

language and a list of arguments to apply to it. It produces as output the result of this application. Each of the inputs and the output are S-expressions. The function is a single S-expression, consisting mainly of numeric operation codes, and the arguments are a sequence of S-expressions. The result is a single S-expression. By inventing suitable operations to read S-expressions, to print S-expressions and to apply a function to its arguments, we can give a very simple abstract program for the principal control operation of the machine:

$$\textbf{pointer } fn,args,result;$$
$$getexp(fn); \; getexplist(args);$$
$$result := exec(fn,args);$$
$$putexp(result)$$

Here we presume that *getexp(fn)* will read a single S-expressioin from the input, build a representation of it in list space and set the pointer variable *fn* to point to it. Similarly we assume that *getexplist(args)* will read a sequence of S-expressions from the input, terminated by end-of-file or some such indication, build a list of them in list space and set the pointer variable *args* to point to this list. The function *exec* will implement the interpretation of SECD machine code, returning a pointer to the result. The final invented operation *putexp(result)* is to print the result as an S-expression on the line printer.

Thus in good structured programming fashion we have separated the concerns of reading S-expressions, of printing them and of executing SECD machine instructions. The remainder of the higher-level design will be concerned with the implementation of these features.

11.3 THE INPUT OF S-EXPRESSIONS

In order to read S-expressions which are formatted as freely as we have used them in this book, we necessarily get involved in a little syntax analysis. The techniques we adopt here are conventional compiler construction practices, for example as described by Wirth, but we do not rely upon the reader having had any experience with them. The objective is to read an S-expression and to build a record structure in list space which represents it. Let us formalize the syntax description which we have for S-expressions:

$$\langle\text{S-expression}\rangle::=\langle\text{atom}\rangle\ |$$
$$(\langle\text{S-expression list}\rangle)$$
$$\langle\text{S-expression list}\rangle::=\langle\text{S-expression}\rangle\ |$$
$$\langle\text{S-expression}\rangle.\langle\text{S-expression}\rangle\ |$$
$$\langle\text{S-expression}\rangle\ \langle\text{S-expression list}\rangle$$

This description defines two categories of phrase, ⟨S-expression⟩ and ⟨S-expression list⟩, and assumes that we have elsewhere defined the phrase ⟨atom⟩. As rules for writing phrases, this description is used as follows. There are two ways of writing an ⟨S-expression⟩. We can write an ⟨atom⟩ or we can write an ⟨S-expression list⟩ enclosed in parentheses. There are three ways of writing an ⟨S-expression list⟩. We can write a single ⟨S-expression⟩ or a pair of ⟨S-expression⟩s separated by a dot or an ⟨S-expression⟩ followed by an ⟨S-expression list⟩. This last alternative gives us the facility to write any sequence of ⟨S-expression⟩s to form an ⟨S-expression list⟩. We can show, by means of a syntax tree (Fig. 11.9), how an ⟨S-expression⟩ (*A B.C*) is constructed according to these rules.

When analyzing input structures according to this syntax, for each ⟨S-expression⟩ recognized on the input we wish to allocate a record of appropriate type and set its fields to the necessary values. In the case

$$\langle\text{S-expression}\rangle::=\langle\text{atom}\rangle$$

we will allocate a record of type symbol or number and set its field to the value of the actual atom appearing on the input. In the case

$$\langle\text{S-expression}\rangle::=(\langle\text{S-expression-list}\rangle)$$

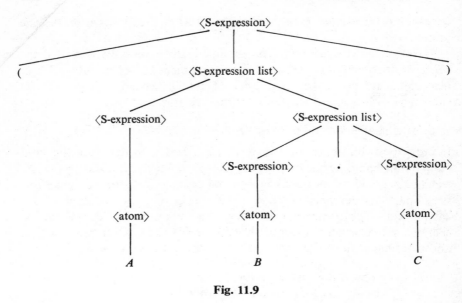

Fig. 11.9

we will allocate a record of type *cons* and set its fields according to what kind of ⟨S-expression-list⟩ we find. If we find

$$⟨S\text{-expression-list}⟩ ::= ⟨S\text{-expression}⟩$$

the *car* field of the allocated record is set to the value of the pointer returned for the (enclosed) ⟨S-expression⟩ and the *cdr* field is set to the value of the pointer *nil*. That is to say, for example, (*A*) causes the construction shown in

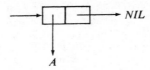

Fig. 11.10

Fig. 11.10, as we would expect. Thus in general we have for (⟨S-expression⟩)

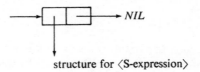

structure for ⟨S-expression⟩

Fig. 11.11

the construction shown in Fig. 11.11. Similarly, when we find

$$\langle\text{S-expression-list}\rangle ::= \langle\text{S-expression}\rangle . \langle\text{S-expression}\rangle$$

we obtain Fig. 11.12, and for

$$\langle\text{S-expression-list}\rangle ::= \langle\text{S-expression}\rangle\ \langle\text{S-expression-list}\rangle$$

we obtain Fig. 11.13.

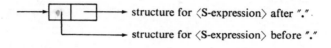

Fig. 11.12

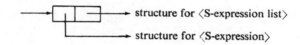

Fig. 11.13

It happens that these rules for the construction of ⟨S-expressions⟩ are such that we can build an analyzer of the kind called *recursive descent*. This is nothing more than writing a recursive procedure for each category of phrase (here ⟨S-expression⟩ and ⟨S-expression-list⟩) whose job it is to scan the input and recognize (that is, scan past) the phrase with which it is associated. The ability to do this depends upon being able to predict, based only on the next symbol on the input, which of the various alternatives must be taken. By presuming that the input will be presented as a sequence of "tokens" which have been suitably characterized, this can be easily achieved.

We presume (and we will design it in the next section) that we have a procedure

       gettoken(token,type)

which, each time it is called, returns the next token from the input, along with an indication as to its type. There are four types of token:

ALPHANUMERIC   i.e. symbolic atoms
NUMERIC   i.e. numeric atoms
DELIMITER   i.e. parentheses and other punctuation
ENDFILE   a special token marking the end of the input

While spacing is used in the input to separate tokens, the user of *gettoken* is not aware of spaces: he sees only the tokens. Thus, successive calls of *gettoken(token,type)* with the input (*A BAY* 73) would return the values shown in Table 11.2.

Table 11.2

Token	type
(	*DELIMITER*
A	*ALPHANUMERIC*
BAY	*ALPHANUMERIC*
73	*NUMERIC*
)	*DELIMITER*
not defined	*ENDFILE*

It is simplest to describe the working of a recursive-descent analyzer by drawing some syntax diagrams, one for each phrase name which will become a procedure in the analyzer. In this case Fig. 11.14 gives the diagram for ⟨S-expression⟩ (abbreviated to *exp*).

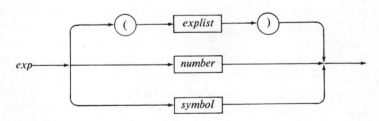

Fig. 11.14

Here we can see that, if we require to recognize an *exp* we can determine which of the three alternatives to take simply by looking at the next token. If it is an opening parenthesis, then we take the first, if it is of type numeric then we take the second, and if it is of type alphanumeric, then we take the third. Similarly, the syntax diagram for ⟨S-expression-list⟩ (abbreviated to *explist*) is as shown in Fig. 11.15.

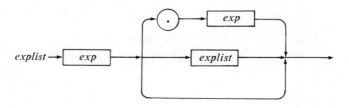

Fig. 11.15

On first sight this seems to present some difficulty. It is resolved by recognizing that an *explist* is always followed by a closing parenthesis. Therefore in Fig. 11.15, after recognizing an *exp* we can determine which way to go according to whether the next token is a dot (first alternative) or a closing parenthesis (third alternative) or something else (second alternative).

Now let us program the analyzer. First we introduce in (11.1) the variables *token* and *type* which will be used to contain the next (as yet unrecognized) token and its type, and the procedure *scan* which will be used to update them.

---

        string *token*; **string** *type*;
        procedure *scan*;
        begin *gettoken(token,type)*;   (11.1)
            if *type* = *"ENDFILE"* **then** *token*:=*")"*
        end;

Here we see that *scan* simply reads the next token. However, on end of file it supplies a closing parenthesis. If *scan* is called repeatedly after end of file, then a series of extra closing parentheses will be supplied. This will have the useful effect of properly terminating a bad S-expression on the input.

In (11.2) we write the main analyzer routines as procedures which return, as a result parameter, a pointer to the structure representing the phrase they have recognized.

```
procedure getexp(e);
if token = "(" then
  begin scan; getexplist(e);
        scan
  end
else if type = "NUMERIC" then
  begin e: = number; ivalue(e): = tointeger(token);
        scan
  end
else
  begin e: = symbol; svalue(e): = token;
        scan                                                    (11.2)
  end;

procedure getexplist(e);
begin e: = cons; getexp(car(e));
      if token = "." then
        begin scan; getexp(cdr(e)) end
      else if token = ")" then
        cdr(e): = nil
      else
        getexplist(cdr(e))
end
```

These procedures cooperate by using the convention that, when they return they will have scanned past all the tokens in the phrase which they recognize, leaving the first token of the next phrase in the variables *token* and *type*. This explains the occurrences of *scan*. This pseudo-code can be seen to correspond very closely to the syntax diagrams. Note how in *getexplist* we call *getexp(car(e))* to assign to the *car* field of the *cons* type record we have just allocated. It might have been clearer to write

$$getexp(p); car(e): = p;$$

where p is some local (temporary) pointer variable.

The other item which needs a word of explanation is the operation *tointeger*, which we shall design in a later section, and which is used to map a numeric string into an integer value.

Let us consider the working of this analyzer when we call *getexp* with $(A\ B)$ on the input. The opening parenthesis causes *getexplist* to be called from *getexp* after scanning past the opening parenthesis. This in turn causes an immediate call of *getexp* to recognize *A*. Table 11.3 lists the various procedure calls and their effects (up until the next call). Observing the

Table 11.3

Call	Input	Effect
getexp(f)	(*A B*)	*scan*
getexplist(f)	*A B*)	*f: =cons*
getexp(car(f))	*A B*)	*car(f): =symbol;*
		svalue(car(f)): ="*A*"; *scan;*
getexplist(cdr(f))	*B*)	*cdr(f): =cons*
getexp(car(cdr(f))	*B*)	*car(cdr(f)): =symbol;*
		svalue(car(cdr(f)): ="*B*"; *scan*
getexplist(cdr(cdr(f)))	)	*cdr(cdr(f)): =nil*
on returning to *getexp*	)	*scan*
	empty	

cumulative effect shown above, we see that *f* rightly has the value shown in Fig. 11.16.

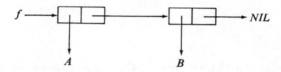

Fig. 11.16

Finally, it is necessary to observe that the syntax analyzer must be primed (initialized) by a single call of *scan* to set *token* and *type* to their values for the first input token.

11.4 THE INPUT OF TOKENS

The syntax analyzer requires the routine

gettoken(token,type)

which assembles each token on the input, determines its type and returns these values as the result of successive calls. This process is called lexical analysis. We can most easily describe the process of lexical analysis using a state diagram (Fig. 11.17). Here the states are denoted by the ovals and the transitions between states by the arrows. Each transition is labeled by the category of character which will cause us to follow it. We assume four categories *blank*, *letter*, *digit* and the anything-else category which we have called *delimiter*.

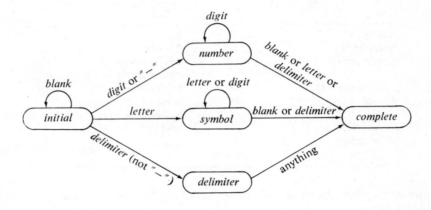

Fig. 11.17

To recognize a token we begin in the initial state and look at the next input character. As long as it is blank we remain in that state. Any other category of character will cause us to switch to one of the states labeled by the class of token which that character heralds. We stay in that state just as long as we receive relevant characters and finally switch to the complete state. The character which causes this final transition may be the first character of the next token and so must be held over to begin assembly at that token. Now we must also deal with end-of-file on the input. To avoid repeated testing for end-of-file, we shall contrive to guarantee that end-of-file will always be preceded by a blank character. This means that we shall always encounter it in the initial state.

Let us assume that we have the routine *getchar* which, when called, sets the variables *ch* and *eof* to the next character from the input and the end-of-file indication, respectively. These variables are declared as

character *ch*; **logical** *eof*;

and with these, we program *gettoken* as shown in (11.3)

```
            procedure gettoken(token,type);
            begin token:=emptystring;
                  while ¬ eof and ch=blank do getchar;
                  if eof then type:="ENDFILE" else
                  if isdigit(ch) or ch = " −" then
                  begin type:="NUMERIC";
                        token:=token^ch; getchar;
                        while isdigit(ch) do
                        begin token:=token^ch; getchar end;
                  end                                           (11.3)
                  else if isletter(ch) then
                  begin type:="ALPHANUMERIC";
                        token:=token^ch; getchar;
                        while isletter(ch) or isdigit(ch) do
                        begin token:=token^ch; getchar end
                  end else
                  begin type:="DELIMITER";
                        token:=token^ch; getchar end
            end
```

In the pseudo-code we have assumed a string-handling capability which, as well as allowing us to assign whole strings, allows us to append characters to strings by the statement

$$token := token^\wedge ch$$

In any particular programming language such facilities will be implemented in a way peculiar to that language. We have chosen for the pseudo-code facilities which can be emulated in any programming language with only a little effort. Note how, in *gettoken*, the variable *ch* is always left containing the character *after* the token which was recognized. Thus *gettoken* presumes on entry that *ch* is significant. It is necessary therefore to initialize it, before the first call of *gettoken*, by a call of *getchar*.

Let us program *getchar* in terms of a routine *getline* which, when called, returns a line of up to (say) 80 characters. After the call

$$getline(line,len,eof)$$

the character array *line* contains these characters in positions 1 to *len* and *eof* is set false. When the input is exhausted, *eof* is set true and a line of at

least one blank is returned. Now to implement *getchar* we must buffer the
input, one line at a time, and supply the characters from that buffer. Let us
declare

character array *inbuffer*(1:80); **integer** *inbufend*;
integer *inbufptr*;

where *inbufend* is to be used to point to the last significant character in a
partially filled buffer and *inbufptr* is to point to the next character to be selected. Initially *inbufptr* will be set to one. Thus we have the procedure *getchar*
as shown in (11.4).

```
procedure getchar;
begin
  if inbufptr > inbufend then
  begin getline(inbuffer,inbufend,eof);                    (11.4)
        inbufptr := 1
  end;
  ch := inbuffer(inbufptr); inbufptr := inbufptr+1
end
```

Here we see that (last line) the next character is selected from the buffer
and the buffer pointer is moved on. Before that can be done we must guarantee that the buffer is non-empty. The conditional call of *getline* does this,
calling *getline* only if the pointer has moved beyond the end of the buffer.
Note that this *presumes* that *getline* will not return an empty buffer (i.e.
inbufend=0). A blank line on the input must be represented by a line of at
least one blank. We consider *getline* to be part of the *system interface*. That
is to say, any system supporting Lispkit must provide such a routine and it
must satisfy the constraints given for it here.

11.5 THE OUTPUT OF S-EXPRESSIONS

Let us turn now to the process of printing S-expressions. We presume we
are given a pointer to a structure of records in list space and we have to
print an S-expression corresponding to it. Since there are many possible
S-expressions, owing to the equivalence of certain dotted and undotted
expressions, for example

$(A.(B.NIL))$ and $(A\ B)$

we choose to print the shortest, that is the one with the minimum number of dots.

To describe this process, let us rewrite the syntax diagrams of Figs. 11.14 and 11.15 as in Fig. 11.18. A careful consideration of this diagram will

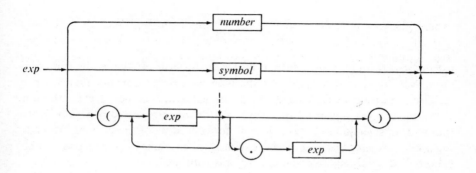

Fig. 11.18

convince you that it is equivalent to Figs. 11.14 and 11.15. For the purpose of obtaining the shortest output, the only kind of *exp* we will print after a dot will be an atom. This decision allows us to loop back, at the point marked with the dashed arrow, whenever the next item in the list is a *cons* type record.

By assuming the existence of a routine *puttoken(token)*, which will print the string in the parameter *token* (without needing to know its type), we can program the procedure *putexp* as in (11.5). Remember, *putexp(e)* has as parameter a pointer to the storage structure to be printed.

```
procedure putexp(e);
if issymbol(e) then puttoken(svalue(e)) else
if isnumber(e) then puttoken(tostring(ivalue(e))) else
begin pointer p; puttoken("("); p:=e;
    while iscons(p) do                                        (11.5)
    begin putexp(car(p)); p:=cdr(p) end;
    if issymbol(p) and svalue(p) = "NIL" then skip
    else begin puttoken("."); putexp(p) end;
    puttoken(")")
end
```

We use a local variable *p* to point to the successive members of a list of *cons* records (Fig. 11.19). We call *putexp* recursively to print the *car* of the

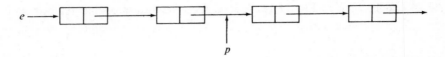

Fig. 11.19

list pointed to by *p*, until finally *p* points to an atom. If this is the symbolic atom *NIL*, then we do nothing; otherwise we print a dot and then (rather craftily I'm afraid) call *putexp* to print the value of the record even though we know it to be an atom. It just saves a little bit of repeated program. Note that with this version of *putexp* there is no formatting of the output. Depending upon how *puttoken* deals with individual tokens, long S-expressions can be expected to be unreadable when using this routine.

11.6 THE OUTPUT OF TOKENS

Let us presume that we can refer to the characters in a string as if they were in a character array indexed from 1 upward. Let us also presume that the function *length* can be used to determine the number of significant characters in the string. Then, in terms of a routine *putchar*, the programming of *puttoken* is simple, as shown in (11.6).

```
procedure puttoken (token);
begin integer len;
    len: = length(token);                                    (11.6)
    for i = 1 until length do putchar(token(i));
    putchar(" ")
end
```

Here we see that we first determine how many characters are to be printed and then print them in order, where *putchar* is called to print each character in turn. Finally we print a blank to guarantee separation between consecutive tokens on the output.

It remains to program *putchar*, which we do in terms of an interface procedure

$$putline(line, len)$$

which, given a character array line of up to (say) 80 characters, will print those in positions 1 through *len* on a line to themselves. Hence, as for the input, we buffer the output in the variables

character array *outbuffer* (1:80); **integer** *outbufptr*;

where *outbufptr* is used to point to the last character put in the buffer. Initially it is set to zero. We then have the procedure *putchar* as shown in (11.7).

---

procedure *putchar(c)*;
begin
    if *outbufptr* = 80 **then** *forcelineout*;
    outbufptr := *outbufptr* + 1;
    outbuffer(outbufptr) := *c*
end;   (11.7)

procedure *forcelineout*;
begin *putline(outbuffer,outbufptr)*;
    outbufptr := 0
end;

First, in *putchar*, we must check that there is room in the buffer before we put a character in it. If there is no room, then we call *forcelineout* to print the buffer and empty it. There are two important operational characteristics of this set of procedures. The first is that when using them we must remember to call *forcelineout* at the end of all printing to empty the final buffer. The second is that these routines will quite arbitrarily split atoms (the only multicharacter tokens) across output lines. It turns out, although we did not comment on the fact at the time, that the input routines which we wrote will also read such split atoms correctly. It is most important that Lispkit implementations can read everything they can write, much more important than that their output should be nicely formatted. Changes to the specifications written here should always bear that fact in mind.

11.7 THE CONVERSION ROUTINES

For completeness, we include here a description of the design of the routines for converting a numeric string to an integer and the reverse. These procedures have been called *tointeger* and *tostring* in the preceding sections. We deal with the conversion of a string to an integer first, as shown in (11.8).

integer procedure *tointeger*(*t*);
begin logical *neg*; **integer** *s*;
    neg: = *t*(1) = " − "; *s*: = 0;
    for *i*: = (**if** *neg* **then** 2 **else** 1) **until** *length*(*t*) **do**   (11.8)
    s: = 10 × *s* + *decimal*(*t*(*i*));
    return (**if** *neg* **then** − *s* **else** *s*)
end;

We use the local integer variable *s* to accumulate the value of the integer which we compute using

$$s: = 10 \times s + d_i$$

where d_i is the decimal equivalent of the *i*th digit. We have written this in the program as a function *decimal* which maps the digit character to the digit value. This is clearly a machine-dependent operation. First, the sign of the number is inspected (only a minus sign being allowed) and the presence or absence of the minus sign is recorded in the variable *neg*. Then each digit in turn is inspected, beginning at the second if a minus sign was encountered. Finally the result is returned after negation if necessary.

The conversion routine in the other direction is a little longer, but just as straightforward. Again, we introduce a new abstract operation

$$t: = c^\wedge t$$

which allows us to concatenate a character *c* to the left of a string *t*, and we obtain (11.9).

string procedure *tostring*(*i*);
if *i* = 0 **then return** "0" **else**
begin string *t*; **logical** *neg*;
    neg: = *i* < 0; *i*: = *abs*(*i*); *t*: = *emptystring*;
    while *i* > 0 **do**
    begin   (11.9)
        t: = *digit*(*i* **rem** 10)^*t*;
        i: = *i* **div** 10
    end;
    if *neg* **then** *t*: = " − "^*t*;
    return *t*
end

First, we must deal with the special case of the integer value zero which is represented by the string "0". This is the only value which requires that a leading zero be included in its string representation. Next, if the number to be converted is not zero, we record whether or not it is negative and then make it positive. Each digit in the number is then selected by dividing by ten. We assume *i* **rem** 10 gives the remainder on division and *i* **div** 10 the quotient. The function *digit* is used to determine the character equivalent of each digit and then that is concatenated to the left of the string *t*, which is accumulating the digits in their proper order. Eventually, the number will become zero because of successive division by 10. Finally, if necessary, a minus sign is concatenated to the string representation.

11.8 THE EXECUTION CYCLE

In Chapter 6 we described the machine language of the SECD machine. There each operation code was represented by a symbolic atom, for readability. In practice, however, each operation code will be represented by a numeric atom in order that we can most efficiently execute that code. The actual numeric equivalents we shall use are as shown in Table 11.4.

Table 11.4

1	*LD*	8	*SEL*	15	*ADD*
2	*LDC*	9	*JOIN*	16	*SUB*
3	*LDF*	10	*CAR*	17	*MUL*
4	*AP*	11	*CDR*	18	*DIV*
5	*RTN*	12	*ATOM*	19	*REM*
6	*DUM*	13	*CONS*	20	*LEQ*
7	*RAP*	14	*EQ*	21	*STOP*

Thus, the machine-language program which we would have written in the previous chapter as

$$(LDC\ (A.B)\ LD\ (0.1)\ CONS)$$

will actually appear to the SECD machine as

$$(2\ (A.B)\ 1\ (0.1)\ 13)$$

We have so contrived the machine code that during normal execution of a correct SECD machine-language program the control expression will always have the form

$$(operation\ ...)$$

That is the form of the control will always be such that it is composite and its *car* is a numeric operation code. Hence, if the control is pointed to by the variable c, the structure of the execution cycle can be as shown in (11.10).

$$cycle\colon \textbf{case } ivalue(car(c)) \textbf{ of}$$
$$\textbf{begin}$$
$$\qquad 1\colon \quad \ldots$$
$$\qquad 2\colon \quad \ldots$$
$$\qquad \vdots$$
$$\qquad 21\colon \textbf{goto } endcycle;$$
$$\textbf{end};$$
$$\textbf{goto } cycle;$$
$$endcycle\colon$$

(11.10)

Thus, on the basis of the value at the head of the control, the case statement switches to one of 21 separate arms. Each arm will carry out the appropriate machine transition for the machine instruction it represents, including an adjustment to the control, and then normal exit from the case statement causes a jump back to repeat the cycle. Only execution of the *STOP* instruction (operation code 21) can terminate this process.

The four principal registers of the SECD machine are declared as pointer variables. In addition we shall require four additional registers, three to hold the constant values to represent *true*, *false* and *nil*, and one as a temporary working register. These four new registers do not figure in the machine state as we have used it until now, for the following reasons. By their nature, the three constant registers never alter as the result of executing an operation. Therefore, indicating at the end of each instruction that these three registers are still respectively *true*, *false* and *nil* is redundant and tedious. The working register will be considered to be undefined before and after the execution of each instruction. That is, it will only be used to hold values temporarily during the execution of an instruction. We declare the registers of the SECD machine as follows:

pointer $s, e, c, d, t, f, nil, w;$

Recall that the operation which invokes the SECD machine execution is called *exec* and has two parameters (see Section 11.2 and Section 6.5). The first parameter is an SECD machine-language program which has been compiled from a function-valued Lispkit Lisp expression. The compiler will have appended two instructions to this code: the first an *AP* instruction, the second a *STOP* instruction. Executing the code will then cause a closure to be loaded onto the stack, which is then applied before the machine halts. The closure is applied to the second parameter of *exec*, which is a list of arguments. Thus we have the skeleton (11.11) for the execution phase.

---

pointer procedure *exec*(*fn,args*);
begin
    $t:=symbol$; $svalue(t):="T"$;
    $f:=symbol$; $svalue(f):="F"$;
    comment *nil was initialized in Section* 11.1;   (11.11)
    $s:=cons$; $car(s):=args$; $cdr(s):=nil$;
    $e:=nil$; $c:=fn$; $d:=nil$;
    cycle: . . .
    endcycle: **return** *car*(*s*)
end

Recall that, when an expression is compiled and the code executed, the value of the expression is found on top of the stack. This explains how, at *endcycle*, it is appropriate to return *car*(*s*) as the result of *exec*. It remains to detail the programming of each of the instructions.

In order to do that, we introduce a convention which will help us design the interpretation of each instruction more uniformly. The convention concerns the use of the working register and is such that it allows us to write clearer implementations of the machine instruction by avoiding explicit mention of the working register. Thus we shall allow ourselves to write

$$e_1:=cons(e_2,e_3)$$

where e_1, e_2 and e_3 are suitable (i.e. pointer-valued) expressions. We take this to mean, allocate a new record of type *cons*, set its fields to e_2 and e_3 respectively, and assign the pointer (to the newly constructed record) to e_1. Often this can be implemented as

$$e_1:=cons; \quad car(e_1):=e_2; \quad cdr(e_1):=e_3;$$

The occasion when it cannot is when e_2 or e_3 refer to the value of e_1. For example, in

$$s:=cons(nil,s)$$

When this happens, we will use the sequence

$$w := cons; \; car(w) := e_2; \; cdr(w) := e_3; \; e_1 := w$$

Consider the example

$$s := cons(cons(car(cdr(s)),e),s)$$

which first expands to

$$w := cons; \; car(w) := cons(car(cdr(s)),e); \; cdr(w) := s; \; s := w;$$

and then to

$$w := cons; \; car(w) := cons;$$
$$car(car(w)) := car(cdr(s)); \; cdr(car(w)) := e;$$
$$cdr(w) := s; \; s := w;$$

This clearly shows how the use of the convention (of expanding from an abbreviation) makes uniform use of the working register. It also shows clearly the need for this register, for we cannot begin the above sequence with $s := cons$ without losing essential information held in s. A similar convention can be used for the records of type *number* and *symbol*.

Each machine instruction has been specified by a transition

$$s \; e \; c \; d \to s' \; e' \; c' \; d'$$

and can therefore be realized by a sequence of assignments to the pointer variables s, e, c and d respectively. For example, the transition for LDC is

$$s \; e \; (LDC \; x.c) \; d \to (x.s) \; e \; c \; d$$

and this can be implemented by the two assignments

$$s := cons(car(cdr(c)),s); \quad c := cdr(cdr(c))$$

Note that we do not try to deal with malformed control lists, allowing the system to fail arbitrarily if this happens. It is unnecessary to assign to either e or d to implement this transition, for they do not change. Consider one complete cycle of the machine when these two assignments are correctly installed in the execution loop. The case statement inspects $car(x)$ and finds it equal to 2 (operation code for LDC). The first assignment then installs the operand of the *LDC* instruction on the stack, the second resets the control list to beyond the operation and its operand and then the cycle repeats with the next instruction.

Let us deal now with the *LD* instruction which has transition

$$s \ e \ (LD \ i.c) \ d \ \rightarrow \ (locate(i,e).s) \ e \ c \ d$$

We can implement this by means of (11.12).

$w := e;$
for $i := 1$ **until** $car(car(cdr(c)))$ **do** $w := cdr(w);$
$w := car(w);$
for $i := 1$ **until** $cdr(car(cdr(c)))$ **do** $w := cdr(w);$ (11.12)
$w := car(w);$
$s := cons(w,s); \quad c := cdr(cdr(c))$

The operand of the *LD* instruction has the form $(b.n)$, where b and n are integers. It means that the value to be loaded can be found in the nth position of the bth sublist of e. We use w to locate this value, by first taking b *cdr*s of e, then selecting the sublist which we find, and then taking n *cdr*s of that and finally selecting the value we require. The last two assignments, to s and c, are similar to those for *LDC*, installing the value on the stack and then moving on past the instruction.

Rather than deal with the instructions in numerical order, we will deal with them in order of increasing complexity and in related groups. Let us take the basic operations next. The transition for *CAR* is

$$((a.b).s) \ e \ (CAR.c) \ d \ \rightarrow \ (a.s) \ e \ c \ d$$

which can be implemented by the assignments

$$s := cons(car(car(s)),cdr(s)); \ c := cdr(c)$$

The implementation of *CDR* is almost identical

$$s := cons(cdr(car(s)),cdr(s)); \ c := cdr(c)$$

Consider next *ATOM*. Here we must inspect the value at the top of the stack and replace it by true or false according to whether or not it is an atom. This is accomplished by the statements:

$$\text{if } isnumber(car(s)) \text{ or } issymbol(car(s)) \text{ then}$$
$$s:=cons(t,cdr(s)) \text{ else } s:=cons(f,cdr(s)); \quad c:=cdr(c)$$

Binary operations have much the same kind of implementation as unary ones, but we must be careful to get the operands the right way round. Let us take *CONS* first, which has the transition

$$(a\ b.s)\ e\ (CONS.c)\ d \rightarrow ((a.b).s)\ e\ c\ d$$

and is implemented by the assignments

$$s:=cons(cons(car(s),car(cdr(s))),cdr(cdr(s))); \quad c:=cdr(c)$$

It may be instructive for the reader to expand this by the convention we have given for the use of working registers, to determine that the effect is precisely what it should be.

The arithmetic operations, apart from requiring their operands the other way round, require that a new record is allocated to hold their result. This is because, as we have explained, there can be sharing of storage and hence we cannot change the value in an existing record of type *number*. The *SUB* instruction has the transition

$$(a\ b.s)\ e\ (SUB.c)\ d \rightarrow (b-a.s)\ e\ c\ d$$

which is implemented by the sequence

$$s:=cons(number(ivalue(car(cdr(s)))-ivalue(car(s))),cdr(cdr(s))); \quad c:=cdr(c)$$

Here we see that the values at the top of the stack are replaced by a new record of type *number* containing the difference. Each of *ADD*, *MUL*, *DIV* and *REM* can be implemented in the same way, using the appropriate arithmetic operator in place of minus.

The relational operators come next. Let us deal with *LEQ* first because, since it takes only arithmetic operands, its implementation is not unlike those of the arithmetic operators. We have

$$\text{if } ivalue(car(cdr(s))) \leqslant ivalue(car(s)) \text{ then}$$
$$s:=cons(t,cdr(cdr(s))) \text{ else } s:=cons(f,cdr(cdr(s)));$$
$$c:=cdr(c)$$

Here we replace the values at the top of the stack by one of the logical values T or F. The instruction EQ is defined not only for numeric values, but also for symbolic and composite ones. Hence the implementation (11.13).

$$
\begin{aligned}
&\textbf{if } issymbol(car(s)) \textbf{ and } issymbol(car(cdr(s))) \textbf{ and} \\
&\quad svalue(car(s)) = svalue(car(cdr(s))) \\
&\textbf{or } isnumber(car(s)) \textbf{ and } isnumber(car(cdr(s))) \textbf{ and} \\
&\quad ivalue(car(s)) = ivalue(car(cdr(s))) \\
&\textbf{then } s := cons(t,cdr(cdr(s))) \\
&\quad \textbf{else } s := cons(f,cdr(cdr(s))); \\
&c := cdr(c);
\end{aligned}
\qquad (11.13)
$$

The values at the top of the stack are first checked to see that they are of the same type and then the appropriate comparison is invoked if they are.

Consider next the transition for LDF.

$$s \; e \; (LDF \; c'.c) \; d \rightarrow ((c'.e).s) \; e \; c \; d$$

The implementation for this is as follows.

$$s := cons(cons(car(cdr(c)),e),s); \quad c := cdr(cdr(c));$$

This is very straightforward. AP has the transition

$$((c'.e') \; v.s) \; e \; (AP.c) \; d \rightarrow NIL \; (v.e') \; c' \; (s \; e \; c.d)$$

which is implemented as

$$
\begin{aligned}
&d := cons(cdr(cdr(s)),cons(e,cons(cdr(c),d))); \\
&e := cons(car(cdr(s)),cdr(car(s))); \quad c := car(car(s)); \\
&s := nil;
\end{aligned}
$$

RTN has the transition

$$(a) \; e' \; (RTN) \; (s \; e \; c.d) \rightarrow (a.s) \; e \; c \; d$$

which is implemented as

$$
\begin{aligned}
&s := cons(car(s),car(d)); \quad e := car(cdr(d)); \\
&c := car(cdr(cdr(d))); \qquad d := cdr(cdr(cdr(d)));
\end{aligned}
$$

The transition for *DUM* is simply

$$s \ e \ (DUM.c) \ d \ \rightarrow s \ (\Omega.e) \ c \ d$$

We shall not implement the "Ω" feature in any special way. Rather we shall simply use *NIL* as the dummy entry in the environment. Hence we have the implementation

$$e := cons(nil, e); \quad c := cdr(c);$$

RAP has the transition

$$((c'.e') \ v.s) \ (\Omega.e) \ (RAP.c) \ d \ \rightarrow NIL \ rplaca(e', v) \ c' \ (s \ e \ c.d)$$

which is programmed as

$$d := cons(cdr(cdr(s)), cons(cdr(e), cons(cdr(c), d)));$$
$$e := cdr(car(s)); \quad car(e) := car(cdr(s));$$
$$c := car(car(s)); \quad \quad \ \ s := nil;$$

Since *DUM* and *RAP* work together in a rather special way, it is worthwhile here to see how our implementation deals with this particular pair of instructions. Let us consider the code which we get from the expression

$$\begin{aligned}
&(LETREC \ e \\
&\quad (f \ LAMBDA \ \text{———)} \\
&\quad (g \ LAMBDA \ \text{———))}
\end{aligned}$$

which has the form

$$(DUM \ LDC \ NIL \ LDF \ c_g \ CONS \ LDF \ c_f \ CONS \ LDF \ c_e \ RAP)$$

Here c_g, c_f and c_e are sublists generated from the *LAMBDA* expressions for *f* and *g* and the body of the block respectively. We shall not be concerned with their content. The *DUM* instruction gives the environment the structure shown in Fig. 11.20.

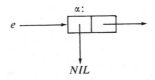

Fig. 11.20

Now the values of f and g are computed and formed into a list on top of the stack. Since f and g are both functions, their values are both closures (Fig. 11.21). Next the closure for c_e is loaded on the stack and then the *RAP*

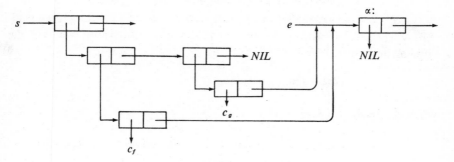

Fig. 11.21

instruction is executed. This causes, among other things, the environment with the dummy first component to be updated to be as shown in Fig. 11.22.

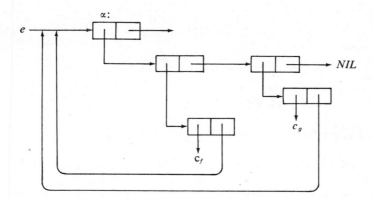

Fig. 11.22

Notice that we have built a circular list structure. The environment contains closures which contain the environment. This is exactly what is meant by a mutually recursive definition.

There remain two unimplemented instructions, *SEL* and *JOIN*. The transition for *SEL* is

$$(x.s)\ e\ (SEL\ c_T\ c_F.c)\ d \rightarrow s\ e\ c_x\ (c.d)$$

which is implemented by

$$d := cons(cdr(cdr(cdr(c))),d);$$
if $svalue(car(s)) = "T"$ **then** $c := car(cdr(c))$ **else**
$$c := car(cdr(cdr(c))); \quad s := cdr(s);$$

Finally, *JOIN* has the transition

$$s \ e \ (JOIN) \ (c.d) \rightarrow s \ e \ c \ d$$

which is trivially implemented by

$$c := car(d); \ d := cdr(d);$$

This completes our implementation of the instructions. Each piece of pseudo-code which implements an instruction is embedded in the instruction execution cycle described at the beginning of the section. Since each instruction sets the control list to the next instruction to be executed, we see that the execution cycle behaves as we expect it to. Apart from the decisions about how to arrange all the text of this first-level design into manageable modules and arranging for their correct initialization (which is left to the reader), this completes our design of the higher level of the Lispkit System.

12 BASIC MACHINE SUPPORT FOR THE FUNCTIONAL PROGRAMMING KIT

12.1 STORAGE FOR LISTS

A most important difficulty arises because of the way in which we have allowed ourselves to handle lists of records. This is that some records effectively disappear in the sense that we become unable to access them. To see how this happens, consider the statement

$$c := cdr(c)$$

If, before execution of the statement, we have the situation depicted in Fig. 12.1, and after it we have that depicted in Fig. 12.2, and we can no

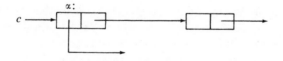

Fig. 12.1

longer access the cell marked α, nor the structure hanging from its *car*, from

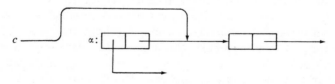

Fig. 12.2

the register c. It is possible (even likely) that other registers, or accessible records, point at α and so α has not been lost. It is, however, also possible that there are no remaining pointers to α and that therefore we could never again reach this record. Similarly, some of the records hanging from the *car* of α may have become inaccessible. This would not be a problem except for two characteristics. The first is that we have only a finite supply of records and when this is exhausted, computation cannot proceed. It would be annoying, to say the least, if computation had to cease when there were many inaccessible records which we could reuse, if only we knew where they were. The second characteristic which makes the problem of inaccessible records a little difficult is that when we make a record inaccessible it is not trivial to determine that we have done so. In the above example, while the operation reduces the number of outstanding references to α by one, we do not know that this number has reduced to zero. If we did, we could return the record α to the pool from which records are allocated.

The process of determining which cells are inaccessible and returning them to a pool for reallocation is called *garbage collection*. There are various strategies that one can use for garbage collection: the type we shall design here is called a *mark and collect* garbage collector. In this garbage collector nothing is done until the supply of records is exhausted. Then all record structures are traced and each accessible cell is marked. Next, the entire storage area used for records is scanned and any unmarked records (which must be inaccessible) are collected and formed into a pool for reallocation. Typically, when such a garbage collector is used with, say, a supply of 10 000 records, if each time it is used it collects about 5000 records we should be satisfied that it is not too gross an overhead. Of course, the actual proportion of records collected will depend not only on the size of the supply but also on the application. We intend here merely to indicate that a certain frequency of calling the garbage collector is tolerable. We shall return to the design of the garbage collector after a discussion of storage formats.

Recall that we require to support three kinds of record: a *number*, a *symbol* and a *cons*. These have space respectively for an integer value, a string and two pointers. There are many advantages which accrue from making each of the records occupy the same amount of physical storage. Principally these are that we only need maintain a single pool of unallocated records, and that when a record is deallocated it can be reallocated to be of a different type if this is appropriate. There are many ways in which we can achieve this. We can make each record large enough to hold the largest value (here, probably the string in a symbolic atom) or we can place restrictions on the maximum size of values which can be placed in records. Each of these extremes can be criticized. In the first case there is almost certain to be considerable waste of storage, and in the second certain decisions could be intolerable. For example, we would certainly not tolerate symbolic atoms of up to only four characters or numeric atoms with absolute value less than 128.

There are also advantages to working with the storage units which are natural for the particular computer on which the implementation is being made. Thus, for example, if the arithmetic operations are defined for 32-bit integers, choosing integer values which are longer or shorter than this may involve many more machine instructions than if we chose integers of exactly that size. So the actual design of a storage structure must be a compromise, and which compromise is best for any particular circumstance will depend upon many factors. Here we shall describe a choice which we have found particularly useful without suggesting that it is in any sense best, and without very much discussion of the alternatives.

The first design decision we make is a logical one. We determine that in order to distinguish each kind of record, it must carry with it two logical values (bits), and we decide that the first of these will be used to distinguish *cons* records from atomic records and the second to distinguish numeric atoms from symbolic ones. Thus, logically we need to implement the structures shown in Fig. 12.3. The bits associated with each record will be referred to as the *isatom bit* and the *isnumber bit* respectively.

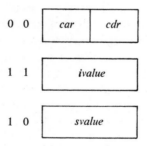

Fig. 12.3

The next design decision we make is that the part of the record excluding the bits will be large enough to hold a standard integer for the implementation machine. That is, the *ivalue* field will be the usual integer value. Now, if we decide that 2^k list cells is adequate, then a pointer field requires k bits, and if an integer requires n bits we will choose a record size which is large enough to hold either n bits or $2k$ bits. For example, on an IBM 370 with $n = 32$ we can choose a record size of 32 bits, which is extremely convenient for that machine, and ideal if $k \leqslant 16$ is adequate. This would allow up to 64K list cells. Since a minimum number of list cells (for the compiler to compile itself) is about 6K, and 10K is a good working size, 64K would seem adequate. However, if much larger applications were envisaged, this might have a fundamental effect upon the design of the list storage.

We shall return to the design of the record of type *symbol* later. Suffice it to comment here that we shall store the actual string in a separate area and a pointer to it in the record. This overcomes the difficulty of packing the string into the record. We can record the design decisions we have made so far by declaring the space to be used for list storage as a set of arrays, as given in (12.1).

$$\begin{aligned} &\textbf{bit array } isatom(1:size); \\ &\textbf{bit array } isnumb(1:size); \\ &\textbf{integer array } ivalue(1:size); \\ &\textbf{pointer array } car(1:size); \\ &\textbf{pointer array } cdr(1:size); \end{aligned} \qquad (12.1)$$

A pointer is effectively a short integer, with a value in the range 0..*size*. We use the pointer value 0 in a special way to be described later. However, we allocate space equivalent to exactly half of an integer value to it and then overlay arrays *car* and *cdr* on the array *ivalue* as indicated in Fig. 12.4. That

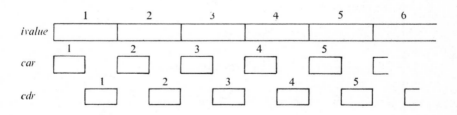

Fig. 12.4

is to say, the *p*th element of *ivalue* occupies exactly the same space as the *p*th elements of *car* and *cdr*, which together make up a *cons* record.

These declarations of arrays allow us to deal, in a relatively machine independent way, with the design of the garbage collector and the interface routines to the list storage module. Indeed, the judicious choice of array names has to a large extent completed the latter process. First, let us consider the predicates. These have simple implementations, as given in (12.2).

```
            logical procedure iscons(p);
            begin
              return isatom(p)=0 and isnumb(p)=0
            end;
            logical procedure issymbol(p);
            begin                                                    (12.2)
              return isatom(p)=1 and isnumb(p)=0
            end;
            logical procedure isnumber(p);
            begin
              return isatom(p)=1 and isnumb(p)=1
            end;
```

Similarly the selectors *ivalue*, *car* and *cdr* are trivially implemented by the usual array-indexing mechanism. The selector *svalue* will need a little more explanation. We are going to store the string values of symbolic atoms in a separate area. Let us postpone the design of this mechanism by (the usual structured programming technique of) introducing procedures which do what we require. Assume we have the procedure

integer procedure *store(s)*; ...;

which stores the string *s* and returns an integer value with which we can subsequently retrieve it using the procedure

string procedure *load(i)*; ...;

Wherever in the higher-level design we have used

$svalue(p):=s$

or its equivalent, we should now replace this by

$ivalue(p):=store(s).$

Similarly, wherever we have used

$s:=svalue(p)$

or something equivalent, we should replace this by

$s:=load(ivalue(p))$

Thus, we are using the *ivalue* selector as a convenient way of expressing the fact that, if the record is of type symbol, it contains an integer which (in some way) identifies the string which is its value.

Now we can consider allocation of records. Since every record can be allocated to be of any of the three types, we will consider all unallocated records to be of type *cons* and link them together in a list called the *free list*, *ff* (Fig. 12.5).

Fig. 12.5

The free list is linked on the *cdr* field and its end is marked by a *cdr* field set to the special pointer value 0. If the free list is not exhausted, we can allocate a cell from it simply by writing

$$p := ff; \quad ff := cdr(ff)$$

Eventually the free list will become exhausted, that is we will have $ff = 0$. We therefore must guard against this by writing, instead of the above allocation sequence,

> **if** $ff = 0$ **then** *collect–garbage*;
> $p := ff; \quad ff := cdr(ff)$

There is of course, the possibility that the garbage collector will collect no cells, but we assume that in this case the garbage collector itself will terminate the computation.

We must specialize this allocation sequence for each different type of record. This is straightforward. Where in the abstract program we have written

> $w := cons$

we must replace this by

> **if** $ff = 0$ **then** *collect–garbage*;
> $w := ff; ff := cdr(ff)$;
> *isatom*$(w) := 0$; *isnumb*$(w) := 0$;

The allocation sequence for records of type symbol and number is identical except for the values used for each of the type bits.

12.2 THE GARBAGE COLLECTOR

In the previous section, we have described how records disappear, in that no register nor record points at them and hence there is no way to access them. In this section we will describe a mark and collect garbage collector which is used to return these records to the free list. First we consider the mark phase. It is necessary to declare one bit per record as the bit which gets set when that record is marked. Thus, logically we have an extra array

bit array *marked* (1 :*size*);

We can mark the record structure *n* with the algorithm (12.3).

---

      procedure *mark*(*n*);
      begin
        marked(*n*): = 1 ;
        if *isatom*(*n*) = 0 **then**
        begin   (12.3)
          mark(*car*(*n*));
          mark(*cdr*(*n*));
        end
      end

Here, we see that the record pointed to by *n* is marked by setting *marked*(*n*) to 1. Then, if the record is composite, we call the procedure recursively, first to mark its *car*, then to mark its *cdr*. Unfortunately, this does not work for circular lists, but we can make it do so simply by taking advantage of the marked bit to indicate that we have previously visited that record, as indicated in (12.4).

---

      procedure *mark*(*n*);
      if *marked*(*n*) = 0 **then**
      begin
        marked(*n*): = 1 ;
        if *isatom*(*n*) = 0 **then**   (12.4)
        begin
          mark(*car*(*n*));
          mark(*cdr*(*n*))
        end
      end

Next, we must concern ourselves with the collect phase. Here, we want to make a sequential scan over the whole of the area used for storing records, and collect all those records which are not marked. This is accomplished by the algorithm (12.5). We simply check each record and if it is not marked we link it onto the front of the free list.

---

procedure *collect*;
begin
   for $i := 1$ **until** *size* **do**
   if $marked(i) = 0$ **then**
   begin   (12.5)
     $cdr(i) := ff$;
     $ff := i$
   end
end

Since $ff = 0$ when the garbage collector is called, this algorithm will correctly build a free list again terminated by zero. This explains how records are returned to the free list. A similar process (12.6) is used to set up the free list initially.

---

procedure *init–storage*;
begin $ff := 0$;
   for $i := 1$ **until** *size* **do**
   begin $cdr(i) := ff$;   (12.6)
     $ff := i$
   end
end

It remains to decide which records must be traced by the garbage collector in its mark phase. Clearly those records accessible from the registers of the SECD machine must be traced and hence the garbage collector must have access to them. Since the input routines are such that they are called only before the SECD machine commences execution it is sensible to assume that they will not run out of storage. It is necessary then only to trace the structures emanating from the SECD machine registers, as we have done in (12.7).

---

procedure *collect–garbage*;
begin
  for $i := 1$ **until** *size* **do** *marked(i)* := 0;

  mark(s); *mark(e)*; *mark(c)*; *mark(d)*;   (12.7)
  mark(w); *mark(t)*; *mark(f)*; *mark(nil)*;

  collect; **if** *ff* = 0 **then error**;
end

The reason that it is necessary to mark only cells reachable from the eight registers of the SECD machine is the result of a combination of circumstances. The only time the garbage collector can be invoked is when a new record is allocated. New records are allocated only in two places, when S-expressions are being input and during the execution cycle of the SECD machine. S-expressions are input only at the very beginning of execution of the interpreting program, and since tree representations are built for them progressively in list storage, no garbage is created. Hence if we run out of space during this process we cannot do anything useful, we must abort the execution. If it were ever necessary to extend the machine to be able to read S-expressions during the execution of a program, this could be done satisfactorily by ensuring that the garbage collector was called before the reading was begun.

The garbage collector as programmed here can be slightly optimized by resetting the *marked* array to zero during the collect phase. This would avoid the need to initialize it at the beginning of the next mark phase, thus saving one sequential scan of the storage allocated for records. The marked array would then have to be set to zero only once at the very beginning of execution, but it would mean that its space could not be used for any other purpose. Another important point to note is that, since the mark algorithm is recursive, it requires stack space in order to be able to execute. If we are writing in a language which does not support recursion and so need to implement it ourselves, this means that we must have sufficient space for it. It probably need not be large in comparison with the list storage itself.

12.3 THE STRING STORE

We were able to handle records uniformly by the device of separating the string part of a symbolic atom and storing it elsewhere. We stored an integer value in the record in order that the string could be subsequently retrieved. We postponed the design of the actual mechanism of storing and retrieving strings until this section. The main consideration is how much space would be required. Let us consider a typical Lispkit Lisp program (for example the compiler). There are about 20 standard Lispkit Lisp reserved words, about 10 function names and about 10 different variable names (although up to 20 could have been used). In any case this is less than 50 different symbolic atoms. On the other hand there are nearly 300 different occurrences of symbolic atoms. The average number of characters in a symbolic atom is about 4. We have to decide whether it is better to save space by trying not to duplicate strings in storage or to save time required to search for strings by allowing duplicates. From the above figures, while allowing duplicates would require up to 6 times the space, even then the space requirement is not large. Conversely the small number of different symbolic atoms would not impose an onerous search time and further, since searching would be done only on storing and this is done only when S-expressions are input, the number of times searching would be required is only equal to the number of occurrences of symbolic atoms. It is not a recurring overhead. It seems that either choice would be satisfactory.

However, there is an overwhelming argument in favor of not allowing duplicates. If equal strings are encoded as the same integer, we can avoid inspecting the string values when we need to see if two strings are equal. Since, as we can infer and indeed shall see, such comparisons are very frequent, this could be an important time saving. Thus we decide not to allow duplicates and to design a store algorithm which searches all previously stored strings to avoid duplicating strings in storage.

We will store the strings in consecutive locations in a string array. We have assumed throughout that the abstract data type **string** represents a sequence of characters and now we will allow a finite but reasonable bound on its length. This in turn will set a bound on the length of symbolic atoms. About 12 characters would be reasonable, but even allowing up to 32 characters would be acceptable from the point of view of storage. If it is considered onerous to allocate so much space for strings whose average length is just four characters, then they can be packed into a character array with only a little more programming effort.

Let us declare the string store to be of size *total*.

> **string array** *stringstore*(1 :*total*);
> **integer** *top*;

Strings will be stored in this array in locations 1 to *top*, thus initially we set *top* to 0. We store a string in the array by first searching to see if it is already there. This is done in the abstract program (12.8) by setting the integer variable i to 1 and then inspecting each of the locations 1 through *top* to see if any of the strings stored there is the same as *t*.

```
        integer procedure store(t);
        begin integer i; i:=1;
          while i⩽top and stringstore(i)≠t do i:=i+1;
          if i⩽top then return i else ·
          begin                                                    (12.8)
            top:=top+1;
            stringstore(top):=t;
            return top
          end
        end
```

If the search succeeds, then the value i, which will be less than or equal to top, will be the position of the string t in the store. This is then returned as the result of the procedure. If the search is unsuccessful, indicated by the fact that at the end of it i will have value $top+1$, then we place the string in the next free location and return its index as the result. It would probably be necessary to program an error trap to take care of the case when we try to store more strings than there is space for.

It is trivial to obtain the strings if their index is given, and we program it as follows:

```
        string procedure load(i);
        begin
          return stringstore(i);
        end
```

For any implementation language or computer, the process of copying or extending a string will probably be a character-by-character operation. We have not gone down to that level of detail here. Suffice it to say that we have used two different ways of encoding strings in character arrays and found each satisfactory for different situations. The first technique involves simply padding short strings to the right with blanks. The second encodes the length of the string and packs this information into an extra leading character position. The second is probably better if your implementation language or machine does not provide any operations on whole strings, and is probably more efficient even then. However, efficiency ought not to worry us unduly since, as we have observed, string comparison is something which takes place only during input.

12.4 BUILDING AND TESTING A LISPKIT SYSTEM

In writing the routines for input and output of S-expressions in Chapter 11 and in writing the garbage collector in this chapter, we have liberally allowed ourselves to use recursive procedures. It is highly likely that, when implementing a Lispkit system, we shall have to transliterate these into an implementation language which does not support recursion. Of course, dealing with recursion by organizing one's own stack is a straightforward and well-known process. Indeed, we have dealt with the process of implementing recursive functions in some detail in this book. However, for algorithms of the complexity of *getexp*, *getexplist*, *putexp* and *mark*, a great deal of care is needed when programming them by hand using a stack. The reader who plans to make a Lispkit implementation is encouraged to devise a set of conventions for transliterating these procedures and to consistently apply these conventions rather than to make an *ad hoc* encoding of the procedures. Not least of all, the structure of the resulting program will have a simple relationship to the pseudo-code given here, thus making subsequent modification of it much easier.

The entire task of putting together all the parts of the SECD machine interpreter is a reasonably complex task and should be approached with care. In particular, each separate part of the implementation should be carefully tested in isolation. In this section we will describe a process whereby this is done. For any particular implementation it will be necessary to vary some of the details, but the general organization of this approach can be followed. We begin with the observation that, if we simply code the entire machine interpreter, then load the compiler from Appendix 2 and a simple piece of Lisp for it to compile, it is extremely likely that this execution will fail. What is important here is that if it fails we do not know where the fault lies. It could be in any part of the interpreter, or our copying of the compiler from Appendix 2 could be erroneous or even the program we are trying to compile could be at fault. Rather than get into this unfortunate position, we shall adopt the kind of testing methodology suggested for developing functional programs in Chapter 3. That is, we shall build the interpreter bottom-up, progressively testing more and more of its logic so that, whenever a test fails, the amount of untested logic participating in that test is reasonably small and the fault can therefore be more easily traced. It should be obvious that this approach is sensible. The duration of the testing period as a whole can be kept within controllable bounds, and confidence that everything has been exercised and appears satisfactory can be gained. On the other hand the more haphazard approach of loading up everything, watching it fail and then looking for a bug provides no such assurances.

We can begin by testing the input and output of characters. This is properly part of the lexical phase, but buffering is a notoriously easy area in which to make a mistake. We should write a simple test program which copies characters from input to output, then use it to copy some of the data to be used in the later tests. This has the advantage that when we are running those later tests we can be certain that the input routines are coping properly with the data. In particular, we should ensure that this test program can cope with the copying of input with 80 character lines and with intermediate null lines.

The next level of testing is to exercise the input and output of tokens. A similar copying program (12.9), as suggested above, can be used. This time, however, we copy a token at a time. The initialization and finalization code is omitted, only the essential logic being shown.

---

string *token, type*;
gettoken(token,type);
while *type* ≠ *"ENDFILE"* **do**   (12.9)
begin *puttoken(token)*;
        gettoken(token,type)
end;

It would be a good idea also to run a test in which the type of the token is also printed, for the above test program will work even if all numbers are recognized (incorrectly) as *ALPHANUMERIC*. Again, we should exercise this on data to be used in later tests, especially some of the SECD programs and Lispkit Lisp programs.

Now, the above test program can be modified in two respects. Firstly, the conversion routines can be tested by some such insertion as

if *type="NUMERIC"* **then**
begin $i:=tointeger(token);\quad i:=i+1$;
        $token:=tostring(i)$
end;

Secondly, we can test the string storage module by

if *type="ALPHANUMERIC"* **then**
begin $i:=store(token)$;
        $token:=load(i)$
end;

Suspicion of the string storage module can be followed up using the conversion routines to print the value of the index. Hence it is a good idea to do these tests in this order.

The next logical recipient of our attention for testing should be the list storage module. Here, we would write some simple test programs which build lists and manipulate them. An example of such as test program is given as (12.10).

```
l: = nil;
for i: = 1 until 10 do
begin n: = number; ivalue(n): = i;
        r: = cons; car(r): = n; cdr(r): = l;
        l: = r;
end;                                              (12.10)

while l ≠ nil do
begin n: = car(l); i: = ivalue(n);
        puttoken(tostring(i));
        l: = cdr(l)
end
```

It is important to exercise the garbage collector. This can probably best be done by adding some instrumentation (or tracing) to the garbage collector itself. It is important to ensure that all garbage is collected. By running some such example as (12.11), where the garbage collector marks lists *l* and *nil*, and by adjusting *M* and *N* to suit the particular size of list space in use, we

```
for j: = 1 until M do
begin
        l: = nil;
        for i: = 1 until N do                     (12.11)
        begin n: = number; ivalue(n): = i;
                r: = cons; car(r): = n; cdr(r): = l;
                l: = r;
        end;
end
```

can create known amounts of garbage and check that exactly the right amount is collected. It is probably a good idea to use only a small amount of list space for the test and to choose the amount to simplify these calculations. The garbage collector should not be invalidated by an upward change in this value.

Having tested the garbage collector, it is advisable to test our scheme for handling recursion, even if the implementation language supports recursion. It is easier to find faults in the recursion-handling scheme if we do this now, rather than at the next stage, when we shall be concerned with syntax analysis. A good example to use would by the recursive *append* function given in Chapter 2. We can use some such program as

> *build list of integers* 1 *to* 10;
> *append it to itself*;
> *print result.*

Now, when we come to test the input and output of S-expressions, we should be confident in the working of our modules for reading and writing tokens, for storing and converting tokens, for storing list structures and in our scheme for supporting recursion. If we now write the very simple test program

> **pointer** p;
> *getexp*(p);
> *putexp*(p)

we can test the coding of these procedures progressively. We give this program successively more elaborate data.

APPLY	a symbolic atom
127	a numeric atom
-127	a negative numeric atom
(*APPLE.*127)	a dotted pair
(*APPLE*)	a list
(*APPLE* 127)	a longer list
(*APPLE* (*PIE* 127))	and so on

We follow this up with the data to be used in later tests, especially the object and source forms of the compiler from Appendix 2.

Now, when we finally come to install the interpreter of the machine and to exercise the main program, the only untested component is the instruction execution part itself. Hence we run

> **pointer** *fn, args, result*;
> *getexp*(*fn*); *getexplist*(*args*);
> *result*: = *apply*(*fn,args*);
> *putexp*(*result*)

with progressively more demanding machine-code programs, thus testing each of the instructions independently.

Recall that the *exec* function loads the argument *fn* into the control register and the argument *args* onto the top of the stack. The value returned in *result* is the value at the top of the stack when the *STOP* instruction is executed. Hence if we give the data

$$(STOP) \ (B \ C)$$

to the program, or more correctly, since we have to give numeric instructions

$$(21) \ (B \ C)$$

we should test that the *STOP* instruction functions as we would expect, that is, the result is $((B \ C))$. Being a little more adventurous, suppose we use the test data (again, we will use mnemonic instructions where in practice we would have to substitute numeric ones).

$$(LDC \ A \ STOP) \ (\ B \ C)$$

Here we would expect the result *A*. Proceeding in this way we can progressively test the instructions with the SECD programs, shown in Table 12.1.

Table 12.1

fn	args	result	operations tested
(STOP)	(B C)	((B C))	STOP 21
(LDC A STOP)	any	A	LDC 2
(LDC A ATOM STOP)	any	T	} ATOM 12
(LDC (A) ATOM STOP)	any	F	
(LDC (A) CAR STOP)	any	A	CAR 10
(LDC A LDC B CONS STOP)	any	(B.A)	CONS 13
(LDC A LDC B EQ STOP)	any	F	EQ 14 also
(LDC A LDC A EQ STOP)	any	T	supply *numeric* and *cons* operands
(LDC 271 LDC 127 ADD STOP)	any	398	ADD 15
(LDC 271 LDC 127 SUB STOP)	any	144	SUB 16
(LDC 271 LDC 127 MUL STOP)	any	34417	MUL 17
(LDC 271 LDC 127 DIV STOP)	any	2	DIV 18
(LDC 271 LDC 127 REM STOP)	any	17	REM 19
(LDC 271 LDC 127 LEQ STOP)	any	F	
(LDC 127 LDC 127 LEQ STOP)	any	T	LEQ 20
(LDC 127 LDC 271 LEQ STOP)	any	T	
(LDC T SEL (LDC A STOP) (LDC B STOP))	any	A	SEL 8
(LDC F SEL (LDC A STOP) (LDC B STOP))	any	B	

```
(LDC T                                                    ⎫
      SEL (LDC A JOIN)                                     ⎪
           (LDC B JOIN) STOP) any        A                ⎪
(LDC F                                                    ⎬  JOIN 9
      SEL (LDC A JOIN)                                     ⎪
           (LDC B JOIN) STOP) any        B                ⎭
(LDF (LDC A) STOP)            (B C)      ((2 A))      LDF 3
(LDF (LDC A STOP) AP)         (B C)      A         ⎱   AP 4
(LDF (LDC A RTN) AP STOP)     (B C)      A         ⎰   RTN 5
(LDF (LD (0.0) RTN) AP STOP)  (B C)      (B C)     ⎫
(LDF (LD (0.1) RTN) AP STOP)  (B C)(DE)  (D E)     ⎪
(LDF (DUM LD (1.0) RTN)                            ⎬   LD 1
      AP STOP)                (B C)      (B C)      ⎪   DUM 6
(LDF (DUM LD (1.1) RTN)                            ⎪
      AP STOP)                (B C)(DE)  (D E)     ⎭
(DUM LDF (LD (0.0) STOP) RAP)(B C)       (B C)        RAP
```

In this sequence, each new test exercises one new instruction and there-fore, if it fails, then the first place to look for a fault is in the encoding of that instruction. In the case of *AP*, the full function of *AP* is not observed by the test, and therefore *AP* and *RTN* have been bracketed. We have used *DUM* in an unusual way (to push the environment out one place) in order to test higher index values for the *LD* instruction. In fact, if more *DUM*s are inserted, even higher values can be tested.

It would be appropriate now to test the SECD machine executing a fairly lengthy sequence of instructions in order to check that each instruction leaves the machine in the correct state. Such sequences can be invented very simply. Alternatively, it is possible (even desirable) to perform the above sequence with some extra instrumentation in the machine. For example, the values of *s*, *e*, *c* and *d* can be dumped after each instruction (using *putexp*). Before attempting to execute the compiler, it is a good idea to hand-compile the *append* function and test that, for then any remaining error will be more easily determined.

Now it is time to load the compiler which must be copied from Appendix 2. Clearly, this must be done with the greatest care. The use of some kind of data verification capability would be wise. At the very least, one person can read aloud from the machine prepared data while the other checks against the appendix. The compiler is fed into the machine as the code to be executed and the program to be compiled as the argument, that is imme-diately following the compiler. The compiler expects to be presented with a Lispkit Lisp expression whose value is a function, for example (*LAMBDA* (*X*)(*CONS X X*)). The code it then compiles for this expression has appended to it the instructions (*AP STOP*).

To test the compiler, we first present it with expressions which do not have functions as values so that it generates code which will not execute. We simply inspect this code to see that it is what we expect (Table 12.2).

Table 12.2

Source	Object
(QUOTE A)	(LDC A AP STOP)
(CAR (QUOTE A))	(LDC A CAR AP STOP)
(CDR (QUOTE A))	(LDC A CDR AP STOP)
(ATOM (QUOTE A))	(LDC A ATOM AP STOP)
(CONS (QUOTE A) (QUOTE B))	(LDC B LDC A CONS AP STOP)
(ADD (QUOTE A) (QUOTE B))	(LDC A LDC B ADD AP STOP)
(SUB (QUOTE A) (QUOTE B))	(LDC A LDC B SUB AP STOP)
(MUL (QUOTE A) (QUOTE B))	(LDC A LDC B MUL AP STOP)
(DIV (QUOTE A) (QUOTE B))	(LDC A LDC B DIV AP STOP)
(REM (QUOTE A) (QUOTE B))	(LDC A LDC B REM AP STOP)
(EQ (QUOTE A) (QUOTE B))	(LDC A LDC B EQ AP STOP)
(LEQ (QUOTE A) (QUOTE B))	(LDC A LDC B LEQ AP STOP)
(LAMBDA (X) (QUOTE A))	(LDF (LDC A RTN) AP STOP)
(LAMBDA (X) X)	(LDF (LD (0.0) RTN) AP STOP)
(LAMBDA (X Y) Y)	(LDF (LD (0.1) RTN) AP STOP)
((LAMBDA (X) X) (QUOTE A))	(LDC NIL LDC A CONS LDF (LDC (0.0) RTN) AP AP STOP)
(LET X (X QUOTE A))	as above
(LETREC X (X QUOTE A))	(DUM LDC NIL LDC A CONS LDF (LDC (0.0) RTN) RAP AP STOP)
(IF (QUOTE A) (QUOTE B) (QUOTE C))	(LDC A SEL (LDC B JOIN) (LDC C JOIN) AP STOP)

Of course, where Table 12.2 uses symbolic operation codes we would actually see numeric values.

Again, we have progressively exercised various parts of the compiler in such a way that failure leads us to suspect a fault in a particular part. A fault in the object of the compiler, however, is difficult to locate, and the above tests only help a little in this respect. However, doing them is important, because for the next stage we need to be certain that, if a compiled program fails, it is the program and not the compiler which is at fault.

So now, at last, we will compile programs and execute them. We should again begin with something very trivial, for example:

$$(LAMBDA \ (X) \ (CONS \ X \ X))$$

and eventually move to some of the examples given in this book. It is time to feel comfortable when the *append* function compiles and executes and to feel confident when the compiler compiles itself. But that is the subject of the next, and last, section of this chapter.

12.5 BOOTSTRAPPING AND OPTIMIZATION

Now that we are able to compile the compiler, we have the opportunity to make extensions to the language and to the machine which supports it. The process of using the compiler to compile new versions of itself is called *bootstrapping*. In order that we do not have to support a multiplicity of versions of the machine interpreter and the compiler, we should always try to return to the steady state in which the object form of the compiler, when run on the machine, produces from the source form an identical copy of the object form. We have then freed ourselves from earlier generations of both the machine and the compiler. As an example, we shall consider the (unusual) process of exchanging the operation codes of the CAR and CDR instructions.

Let us denote the process of running a compiled program f on the machine m with the arguments x giving the result y by

$$y = m(f,x)$$

Thus, in the case of compilation, if Co is the object of the compiler and Ps the source of some program, then Po, the object of that program, is

$$Po = m(Co,Ps)$$

In particular, in the steady state we will have

$$Co = m(Co,Cs)$$

where Cs is the source of the compiler.

For the example we have chosen, let us denote the various machines and programs as follows:

m_0 original machine with $CAR=10$, $CDR=11$
m_1 new machine with $CAR=11$, $CDR=10$
Cs_0 source of original compiler, generates code for m_0
Co_0 object of original compiler, $Co_0=m_0 (Co_0,Cs_0)$
Cs_1 source of new compiler, generates code for m_1.

First we compile Cs_1 as follows

$$Co_t = m_0(Co_0,Cs_1)$$

Now, Co_t (t for temporary) is code which will execute on the m_0 machine. So now we compile Cs_1 again, under itself, on this machine:

$$Co_1 = m_0(Co_t, Cs_1)$$

This time we get code which will run on the m_1 machine and so, if we compile Cs_1 for a third time we should have again reached a steady state:

$$Co_1 = m_1(Co_1, Cs_1)$$

We can show this bootstrapping process, diagramatically, as in Fig. 12.6. From this diagram it is clear that if we had made no change to the

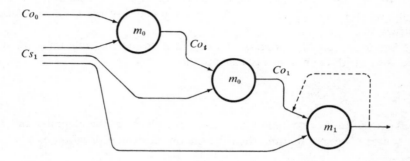

Fig. 12.6

machine, i.e. if $m_1 = m_0$, then we might have obtained Co_1 directly and not needed to go through the middle stage. That is we would simply have had the situation shown in Fig. 12.7.

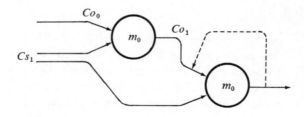

Fig. 12.7

In both cases, however, it is possible that we could need to make additional steps. That is, we might find that the first version of Co_1 is not identical to later versions. At worst, we might find that Co_1 generates incorrect code. Therefore, unless Co_1 were textually identical to the final output in either of the above processes, it is necessary to take additional steps (shown by the dotted line) until it is. It is also necessary to run other tests than just having the compiler compile itself. Indeed, all the machine tests of the previous section should be repeated. This is because not all the instructions of the machine (or parts of a new compiler) are exercised by the process of the compiler compiling itself.

This capability for bootstrapping a new system makes the extension and optimization of a Lispkit system reasonably straightforward. It is, however, sensible to make some elementary calculations before tackling optimization. In particular, it is important to investigate what the possible gains are before attempting an optimization.

An important and simple kind of data to collect in order to make good decisions concerning optimization is the frequency with which each SECD machine instruction is executed. The data in Table 12.3 are typical for an SECD machine program execution. From these data, even without accurate measurement of the *time* spent executing each instruction, it is easy to see that more gains are likely from optimizing the LD instruction than from (say) the EQ instruction, both of which have lengthy interpretations.

Table 12.3

LD	14528	SEL	5894	ADD	278
LDC	7959	JOIN	5894	SUB	0
LDF	14	CAR	4380	MUL	0
AP	2909	CDR	1490	DIV	0
RTN	2910	ATOM	1350	REM	0
DUM	1	CONS	6939	LEQ	0
RAP	1	EQ	3570	STOP	1

The reader who sets out to build a Lispkit Lisp system for himself will doubtless wish to refine the very simple implementation given here, for example to include the sophisticated primitives discussed in Chapters 7 and 8. There are significant advantages, however, to making sure that each extension is contributing enough power to the system to make the lengthy bootstrap process, with the necessary checking which it involves, worthwhile. Clearly, with many extensions, such as delayed evaluation, this will be the case, but in general it is something which the reader must judge carefully for himself.

APPENDIX 1 ANSWERS TO SELECTED EXERCISES

CHAPTER 2

2.1 $product(x) \equiv$ **if** $eq(x,NIL)$ **then** 1 **else** $car(x) \times product(cdr(x))$

2.2 $declist(x) \equiv$ **if** $eq(x,NIL)$ **then** NIL **else**
$$cons(car(x)-1,declist(cdr(x)))$$
$declist(x,n) \equiv$ **if** $eq(x,NIL)$ **then** NIL **else**
$$cons(car(x)-n, declist(cdr(x),n))$$

2.3 $position(x,y) \equiv$ **if** $eq(x,car(y))$ **then** 1 **else**
$$1+position(x,cdr(y))$$

2.4 $position1(x,y) \equiv$ **if** $member(x,y)$ **then** $position(x,y)$ **else** 0

2.5 $index(i,y) \equiv$ **if** $i=1$ **then** $car(y)$ **else** $index(i-1,cdr(y))$

2.6 $flatten(x) \equiv$ **if** $eq(x,NIL)$ **then** NIL **else**
if $atom(car(x))$ **then** $cons(car(x),flatten(cdr(x)))$ **else**
$append(flatten(car(x)),flatten(cdr(x)))$

2.11 $mapset(x,f) \equiv$ **if** $eq(x,NIL)$ **then** NIL **else**
$$addtoset(f(car(x)),mapset(cdr(x),f))$$

2.12 $reduce2(x,g;a) \equiv$ **if** $eq(x,NIL)$ **then** a **else**
$$reduce2(cdr(x),g,g(a,car(x)))$$

2.13 $((A\ B)\ (C\ D))$
$(((A)).B)$
$(A\ B\ C\ D\ E\ F)$
$((A.B)\ C.D)$

2.14 $flatten(x) \equiv$ **if** $atom(x)$ **then** $cons(x,NIL)$ **else**
$\qquad\qquad\qquad append(flatten(car(x)),flatten(cdr(x)))$

2.15 $samefringe(x,y) \equiv$ **if** $atom(x)$ **then**
$\qquad\qquad\qquad$ **if** $atom(y)$ **then** $eq(x,y)$ **else** F **else**
$\qquad\qquad\qquad$ **if** $atom(y)$ **then** F **else**
$\qquad\qquad\qquad$ {**let** $x = adjust(x)$
$\qquad\qquad\qquad\quad$ **and** $y = adjust(y)$
$\qquad\qquad\qquad\qquad$ **if** $eq(car(x),car(y))$ **then** $samefringe(cdr(x),cdr(y))$
$\qquad\qquad\qquad\qquad$ **else** F}
$\qquad adjust(x) \equiv$ **if** $atom(car(x))$ **then** x **else**
$\qquad\qquad\qquad$ {**let** $x' = adjust(car(x))$
$\qquad\qquad\qquad\quad cons(car(x'),cons(cdr(x'),cdr(x)))$}

CHAPTER 3

3.2 $findseq(s) \equiv findseqlist(cons(s,NIL),NIL)$
$\qquad findseqlist(S,a) \equiv$ **if** $S = NIL$ **then** $NONE$ **else**
$\qquad\quad$ **if** $p(car(S))$ **then** $cons(car(S),a)$ **else**
$\qquad\quad$ {**let** $t = findseqlist\ (suc(car(S)),cons(car(S),a))$
$\qquad\quad$ **if** $t = NONE$ **then** $findseqlist\ (cdr(S),a)$ **else** t}

3.4 $find(s) \equiv findlist(cons(s,NIL),NIL)$
$\qquad findlist(S,t) \equiv$ **if** $S = NIL$ **then**
$\qquad\qquad\qquad$ **if** $t = NIL$ **then** $NONE$ **else** $findlist(car(t),cdr(t))$ **else**
$\qquad\qquad\quad$ **if** $p(car(S))$ **then** $car(S)$ **else**
$\qquad\qquad\quad findlist(cdr(S),cons(suc(car(S)),t))$

3.6 $map(x,f) \equiv mapf(x)$
$\qquad$ **whererec** $mapf(x) \equiv$ **if** $x = NIL$ **then** NIL **else**
$\qquad\qquad\qquad\qquad cons(f(car(x)),mapf(cdr(x)))$

3.7 $singset(s) \equiv$
$\qquad$ **if** $atom(s)$ **then** $cons(cons(s,NIL),cons(s,NIL))$ **else**
$\qquad$ {**let** $c = singset(car(s))$
$\qquad\quad$ **and** $d = singset(cdr(s))$
$\qquad\quad cons(union(difference(car(c),cdr(d)),difference(car(d),cdr(c))),$
$\qquad\qquad union(cdr(c),cdr(d)))$}

3.8 $followers(x,y) \equiv$
$\qquad\qquad$ **if** $y = NIL$ **then** NIL **else**
$\qquad\qquad\qquad$ **if** $car(y) = x$ **then** $union(prefix(cdr(y)),followers(x,cdr(y)))$ **else**
$\qquad\qquad\qquad\qquad followers(x,cdr(y))$
$\qquad prefix(y) \equiv$ **if** $y = NIL$ **then** NIL **else** $cons(car(y),NIL)$

3.10 $add(x,f) \equiv \lambda(y)$ **if** $y = x$ **then** T **else** $f(y)$

3.11 $rem(x,f) \equiv \lambda(y)$ **if** $y = x$ **then** F **else** $f(y)$

3.12 The empty set is $\lambda(n)0$.

$add(x,f) \equiv \lambda(n)$ **if** $member(x,f)$ **then** $f(n)$ **else**
$\qquad\qquad\qquad\qquad$ **if** $n = 0$ **then** $f(0) + 1$ **else**
$\qquad\qquad\qquad\qquad$ **if** $n = 1$ **then** x **else** $f(n-1)$

$member(x,f) \equiv scan(x,f,f(0),1)$

$scan(x,f,n,i) \equiv$ **if** $i > n$ **then** F **else**
$\qquad\qquad\qquad\qquad$ **if** $f(i) = x$ **then** T **else** $scan(x,f,n,i+1)$

CHAPTER 4

4.7 The result of $(VALOF\ e)$ is the value of the variable whose name is computed as the value of e. This makes it possible to import names into internal contexts, which is not a very desirable feature since it is very complex to use.

4.10 $eval(e,n,v) \equiv$
$\qquad$ **if** $atom(e)$ **then** $assoc(e,n,v)$ **else**
$\qquad$ **if** $car\ (e) = QUOTE$ **then** $car(cdr(e))$ **else**
$\qquad$ **if** $car(e) = AND$ **then**
$\qquad\quad$ **if** $eval\ (car(cdr(e)),n,v)$ **then**
$\qquad\qquad\qquad\qquad$ $eval(car(cdr(cdr(e))),n,v)$ **else** F **else**
$\qquad$ **if** $car(e) = OR$ **then**
$\qquad\quad$ **if** $eval\ (car(cdr(e)),n,v)$ **then** T **else**
$\qquad\qquad$ $eval\ (car(cdr(cdr(e))),n,v)$ **else**
$\qquad$ **if** $car(e) = NOT$ **then**
$\qquad\quad$ **if** $eval(car(cdr(e)),n,v)$ **then** F **else** T **else**
$\qquad$ **if** $car(e) = ALL$ **then**
$\qquad\quad$ $\{$**if** $eval(e,cons(x,n),cons(T,v))$ **then**
$\qquad\qquad$ $eval(e,cons(x,n),cons(F,v))$ **else** F
$\qquad\quad$ **where** $e = car(cdr(cdr(e)))$
$\qquad\qquad$ **and** $x = car(cdr(e))\}$ **else**
$\qquad$ **if** $car(e) = SOME$ **then**
$\qquad\quad$ $\{$**if** $eval(e,cons(x,n),cons(T,v))$ **then** T **else**
$\qquad\qquad$ $eval(e,cons(x,n),cons(F,v))$
$\qquad\quad$ **where** $e = car(cdr(cdr(e)))$
$\qquad\qquad$ **and** $x = car(cdr(e))\}$ **else error**

$assoc(e,n,v) \equiv$ **if** $e = car(n)$ **then** $car(v)$ **else**
$\qquad\qquad\qquad\qquad\qquad\qquad\qquad\qquad$ $assoc(e,cdr(n),cdr(v))$

(*Note*: simpler namelist/valuelist structure.)

CHAPTER 5

5.2 $assoc(e,\sigma) \equiv \sigma(e)$
$\qquad$ $update(\sigma,x,y) \equiv \lambda(z)$ **if** $z = x$ **then** y **else** $\sigma(z)$

5.4 $val(\{e_1 \text{ and } e_2\},n,v) \equiv$ **if** t_1 **then** t_2 **else** F
$\qquad\qquad\qquad\qquad\qquad\qquad$ **where** $t_1 = val(\{e_1\},n,v)$
$\qquad\qquad\qquad\qquad\qquad\qquad\quad$ **and** $t_2 = val(\{e_2\},n,v)$

$\qquad$ $val(\{e_1 \text{ cand } e_2\},n,v) \equiv val$ (**if** t_1 **then** $\{e_2\}$ **else** $\{F\},n,v$)
$\qquad\qquad\qquad\qquad\qquad\qquad$ **where** $t_1 = val(\{e_1\},n,v)$

CHAPTER 6

6.1 $((c'.e').s)\ e\ (AP0.c)\ d \rightarrow NIL\ (NIL.e')\ c'\ (s\ e\ c\ .\ d)$

6.2 $((c'.e')\ y.s)\ e\ (AP1.c)\ d \rightarrow NIL\ ((y).e')\ c'\ (s\ e\ c.d)$
equivalent using AP is
$(LDC\ NIL\ \ldots$ code to load argument $\ldots CONS\ \ldots$ code to load
closure $\ldots AP)$

6.4 $(e)*n = e*n\ |\ AP0$
$(e\ e_1)*n = e_1*n\ |\ e*n\ |\ AP1$

6.5 $(CAND\ e_1\ e_2)*n = e_1*n\ |\ (SEL\ e_2*n\ |\ (JOIN)\ (LDC\ F\ JOIN))$
$(COR\ e_1\ e_2)*n = e_1*n\ |\ (SEL\ (LDC\ T\ JOIN)\ e_2*n\ |\ (JOIN))$

6.8 $goodif(a,b,c) \equiv$ **if** a **then** $b()$ **else** $c()$
$goodif(atom(x),\lambda()x,\lambda()car(x))$

6.9 $badfac(n)$ never terminates

CHAPTER 7

7.2 $split(x) \equiv cons(cons(car(x),NIL),\ cdr(x))$ **or**
$\qquad$ **if** $eq(cdr(cdr(x)),NIL)$ **then none else**
$\qquad \{$**let** $s = split\ (cdr(x))$
$\qquad\qquad cons(cons(car(x),car(s)),cdr(s))\}$
$tree(x) \equiv$ **if** $x = NIL$ **then none else**
$\qquad$ **if** $cdr(x) = NIL$ **then** $car(x)$ **else**
$\qquad \{$**let** $s = split(x)$
$\qquad\quad cons(tree(car(s)),\ tree(cdr(s)))\}$
(*Note:* $split(x)$ generates a pair of sublists representing an arbitrary split of
the list x.)

CHAPTER 8

8.1 $integersfrom(m) \equiv$ **delay** $cons(m,integersfrom(m+1))$
$first(k,x) \equiv$ **if** $k = 0$ **then** NIL **else**
$\qquad cons(car(\textbf{force}\ x),first(k-1,cdr(\textbf{force}\ x)))$

8.20 $filter(p,x) \equiv omit(1,p,x)$
$omit(j,p,x) \equiv$ **if** $j = p$ **then** $cons\ (OMITTED,omit(1,p,cdr(x)))$ **else**
$\qquad cons(car(x),omit(j+1,p,cdr(x)))$
(*Note:* The list *primes* will now contain redundant *OMITTED*s.)

CHAPTER 9

9.4
$$cons: X \times Delayed(Delayedlist(X)) \rightarrow Delayedlist(X)$$
$$car: Delayedlist(X) \rightarrow X$$
$$cdr: Delayedlist(X) \rightarrow Delayed(Delayedlist(X))$$
$$append: Delayedlist(X) \times Delayedlist(X) \rightarrow Delayedlist(X)$$
$$x: Delayedlist(X)$$
$$y: Delayedlist(X)$$
$$cdr(x): Delayed(Delayedlist(X))$$
$$\textbf{force } cdr(x): Delayedlist(X)$$
$$car(x): X$$
$$cons(car(x), \textbf{delay}(append(\textbf{force } cdr(x),y))): Delayedlist(X)$$

9.5
$$dot: (Y \rightarrow Z) \times (X \rightarrow Y) \rightarrow (X \rightarrow Z)$$
$$map: (U \rightarrow V) \rightarrow (List(U) \rightarrow List(V))$$
$$dot(map,map): (U_2 \rightarrow V_2) \rightarrow (List(List (U_2)) \rightarrow List(List(V_2)))$$

Note: Take
$$Y = U_1 \rightarrow V_1$$
$$Z = List(U_1) \rightarrow List(V_1)$$
$$X = U_2 \rightarrow V_2$$
$$Y = List(U_2) \rightarrow List(V_2)$$
i.e. $U_1 = List(U_2)$
$$V_1 = List(V_2)$$

9.7 $B: (Y \rightarrow Z) \rightarrow ((X \rightarrow Y) \rightarrow (X \rightarrow Z))$
$$map: (U \rightarrow V) \rightarrow (List(U) \rightarrow List (V))$$
$$B(map): (X \rightarrow (U \rightarrow V)) \rightarrow (X \rightarrow (List(U) \rightarrow List(V)))$$

9.9 $andp(p,q) \equiv \lambda(x)$ **if** $p(x)$ **then** $q(x)$ **else** F
can be used to check that a phrase satisfies both p and q.

CHAPTER 10

10.1 $order(x,y) \equiv \langle$**if** $x \leqslant y$ **then** x **else** y, **if** $x \leqslant y$ **then** y **else** $x \rangle$
or
$order(x,y) \equiv$**if** $x \leqslant y$ **then** $\langle x,y \rangle$ **else** $\langle y,x \rangle$

10.2 $sort3(a,b,c) \equiv$
$\{$**let** $\langle a,b \rangle = order(a,b)$
$\quad \{$**let** $\langle b,c \rangle = order (b,c)$
$\quad \quad \{$**let** $\langle a,b \rangle = order(a,b)$
$\quad \quad \quad \langle a,b,c \rangle \}\}\}$

10.4 $addnd(cons(a1,NIL),cons(b1,NIL))$
$\quad = add1d(a1,b1,0)$
$addnd(cons(a1,a),cons(b1,b))$
$\quad = \langle c0,cons(d,s) \rangle$
$\quad \quad$**where** $\langle c0,d \rangle = add1d(a1,b1,ci)$
$\quad \quad \quad$**where** $\langle ci,s \rangle = addnd(a,b)$

10.5 $length(s)\equiv$**if** $unitsequence(s)$ **then** 1 **else**
$$length(left(s)) + length(right(s))$$
$max(s)\equiv$**if** $unitsequence(s)$ **then** $element(s)$ **else**
$$greater(max(left(s)),max(right(s)))$$
$greater(x,y)\equiv$**if** $x<y$ **then** y **else** x

APPENDIX 2   THE LISPKIT COMPILER

The following text, if faithfully copied and used with an implementation of the Lispkit system as described in Chapters 11 and 12, will compile Lispkit Lisp programs into SECD machine code. The text consists of two parts—respectively the compiler in source form and in object form.

```
(LETREC COMPILE
  (COMPILE LAMBDA (E)
    (COMP E (QUOTE NIL) (QUOTE (4 21))))
  (COMP LAMBDA (E N C)
    (IF (ATOM E)
        (CONS (QUOTE 1) (CONS (LOCATION E N) C))
     (IF (EQ (CAR E) (QUOTE QUOTE))
         (CONS (QUOTE 2) (CONS (CAR (CDR E)) C))
      (IF (EQ (CAR E) (QUOTE ADD))
          (COMP (CAR (CDR E)) N (COMP (CAR (CDR (CDR E))) N (CONS (QUOTE 15) C)))
       (IF (EQ (CAR E) (QUOTE SUB))
           (COMP (CAR (CDR E)) N (COMP (CAR (CDR (CDR E))) N (CONS (QUOTE 16) C)))
        (IF (EQ (CAR E) (QUOTE MUL))
            (COMP (CAR (CDR E)) N (COMP (CAR (CDR (CDR E))) N (CONS (QUOTE 17) C)))
         (IF (EQ (CAR E) (QUOTE DIV))
             (COMP (CAR (CDR E)) N (COMP (CAR (CDR (CDR E))) N (CONS (QUOTE 18) C)))
          (IF (EQ (CAR E) (QUOTE REM))
              (COMP (CAR (CDR E)) N (COMP (CAR (CDR (CDR E))) N (CONS (QUOTE 19) C)))
           (IF (EQ (CAR E) (QUOTE LEQ))
               (COMP (CAR (CDR E)) N (COMP (CAR (CDR (CDR E))) N (CONS (QUOTE 20) C)))
            (IF (EQ (CAR E) (QUOTE EQ))
                (COMP (CAR (CDR E)) N (COMP (CAR (CDR (CDR E))) N (CONS (QUOTE 14) C)))
             (IF (EQ (CAR E) (QUOTE CAR))
                 (COMP (CAR (CDR E)) N (CONS (QUOTE 10) C))
              (IF (EQ (CAR E) (QUOTE CDR))
                  (COMP (CAR (CDR E)) N (CONS (QUOTE 11) C))
               (IF (EQ (CAR E) (QUOTE ATOM))
                   (COMP (CAR (CDR E)) N (CONS (QUOTE 12) C))
                (IF (EQ (CAR E) (QUOTE CONS))
                    (COMP (CAR (CDR (CDR E))) N (COMP (CAR (CDR E)) N (CONS (QUOTE 13) C)))
                 (IF (EQ (CAR E) (QUOTE IF))
                     (LET (COMP (CAR (CDR E)) N (CONS (QUOTE 8)
                                                      (CONS THENPT (CONS ELSEPT C))))
                       (THENPT COMP (CAR (CDR (CDR E))) N (QUOTE (9)))
                       (ELSEPT COMP (CAR (CDR (CDR (CDR E)))) N (QUOTE (9)))  )
                  (IF (EQ (CAR E) (QUOTE LAMBDA))
                      (LET (CONS (QUOTE 3) (CONS BODY C))
                        (BODY COMP (CAR (CDR (CDR E))) (CONS (CAR (CDR E)) N)
                                                      (QUOTE (5))) )
                   (IF (EQ (CAR E) (QUOTE LET))
                       (LET  (LET  (COMPLIS ARGS N (CONS (QUOTE 3)
                                            (CONS BODY (CONS (QUOTE 4) C))))
                               (BODY COMP (CAR (CDR E)) M (QUOTE (5))))
                         (M CONS (VARS (CDR (CDR E))) N)
                         (ARGS EXPRS (CDR (CDR E))))
                    (IF (EQ (CAR E) (QUOTE LETREC))
                        (LET  (LET  (CONS (QUOTE 6) (COMPLIS ARGS M
                                     (CONS (QUOTE 3) (CONS BODY (CONS (QUOTE 7) C)))))
                                (BODY COMP (CAR (CDR E)) M (QUOTE (5))))
                          (M CONS (VARS (CDR (CDR E))) N)
                          (ARGS EXPRS (CDR (CDR E))))
                     (COMPLIS (CDR E) N (COMP (CAR E) N (CONS (QUOTE 4) C))))))))))))))))))))))
  (COMPLIS LAMBDA (E N C)
    (IF (EQ E (QUOTE NIL)) (CONS (QUOTE 2) (CONS (QUOTE NIL) C))
        (COMPLIS (CDR E) N (COMP (CAR E) N (CONS (QUOTE 13) C)))))
  (LOCATION LAMBDA (E N)
    (LETREC
      (IF (MEMBER E (CAR N)) (CONS (QUOTE 0) (POSN E (CAR N)))
          (INCAR (LOCATION E (CDR N))))
      (MEMBER LAMBDA (E N)
          (IF (EQ N (QUOTE NIL)) (QUOTE F)
            (IF (EQ E (CAR N)) (QUOTE T) (MEMBER E (CDR N)))))
      (POSN LAMBDA (E N)
        (IF (EQ E (CAR N)) (QUOTE 0) (ADD (QUOTE 1) (POSN E (CDR N)))))
      (INCAR LAMBDA (L) (CONS (ADD (QUOTE 1) (CAR L)) (CDR L)))))
  (VARS LAMBDA (D)
    (IF (EQ D (QUOTE NIL)) (QUOTE NIL)
        (CONS (CAR (CAR D)) (VARS (CDR D)))))
  (EXPRS LAMBDA (D)
    (IF (EQ D (QUOTE NIL)) (QUOTE NIL)
        (CONS (CDR (CAR D)) (EXPRS (CDR D))))))
```

(6 2 NIL 3 (1 (0 . 0) 2 NIL 14 8 (2 NIL 9) (2 NIL 1 (0 . 0) 11 13 1 (1 . 5) 4 1
(0 . 0) 10 11 13 9) 5) 13 3 (1 (0 . 0) 2 NIL 14 8 (2 NIL 9) (2 NIL 1 (0 . 0) 11
13 1 (1 . 4) 4 1 (0 . 0) 10 10 13 9) 5) 13 3 (6 2 NIL 3 (1 (0 . 0) 11 2 1 1 (0
. 0) 10 15 13 5) 13 3 (1 (0 . 0) 1 (0 . 1) 10 14 8 (2 0 9)· (2 1 2 NIL 1 (0 . 1)
11 13 1 (0 . 0) 13 1 (1 . 1) 4 15 9) 5) 13 3 (1 (0 . 1) 2 NIL 14 8 (2 F 9) (1
(0 . 0) 1 (0 . 1) 10 14 8 (2 T 9) (2 NIL 1 (0 . 1) 11 13 1 (0 . 0) 13 1 (1 . 0)
4 9) 9) 5) 13 3 (2 NIL 1 (1 . 1) 10 13 1 (1 . 0) 13 1 (0 . 0) 4 8 (2 NIL 1 (1 .
1) 10 13 1 (1 . 0) 13 1 (0 . 1) 4 2 0 13 9) (2 NIL 2 NIL 1 (1 . 1) 11 13 1 (1 .
0) 13 1 (2 . 3) 4 13 1 (0 . 2) 4 9) 5) 7 5) 13 3 (1 (0 . 0) 2 NIL 14 8 (1 (0 .
2) 2 NIL 13 2 2 13 9) (2 NIL 2 NIL 1 (0 . 2) 2 13 13 13 1 (0 . 1) 13 1 (0 . 0)
10 13 1 (1 . 1) 4 13 1 (0 . 1) 13 1 (0 . 0) 11 13 1 (1 . 2) 4 9) 5) 13 3 (1 (0
. 0) 12 8 (1 (0 . 2) 2 NIL 1 (0 . 1) 13 1 (0 . 0) 13 1 (1 . 3) 4 13 2 1 13 9)
(1 (0 . 0) 10 2 QUOTE 14 8 (1 (0 . 2) 1 (0 . 0) 11 10 13 2 2 13 9) (1 (0 . 0)
10 2 ADD 14 8 (2 NIL 2 NIL 1 (0 . 2) 2 15 13 13 1 (0 . 1) 13 1 (0 . 0) 11 11 10
13 1 (1 . 1) 4 13 1 (0 . 1) 13 1 (0 . 0) 11 10 13 1 (1 . 1) 4 9) (1 (0 . 0) 10
2 SUB 14 8 (2 NIL 2 NIL 1 (0 . 2) 2 16 13 13 1 (0 . 1) 13 1 (0 . 0) 11 11 10 13
1 (1 . 1) 4 13 1 (0 . 1) 13 1 (0 . 0) 11 10 13 1 (1 . 1) 4 9) (1 (0 . 0) 10 2
MUL 14 8 (2 NIL 2 NIL 1 (0 . 2) 2 17 13 13 1 (0 . 1) 13 1 (0 . 0) 11 11 10 13 1
(1 . 1) 4 13 1 (0 . 1) 13 1 (0 . 0) 11 10 13 1 (1 . 1) 4 9) (1 (0 . 0) 10 2 DIV
14 8 (2 NIL 2 NIL 1 (0 . 2) 2 18 13 13 1 (0 . 1) 13 1 (0 . 0) 11 11 10 13 1 (1
. 1) 4 13 1 (0 . 1) 13 1 (0 . 0) 11 10 13 1 (1 . 1) 4 9) (1 (0 . 0) 10 2 REM 14
8 (2 NIL 2 NIL 1 (0 . 2) 2 19 13 13 1 (0 . 1) 13 1 (0 . 0) 11 11 10 13 1 (1 .
1) 4 13 1 (0 . 1) 13 1 (0 . 0) 11 10 13 1 (1 . 1) 4 9) (1 (0 . 0) 10 2 LEQ 14 8
(2 NIL 2 NIL 1 (0 . 2) 2 20 13 13 1 (0 . 1) 13 1 (0 . 0) 11 11 10 13 1 (1 . 1)
4 13 1 (0 . 1) 13 1 (0 . 0) 11 10 13 1 (1 . 1) 4 9) (1 (0 . 0) 10 2 EQ 14 8 (2
NIL 2 NIL 1 (0 . 2) 2 14 13 13 1 (0 . 1) 13 1 (0 . 0) 11 11 10 13 1 (1 . 1) 4
13 1 (0 . 1) 13 1 (0 . 0) 11 10 13 1 (1 . 1) 4 9) (1 (0 . 0) 10 2 CAR 14 8 (2
NIL 1 (0 . 2) 2 10 13 13 1 (0 . 1) 13 1 (0 . 0) 11 10 13 1 (1 . 1) 4 9) (1 (0 .
0) 10 2 CDR 14 8 (2 NIL 1 (0 . 2) 2 11 13 13 1 (0 . 1) 13 1 (0 . 0) 11 10 13 1
(1 . 1) 4 9) (1 (0 . 0) 10 2 ATOM 14 8 (2 NIL 1 (0 . 2) 2 12 13 13 1 (0 . 1) 13
1 (0 . 0) 11 10 13 1 (1 . 1) 4 9) (1 (0 . 0) 10 2 CONS 14 8 (2 NIL 2 NIL 1 (0 .
2) 2 13 13 13 1 (0 . 1) 13 1 (0 . 0) 11 10 13 1 (1 . 1) 4 13 1 (0 . 1) 13 1 (0
. 0) 11 11 10 13 1 (1 . 1) 4 9) (1 (0 . 0) 10 2 IF 14 8 (2 NIL 2 NIL 2 (9) 13 1
(0 . 1) 13 1 (0 . 0) 11 11 10 13 2 NIL 2 (9) 13 1 (0 . 1) 13
1 (0 . 0) 11 11 10 13 1 (1 . 1) 4 13 3 (2 NIL 1 (1 . 2) 1 (0 . 1) 13 1 (0 . 0)
13 2 8 13 13 1 (1 . 1) 13 1 (1 . 0) 11 10 13 1 (2 . 1) 4 5) 4 9) (1 (0 . 0) 10
2 LAMBDA 14 8 (2 NIL 2 NIL 2 (5) 13 1 (0 . 1) 1 (0 . 0) 11 10 13 13 1 (0 . 0)
11 11 10 13 1 (1 . 1) 4 13 3 (1 (1 . 2) 1 (0 . 0) 13 2 3 13 5) 4 9) (1 (0 . 0)
10 2 LET 14 8 (2 NIL 2 NIL 1 (0 . 0) 11 11 13 1 (1 . 5) 4 13 1 (0 . 1) 2 NIL 1
(0 . 0) 11 11 13 1 (1 . 4) 4 13 13 3 (2 NIL 2 NIL 2 (5) 13 1 (0 . 0) 13 1 (1 .
0) 11 10 13 1 (2 . 1) 4 13 3 (2 NIL 1 (2 . 2) 2 4 13 1 (0 . 0) 13 2 3 13 13 1
(2 . 1) 13 1 (1 . 1) 13 1 (3 . 2) 4 5) 4 5) 4 9) (1 (0 . 0) 10 2 LETREC 14 8 (2
NIL 2 NIL 1 (0 . 0) 11 11 13 1 (1 . 5) 4 13 1 (0 . 1) 2 NIL 1 (0 . 0) 11 11 13
1 (1 . 4) 4 13 13 3 (2 NIL 2 NIL 2 (5) 13 1 (0 . 0) 13 1 (1 . 0) 11 10 13 1 (2
. 1) 4 13 3 (2 NIL 1 (2 . 2) 2 7 13 1 (0 . 0) 13 2 3 13 13 1 (1 . 0) 13 1 (1 .
1) 13 1 (3 . 2) 4 2 6 13 5) 4 5) 4 9) (2 NIL 2 NIL 1 (0 . 2) 2 4 13 13 1 (0 .
1) 13 1 (0 . 0) 10 13 1 (1 . 1) 4 13 1 (0 . 1) 13 1 (0 . 0) 11 13 1 (1 . 2) 4
9) 9) 9) 9) 9) 9) 9) 9) 9) 9) 9) 9) 9) 9) 9) 9) 9) 5) 13 3 (2 NIL 2 (4 21) 13 2
NIL 13 1 (0 . 0) 13 1 (1 . 1) 4 5) 13 3 (1 (0 . 0) 5) 7 4 21)

APPENDIX 3 BIBLIOGRAPHY

The reader who wishes to explore further the ideas presented in this book may feel inclined to set out in any one of three directions. He may wish to study further the techniques of programming with pure functions, or the methods of giving a formal specification to the semantics of a programming language or further details of Lisp and its implementation. To this end we give here a brief guide to some of the literature in these areas, specifically to those books and papers on which the author has drawn for his own studies. Rather than present the references in order of importance, which would be difficult to do because they are so interrelated, we shall review them in the order in which topics are introduced in the book.

The purely functional language introduced in Chapter 2 and used throughout the book is based on Landin's ISWIM notation (1966). The programming style is developed by many authors, in particular Barron (1968), Burge (1975), Burstall et al. (1971), and Foster (1967), while the compendium of papers edited by Fox (1966) is particularly recommended in this connection. In Chapter 3, the searching programs are based on a method described by Nilsson (1971). The reader interested in larger applications of functional programming is referred to the artificial intelligence literature in general and the references on Lisp described below. A particularly interesting application is described by Robinson (1979) who gives a Lisp program for proving theorems, albeit written in full Lisp rather than a purely functional subset.

The variant of Lisp introduced in Chapter 4 is based on the original definition of Lisp given by McCarthy (1960). This original paper is highly recommended, both as an alternative source for the basic ideas of Lisp and for a description of a Lisp interpreter. Equally important is the standard work on Lisp by McCarthy et al. (1962), which also describes an alternative Lisp interpreter. There are many works on Lisp as a programming language. Those which the author has found of value are Friedman (1974), Maurer (1973), Siklossy (1976) and Weissman (1968). However, it must be noted that full Lisp, as presented by these authors, is far from being a purely functional language. The interpreter presented in Chapter 4, while clearly based on McCarthy (1960) borrows ideas from Landin (1964) and Reynolds (1972).

Again, the interpreter for the Algol fragment in Chapter 5 is based on the work of Landin (1965), as is much of the subsequent development in that chapter. The method of transforming flow diagrams to recursive functions is due to McCarthy (1960), while the idea of giving a functional equivalent to each construct in a programming language is the basis of mathematical semantics developed at Oxford by Scott and Strachey. The interested reader is referred to Milne and Strachey (1976), Scott (1977) and Stoy (1977). The paper by Scott is the shortest and will act as an introduction to his many works in this area, while the book by Stoy is a comprehensive introduction. The two-volume work of Milne and Strachey is not for the timid but is highly recommended as a source of ideas about using pure functions to define programming-language semantics.

The SECD machine in Chapter 6 is based on the abstract machine designed by Landin (1964) which is also described by Burge (1975) and Wegner (1968). Alternative methods of implementing a purely functional language are not discussed in the book, apart from direct interpretation. However, the interested reader is recommended to look at the alternative proposals of Berkling (1975) and Turner (1979).

The solution to the Queen's problem, described in Chapter 7, is based on a solution given by Dijkstra in Dahl et al. (1972). The notions of delayed and lazy evaluation described in Chapter 8 are based on similar ideas presented by Burge (1975), Friedman and Wise (1976) and Vuillemin (1973). Indeed, these ideas can be traced back to streams as described by Landin (1965). The problem attributed by Dijkstra (1976) to Hamming is solved by a method based on Kahn and McQueen (1977).

Higher-order functions as a method of building practical programs is discussed at length by Backus (1978). Burge (1975) also bases almost all of his presentation on the use of such functions. The interested reader can hardly proceed without some attention to the beautiful theory of combinatory logic (Hindley et al., 1972). The notion of continuation, introduced in Chapter 9 and used in Chapter 10, is based on an idea of Strachey and Wadsworth (1974) which is also discussed by Reynolds (1972).

The implementation of Lispkit Lisp uses standard structured programming ideas. Specific sources of study for the interested reader are Wirth (1976) for compilation techniques, McCarthy (1960) for details of S-expressions, list structures and mark and collect garbage collectors, and Knuth (1968) for alternative garbage collectors.

BACKUS, J. (1978), Can programming be liberated from the von Neumann style? A functional style and its algebra of programs. *Comm. ACM* **21** (8), 613–41.
BARRON, D. W. (1968), *Recursive Techniques in Programming*, McDonald, London (also American Elsevier, Amsterdam).
BERKLING, K. J. (1976), *Reduction Languages for Reduction Machines*, ISF–76–8, GMD, Bonn (also shorter version in *2nd Annual Symposium Computer Architecture, Houston*, 1975).
BURGE, W. H. (1975), *Recursive Programming Techniques*, Addison-Wesley, Reading (Mass.).
BURSTALL, R. M., COLLINS, J. S. and POPPLESTONE, R. J. (1971), *Programming in POP-2*, Edinburgh University Press, Edinburgh.
DAHL, O-J., DIJKSTRA, E. W. and HOARE, C. A. R. (1972), *Structured Programming*, Academic Press, London.

DIJTKSRA, E. W. (1976), *A Discipline of Programming*, Prentice-Hall, Englewood Cliffs (N.J.).

FOSTER, J. M. (1967), *List Processing*, McDonald, London (also American Elsevier, Amsterdam).

FOX, L. (ed.) (1966), *Advances in Programming and Non-numerical Computation*, Pergamon Press, London.

FRIEDMAN, D. P. (1974), *The Little Lisper*, Science Research Associates, London.

FRIEDMAN, D. P. and WISE, D. S. (1976), CONS Should Not Evaluate Its Arguments, in *Automata, Languages and Programming*, S. Michaelson and R. Milner (eds.), Edinburgh University Press, Edinburgh.

HINDLEY, J. R., LERCHER, B., and SELDIN, J. P. (1972), *Introduction to Combinatory Logic*, Cambridge University Press, Cambridge.

KAHN, G. and McQUEEN D. (1977), Coroutines and Networks of Parallel Processes. *Information Processing 77*, North-Holland, Amsterdam.

KNUTH, D. E. (1968), *The Art of Computer Programming: Vol. 1, Fundamental Algorithms*, Addison-Wesley, Reading (Mass.).

LANDIN, P. J. (1963), The Mechanical Evaluation of Expressions, *Computer Journal*, **6** (4), 308–20.

LANDIN, P. J. (1965), A Correspondence between Algol 60 and Church's Lambda Calculus, *Comm. ACM*, **8** (3), 158–65.

LANDIN, P. J. (1966), The Next 700 Programming Languages, *Comm. ACM*, **9** (3), 157–64.

McCARTHY, J. (1960), Recursive Functions of Symbolic Expressions and Their Computation by Machine, *Comm. ACM*, **3** (4), 184–95.

McCARTHY, J. ABRAHAMS, P. W., EDWARDS, D. J., HART, T. P. and LEVIN, M. I. (1962), *The Lisp 1.5 Programmer's Manual*, MIT Press, Cambridge (Mass.).

MANNA, Z. (1974), *Mathematical Theory of Computation*, McGraw-Hill, New York.

MAURER, W. D. (1973), *A Programmer's Introduction to Lisp*, American Elsevier, Amsterdam.

MILNE, R. E. and STRACHEY, C. (1976), *A Theory of Programming Language Semantics*, Chapman and Hall, London.

NILSSON, J. N. (1971), *Problem Solving Methods in Artificial Intelligence*, McGraw-Hill, New York.

REYNOLDS, J. C. (1972), Definitional Interpreters for Higher-Order Programming Languages, *Proc. ACM Annual Conference*.

ROBINSON, J. A. (1979), *Logic: Form and Function. The Mechanisation of Deductive Reasoning*, Edinburgh University Press, Edinburgh.

SCOTT, D. S. (1977), Logic and Programming Languages, *Comm. ACM*, **20** (9), 634–41.

SIKLOSSY, L. (1976), *Let's Talk Lisp*, Prentice-Hall, Englewood Cliffs (N.J.).

STOY, J. E. (1977), *Denotational Semantics: The Scott–Strachey Approach to Programming Language Theory*, MIT Press, Cambridge (Mass.).

STRACHEY, C. and WADSWORTH, C. P. (1974), *Continuations, A Mathematical Semantics for Handling Full Jumps*, Technical Monograph PRG-11, Oxford University Computing Laboratory.

TURNER, D. A. (1979), A New Implementation Technique for Applicative Languages, *Software Practice and Experience*, **9**, 31–49.

VUILLEMIN, J. E. (1973), *Proof Techniques for Recursive Programs*, Memo AIM–318, STAN–CS–73–393, Stanford University.

WEGNER, P. (1968), *Programming Languages, Information Structures and Machine Organisation*, McGraw-Hill, New York.

WEISSMAN, C. (1968), *Lisp 1.5 Primer*, Dickenson, Encino (Calif.).

WIRTH, N. (1976), *Algorithms + Data Structures = Programs*, Prentice-Hall, Englewood Cliffs (N.J.).

INDEX

A

abbreviation in dot notation 50
absolute units in dimensions 65
abstract form of Lisp program 94
abstract program 282
abstract syntax 128
access to variables 82
accumulating parameters 33, 56, 87, 148
activation record 154, 166
actual parameters, extra 193
addition of vectors 256
addition, + 22
ADD, compilation 180
  syntax 98
  SECD machine instruction
    transition 170
    implementation 308
adder 270
addtoset(s,x), set operation 30
Algol fragment 126
Algol fragment, well formed
    expressions 128
  well formed statements 128
Algol interpreter 130
allocation of records in list
    space 318
allocation of variables to
    parameters 153

ambiguity, syntactic 128
and, logical connective 157, 253
  used to separate definitions 38
AP, SECD machine instruction
  transition 174
  implementation 309
append(x,y) 23
  infix form 178
application of a function 3, 5
applicative language 7
applicative structure of language 7
apply(f,x) 94, 120, 163
APO, SECD machine instruction
  transition 221
arbitrary choice 211
argument (*see* parameter)
arrays 273, 274, 278
assignment statement 128, 277
association list 62 (*see also*
    namelist, valuelist)
assoc(v,a), for association list 62
assoc(x,n,v), for Algol 131
  for Lisp interpreter 112
atom 14, 21
ATOM, compilation 181
  interpretation 114
  syntax 98
  SECD machine instruction
    transition 171
    implementation 307

atomsin(t) 30
atomsize(s) 53
availability mode evaluation 233

B

backtrack programming 206
backtrack search, explicit
    encoding 209
Backus, J. 248, 249
Barron, D. W. 342
Berkling, K. J. 343
binary tree equivalent to
    S-expression 57
binding 103, 277
  fluid 123
  proper 47
  static 47
bootstrapping 331
bound variable (*see* parameter)
bottom up testing 70, 324
breadth first search 76, 78
brick-walls 263
bundles of wires, as data
    domain 275
Burge, W. H. 343
Burstall, R. M. 342

C

caar(x) 188
cadr(x) 188
call by name 164, 192, 223, 225
call by need 225
call by value 164, 192, 223, 225
call of function 5
CAND, logical connective 196
cand, logical connective 157
CAR, compilation 181
  interpretation 114
  syntax 98
  SECD machine instruction
    transition 171
    implementation 307
car, 19

case analysis, for lists 23
  for S-expressions 52
CDR, compilation 181
  interpretation 114
  syntax 98
  SECD machine instruction
    transition 171
    implementation 307
cdr, 19
chess board, representation 17
choice, arbitrary 211
choice(n), non-deterministic
    choice 199
clarity of expression 269
closure 107, 174
code generation, for function
    call 155
  for function definition 156
collect free storage 319
combinator 248
combinatory logic 248, 343
compiler for Lisp 176
compilers and interpreters 94
compositon of functions 6
computation by effect, value 10,
    126, 269
compile(f) 165
concrete form of Lisp program 94
constant in Lisp, compilation 180
constructors 18
CONS, compilation 181
  interpretation 114
  syntax 98
  SECD machine instruction
    transition 171
    implementation 308
cons 20
  and dot-notation 285
  record for 283
  number of calls by reverse 29,
    35
context 103
  recursive 109
context-free language 251
continuation 250, 343
  for multiple results 271

for non-determinism 266
control, SECD machine
    register 167
conventional machines, functional
    programs on 149
copying array values 278
coroutines 223
  functional equivalent 217
correct programs 85
  by inspection 255
cut point in loop 139, 143
cut-out tetrahedra 74

D

data domains 272
data representation 66
data structuring 12
data structures embedding
    functions 90
data, symbolic 13
definition of function 4
delayed evaluation 214, 343
Delayed(X), type 266
DELAY, compilation 220
delay 216
demand mode evaluation 233
depth first search 76
differentiation, symbolic 39
difference(x,y), set operation
    56, 86
Dijkstra, E, W. 235, 343
dimensional analysis 60
dimensions, representation 61
DIV, compilation 181
  syntax 98
  SECD machine instruction
    transition 170
    implementation 308
division, ÷ or **div** 22
domain of a function 2
dot notation 48, 285
  abbreviation 50
dot(f,g) 47
DUM, use by LETREC 186

SECD machine instruction
  transition 175
  implementation 310
dummy statement, **skip** 128
dump, SECD machine
  register 167

E

easy solutions 69
effect, computation by 10, 126,
    269
effect(e,n,v), for Algol
    expressions 131
efficient programs 85
empty list 20
environment in SECD
    machine 171
environment, SECD machine
    register 167
EQ, compilation 181
  syntax 98
  SECD machine instruction
    transition 170
    implementation 309
eq 22
equation form of functional
    program 133, 272
equal(x,y) 53
Eratosthenes, prime sieve 237
erroneous programs 193
Euclidean algorithm 143
eval(e,n,v), for Lisp
    interpreter 112
exclusiveunion(x,y), set
    operation 56
exec(fn,args), 165, 191, 305
expression evaluation on
    stack 150
expressions, net-effect
    property 151
  net-effect property for Lisp 176
exprs(d) 120, 188
extra function definitions 26

F

Fibonacci sequence 235
flatten(x), for lists 55
  for S-expressions 57
flow diagrams 137
  with more than one
    variable 140
  transformation 343
fluid binding 123
FORCE, compilation 220
force 216
formulae, representation of
    algebraic 16
Fortran 8
Foster, J. M. 342
fragment of Algol 126
free list 318, 319
free variable 47, 103
Friedman, D. P. 342
function 2
  as a value 106, 273
  call, compilation 183
    interpretation 115
    outermost 150
  definition 19
  equivalent to statement 135
  equivalent to Algol variable 134
  evaluation on stack 155
  producing function 46
  with multiple result 35, 269
  with no parameters 194, 219
  definition 4
  domain 2
  name 244
  parameter 4
  partial 5, 245
  range 2
  recursive 23
  total 5
  higher order 40, 242
  programming with 2
functional equivalents of
    imperative programs 134
functional language 13
functional program 27

functional program, equational
    form 133
functional programs on
    conventional machines 149

G

garbage collector 343
garbage collection 314, 319
geometrical concept of vector 255
global organization of program 83
global variable 47, 81, 103
goto statement 143, 251
graph, state 75

H

hardware 274
higher order functions 40, 242,
    343
  syntax of 102
  for expressing syntax 254
  type of 243

I

IF, compilation 182
  interpretation 114
  syntax 98
if statement 128
image 3
imperative language 127
imperative program, functional
    equivalent 134
  transformation 136
inaccessible records 314
index pair in SECD machine 171
indexing memory 277
infinite structures 218
interpreter 95
  for Algol 130
  for Lisp 110
integers, list of all integers 232

intersection(x,y), set
    operation 56
ISWIM notation 342
iterative form of function 150

J

JOIN, SECD machine instruction
    transition 173
    IMPLEMENTATION 312

K

Kahn, G. 343
Knuth, D. E. 343

L

labels on flow diagrams 138
lambda expression 42
lambda, let equivalence 108, 116,
    185
LAMBDA, compilation 182
    interpretation 115
    syntax 98
Landin, P. J. 7, 165, 167, 342,
    343
language
    applicative 7
    applicative structure 7
    context-free 251
    imperative 127
    purely functional 7, 13
    semantic revision 269
    syntax 251
    purely syntactic extensions 269
lazy evaluation 223, 226, 228,
    343
LD, SECD machine instruction
    transition 172
    implementation 307
LDC, SECD machine instruction
    transition 168

implementation 306
LDE, SECD machine instruction
    transition 220
LDF, SECD machine instruction
    transition 174
    implementation 309
length(x) 23
LEQ, compilation 181
    syntax 98
    SECD machine instruction
        transition 170
    implementation 308
LET, compilation 185
    interpretation 116
    syntax 98
let block 37, 104
let, lambda equivalence 108, 116,
    185
LETREC, compilation 186
    execution by Lispkit 310
    interpretation 118
    syntax 98
letrec 44
    proper interpretation 227
    evaluation 109
line(a,b) 258
Lisp 342
    compiler 176
    program, concrete form 94
        complete example 101
    compiler for 176
    interpreter 110
    real and Lispkit 93
Lisp expressions, net-effect
        property for 176
Lispkit Lisp 93
list of functions 247
list space, allocation of
        records 318
list 15
    free 319
    empty 20
    simple 14
List(x), type 245
local definitions 37, 105
    of functions 43

local variables 81
locate(i,e) 172
location(x,n) 179
loop, cut point 143

M

McCarthy, J. 13, 112, 342, 343
machine transition 304
machine, SECD 165, 288
  transition 167
  multiple, for
      non-determinism 201, 205
maps 3
map(x,f) 41, 91
  type of 245
mapset(x,f) 56
mark used storage 319
Maurer, W. D. 342
McQueen, D. 343
member(x,s), set operation 31, 86
memory 277 (*see* storage)
multiplication 22
MUL, compilation 181
  syntax 98
  SECD machine instruction
    transition 170
    implementation 308
multiple machine interpretation of
      non-determinism 201, 205
multiple results from functions 37,
      269
  continuation for 271
mutual recursion 45, 109

N

name, call by 164, 192, 223, 225
namelist in Algol interpreter 130
  in Lisp interpreter 111
need, call by 225
nested well-formed expressions 96
net-effect property, for
      expressions 151

  for Lisp 176
networks of communicating
      processes 231
NIL 19
  rules for omitting 51
Nilsson, J. N. 73, 75, 342
non-commutative operation on
      stack 152
non-determinism using
      continuations 266
  using multiple machines 201,
      205
non-deterministic programs 198
NON, SECD machine
      instruction 205
NONE, terminate
      computation 204
none, terminate computation 201
number, record for 283
numeric atom 14
  record for 283
numeric codes for SECD machine
      instructions 304

O

operational semantics 195
OR, non-deterministic choice 203
or, non-deterministic choice 199
orp(p,q) 252
outermost function call 150
overwriting memory 277

P

pairs using *cons* and *twolist* 52
parallel assignment statement 161
parallelism, quasi 214
parallelogram rule for vectors 256
parameter of function 4
  accumulating 35, 56, 87
  allocation of variables to 153
  function with no 194, 219
partial function 5, 22, 245

Pascal 8
pending value, use by *rplaca* 117
picture(p,q) 258
PL/1 8
pointer 283
postfix or reverse form of
    expression 181
pop operation on stack 151
position(x,y) 55, 179
postponed decisions in design 28
predicate 252, 284
  of S-expressions 21
prime sieve of Eratosthenes 237
primitive functions of
    S-expressions 18
procedures, programming with 8
processes, networks of 231
product of two dimensions 68
product(x) 54
program is a well-formed
    expression 96
program, functional 27
programming with functions 2
programming with procedures 8
progressive testing of code 327
proper binding 47
pseudo-code 282
purely functional language 7
purely syntactic extensions to
    language 269
push operation on stack 151
putatendof(x,y) 27

Q

Quarendon, P. 237
quasi-parallelism 214, 223
queens, problem of the eight 206
QUOTE, interpretation 113
  syntax 97

R

range of a function 2

RAP, use of LETREC 187
  SECD machine instruction
    transition 175
  implementation 310
ratio of two dimensions 69
real Lisp 93
real machines 277
real world 73
recipe 216
  representation 220
records for symbol, number and
    cons 283, 314
recursion, mutual 45, 109
recursive descent analyzer 291
recursive function 23
  local definition of 44
recursive procedures 324
reduction of dimensional
    expressions 67
redundancy in dot notation 50
redı:ce(x,g,a) 41
reduce2(x,g,a) 57
REM, compilation 181
  syntax 98
  SECD machine instruction
    transition 170
  implementation 308
remainder, **rem** 22
representation of data 66
  of set by function 89
  of stack by S-expression 166
result expression 144
resumption register in SECD
    machine 203
reverse(x) 27
  using accumulating
    parameters 35
Reynolds, J. C. 342
rf, repeatedly force 226
Robinson, J. A. 342
rotations of a tetrahedron 73
rplaca(x,y) 116, 175
RTN, SECD machine instruction
    transition 175
  implementation 309

S

samefringe(x,y) 57, 230
scope of variable in Lisp
     program 171
Scott, D. S. 343
search 76, 78
SECD machine 165, 288, 343
  instruction mnemonics 169
  registers 167
  execution cycle 303
SEL, SECD machine instruction
  transition 173
  implementation 311
selectors 18
semantic revision of language 269
semantics as defined by
     interpreters 122
semantics, operational 195
seq(p,q) 253
sequence for testing functions 71
sequence of machine
     transitions 169
sequence of statements 128
sequences as data domain 280
set operations 30, 56, 86
set, representation by function 89
sets 273
S-expression 13, 15, 52, 272
  syntax 289
  predicates 21
  equivalent binary tree 57
  primitive functions of 18
sharing storage 287, 308
Siklossy, L. 342
simple list 14
singletons(t) 56, 84
skeletons of pictures 260
skip, dummy statement 128
SOR, SECD machine
     instruction 204
stack for expression
     evaluation 150
  represented by S-expression 166
  push and pop operation 151
  SECD machine register 167

state graph 75
static binding 47
STOP, SECD machine
     instruction 169
storage for lists 313
storage management for
     functions 274
storage, sharing 287, 308
Stoy, J. E. 343
Strachey, C. 343
string storage 321
structure of a picture 255
structure of functional
     programs 80
structured programming 343
subtraction, − 22
SUB, compilation 181
  syntax 98
  SECD machine instruction
     transition 170
     implementation 308
substitution operator 145
substitutivity 200, 211
successor in state graph 75, 79
sum(x) 23
syllables 252
symbol, record for 283
symbolic atom 14
symbolic data 13
symbolic differentiation 39
syntactic ambiguity 128
syntax analysis 289
syntax diagrams 292, 299
syntax of a language 251
syntax, abstract 128

T

testing a Lispkit system 323
testing functional programs 65
testing 70
toss of coin 201
total function 5
transformation of imperative
     programs 136

transition, machine 304
Tree(X), type 265
Turner, D. A. 343
2-list 36
type of function 243
type-expression 242

U

union(u,v), set operation 32, 56, 86
UNDEFINED, functions which return 67
UPD, SECD machine instruction transition 221
update in place 221, 279
update(a,i,x), array operation 278

V

val(e,n,v), for Algol expressions 131
value, call by 164, 192, 223, 225
value, computation by 10, 126, 268
valuelist, in Algol interpreter 130
in Lisp interpreter 111

variable, free 47, 103
global 47, 81, 103
scope in Lisp program 171
access to 82
local 81
in Lisp, compilation of 180
interpretation of 113
vars(d), 120, 188
vectors 255
addition 256
parallelogram rule 256
Vuillemin, J. E. 343

W

Wegner, P. 343
Weissman, C. 342
well-formed expressions for Algol 128
for Lisp 97, 102
degenerate cases 103
well-formed statements for Algol 128
where block 37, 82, 104
whererec, 44, 82, 109
while statement 128
Wirth, N. 343
working register 305